THE CONSTITUTION RECONSIDERED

THE CONSTITUTION
RECONSIDERED

Edited for the

American Historical Association

by

Conyers Read

Revised Edition
with a new Preface by
Richard B. Morris

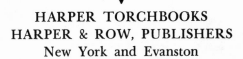

HARPER TORCHBOOKS
HARPER & ROW, PUBLISHERS
New York and Evanston

Contents

Preface to the Revised Edition, by RICHARD B. MORRIS   viii

Preface, by CONYERS READ   xi

1937 to 1787, Dr., by WALTON H. HAMILTON   xiii

PART ONE

THE BACKGROUND OF POLITICAL, ECONOMIC, AND SOCIAL IDEAS BEHIND THE CONSTITUTION

The Fundamental Law behind the Constitution of the United States, by CHARLES H. MCILWAIN   3

The Constitution and the Courts: a Reëxamination of the Famous Case of Dr. Bonham, by S. E. THORNE   15

The Beginnings of Representative Government in England, by CARL STEPHENSON   25

The Theory of Balanced Government, by STANLEY PARGELLIS   37

European Doctrines and the Constitution, by R. M. MacIVER   51

Mercantilism: the Old English Pattern of a Controlled Economy, by CONYERS READ   63

English and French Industrial History after 1540 in Relation to the Constitution, by JOHN U. NEF   79

The Concepts of Democracy and Liberty in the Eighteenth Century, by GAETANO SALVEMINI   105

The Appeal to Reason and the American Constitution, by ROLAND BAINTON   121

The Puritan Background of the First Amendment, by WILLIAM HALLER   131

Philosophical Differences between the Constitution and the Bill of Rights, by HERBERT W. SCHNEIDER   143

Contents

PART TWO

THE CONSTITUTION AND ITS INFLUENCE UPON AMERICAN THOUGHT

Historiography and the Constitution, by CHARLES A. BEARD   159

The Path of Due Process of Law, by WALTON H. HAMILTON   167

Minority Rule and the Constitutional Tradition, by MAX
LERNER   191

✓ *The Constitution as the American Social Myth, by* W. Y.
ELLIOTT   209

Constitutional History and the Higher Law, by HENRY STEELE
COMMAGER   225

Constitutional Democracy: a Nineteenth-Century Faith, by
RALPH HENRY GABRIEL   247

PART THREE

*REPERCUSSIONS OF THE CONSTITUTION OUTSIDE
THE UNITED STATES*

The Constitutional Cult in the Early Nineteenth Century, by
GEOFFREY BRUUN   261

*The Holy Roman Empire versus the United States: Patterns
for Constitution-Making in Central Europe, by* ROBERT C.
BINKLEY   271

*The Influence of the American Constitution on the Weimar
Constitution, by* HAJO HOLBORN   285

American Influence on British Federal Systems, by W. MENZIES
WHITELAW   297

The Judicial Interpretation of the Canadian Constitution, by
C. P. WRIGHT   315

The Frontier and the Constitution in South Africa, by
C. W. DE KIEWIET   329

Federalism in Latin America, by C. H. HARING   341

Contents

PART FOUR

THE CONSTITUTION IN THE NUCLEAR AND SPACE AGE

Some Reflections on Current Constitutional Controversies,
  by LOUIS HENKIN — 350

The Founding Fathers: a Reform Caucus in Action, by JOHN
  P. ROCHE — 380

EPILOGUE

Afterthoughts on Constitutions, by CARL BECKER — 417

Index — 431

Preface to the Revised Edition

BY ONE of those ironies of historical coincidence the sesquicentennial anniversary of the Constitution of the United States, the occasion for the original publication of these essays, proved to be a decisive turning-point in the history of the Constitution. It was early in 1937 that Franklin Delano Roosevelt, reacting to the nullifying by the Supreme Court of so much of the New Deal, proposed his court-packing bill. Although Roosevelt's ill-conceived measure went down to thumping defeat, the President did in fact achieve his real purpose, which was to secure a Court that would be more responsive to public opinion and to the changing social and economic climate of the nation.

Within a month after F. D. R. had sent to Congress his bold design for revamping the Court, the Supreme Court reversed itself and upheld a state minimum wage law. Two weeks later, the Court found the Wagner Act constitutional. Within the next two-and-a-half years Roosevelt had the opportunity of naming five of his own appointees to the nine-man bench. The "Roosevelt Court" greatly extended the area of permissible regulation of the economy by the federal government and, in the area of civil liberties, this new court was to lay the groundwork for a judicial revolution.

It is because the Constitution as the Court has interpreted it is not the same document that it was when this volume was originally published that it has been deemed desirable, in issuing this new edition, to include an updated analysis of more recent Constitutional issues. Thus, Walton Hamilton's provocative essay, "The Path of Due Process of Law," correctly pointed out that the Court, through its interpretation of the Fourteenth Amendment, had turned "liberty and property" into a single word, "with a constant shift of accent to the right." Mr. Justice Holmes might protest against the Court's freezing the law into "Mr. Herbert Spencer's *Social Statics*," but he and other dissenters were unable to prevent a constitutional doctrine contrived to protect the natural rights of men against corporate monopoly from being commuted into a formula for safeguarding the domain of business against the regulatory power of the state.

All that was before 1937. In the last three decades many of the old shibboleths like "freedom of contract" and "due process" have undergone drastic revision while the general welfare and commerce clauses have been stretched and the police power has been expanded to buttress the welfare state. The sharp shift in the direction of judicial statesmanship is the subject of a new paper by Professor Louis Henkin included in this revised edition. The area of permissible Congressional action under the Fourteenth Amendment has greatly expanded, but controversy now rages about the meaning and scope of prohibitions on governmental power, federal or state, primarily in the field of personal liberty. By its interpretations of the Equal Protection and Due Process clauses of the Fourteenth Amendment the Supreme Court has extended national protection to civil rights and liberties. At the same time many of the issues of federalism are evaporating, and as Professor Henkin remarks, in his perceptive analysis, the constitutional issues before the Court "begin to resemble those of a unitary state with a written constitution." In short, since 1937 new challenges have been posed by the enormously enlarged responsibilities of the United States, by the revolution in technology, and by the rising expectations of the less privileged and minority groups. The Constitution has met these new challenges, thereby enabling the Federal Government to assume a far more dominant role in the national life than a generation ago.

Charles A. Beard calls attention in this volume to the importance of giving due weight to interests alongside ideas in the shaping of the Constitution. No man did more than Beard himself to suggest that economic interests played a dominant role in the making and ratifying of the Constitution. As late as 1937 those who pursued Beard's line of economic interpretation were prepared to go much further than he was, and to postulate the thesis that the Constitution amounted to a counter-revolution, a repudiation of the goals of the Great Declaration.

As a result of the close research conducted by investigators over the past generation it is no longer fashionable to advance the argument that the Constitution was the result of an undemocratic maneuver carried out in a society that was undemocratic, or that its adoption was the result of some kind of conspiracy by substantial holders of personal property working against the interests of small farmers and debtors. Neither of these propositions is generally accepted today. Looking back at the closing years of the Confederation it would seem that few Americans challenged the notion that the Federal government must have effective control over commerce or adequate powers to deal with national defense and foreign affairs. From that point of view the Constitutional period marks a continuation of the Revolutionary Age, and the ratifying conventions proved revolutionary instruments of the people.

In their capacity to distinguish between the possible and the unacceptable the Founding Fathers demonstrated both sound judgment and remarkable flexibility of mind, and it was that very flexibility that has made the Constitution so wonderfully adaptable an instrument of government. They also demonstrated political prudence in the purposeful ambiguity with which they clothed crucial powers, which the courts were later impelled to spell out.

In retrospect, as Professor Roche herein demonstrates in his brilliant essay, the drafting of the Constitution and its ratification evidenced exceptionally skillful operatives at work, men who, placing the national interest uppermost, over came formidable obstacles to secure from the country at large a consensus endorsing a federal system of tremendous potentialities. Time has vindicated that consensus.

RICHARD B. MORRIS

Preface

THIS book is the offspring of the meeting of the American Historical Association in December, 1937, at Philadelphia on the occasion of the sesquicentennial anniversary of the United States Constitution. The papers printed here were read on that occasion. As originally designed, the program provided for: (1) a consideration of the background of political and economic and social ideas which determined the thinking of the authors of the Constitution and which found expression in their work; (2) an analysis of some phases of the Constitution itself; and (3) a study of its influence, not only upon American political thought and action, but also upon political thought and action in the world outside the United States.

It was no easy matter to plan such a program, to find the scholars competent to participate in it, and to induce them to contribute their time and their services. That task fell upon the shoulders of the Program Committee, and particular acknowledgment should be made here of the work of Professor Walton H. Hamilton of Yale, its Chairman; of Professor John H. Wuorinen of Columbia, its Secretary; and of Professor Dora Neill Raymond of Sweet Briar College, Professors Austin P. Evans and John A. Krout of Columbia, Professors Roy F. Nichols and A. P. Whitaker of the University of Pennsylvania, Professor J. Salwyn Schapiro of the College of the City of New York, Professor Stanley Pargellis of Yale, and Professor W. K. Jordan of Scripps College, California. The other members of the Program Committee: Professor Elizabeth S. Rogers of Wilson College, Professor Robert C. Binkley of Western Reserve University, Professor W. T. Root of the University of Iowa, and Professor Richard H. Shryock, then of Duke University, were unfortunately too far away to participate actively in the discussions, although they contributed much by correspondence.

The actual selection of papers to be published was made by this group, though the business of seeing the book through the press was referred by the Council of the Association to a smaller committee made up of Professors Hamilton, Krout, Nichols, and Wuorinen, with Conyers Read as chairman.

It is unfortunate that all the papers read on that occasion could not be included in this volume. A few of them were not offered. From those that were, the Publication Committee, forced by the exigencies of space to establish some principle of selection, has given the preference to those which have seemed to them most pertinent. It particularly regrets the omission of Dr. Max Farrand's paper, "If James Madison Had Had a Sense of Humor," of Professor Edward S. Corwin's paper, "What Kind of Judicial Review Did the Framers Have in Mind?" and of Professor Francis S. Philbrick's paper, "Changing Conceptions of Property in Law." Fortunately, Dr. Farrand's paper has appeared in *The Pennsylvania Magazine of History* (Vol. LXII, No. 2, April 1938, pp. 130–39) and Professor Philbrick's paper in *University of Pennsylvania Law Review* (Vol. LXXXVI, No. 7, May 1938, pp. 691–732). Professor Corwin's paper is soon to be published.

The Publication Committee wishes to express its gratitude to the Columbia University Press, particularly to Mr. Charles G. Proffitt, Mr. Donald P. Geddes, and Miss Elizabeth J. Sherwood, for their constant coöperation. The actual editorial work has been divided between Miss Sherwood of the Press and the Chairman of the Publication Committee, with Miss Sherwood taking the lion's share. Miss Lucie E. Wallace has prepared the Index.

CONYERS READ

Philadelphia
August 15, 1938

1937 to 1787, Dr.

I

THROUGH a great event the whole course of history flows. The dates 1492, 1776, 1787, 1868, 1918, fall glibly from the lips as points of time that can be definitely marked, yet each emerges out of all that has gone before and each feeds the stream of things that will be.

Cause, at home amid the severities of theology or mathematics, is not an apt word to apply to the historical process. For the course of human events is a multiple and turbulent affair, with innumerable actors, an open catalogue of motives, and a dramatic action which reaches its climaxes and yet runs on. In endless disarray incident jostles incident, usage emerges from usage, and idea joins idea to beget progeny not after its kind. A continuity of mutual influence alike pervasive and cumulative cannot be captured within any formula which a physicist or a logician can offer. As it stretches away into its past and its future the actuality of an event is exhaustless. At best the historian can follow only a little way a few of the strands which converge to give significance to his subject. Even a group in a planned venture can only report soundings in the domains they went out to explore. The very task of the interpreter denies him a definitive statement. The order he imposes upon his sample of materials is that of the artist.

It is easy to scribble down a time, a place, and an event. Any schoolboy can recite, "1787, Philadelphia, the Constitution of the United States." And it is the right answer. The men who foregathered in Independence Hall can be named, the conditions which drew them there are on record, the interests which impelled them to form "a more perfect union" can be specified, and the document which emerged from compromise is available for everyman to read. But no body of historians, in spite of plenary wisdom and composite learning, can set down in their fullness or without peradventure what these cryptic words mean.

The crisis caused by independence drew them together. The separation of the United States from Great Britain had many an aspect; it was a schism in a colonial economy, a division within an imperial state, a rift within the scheme of common amenities. A breach had come into an emergent culture—and a bit of national planning was in order. The names of the actors as names are empty nomenclature; a more colorful array of proper nouns can be picked up any day at the Hadley town meeting, within the New Haven Green, or on some village Hyde Park Corner. The meaning lies in the associations—meager and exhaustless—which such verbal symbols conjure up. The select company were almost all Englishmen by birth who had been Americanized under the stress of Revolution. They were creatures of a culture filled with conflict and in need of a new synthesis. The majority had been driven to a new political allegiance just as they reached manhood; at the time of the convention their average age was a scant forty-three. Here are questions of personality—caught up in an enduring event—that ramify to the limits of a society.

So, too, with the date itself. A statesman of fading repute—his reputation does not derive from the statement—has referred to the Constitution as the greatest document ever struck off by the pen of man at one moment. Such a dictum testifies rather to ignorance of the historical process than to the character of the event. The men who by nag or stage came into history had a variety of eighteenth-century universes beneath their hats; they lived in a world through which blew distinctive winds of opinion; they were blessed with the common sense appropriate to their stations in life —and all these matters had been long in the making. In erecting a government they had a social heritage—of idea, usage, and institution—upon which to draw. The necessities of the times, the interests to be guarded, the temperaments of the men guided selection among alternatives provided by the slow accumulations of the past. In a sense all history conspired that the Constitution should be written.

As the past converges upon it, so the event diverges into all that is the future. The writing on parchment is verbal currency intended to pass between the generations. Its succinct clauses, its general words, its crisp imperatives and injunctions are brevity itself. Abstractions carry lightly and uncertainly the wealth of detail with which they are freighted. The Constitution is as it is expounded; and in its interpretation principles intended to endure

are forever newly pointed. As decade has followed decade the supreme law of the land has made its adjustment to other times,
novel problems, fresh currents of opinion. It has failed in its national office only as the expediencies of the past, converted into
verbalisms, have carried across the years to blur vision and to confuse action. So long as it is the Constitution that is interpreted,
the spirit of 1787 carries on. It has provided a framework within
which a body of living usages has come into being. It has imposed
a flexible pattern upon an economic order, a political state, a culture in the making. It has channeled elastic grooves within which
the life of the nation must run. As functions once vital harden into
vestigial structure, it currently muddles the attack direct upon an
unruly industrial system. Nor has its force been spent at home;
the lines of its influence have gone out to the ends of the earth.

Thus the emergent event is focused upon, rather than fixed at,
Philadelphia in 1787. On the march idea, custom, institution, forever change their identity. However viewed—as raw material, document, or corpus of living usage—the Constitution is forever on
the make. As the eighteenth century recedes into the distance, the
world that moved within contemporary heads becomes more and
more a closed book to us. As the years pass, more and more uncertainly we seek the meaning in the authority we invoke. Usage
knows crisis as well as growth, and the Constitution of the United
States is unique in that the incident of a single event is still so
deeply grooved in its design. The signing of the document is
among the greatest of events. It marks the point of time at which
the heritage of a culture became the promise of American life.

II

As a step toward understanding let us commute the reality of
idea and usage into the symbol of person. It is customary to set
down the Constitution as the creation of the Fathers. Even if there
was none at the event who ever cast himself in so venerable a rôle,
the patronymic has—in defiance of their injunction against *ex post
facto* legislation—been thrust upon them.

If, then, the Fathers created the Constitution, who were the
Fathers? Certain gentlemen of substance and standing assembled
at Philadelphia in 1787? Authentic record holds their number to

be fifty-five; but—such a closed club aside—are these the fifty-five whose portraits should go into a gallery intended to give a fleeting immortality to doctrinal paternity. A number of the original group have unquestioned positions: Madison, Franklin, Washington, James Wilson, and Roger Sherman must go there. Tradition triumphs over irregular attendance to accord place to Alexander Hamilton; and Gouverneur Morris and the young Pinckney, in spite of a loquacity that knew no quenching, are hardly to be denied.

Yet are all of their colleagues entitled to the honor? What of the tardy delegates from New Hampshire who missed the formative period yet got in on the result? The unappointed delegate from Rhode Island lost his chance at immortality by never showing up; and Patrick Henry, because he "smelt a rat" and stayed away. What of the delegates from New York—Yates and Lansing —whose diaries tell much of what transpired, yet who left in midsummer in disgust at the nationalistic trend. What of the men who signed after remaining mute during all the exciting days? Is paternity to be imputed to so passive a performance? Are niches to be accorded them as against men, generous with ideas and prodigal with words, whose faith faltered at the end? Such as Edmund Randolph, whose speech opened the convention and who was to become Washington's Attorney General, but whose signature was enjoined by political expediency? Or Oliver Ellsworth, who presently as Chief Justice was to become oracle to the document he could not accept? Or George Mason of Virginia, a man of the people in an assembly of the just and the good, who did not find the document democratical enough?

What, too, of men of old who fashioned the ideological material with which the Fathers would build the edifice? Places must go to those who made the old feudal document Magna Carta glow with a seventeenth-century meaning. To those who hammered authority into responsibility with the Petition and the Bill of Rights. To a group of Johns—Pym, Hampden, Milton, and Locke —who in varied assaults against the pretensions of the Stuarts cleared the way for constitutional government. To the British Tories who bequeathed the system of checks and balances, with all its hampering obstinacy, to the American democracy. To William Blackstone, whose Tory commentaries became the Bible of the law to judges in a republican United States. To the authors of common law doctrines which fetter with safeguard and irrelevance an instrument designed "to insure the blessings of liberty" to the Fathers and their posterity.

As often as not the expositor is the creator. Places must be found for those who have suited the Constitution to the times. For John Marshall, whose dogmatic exposition still has a cathedral authority to which the original document cannot aspire. For Roger Taney, who garnered fragments into a police power which is today the safeguard of the common good. For Mr. ex-Justice Campbell, who first discovered the possibilities lurking within the "due process" clause; and to the satisfaction of four out of nine justices read "the rights of man" into the classic phrase. For Mr. Justice Field, who, as the Campbell interpretation became the law, harnessed to property sanctions which had come into the law to serve the cause of personal liberty. For Mr. Justice Brewer, haunted always by the ghost of Karl Marx, who innovated the judicial review of rate structure, distorted a question of price policy into a solicitude over the value of property, and eternally confused the regulation of public utilities. For Mr. Justice Holmes, whose "it is not unconstitutional" explored the possibilities of the double negative and harnessed a redundancy to the cause of social legislation. For President after President who appointed a Justice because "he is of a mind with me in matters that count."

The bother is that the work of selection is never done. As the Constitution is remade, the list of Fathers must be brought up to date. Until 1877 no one would have acclaimed Sir Matthew Hale a Father of the American Constitution. He had been a person of some repute two centuries earlier—an English Chief Justice of the Restoration period whose learned works were still known to a few scholars. In that year his words were borrowed to "affect" grain elevators "with a public interest" and so justify their regulation. In the twenties, when he was least understood, his prestige rode highest as industry after industry was found *not* to be "affected with a public interest." In 1934 he was rather unceremoniously discharged from his office as Father, when Mr. Justice Roberts discovered that the whole matter rested upon "historical error." A doctrine comes into the law to serve a cause; presently it wears the livery of another master; eventually it is dismissed as a dialectical imposition—even though its author is no imposter. Such are the hazards which lie in wait for constitutional paternity.

As 1937 acknowledges its debt to 1787, a reconsideration of the list of the Fathers seems inevitable. A grim necessity for a people, such as social security, no longer lies beyond judicial tolerance. The economic system, in all its disorderly detail, belongs no more to a sacred domain of "liberty and property" which the state is powerless to invade. A seething cauldron of "labor relations" has just been entrusted to the oversight of the federal government. The Congress has a qualified power to protect the investor, to indulge an experiment in community building such as the TVA, to bring a semblance of discipline to industries whose affairs refuse to respect state boundaries. A novice on the Supreme Court finds a judicial muddling in matters of price an unrealistic trial by ordeal and urges that rate cases be dismissed from the courts for "want of jurisdiction." His novel attitude is not yet the law; but his demand represents an advance point in the direction the Constitution is moving. He proposes no more than that the fading picture of Mr. Justice Brewer be removed from the Hall of Constitutional Fame. All along the line the march of laissez faire into the Constitution has been halted—and the catalogue of the Fathers must be revised to conform to current reality.

As the Constitution takes its uncharted course, paternity must ever assume a fresh pattern. If one has faith in the supreme law of the land, he can accord to only a few abiding places among the elect. He can write finis to his list of portraits only if he has stereotyped the clauses on parchment into Mr. Herbert Spencer's Social Statics. An instrument of government designed to "establish justice," "insure domestic tranquillity," and "promote the general welfare" can be endowed with no such arrested perfection. A Constitution which serves the necessities of a people is an enabling act that keeps relevant a group of living usages. New faces must appear as older ones vanish; and portraits that endure must be rehung as contributions wax and wane. The Fathers must ever be what the Sons make them.

III

The Sons cannot recapture, they can only recreate, the Fathers. The quest is as certainly fixed in time and place as its subject. As the Fathers were creatures of their own day, so are those who currently scribble about them. In the most pristine of historical accounts narrative involves selection, and selection touches off appraisal. In his portrait the artist reveals himself as well as his sitter, and the impinging culture leaves its indelible marks upon both. The attempt to capture the spirit of 1787 recorded here is itself a historical document. It reveals the craft and the world of the historian as of 1937.

As an event the Constitution of the United States is not easy to recreate. Like things of its kind its focus is fixed, but its penumbra is uncertain. Its identity can be reduced to a name. Its verbal symbols may take on enhanced significance. A myth may arise to dispute dominion over men and their government. But the reality of the Constitution cannot be pent in by the sharp line of definition. Any lordlet of industry knows that something which somehow has to do with his rights happened at Philadelphia during the long hot summer months of 1787. No philosopher, endowed with understanding and buttressed with documents, can set down the significance of it all.

In this volume the event appears in a series of miniatures. Here is no reduction of "the giving of the law" to the articulate lines of a marching narrative. Instead an attempt has been made to capture something of its significance in a sequence of surprise attacks. A number of adventurers—unlike in objective, in point of view, in distinctive capacity, in all save interest—are enlisted in a loosely formed conspiracy. Each, within the catholic tolerance of the program committee, is allowed his own point of attack, his own historical strategy, his chance to bring back his own loot from the front. Another period, whose fashions in truth turned to the trim and the tidy, would have found the accounts here set down incomplete and disorderly. But ours is not one of the great ages of faith; we talk of "samples" and "soundings" as the way of inquiry; we affect uncertainty and parade the word "perhaps"; we take pride in our incapacity to master a subject. In this volume there is little to satisfy the demand for authority. There are here more trails than any wayfarer can take; many of them are too novel easily to be trodden; they cross and recross each other in bewildering and miscellaneous wise. Here is no eternal verity or its fraction. Instead there is interpretation, suggestion, provocation, each in its finiteness. Our generation demands raw materials for its own process of understanding—and here is such stuff in abundance.

It is the way of the historian to flit deftly through the ages. If this volume has a sweep in time and space which no master of sliding rule and test tube would tolerate, the fault is with the subject. The "secret chamber" within which the Fathers met was no isolated laboratory of politics; a single step beyond the "closed doors" lay the open corridor of the eighteenth century. It is essential to know what was done and said and thought on the eventful occasion. But such behavior stemmed from the stream of the things that had gone before. So if in these pages the discussion runs off into the conduct of new and self-styled states, or the mercy ladled out by assemblies to those who would not pay their "just debts," or the reprisals which neighbor commonwealths visited upon each other, or the plight into which commerce had been placed by the separation from Great Britain, we are still engaged with matters of insistent concern to the founding Fathers. If the argument turns to the conversion of a humid little isle dotted with sheep pastures into an empire, to a system of national planning called mercantilism, to the invention of devices of obstruction in Tory politics, to petitions and bills by which a pretentious monarchy was beaten into a responsible government, or to a world of nature all complete with a god and reason and laws, we are still well within the universe that lay beneath the Fatherly periwig. And if at times the account strays to the usages of a monastic order or reaches through the centuries to capture the institutions—or what the eighteenth century thought were the institutions—of the "ancient" Greeks and Romans, we are not outside the streams which converged upon Philadelphia.

As from the past, so from 1787 into the future. The document was a pattern for the commonwealth. It set up a framework for the new republic, effected a rough division of labor between nation and state, and in its first ten amendments appointed limits to the province of government. The affairs of an emergent nation were to be shaped to its orderly processes. But as it bore upon the course of events with imperative and injunction, its flexible provisions yielded to circumstance and necessity. Unwritten usage grew up to temper its commands, and novel ideas found lodging within its classic clauses. It is the nature of the written law to create in its uncertain likeness another constitution. And when a document becomes the reference, expediencies emerge, grow up into doctrines, and pass through their life histories. The words on parchment may remain unaltered; yet, so long as the process is gradual enough to obscure the identity, usage usurps the place of usage and still claims the blessing of ancient sanction.

The links that bind 1937 to 1787 are strong and uncertain. Now as then a President is the Chief Executive; but the mechanisms of selection are as different as the offices to be filled. The Fathers—at least the amending Fathers—believed in "due process of law" and so do we. But their narrow category was too crowded with decorous procedures to have room for the privileges and immunities accorded by another age to corporations. It takes a heroic act of reconstruction even to approximate what they had in mind by "commerce"; but today as yesterday the Congress has the power to regulate commerce "among the several states." The group at Philadelphia may—or it may not—have intended to encourage "judicial review." It is not set down in the document; but he must be poor indeed in powers of inference who cannot find it there. Yet no master of the documents can tell us what manner of judicial review was intended. The thing we know by that name stems rather from *Marbury* v. *Madison* than from any clause on parchment. It is so much the creature of growth that John Marshall could today hardly recognize the adult who was his own child. No one can set down the event of 1787 as causal to what has come about; yet there is little of current consequence that does not bear the mark of the craft of the Founding Fathers.

So this volume appears as a companion on a voyage of discovery. It aims, not to tell everyman what the Constitution is, but to help him find that out for himself. It is fitting, therefore, that the reader should bring to the essays which follow a question which is a veritable *e pluribus unum*. What is the Constitution? A writing set down on parchment in 1787 and some twenty-one times amended? Or a gloss of interpretation many times the size of the original page? Or a corpus of exposition with which the original text has been obscured? Or "the supreme law of the land"—whatever the United States Supreme Court declares it to be? Or the voice of the people made articulate by a bench of judges? Or an arsenal to be drawn upon for sanction as the occasion demands? Or a piling up of the hearsay about its meaning in a long parade of precedents? Or a cluster of abiding usages which hold government to its orbit and impose direction upon public policy? Or "a simple and obvious system of natural liberty" which even the national state must honor and obey? And is the Constitution engrossed on parchment, set down in the United States Reports, or engraved in the folkways of a people?

And, last of all, has the United States a written or an unwritten Constitution?

WALTON H. HAMILTON

PART ONE

*The Background of
Political, Economic,
and Social Ideas behind
the Constitution*

The Fundamental Law behind the Constitution of the United States ⚘ CHARLES H. McILWAIN

IT IS a very curious and interesting fact that in ordinary language we usually speak of a constitutional monarchy as a "limited" monarchy. The characteristic that distinguishes this kind of monarchy from others for us is a negative, not a positive, characteristic. We think first of all of what the monarch may not do, not of what he *may* do. The whole history of modern constitutionalism proves the soundness of this instinct. A constituted authority is one that is defined, and there can be no definition which does not of necessity imply a limitation. Constitutional government is and must be "limited government" if it is constitutional at all. Whatever its form may be, whether monarchical, aristocratic, or democratic, in any state that we may properly call constitutional, the supreme authority must be defined and defined by a law of some kind. That law may be unwritten and entirely customary, as it has been for the greater part of its history; or it may be set forth in a single official document, as in our state and federal constitutions, but in every case it is a law that puts bounds to arbitrary will.

It is true that in such of our early state constitutions as made a formal distinction between the "bill of rights" and the "frame of government," the latter usually took up more space than the former; but this should not blind us to the fact that, in any concession of "enumerated powers," such as these were the very enumeration means a limitation. In many ways the non-enumerated powers are more important practically than the enumerated, for they establish the boundaries of any government that can be called legitimate.

In creating this government of enumerated powers the founders of our state were merely setting forth in explicit form the essential principle of all historical constitutionalism. For most of the past it was the arbitrary power of princes which was hemmed in by these rights of subjects. In a popular state such as we think ours is, it is the arbitrary will of the government to which the rights of the citizens form a barrier. But the principle is the same. A safeguard is provided in our state by the fundamental law of the Constitution; it is an appeal from the people drunk to the people sober. If we have made any contribution to modern constitutionalism, it lies in the effectiveness of these constitutional limitations, in the sanction of individual freedom, in withholding from government what belongs to the citizen.

It is the earlier history of bills and rights, of this negative feature of our constitutional system, that I should like briefly to trace; for it is this negative feature, and not its positive provisions, that constitutes the chief bulwark of liberty, as well during the whole history of modern constitutionalism as in our existing government. It is our most precious heritage from the past constitutional struggles of our race.

The framers of our Constitution were under the constant fear of an arbitrary rule such as they had suffered under as colonists. Therefore they incorporated in our fundamental law the express negative checks of the Bill of Rights, whose historical background I propose briefly to trace, and further restricted the legitimate sphere of the federal government by withholding from it powers of which some have been shown by later developments to be necessary for the public welfare. But not content with these precautions, in their dread of despotism, they added a dissipation of authority in the form of positive checks imposed by one organ of government upon another, and carried to what I must regard as a dangerous extreme, a separation of powers which could only have the effect of rendering the government they set up both feeble and irresponsible. As one foreign observer puts it, in their fear of the government's doing harm, they incapacitated it for doing much good.

These positive checks, I am bold enough to say, are proof that the founders of our state had not thoroughly learned the lesson of all past constitutionalism—that the really effective checks on despotism have consisted not in the weakening of government, but rather in the limiting of it; between which there is a great and a very significant difference. And even today, in the protests that have recently arisen against the "regimentation" of our times, I find a demand for the restoration of all our former "checks and balances," usually without much discrimination between these and the older historic process of putting dangerous powers entirely beyond the government's sphere of legitimate action.

"Mediaeval history," as Professor Pollard observed in his *Factors in American History*, "not only contained the germs of what was made explicit in modern England, but much of what has been made explicit in the history of the United States." In the historical outline which follows I may have to start further back even than the Middle Ages. The outline will include only "modern" history, but for the growth of constitutionalism specifically the tracing of modern tendencies can hardly begin much later than the second or third century, B. C.

The Greeks of the pre-Hellenistic period apparently knew nothing of them. When we translate their word *politeia* by our word "constitution," as we always do, we mistranslate it. There may be no other English word we could use, but it is none the less a very bad misfit, not so much in etymology as in actual content. Plato and Aristotle could think of an ideal of which an actual government must be an approximation if that government was to be considered good, but apparently they had no conception of a definite superior law to which a government must conform if it is to be treated as legitimate. They thought of law in terms of politics, we moderns think of politics in terms of law. This I take to be the most fundamental of the differences between ancient and modern conceptions of government.

As moderns, therefore, we tend to fix our attention on the legitimacy of an act of government, where the ancients looked merely to its desirability or expediency. Such an idea of legitimacy could only arise after men had come to think of a universal law which had more coercive power than mere universal reason, but, like reason, was coterminous with mankind; and, what is more, coeval with man himself. Since states are obviously the creations of men in time, this means therefore that these states are not as old as this law of nature. And granted that there was such a preëxistent law, it became inevitable that governments and their acts should be judged by their conformity to it rather than to reason alone. As St. Thomas says, those conditions must also be observed which are of the essence of a law. From such a law of nature, there was a further and obvious inference of rights defined by such a law; and if the law antedated the creation of actual states, so these "rights of man" were older, more fundamental, more universal, and therefore more binding than the merely "civil" law of any particular state. It is but a step further to say as St. Thomas Aquinas did in the thirteenth century that a state may promulgate a civil law beyond this law of nature but never a binding law contrary to it: that a civil law flatly violating the rights of man is void.

In brief, for the ancients, the state makes the law; for moderns, the law makes the state. The first known extension of the latter idea was in the Hellenistic period by the Stoics, but the fullest surviving expression of it was by the Romans and the *locus classicus* is in the writing of Cicero. "What is a state," he asks, "except a society (or sharing) in law" (*juris societas*)? "Law is the bond of civil society" (*civilis societatis vinculum*).

The newer, more constitutional, idea is expressed at Rome, under the Principate and afterward, in the *lex regia* by which the people conferred on the emperor an authority defined in very broad terms, yet certainly defined. With the gradual growth of absolutism earlier restrictions disappear, and by the sixth century the authors of Justinian's *Institutes* can say that in this *lex regia* the *populus* concedes to the emperor not a part but the *whole* of its authority. Throughout all these changes, however, the basic conception of a fundamental law is never entirely absent, and in the legal sources it survived the encroachments of despotism and the fall of the empire, eventually to influence new races for centuries to come.

These new races in turn brought with them and added the new —or rather the very old—conception of law as the immemorial custom of the tribe, and when their wanderings were finally over and their boundaries permanently fixed, this tribal custom became the common custom of a local community. The last of these stages, this returning phase of territorial law, we characterize by our word "feudal," and from it we are able to trace the growth of constitutionalism up to our own times as a continuous development.

In a peculiar sense, therefore, feudal institutions and ideas may be said to furnish evidence of the beginnings of our distinctive modern constitutionalism. And if it be true, as I have maintained, that constitutional government is essentially limited government, feudalism assumes a special importance, for one of its most striking features is the prominence of the negative check on government inhering in the rights of feudal vassals, which no lord, not even a king, may lawfully infringe. For the Middle Ages the validity of my thesis of limitation, not dissipation, of government depends on the existence of evidence clearly showing that contemporaries drew a distinction between two things that we now usually confound, autocracy and despotism. Autocracy is unmixed government; despotism, lawless government. Under modern conditions they tend in practice to merge (we have some striking instances in almost every morning's news) and we habitually treat the two—unfortunately I think—as practically identical. In feudal times and after this was not so either in practice or in theory. Unmixed government and lawless government were quite different things, and well recognized as such. Autocracy was always accepted as legitimate, despotism never. The king, in other words, was never controlled but always limited. If such a limit existed, we should look for it in a period of customary law primarily in custom, and in a feudal period in the custom of fiefs. If the law defining and protecting the fiefs of his vassals is beyond the king's authority to define or abridge in the Middle Ages, we may say that it constitutes a true limitation of his governmental power. It may be only a feudal and scarcely yet a constitutional limitation, but it is a real and a legal limitation. In France, even down to the Revolution, as Viollet notes, the king's ordinances seldom touched the "private law." In feudal England it was felt that they could not legally do so if this meant arbitrary definition or diminution or transfer of private rights. There is a curious illustration in a side remark of the author of the *Dialogue of the Exchequer,* written in the reign of Henry II, indicating the nature of the current theory and also the difficulty of enforcing it against an unwilling king. Among the royal revenues enrolled in the Exchequer, the master in the dialogue had mentioned chattels of fugitives from justice which were forfeited to the king. "I am amazed at what you have said," the pupil replies. "It is surprising in the case of a lord who has rights over both the person and the goods of a delinquent and has himself committed no offense for which he should be deprived of his possession. It would seem just that an edict of the king should inflict punishment for an offense on the person of the wrongdoer but should relinquish his goods and even his lands for the use of the lord."

"What disturbs you has disturbed me too," the master answers. "I think we are wasting time on these things which are aside from our original topic, but if you must know why this is so, it is solely on account of the edict [*assisa*] of the king. For there is no one who would presume to resist a royal edict which was made for the good of the peace. . . . As I have said it is the king's edict alone, in a case of urgent necessity, made for the good of the peace, that furnishes answer to this important question."

This reply is very significant, but the pupil's amazement is not likely to have been any less after hearing it. "I see that it was not without a cause," he says. "Now, if you please, let us go on to something else."

An even more interesting example in an actual case and a remarkably early one, occurred some years before, during the reign of Stephen, as recorded by the chronicler of Battle Abbey.

In one of the manors on the southeast coast granted by William the Conqueror to the Abbey of Battle, an ancient custom prevailed under which all vessels wrecked on the coast and not repaired within a certain time should belong to the abbot. Henry I, "hating that custom," by an exercise of royal power issued an edict under which a single living survivor of a wreck should have it instead of the lord of the manor. But, as the chronicler says, "when the new king died, the new law died with him." On Henry's death the magnates quashed his edict and restored the ancient custom. Soon after this, a ship sailing from lands of the Archbishop of Canterbury was wrecked on this coast, and the abbot's men by force seized it and the cargo, pursuant to "the maritime customs and the royal dignities of the Church of Battle." The archbishop at once appealed to the king's curia and the abbot was summoned to defend the acts of his men. In his defense he asserted that a king might at will change the ancient rights of a district for his own lifetime, but only by consent of the barons of the realm could this change be treated as legitimate afterward. Therefore, he said, he would concede this claim if the barons should now declare that it was lawful. This the barons denied "with one voice," although the king himself was present and favored the archbishop's cause; and in the end they decreed that the abbot had maintained his right and that no further complaints of the archbishop were to be heard. That was in the year 1139. Have we heard it said that judicial review was a thing undreamt of yet in the Constitutional Convention of 1787?

Here in this case is the same question that disturbed the master and the pupil in the *Dialogue*. No one will dare oppose an administrative order of the king, but if it is against private right, it cannot be maintained as law, at least after that king's death. There certainly is limitation here—some royal acts are *ultra vires;* but there is no hint of positive compulsion, or control, or parceling out of royal authority *intra vires*. There are no "checks and balances."

If we look carefully through the famous assizes of the next reign we find further confirmation of these same views. In this general period, rights embodied in ancient custom are never spoken of as "made." In the *Summa de Legibus* of Normandy, they are said to be "held" from ancient times, "approved" by the prince, and "preserved" by the people; they are "established" and "promulgated" by the king, and "defined" by his council, as Bracton says. But Henry II's assizes are "made" (*facta*), and they turn out on examination to be administrative edicts, not definitions of rights. In the preamble of the Assize of Clarendon in 1166, it is said to be "made" with the assent of the magnates, but its last section declares that it shall be in force as long as the king pleases. It is clearly concerned with government rather than law, and it is a temporary thing totally unlike the definition of an immemorial customary law, which from its nature must be permanent. The king, it implies, can at any time quash his own edict, but a custom enjoyed by his subjects is beyond his power. This earlier difference between a temporary government order concerned with administrative procedure, and an official determination of immemorial custom is the precedent for the later distinction between ordinances and statutes which we find in the rolls of parliament in the fourteenth and fifteenth centuries. The latter are always distinguished in the same way by their temporary or their permanent character. But all are acts of the king, and the king alone can give binding effect to any of them. All government is the king's government, there is no other; and any act which is strictly governmental he may legally do alone and unaided. Even for a period as late as the fourteenth century, Professor Tout declares, "The great fact, never to be forgotten, is that the king governed the country, and, whatever advice he took was ultimately responsible for all executive acts."

In administration the king, as Bracton says, is without a peer, much less a superior. Within his legal sphere he is "absolute," in the medieval sense of that term. And yet that sphere is legally limited; a royal act may be *ultra vires*. The king may be legally an autocrat but he is no despot. Bracton puts it all, both sides of it, into a single sentence in his famous line: *Rex non debet esse sub homine, sed sub Deo et lege:* The king is without control, but he is limited by law. Here we find essentially the same constitutional doctrine that Sir Edward Coke makes his own in the seventeenth century in the famous "Case of Proclamations," and he accepts both parts of it: ". . . it is a grand prerogative of the King to make proclamation (for no subject can make it without authority from the King, or lawful custom) upon fine and imprisonment." And yet: ". . . the King by his proclamation, or other ways, cannot change any part of the common law, or statute law, or the customs of the realm . . . the King hath no prerogative, but that which the law of the land allows him."

When we come to Magna Carta, "the palladium of our liberties," we see as before the same absolute administration within a legally limited sphere. If we took the trouble to trace the quarrel between John and his barons from its beginning to the issuance of the Charter, we should never find a single challenge of the king's sole right to make and to direct a "foreign" war. That is the king's business. What we do find is a stubborn resistance to his attempts to compel by force the attendance of his feudal tenants of English fiefs in a campaign in defense of his other dominions across the Channel. The latter involved no question of royal administration, but a disputed point of feudal law, touching the rights and obligations of the tenants themselves. The determination of such rights could never be legally "made" by the king arbitrarily and alone and enforced by arms; they could be only "defined," and defined by a judgment of peers which "found" what the customary law actually was. In Magna Carta we find much legal limitation, but no strictly governmental checks. Even the committee of twenty-five, in its final section, was no committee for government; it was nothing but a temporary committee for enforcement of the terms of the document, and it was never revived in any of the subsequent reissues of the Charter.

For the long reign of Henry III it may be enough to cite the interesting example of the Provisions of Oxford and their aftermath, and the classic exposition of our distinction in Bracton's great book on the laws and customs of England.

The Provisions of Oxford of 1258 might be considered an early indistinct anticipation of modern English cabinet government, for under them Henry III reigned but did not rule, but one would search in vain for any balances. There was neither diminution nor splitting of royal administration. All that was done was to transfer it whole to a committee of barons. There was as much solidarity in their rule as in that of a modern cabinet. But even this was without precedent, and when barons and king agreed to submit to the arbitration of Louis IX of France, his decision was clear and unambiguous and wholly in favor of the king. Committee government was illegal. The king in person had a right to a *liberum regimen,* that is, an autocratic rule in matters properly belonging to government. There is no denial of the legal limits, but within these limits, the king must be free of all restraint. We have seen that Bracton's constitutional doctrine was the same, but there is one passage in his book, much quoted by parliamentarians in the seventeenth century, which seems to contradict it. It is the famous passage which reads: "Moreover the King has a master, namely God. Likewise the law under which he was created King. Likewise · his curia, to wit the earls and barons; for the earls are so-called as a kind of associates of the King, and one who has an associate, has a master; and so if the King is without a bridle, that is, without law, they ought to put a bridle on him." But as Maitland has said, this doctrine is flatly contradicted "by at least five statements found in all parts of the book," and the passage is lacking in most of the best manuscripts. He concludes that it was "no part of the original text," but was an addition by a later hand. Nevertheless it is repeated in full by the author of *Fleta,* written in the reign of Edward I; but even this statement, it should be noted, is no defense of checks and balances or of a division of authority; at most it merely advocates the substitution of the will of the majority of a single committee of barons for the will of the king in the royal administration.

In the Year Books, which begin in Edward I's reign and cover the whole remaining medieval period, I know of no references to checks and balances, but the discussions of legal limits to the prerogative are many, and in them all the king's legal rights are invariably treated under the same ordinary feudal definitions that apply to any fief in the hands of a subject. Prerogative is a right of the king, standing beside, but not above, the rights of his vassals. These same facts constitute the true interpretation of the famous books of Sir John Fortescue, consideration of which may bring the medieval part of our survey to an end. In 1932 I suggested that Fortescue's well-known phrase *dominium politicum* meant merely medieval limitation, and not modern control as it had always been interpreted. Since then the brilliant studies of a young English historian on English constitutional ideas of the fifteenth century seem to me to have demonstrated the soundness of this thesis beyond a reasonable doubt.

It is notorious that the Tudor period was a period of concentrated administrative authority so far as the central government was concerned. What is not so well understood is the fact of the persistence of the old limits of law which still remained to protect subjects from an exercise *ultra vires* of governmental power. It is true that this power occasionally broke through these barriers, and the cases are dramatic, but, after all, such cases are comparatively few. No better summary of the general situation was ever made than by Sir Francis Bacon when he said, "although the king in his person, be *solutus legibus,* yet his acts and grants are limited by law, and we argue them every day." In the third year of Elizabeth this same doctrine was laid down in the Court of Common Pleas, when it was said that "the common law has so admeasured his [the king's] prerogatives, that they shall not take away nor prejudice the inheritance of any. . . . The King's prerogative by the Common Law cannot prevail against such a Custom as stands with the Right of Inheritance of another." But the most striking case of all in the Tudor period is Cavendish's Case in 1587, which I have often cited, but must cite once more. The late Professor Thayer considered it important enough to print in his casebook of American constitutional law. The queen by letter patent had granted to a hanger-on of Leicester's the lucrative office of writing the writs of *supersedeas* in the Court of Common Pleas, and by letter commanded the justices of that court to admit him to the office. Since it was legally the property of another, the justices ignored the command. It was repeated in a second sharper letter which the justices also ignored. They were then ordered to appear and explain their disobedience. In so doing they said

that they must needs confess that they had not performed the orders; but this was no offence or contempt to her Majesty, for the orders were against the law of the land, in which case it was said, no one is bound to obey such an order. And they said that the queen herself was sworn and took an oath to keep her laws, and the judges also, as regards their willingly breaking them. As to this matter, so far as it concerned the judges, they answered again that if they obeyed these orders they should act otherwise than the laws warranted, and merely and directly against them; and that was contrary to their oath, and in contempt of God, her Majesty, and the country and commonwealth in which they were born and lived.

To the end of the Tudor period there was no balance of control, but a very real limitation of law. As Justice Crawley put it later in the Ship-Money Case, "In the King are two kinds of prerogative *regale* and *legale*"; a statement in which was much truth, although Crawley's interpretation of it was probably as politically dangerous as his grammar was bad. Between the Conquest and the present many have beaten against these legal barriers to despotism; but in the Anglo-Saxon race they have never yet beaten them down. In the Stuart period the disputes and the conflicts did not touch directly this legal aspect of prerogative; that was assumed. They were concerned more with what Crawley called the regal, they began to turn on the king's discretionary powers, control and not mere legal limitation was becoming the new center of a new debate and ultimately the cause of a great civil war.

With the growth of this new quarrel, with the new *formulae* under which it was finally composed, and its modern outcome in cabinet government of a democratic state, I shall not deal—they are dealt with in the paper of Dr. Pargellis; but no one who knows anything of modern English cabinet government would venture to say that it is a system of checks and balances, and what little check survived to the beginning of the century was swept away by the Parliament Act of 1911 in taking from the Lords the legal right permanently to block an action of the cabinet approved by the house of commons. What is more vital for us here in America is the bearing on our own present constitutional problems of this history of the past, and above all the history of the last twenty-five years. Since the English civil wars of the seventeenth century there has been no challenge to constitutional government such as we have witnessed in this last decade and face at the present moment. There is a tidal wave of despotism sweeping over the world. On this anniversary of our Constitution we find constitutionalism itself threatened everywhere as it has never been threatened since the founding of our government. We find ourselves today in circumstances as critical as those the framers of our Constitution faced in 1787. Do we realize as fully as they realized the crisis we have to meet? Does the history of constitutionalism suggest any cause of that crisis? Above all, can past experience furnish any help in finding a remedy?

I have attempted the analysis above because I believe this past history does indicate one important cause, and also the one possible line of defense. The cause, in a word, is the feebleness of government. It must be strengthened. The present danger is despotism. It must be prevented, and by legal limitations on government. If weakness is the cause, no true remedy can lie in increasing that weakness, it can lie only in making government effective, in removing such "balances" as prevent prompt and decisive action; but also in seeing to it that such action can never jeopard the just rights of any. We must preserve and strengthen those bounds beyond which no free government ought ever to go, and make them limits beyond which no government whatever can ever legally go. We must make *ultra vires* all exorbitant acts of government. If the states which are still constitutional hope to remain so for the future, they must make their governments strong enough to defy the despotisms which now threaten their destruction; but above all, as the whole history of constitutionalism also shows, they must never let this strength become the lawless usurpation, divorced from right, under which individual liberty is trampled under foot before our eyes in so many parts of the world today, and may in time become only a memory even here.

The Constitution and the Courts: a Reëxamination of the Famous Case of Dr. Bonham ⌒ S. E. THORNE

TO STUDENTS of the origins of American constitutional law and theory no judicial utterance of Sir Edward Coke can surpass in interest and importance his so-called dictum in Dr. Bonham's case, decided in the court of common pleas in 1610.[1] It is widely regarded as foreshadowing not merely the power which American courts to-day exercise in the disallowance of statutes on the ground of their conflict with the Constitution, but also that very test of "reasonableness" which is the ultimate flowering of that power. We turn here to a determination of these questions: to what extent does Coke's own intention sanction the modern application of his doctrine, and also, on what grounds does the doctrine rest.

In April, 1606, Thomas Bonham was summoned to appear before the president and censors of the Royal College of Physicians for practicing medicine in the city of London without their certificate. A fine of one hundred shillings was imposed upon him, and he was forbidden under pain of imprisonment to practice physic until he had been admitted to do so by the college. Bonham continued to practice, however, and in October he was resummoned. This time he defaulted, and was sentenced in his absence to a fine of ten pounds. Early in November he again appeared, in response to a third summons, and refused either to pay his fine or to refrain from further practice, on the ground that he was a doctor of medicine of the University of Cambridge, and that therefore the Royal College of Physicians had no jurisdiction over him. In the words of the re-

[1] 8 Rep. 114a; 2 Brownl. 255. The literature upon Bonham's case is voluminous and repetitious: McIlwain, *The High Court of Parliament* (1910), pp. 286 ff.; Plucknett, "Bonham's Case and Judicial Review," *Harvard Law Review*, XL (1926), 30; Corwin, "The 'Higher Law' Background of American Constitutional Law," *Harvard Law Review*, XLII (1929), 367 ff.; Allen, *Law in the Making* (2d. ed., 1930), p. 265; Haines, *The Revival of Natural Law Concepts* (1930), pp. 32–36. Other literature will be found collected in these discussions.

porter, he said "he had practiced and would practice within the city, as he conceived he might lawfully do." Thereupon the censors committed him to prison in the Counter of Fleet Street, whither he was conveyed by the servants of the president and censors. Bonham now brought an action of false imprisonment against the leading members of the Royal College of Physicians.

The pleadings of the defendants set forth that letters patent dated 10 Henry VIII had incorporated them as the Royal College of Physicians, with powers to fine practitioners in London who were not admitted by them, and further general powers to govern all the physicians in London and district with fine and imprisonment. In all cases one-half of the fine was to go to the king, and one-half to the college. This patent was confirmed twice by statute, with the addition of a general command to all jailers to keep such persons as the president and college shall commit to them without bail or mainprise, until delivered by the president and censors, or their successors. It was pursuant to these statutory powers that the college claimed to have committed Dr. Bonham.

Protracted argument followed, to which we will return shortly. For the present we may turn directly to the judgment of the chief justice, Sir Edward Coke. He regarded as decisive two legal points. In the first place, a proper construction of the statute indicated that the censors did not possess the power to fine and imprison unlicensed, as distinct from incompetent, physicians; and secondly, even if they did, they had not pursued them aright. It is the fourth of the five reasons adduced in support of the former of these propositions that has since become so famous. Coke pointed out that the censors were to receive one-half of the fines, and therefore are not only judges but parties in any case that comes before them. It is an established maxim of the common law that no man can be judge in his own case. "And it appears in our books that in many cases the common law will controul acts of parliament and sometimes adjudge them to be utterly void: for when an act of parliament is against common right or reason, or repugnant, or impossible to be performed, the common law will controul it and adjudge such act to be void."

The generally received opinion is that Coke was here appealing to natural law, or higher law, or fundamental law. "Although Coke was no canonist," says Sir Frederick Pollock, "we can be pretty sure that his theory was ultimately derived from the canonist doctrines prevailing on the continent," [2] and in this he has been generally followed by contemporary scholars. They have had some difficulty in explaining the appearance of the principle in Bonham's case. They likewise have been troubled by *Rowles* v. *Mason*,[3] decided two years afterward, which they are forced to regard as a retreat by Coke from the position he had taken earlier. The fact that the statement as interpreted makes no appearance in Coke's *Institutes*, though the last three *Institutes* appeared when Coke was quite safe from imprisonment in the Tower, also has been a constant source of embarrassment. Nevertheless, the belief that Coke in Dr. Bonham's case was invoking the doctrine that there were superior principles of right and justice, which acts of parliament might not contravene, is widely held. Without disputing the general truth of this proposition, we believe that some light may be thrown upon the problem by approaching it from the private law rather than from the constitutional law side, and we suggest that to some extent at least later doctrines of natural law have been reflected backward upon Coke's statement, giving it a content it did not in fact have. His words have been read so long in the light of theories Coke did not contemplate that it is difficult now to dissociate them. It is nevertheless to this that we now turn.

The statute under consideration was a negative statute. The words of the patent were clear: no one should practice medicine in the city of London and district if he be not admitted by the letters of the president and college, sealed with their common seal. Now it was a general principle of statutory interpretation that statutes phrased in the negative superseded and defeated common law. A negative statute could neither be extended to include cases in like mischief, or narrowed to exclude cases within its express words. It must be taken literally as it stands; as Coke remarks elsewhere, a statute in the negative is necessary to be observed. This is the burden of Justice Walmesley's remarks, as we see them in Brownlow's report of Bonham's case; Walmesley

doth not know of any case where the words of the statute are negative, that they admit any interpretation against that but only one, and that is the statute of Marlbridge, chapter 4, which provides that no lord shall

[2] *The Expansion of the Common Law* (1904), p. 122.
[3] 2 Brownl. 198.

distrain in one county, and the beasts distrained drive into another county, in which case, though that the words are negative, yet if the lord distrain in one county, he may drive the beasts to his manor in another county, of which the lands, of which the distress was taken, were held, but it is equity and reason in this case, that the statute should admit such exception, for it is not of malice, but for that, that the beasts may remain within his fee, but in the principal case there is not the like reason or equity.

Similarly in Coke's summary of the arguments made for the defendant college, the question of statutes negatively phrased appears again:

They [the defendants] relied upon the letter of the grant, ratified by the said act of 14 Henry VIII, which is in the negative, *scilicet, Nemo in dicta civitate &c.* And this proposition is a general negative, and *nemo* excludes all; and therefore a doctor of the one University or the other is prohibited within this negative word *nemo.* And many cases were put where negative statutes shall be taken *stricte & exclusive,* which I do not think necessary to be recited here.

Thus an obvious way out of the difficulty—by excepting from the general words of the statute graduates of the universities—was closed. It was even more completely closed by another section of the act of 14 Henry VIII, which regulated persons practicing medicine outside London. They were likewise to be examined and certified by the college, but with one exception: graduates of Oxford and Cambridge were to be permitted to practice outside London without examination. The absence of this proviso in the portion of the statute relating to practice in London made it clear that in that case the exception was not to be made. Nevertheless the plaintiff relied completely upon this point, and at least one of the justices, Justice Daniel, agreed with him, for he said that a doctor of physic of the one university or the other was not within the body of the act, and if he were, that he was excepted by the said later section of the act. But the chief justice did not speak to this point, which, we may add, was quite proper.

Coke turned instead to a construction of the letters patent of the college. The provisions were that none should practice in the city of London if he be not admitted by the college. For every month an unlicensed physician practiced there, he was open to a fine of one hundred shillings. A second clause provided that the college should have the overseeing, and searching, correcting, and governing of all the physicians of the city, including foreign physicians practicing there, and the power to punish them for improper practice by fines, amercements, imprisonments of their bodies, and other reasonable and fitting ways. Coke's contention was "that the censors have not power by the letters patent and the act to fine or imprison any for simply practicing physic in London, but only for ill, and not good use and practice of physic." This he proved by five arguments: (1) The clauses are distinct and parallel, and therefore the one does not extend to the other, for a definite penalty of one hundred shillings is attached to the first clause, but no definite penalty is attached to the second. The intention of the makers of the statute, says Coke, must have been to have the penalties for inexpert practice vary with the injuries done in that practice, and thus they left it to the college to fix punishments in each case. But the college was not given that discretion in the first clause. Therefore the two clauses are distinct, and imprisonment cannot attach to one who falls only into the class of unlicensed practitioner. (2) The harm that accrues by improper practice concerns the body of man, and therefore it is reasonable that the offender should be punished in his body, that is, by imprisonment. But he who practices physic in London in a good manner, though he doth it without a license, yet it is not any prejudice to the body of man. (3) The time of a month is fixed by the first clause, and a man doth not offend the statute unless he practice in the city of London a month. But no time is fixed in the second clause, and if a man practice improperly within a month, he doubtless would be punishable. Thus the two are distinct. (4) The censors cannot be judges, ministers, and parties. Judges to give sentence, ministers to make summons, parties to have the moiety of the forfeiture. One cannot be judge in his own case, and it appears in our books that in many cases the common law will control acts of parliament and adjudge them to be utterly void. For when an act of parliament is against common right or reason, or repugnant, or impossible to be performed, the common law will control it and adjudge such act to be void. (5) If the two clauses were not distinct, an unlicensed physician would be liable to a fine of one hundred shillings, fixed by the statute, after practicing a month, and also to fine and imprisonment, under the second clause, for the same thing. But this is absurd, for no one should be twice punished for the same offense. Thus the second clause must be understood to apply only to improper, rather than to both unlicensed and improper, practice.

These are the arguments that Coke brought forward to indicate that the two clauses of the patent were distinct; that therefore the college's power to imprison was confined to imprisoning physicians guilty of improper practice; and that therefore Dr. Bonham's imprisonment had been illegal. As we examine them, all but the fourth seem to be directed toward that end. It may be, as has been urged, that the fourth argument embodied a favorite argument of Coke, which he was anxious to publish, so anxious, indeed, that he did so by placing it in a group of arguments with which it has no apparent connection. This supposition, of course, is unfounded. The fourth argument was directed, just as the others were, toward an interpretation of the statute which on its face seemed to make Dr. Bonham's imprisonment lawful. We must keep well in mind the fact that the question of the legality of Bonham's commitment was the only question before the court in this action against the defendant college for false imprisonment. In view of the first three and the fifth of Coke's arguments, it seems reasonable to suppose that the act was not meant to provide for the imprisonment of merely unlicensed, as against incompetent, physicians. But if Bonham did not fall within the provisions of the second clause, he seemed very clearly to fall into those of the first. He therefore might be fined; indeed this fine Bonham had refused to pay. Now it was clear law that to every fine imprisonment was incident. Coke himself had said those very words in Beecher's case, decided a few months before.[4] Thus the college, if not directly permitted to imprison Bonham under the second clause of the act, was entitled, if entitled to fine at all, to commit him until his fine was paid. Coke's fourth argument is directed toward the fine and the consequent imprisonment. It may be reproduced as follows: just as it would be absurd to interpret the statute to permit an unlicensed physician to be fined one hundred shillings at the end of a month, and also to be punished by imprisonment during the month, for the one offense of engaging in practice without a license, so it would be absurd to interpret it to permit the college to be party and judge, that is, to assess fines in which it shares. Even though the statute apparently gives the college power to fine unlicensed physicians, when upon investigation we find that the college has a direct, pecuniary interest in those fines, it would be impossible, without

[4] 8 Rep. 59b.

absurdity, to adhere even to words so unambiguous. It therefore cannot fine. Thus the fine placed upon Dr. Bonham was not legally placed upon him, and therefore the imprisonment incident to it was unjustified. All five arguments, then, converge to prove Bonham's false imprisonment; all five take their proper place as interpretations of the statute. Coke's fourth point proves to be not a dictum, but a very material portion of his argument. And finally, though Coke's fourth argument is phrased in very wide terms, it visualizes no statute void because of a conflict between it and common law, natural law, or higher law, but simply a refusal to follow a statute absurd on its face.

Far from "evincing a receptive and candid attitude toward natural law ideas, a fresh influx of which from the continent was already setting in," the argument is derived from the ordinary common-law rules of statutory interpretation, with which, we may add, Coke doubtless was more familiar. Let us state the words again: "When an act of parliament is against common right or reason, or repugnant, or impossible to be performed, the common law will controul it and adjudge such act to be void." Repugnancy in statutes was quite familiar to seventeenth-century lawyers. In a contemporary treatise on statutory interpretation, preserved among the Ellesmere papers at the Huntington Library, we find it treated in these words: "If the words of a statute be contraryant or repugnant, what is there then to be said? And surelie therin we ought to make our construction as nigh as we can so that nothing be repugnant. Yet if it cannot be avoided, so that a repugnancy must needs be, then is the thing repugnant void." [5] A repugnancy, then, is a contradiction; it occurs when a statute provides one thing, and then through oversight perhaps, its opposite. When we are faced with a repugnant statute, we are first to construe it so as to save its words, but if that is impossible, then our author tells us, "are the former wordes good, and the latter, because they make a jarre by reason of the repugnancy, shalbe omitted." There is no conscious constitutional problem raised here, but only one of statutory construction. We are looking at a statute from the point of view of a judge called upon to apply it in a particular case. Since a provision and its opposite cannot both be applied, the later contradictory words are regarded as of no effect. How simple to carry this idea over to the case in

[5] El. 2565, fo. 7-7b.

which a man is both party and judge. To be sure, that is not a direct
repugnancy: if it were, none could object, for even Lord Ellesmere,
who did not approve of those who declared statutes void for being
contrary to reason and common right, made two exceptions: "I
speak not of impossibilities or direct repugnances." Though not
technically a repugnancy, certainly a statute making a man judge
in his own case and a self-contradictory statute might well be regarded as cognate, and as Coke, with the facts of Bonham's case before him, turned over his precedents on statutes repugnant and
statutes impossible to be performed, his theory of a statute against
common right and reason took form. There can be no doubt, we
think, that it was from these precedents, rather than from any
natural law theories, that Coke's argument stems. It will be remembered that his fourth argument was one of five interpreting the
statute in Bonham's case. We see that it is phrased in the technical
language of statutory interpretation. But two years after Bonham's
case, in *Rowles* v. *Mason,* Coke felt that common right or reason and
repugnancy were roughly equivalent: "if there is repugnancy in
statute or unreasonableness in custom, the common law disallows
and rejects it, as appears in Dr. Bonham's case." [6] This is, likewise,
the tone of all the relevant passages of the *Institutes.*[7]

Further light on the meaning of Coke's fourth argument is supplied by the precedents he cited in its support. These have been
examined many times, most recently by Mr. Plucknett, who clearly
felt that they did not support the idea of a fundamental law which
limited crown and parliament indifferently. With this we may
wholeheartedly agree, for as we have indicated, the probabilities
that such a theory existed in Coke's mind are small. But we need not
therefore offer apologies for Coke's *bona fides* or for his Year Book
scholarship, for Coke doubtless felt it unnecessary to support a
theory of unconstitutional legislation when propounding one of
strict statutory interpretation. In *Cessavit* 42, cited by Coke from
Fitzherbert's *Abridgement,* and in *Copper* v. *Gederings,*[8] an earlier
case with which it is in complete accord, the court quietly ignored
an unambiguous statute, just as Coke did in the instant case. Mr.
Plucknett tells us that in neither of the earlier cases was the nature

[6] 2 Brownl. 198.
[7] Corwin, *op. cit. supra,* n. 1 at p. 374, n. 32.
[8] Y.B. 3 Edw. II, 105.

of statutes questioned or the constitutional issue raised. Nor was it in Dr. Bonham's case. Tregor's case [9] is a trenchant comment upon the situation in Bonham's case, and the interpolations by Coke introduce an idea of some superior "right" only when read in the light of St. Germain's and Fortescue's natural law. Certainly the legislator who conferred upon the Royal College of Physicians the power to fine and imprison, and thus established it as a court of record,[10] would have repented of his hasty piece of work when he found that the president and censors were judges of record, no more open to attack for false imprisonment than were the judges of the king's bench who committed a defendant to prison. Bound by no common-law rules, required to hold no public trial, and, in addition, permitted to have half the fines collected, they would indeed have had "power to correct or punish any of the subjects of the kingdom at their pleasure." Fitzherbert's *Annuitie* 41, though an opinion only, is clearly in point with the meaning we are giving to Coke's fourth argument, and so too are the Elizabethan cases on the conflict between prerogative and statute. These cases, then, support no theory of higher law, binding upon parliament and making acts that contravene it void. Nor does Coke entertain that theory. We can agree with Mr. Allen's statement that they are "cases merely of strict interpretation which seem to have produced a result other than that which was intended by the legislator," [11] though not with his general discussion of Bonham's case. When the fundamental law theories have been put aside, we can understand Coke's refusal to acknowledge any substantial error in his writings, and his repetition of the offending passage in Bonham's case word for word in reply to the questions put to him in 1617 by the king, apparently at the suggestion of Bacon and Yelverton.[12] We can understand his words in *Rowles* v. *Mason* and his later expressions in the *Institutes*, and similarly the appearance of his doctrine in the language of statutory interpretation and as the fourth of five arguments on the interpretation of the statute in Dr. Bonham's case.

It remains only to account for such criticism as Ellesmere's, the accumulation of which was a material factor in forcing Coke's re-

[9] Y.B. 8 Edw. III, Pasch. 26.

[10] Thorne, "Courts of Record and Sir Edward Coke," *Univ. of Toronto Law Journal,* II (1937), 24.

[11] Allen, *Law in the Making* (1930), p. 266.

[12] Bacon, *Works* (1803 ed.), VI, 405.

moval from the bench. We know that judges had wide powers of statutory interpretation, but Coke's disregard of the express words of the act probably went beyond them. Though even this is not clear, for our manuscript treatise on statutory interpretation permits a statute "to be taken contrary to its words to escape injustice, for statutes come to establish laws, and if any iniquity should be gathered of them, or if any absurdity or contraryty should follow, they do not so much deserve the name of laws." The cases Coke cited technically support his view, but they were early cases, and the feeling was prevalent that acts of parliament should not be disregarded if clear and unambiguous. This we take to be the meaning of Ellesmere's remark implying that the king and parliament should be left to judge what was common right and reason.[18] Then, too, members of the council, such as Bacon and Ellesmere, might very well have a conception of statutes different from that entertained by common lawyers and judges, though we do not believe that Ellesmere regarded Coke's argument as meaning more than this: that unambiguous statutes would not be enforced if unreasonable results might follow. Ellesmere's qualifying adjective: "I speak not of impossibilities or *direct* repugnances," seems to indicate that to him Coke's theory was directed toward interpretation broadened to include indirect repugnances, that is, contradictions not on the statute's face. Finally, anything coming from Coke was open to suspicion. Coke's argument was soon to be read in a new light, and to bear fruits across the sea, but it is difficult to believe that it contained an appeal to fundamental, higher, or natural law. It furnished a form of words which soon became separated from the case in which they had been uttered, but when they are returned to their proper place, Coke's ambitious political theory is found to be not his, but the work of a later generation of judges, commentators, and lawyers.

[13] McIlwain, *op. cit. supra*, n. 1 at pp. 293–94.

The Beginnings of Representative Government in England ~ CARL STEPHENSON

THIS paper, as will be seen, is based upon a series of distinctions, and to some it may appear significant that my plan was drafted between lectures on Gratian and Peter Lombard. Perhaps I *have* developed a scholastic bent; but I can at least affirm that my distinctions are drawn neither from theology nor from canon law. Rather, they have been suggested by an enforced reading of English constitutional sources during the past two years. The first distinction should be familiar to anyone who has studied the political oratory of Great Britain; the others to anyone who has followed the recent discussion of parliamentary origins. Reëmphasizing these distinctions will, I hope, serve to improve our understanding of representative institutions in medieval England.

A Conservative argument frequently heard in the halls of parliament has been that the house of commons holds discretionary power to act for the nation as a whole. A member, no matter how many people vote for him or what may be their local interests, should be regarded and should regard himself as a statesman rather than a mere delegate. The notion of a parliamentary mandate, a binding instruction laid upon either group or individual, is utterly foreign to the British constitution. Every loyal subject must fear and deplore the growing tendency to decide important issues by alleged appeals to the people—by exciting the voters to periodic states of frenzy and substituting a count of heads for political wisdom.

Such opinions—and they are by no means dead yet—rest upon a theory of representation dear to the hearts of the eighteenth-century Whigs. Writing to Sir Hercules Langrishe in 1792, Edmund Burke explained the matter as follows [1] (the *distinctio prima* of this paper):

Virtual representation is that in which there is a community of interests, and a sympathy in feelings and desires, between those who act in

[1] *Works* (Bohn ed., London, 1855), III, 334-35.

the name of any description of people and the people in whose name
they act, though the trustees are not actually chosen by them. This is
virtual representation. Such a representation I think to be, in many
cases, even better than the actual. It possesses most of its advantages and
is free from many of its inconveniences; it corrects the irregularities
in the literal representation, when the shifting current of human affairs,
or the acting of public interest in different ways, carry it obliquely from
its first line of direction. The people may err in their choice; but common interest and common sentiment are rarely mistaken.

Repelling all suggestions for a change in the parliamentary franchise, he supported the thesis—[2]

that neither now nor at any time is it prudent or safe to be meddling
with the fundamental principles and ancient tried usages of our constitution—that our representation is as nearly perfect as the necessary
imperfection of human affairs and of human creatures will suffer it
to be. . . .

Similar views were continually expressed by those who opposed
the Reform Bill of 1832. Even the nomination boroughs, said Peel,
were a worthy feature of the ancient constitution, because they
permitted the ablest representatives of the national interests to be
returned as a matter of course.[3] And anyone with sufficient curi-
osity to search the parliamentary debates can find the same reasoning employed on many other occasions.

Much earlier, though without Burke's support, the British government had declared that the American complaint of taxation
without representation was ill-founded: the colonists, it was true,
elected no deputies to parliament; yet they were as adequately
represented as most Englishmen. Not very long ago the women
were still being told that they had no real need of the suffrage,
for the men represented them better than they could hope to represent themselves. Attacking the Parliament Bill of 1911, the Duke
of Northumberland denounced the house of commons as a body of
paid politicians and proclaimed the house of lords "the most independent assembly in the world." Said he: "We represent, my
lords, in a peculiar degree the education and the intelligence of the
country." [4]

Here, obviously, lies the trouble with Burke's argument. It can

---

[2] *Ibid.*, VI, 144.
[3] *The Speeches of Sir Robert Peel* (London, 1853), II, 276 f.
[4] *Parliamentary Debates: House of Lords*, Fifth Series, VIII, 810.

be used, not merely, as he used it, to defend aristocratic control of the commons, but to justify any regime that the speaker happens to like. May not Hitler assert that, by virtue of a "sympathy in feelings and desires," he represents the German people? Perhaps he has asserted it; and yet others will disagree. Indeed, any government, according to the personal attitude of the critic, may in this way be said to represent or not to represent the governed. On ultimate analysis virtual representation proves to be at its best a somewhat impractical ideal, at its worst a mere figure of speech. And in any case it is not what we normally understand as representative government. In dealing with the beginnings of the latter—as in this paper—we must keep our eyes on actual representation, that is, the practice of electing and commissioning deputies.[5]

Accordingly, I must differ with those who, for the present subject of inquiry, find significance in the fact that the hundred court was anciently called the hundred, and the county court the county.[6] The usage, in my opinion, hardly implies a true theory of representation. Does it not merely reflect the popular identification of a community with its government—as when we say that Russia declared war, that the church forbade the marriage of priests, or that a city regulated traffic? The language suggests at most a lawful spokesman. Nor can I, with Mr. McIlwain, perceive a germ of modern representative institutions in another practice of medieval courts: that of having a body of doomsmen or *scabini* to declare the customary law.[7] Since they were not elected by the suitors, they could have been representatives only in a figurative sense.

More to the point is a famous passage in the *Leges Henrici Primi*. These so-called Laws of Henry I state that the demesnes of a lord may, in either the county or the hundred court, be acquitted by the lord or his steward or, if they are of necessity absent, by the

---

[5] By definition of terms many books on representative institutions would have avoided considerable obscurity—among them Miss M. V. Clarke's recent work, *Medieval Representation and Consent* (London, 1936), although it contains a number of excellent chapters. Mr. Pollard, on the other hand, recognizes the ambiguity in the word representation and sensibly declares, "It is idle to seek the origin of representation in its vaguer sense." But I cannot follow him when he concludes, "It is only in this sense that parliaments were representative during the earlier periods of their existence" (*The Evolution of Parliament*, pp. 151–52).

[6] In this connection Pollock and Maitland (*History of English Law*, I, 536) speak only of a "fleeting representation." But cf. Mr. McIlwain's more positive deductions (*Cambridge Medieval History*, VII, 668).

[7] *Ibid.*, pp. 666–67.

reeve, the priest, and four of the better men of the vill, on behalf of all who are not summoned by name.[8] From that dubious assertion by a private compiler of the twelfth century, illumined by an ardent faith in the self-governing township, the Germanist school of historians once deduced a primeval English constitution based on the representative principle. Writing on the common meeting of the free Teutonic villagers, John Richard Green eloquently expressed the conviction of Freeman, Stubbs, and virtually their entire generation:[9]

Here new settlers were admitted to the freedom of the township, and bye-laws framed and headman and tithing-man chosen for its governance. Here plough-land and meadow-land were shared in due lot among the villagers, and field and homestead passed from man to man by the delivery of a turf cut from its soil. Here strife of farmer with farmer was settled according to the "customs" of the township as its elder men stated them, and four men were chosen to follow headman or ealdorman to hundred court or war. It is with a reverence such as is stirred by the sight of the headwaters of some mighty river that one looks back to these village moots. . . . It was here that England learned to be a "mother of parliaments."

That such an idyllic picture had to be blotted out by a new generation of scholars is indeed a pity. Even one in our own midst, Mr. Charles Beard, has shown himself especially ruthless.[10] Sympathizing with those who wish to save a corner of that once lovely fabric, I yet fear it is gone beyond hope of restoration. Mr. McIlwain would have us believe that the *Leges Henrici Primi* sketch a representative system which at least in part was Anglo-Saxon.[11] To me as to Mr. Beard, however, the passage in question does not portray a scheme of local representative government at all. In the appearance for the vill of the reeve, priest, and four select villeins, the anonymous author seems to be describing—for he is chronically inaccurate —an occasional procedure, such as that adopted for the Domesday

[8] Liebermann, *Gesetze*, I, 553–54; translation in Stephenson and Marcham, *Sources of English Constitutional History* (New York, 1937), No. 26. Subsequent quotation from this book is made by permission of the publishers, Harper & Brothers.

[9] *History of the English People* (New York, 1881), I, 12–13.

[10] "The Teutonic Origins of Representative Government," *American Political Science Review*, XXVI (1932), 28 f.

[11] *Cambridge Medieval History*, VII, 668.

inquest of 1086.[12] The reference, in other words, is not to an ancient routine of administering justice in shire and hundred, but to a Norman adaptation of the jury.

Here, at last, we reach something fairly solid; an opinion touching the origin of the English representative system becomes less an act of faith, as it was with Stubbs, and more a matter of real understanding. And in this connection we are all greatly indebted to Mr. A. B. White. He has convincingly shown that the characteristic self-government of the English people was due rather to the training of their Norman-French kings than to "an urge . . . in Anglo-Saxon blood." [13] The principal stages of the development, as he sees it, are already familiar to students of English constitutional history. In the course of the twelfth century, local juries came to be used more and more frequently for a great variety of governmental business: to secure information concerning the privileges of individuals or communities; to assess persons and estates for maintenance of arms or payment of taxes; to bring charges against dishonest officials; to present the names of suspected criminals; to settle disputed titles to land or other property; to answer all sorts of questions put by the royal justices on eyre. Not uncommonly the desired results could best be obtained when the juries were popularly elected, and occasionally it was found convenient to call together a number of juries to consult with the king or his ministers. In the later thirteenth century such assemblies came to be associated with meetings of the great council; and so, we are told, the house of commons ultimately emerged.

At this point, however, I should like to interpose another distinction: that between a jury system and a system of representative government. The one does not inevitably imply the other. The essence of a jury was not that certain men were elected to represent others, but merely that certain men were put on oath to give true answers to questions. Two hundred years after the Norman Conquest the jury remained primarily a fact-finding institution. What was still demanded of the juror was particular knowledge, rather

[12] Made in the hundred court, where the reeve, the priest, and six villeins attended for each vill: Stephenson and Marcham, No. 21; cf. Round, *Feudal England*, pp. 3 f., 118 f.

[13] *Self-Government at the King's Command* (Minneapolis, 1933), p. 2, and *passim*. See also *The Making of the English Constitution* (New York, 1921), pp. 353 f.

than authority to act on behalf of a community. So long as the king merely wanted information, a system of appointed juries, consulted either singly or in groups, would be entirely adequate. This may be representative government of a sort, but it is not what we recognize by that name in later England.

Sometimes, indeed, it was necessary for juries to be popularly elected—as when the counties were asked to present complaints of official maladministration. Also, when the royal justices made their great eyres through the country, they presumably wanted the juries from the local communities to be free of dictation on the part of sheriffs or bailiffs, and so encouraged a form of popular choice. In any case, there can be no doubt that by 1250 elected deputies of county, hundred, borough, or manor were often being called on for help in assessing and collecting taxes.[14] And by that time the greater towns had formal rights of self-government, with elected magistrates and municipal councils.[15] It is clear, therefore, that representative institutions were more than a by-product of the jury system. They were, in fact, more than a result of convenience in royal administration. To explain their new prominence in the thirteenth century, the economic and social developments of the age must be taken into account.

From this point of view the assembly of 1254 is especially significant, and it was not a mere concentration of juries. In February of that year the king commanded the election in each county court of two lawful and discreet knights, to come before the royal council at Westminster and there represent all and several of the county in granting him an aid for his expedition to France. The sheriff was to explain to the knights and others of the county the urgency of the king's needs and was to induce them to render an efficacious aid, so that the elected knights could make a precise response to the council.[16] For the first time, so far as we can tell, knights of the shires were then summoned to attend parliament. Also for the first time,

---

[14] For examples of such procedure, see Stephenson and Marcham, No. 46C,D,G. The elected men, though put on oath, hardly constituted a jury or juries; rather they shared the responsibilities of the sheriffs and justices.

[15] See especially J. Tait, *The Medieval English Borough* (Manchester, 1936), Chs. VI–XI; C. Stephenson, *Borough and Town* (Cambridge, Mass., 1933), Ch. VI.

[16] Stephenson and Marcham, No. 46J. In addition to the books already cited, see on this assembly D. Pasquet, *An Essay on the Origins of the House of Commons* (Cambridge, 1925), pp. 33 f.

as Mr. J. G. Edwards has remarked,[17] such deputies were required to bear what amounted to powers of attorney from their respective counties.

An authorization of the sort demanded in 1254 was no empty formula; it bound the whole county to the specific action taken by its delegates. And a very similar requirement was placed in the writs of 1268 for the election of burgesses to come before the king and council—the earliest such writs of which we have the complete wording.[18] Indeed, the record contains the actual form of the letters to be sealed and attested by the electing community:

To all faithful in Christ before whom these present letters shall come, the mayor, bailiffs, and entire community of the city of York, greeting in the Lord. For the sake of the affairs concerning our lord king H[enry], illustrious king of England, his kingdom, the community of England, and us [to be considered], in the council called by the legate at London on the approaching quinzime of Easter, we have seen fit to send thither ——, our mayor, and——, our bailiffs, and——, our citizens or fellow burgesses, so that full faith may be given to them in everything which, with regard to the aforesaid matters, they shall see fit on our behalf to set forth in the council or on the occasion of the council. And we shall hold as established and accepted whatever on our behalf those men do in the aforesaid matters. In testimony whereof, etc. Given, etc.

The precedents thus set under Henry III were continuously followed under Edward I. Almost every writ that he issued for the election to parliament of burgesses or knights of the shires includes a provision that the men so chosen must have binding authority to act on behalf of their communities. For a score of years there was considerable variation in the phrases used; then the formula was invented that continued in official use for over five hundred years:[19]

. . . We command and firmly enjoin you that without delay you cause two knights, of the more discreet and more capable of labor, to be elected from the aforesaid county, and two citizens from each city of the aforesaid county, and two burgesses from each borough, and that you have

[17] *Oxford Essays in Medieval History Presented to H. E. Salter* (Oxford, 1934), pp. 141 f. The argument in the next two paragraphs is essentially that of Mr. Edwards.
[18] Stephenson and Marcham, No. 48D. For the little that is known of this meeting, see the article by Mr. Sayles accompanying the original text, *English Historical Review*, XL, 583 f.
[19] Stephenson and Marcham, p. 160.

them come to us on the day and at the place aforesaid; so that the said knights shall then and there have full and sufficient authority on behalf of themselves and the community of the county aforesaid, and the said citizens and burgesses on behalf of themselves and the respective communities of the cities and boroughs aforesaid, to do whatever in the aforesaid matters may be ordained by common counsel; and so that, through default of such authority, the aforesaid business shall by no means remain unfinished. . . .

I heartily agree with Mr. Edwards that this is a fact deserving greater attention than it has hitherto received. Why was the king so insistent, not only upon the election of lawful men from county and borough, but also upon their being formally empowered to bind their constituents? Surely he must have wanted more than information, complaints, or requests. Within the last quarter of a century, for all the modern emphasis on economic factors in history, many writers on parliamentary origins have stressed judicial routine as the dominating influence in the development of both houses. Against that opinion I registered a mild protest in 1929.[20] Now, after a wider reading of the pertinent evidence, I am prepared to strengthen it. The crux of the matter, it seems to me, lies in the distinction—the third and final one of this paper—between the original functions of parliament and the original functions of the commons in parliament.

The research of Messrs. Richardson and Sayles has proved in detail that under the three Edwards the main business of parliament continued to be judicial.[21] Most of the work that later devolved upon the privy council or the chancellor—the settlement of cases lying beyond the jurisdiction of the common law courts—was still in the fourteenth century handled by parliament. But this body, the greatest and highest of the king's courts, was the original parlia-

---

[20] "Taxation and Representation in the Middle Ages," *Anniversary Essays in Medieval History by Students of C. H. Haskins* (Boston, 1929), pp. 291 f. Since this article was published, a number of other writers have rallied to the support of Stubbs's thesis: notably Mr. Edwards, *op. cit.*, p. 147; Miss M. V. Clarke, *Medieval Representation and Consent*, p. 315; and Miss May McKisack, *The Parliamentary Representation of the English Boroughs during the Middle Ages* (Oxford, 1932), pp. 127 ff. Even the scholars who emphasize the judicial functions of parliament give little support to Mr. Pollard's rash statement (*Evolution of Parliament*, p. 153) that the representation of the commons was merely "an unpleasant incident of feudal service."

[21] See especially their articles published in the *English Historical Review*, Vols. XLVI, XLVII, and in the *Bulletin of the Institute of Historical Research*, Vols. VIII, IX.

ment, in which burgesses and knights of the shire had no place. In 1400 the commons set forth to the newly enthroned Henry IV—[22]

that, whereas the judgments of parliament pertained solely to the king and to the lords, and not to the commons except in case it pleased the king of his special grace to show them the same judgments for their satisfaction, no record should be made in parliament concerning the said commons to the effect that they are or shall be parties to any judgments henceforth to be given in parliament. To which, at the king's command, response was made by the archbishop of Canterbury, to the effect that the commons are petitioners and demandants and that the king and the lords have always had and of right shall have the [rendering of] judgments in parliament after the manner described by the same commons; except that the king especially wishes to have their advice and assent in the making of statutes, or of grants and subsidies, or [other] such matters for the common good of the realm.

The action thus taken merely confirmed the established custom of England. The commons were not and never had been judges in parliament. The fact that meetings of the parliament had come to be associated with meetings of deputies from the local communities had, so far as judicial work was concerned, no legal significance. In the words of Mr. H. L. Gray,[23]

The century of the three Edwards remains one during which the commons were practically non-existent for any one who wished to offer a petition in parliament. They stood in the same position as did the petitioner himself.

If, therefore, we take judicial functions as the determining factor in the rise of the commons, we are reduced to the contention that they were somehow invaluable as petitioners. It is, of course, undeniable that before the time of Edward I meetings of deputies were sometimes held for the specific purpose of recording popular grievances, and that in a few of the later parliaments the commons apparently did nothing but present petitions. As acutely remarked by Mr. Richardson, however,[24]

the real problem . . . is not to explain the occasional association of popular representation with a session of parliament in England or elsewhere, but to explain why popular representation became an essen-

[22] Stephenson and Marcham, p. 256.
[23] *The Influence of the Commons on Early Legislation* (Cambridge, Mass., 1932), p. 337.
[24] *Transactions of the Royal Historical Society*, Fourth Series, XI, 170.

tial and inseparable feature of English parliaments. The explanation is not to be found by any examination of the origins of parliament, however far-reaching or ingenious.

Neither, I would add, is it to be found by tracing into earlier times any political practice that did not involve the actual election of deputies with a delegation of binding authority from the communities of England. The assembling of such communal representatives apparently began in 1254 and developed into a regular custom by the end of the century. Why a king like Edward I should have insisted on these assemblies merely to facilitate the presentation of petitions I cannot understand. But I can understand how the bringing of petitions in parliament would be encouraged by the constant election of burgesses and knights of the shires for other purposes. The principal purpose, I am convinced, was to obtain money—a conclusion that agrees with the known character of the king and the social and economic changes of the age.

The euphemistic language of the royal writs should not mislead us. In 1241 Henry III called at Worcester an assembly of the wealthier Jews from all his boroughs *ad tractandum nobiscum tam de nostra quam sua utilitate.* But the matter of mutual advantage of which they were to treat was actually a tallage of 20,000 marks.[25] When Edward I notified his good men of various towns that he had commissioned John of Kirkby to explain to them and expedite through them "certain arduous and especial concerns" of his,[26] no one could have been surprised to discover that he was negotiating for a subsidy. And contemporaries were as little mystified when parliamentary representatives were summoned to consider those other "difficult and momentous affairs" to which the writs constantly refer. They knew that they would be fortunate to escape further demands for taxes.

Mr. McIlwain goes so far as to remark that, if we confine our attention to the innovations affecting parliament under Henry III, "the contemporary evidence is strongly in favour of Bishop Stubbs' view that the original motive behind the beginning of these changes was almost entirely fiscal." [27] To my mind the evidence for a similar motive on the part of Edward I is even stronger. On reëxamining

---

[25] *Close Rolls, 1237–42,* pp. 281, 346–47.
[26] Stephenson and Marcham, No. 49C.
[27] *Cambridge Medieval History,* VII, 678.

the records of his sixteen parliaments that included deputations of the commons, Miss M. V. Clarke has found only three in which no question of a grant was apparently raised. "The evolution of the *premunientes* clause . . . to bring the proctors of the clergy to parliament," she points out, "was frankly fiscal in intention, as there was no other reason why Edward I should require their presence." [28] And it seems idle to assert that the king had the right to tax the freeholders of shire and borough at will. As a matter of fact, the royal tallage on the towns had normally been levied through negotiation with the individual communities, and in the later thirteenth century the tallage was generally supplanted by subsidies officially styled free.[29] Meanwhile, as the burden of taxation was shifted downward from the barons to their knightly tenants, it had become practically imperative for the king to seek formal grants from the county courts according to the plan adopted in 1254.[30]

When, under Edward III, the proceedings of parliament come to be entered in the rolls, they offer continuous proof that the primary task of the commons was to vote supply. The reader almost invariably knows what to expect at the opening session. After the usual preliminaries, the lord chancellor, or some other minister, would explain the reasons for the calling of the parliament. He would set forth the great expense incurred by the king in defending the realm, in promoting worthy projects abroad, in repressing civil disorder, in maintaining the regal estate, and in otherwise assuring to the English people the blessings of a sound administration; so, in the face of the existing emergency, he would urge the commons to make generous provision for his majesty's needs, promising a gracious consideration of whatever requests they might care to make. And it is a very familiar story how the commons, by formulating joint petitions and stipulating royal approval as the necessary condition to a grant of supply, ultimately established their control over the vital functions of the government.[31]

Accordingly, if the view here expressed is justified, the core of

[28] *Medieval Representation and Consent,* pp. 315 f.

[29] See particularly Stephenson and Marcham, Nos. 46F, 49E; also my article in the *Haskins Anniversary Essays.*

[30] This has been clearly demonstrated by Mr. McIlwain, *Cambridge Medieval History,* VII, 674–76.

[31] In this respect, it seems to me, the thesis of Stubbs remains fundamentally sound (*Constitutional History,* Chs. XVI, XVII).

the English representative system has not been a vague sympathy on the part of self-appointed spokesmen, a primitive custom of deeming dooms in the name of the people, or even the selection of jurors for a sort of national inquest. Rather it has been a matter of sheer political necessity, occasioned on the one hand by the king's lack of money and on the other by the growing strength of the social groups who could supply it. Although the king might use communal delegates in a variety of ways, the compelling motive behind their incorporation as an estate of parliament was economic. Without the recurring need for general taxation, there would, I believe, have been no house of commons.

In concluding, it may also be remarked that some of the constitutional features praised by Burke as "the ancient tried usages" of England were by no means so fundamental as he imagined. It was not the original practice for members of the commons to be representatives of the nation at large. Actually, the burgesses and knights of the shires were procurators of the local communities, chosen and instructed by them, responsible to them, and legally bound to be resident within them.[32] Contemporary political thought, of course, embraced no theory of democracy founded on universal suffrage. But it did recognize the interdependence of representation and popular election and, the principle of the mandate was not wholly foreign—all good Tories to the contrary notwithstanding.

[32] See especially the statute of 1413 (Stephenson and Marcham, No. 69D); also Pasquet, *Origins of the House of Commons*, pp. 68 f., 194 f., and McKisack, *Parliamentary Representation of English Boroughs*, pp. 44 f., 119 f., 139 f. How ideas of representation were affected by the social and political changes of the fifteenth century is a subject that lies beyond the scope of the present discussion.

The Theory of Balanced Government ⌒

STANLEY PARGELLIS

SO FAMOUS is the political theory of checks and balances, so well known to Americans, that he is a bold man who tries to say new things about it. I have given it the less familiar title of balanced government only to isolate and to emphasize one aspect of the theory. Ours is not the only form in which it has appeared. It is as old as the Greeks, and it had in England a career longer by half a century than its career with us. Let me define the theory as I shall treat it: in the ideal state governing power should be divided into parts, usually three parts; each part should derive so far as possible from a separate source; each should be as independent as it can be; and each should be held to its own sphere of action by checks. To whatever set of institutions this theory in times past has applied, its key notion has never varied: that government's stability and government's objectives are best accomplished by a delicate equipoise between equal powers, by mutual jealousies. Some think of a balance between abstract powers as did Madison in 1787 and Mr. Justice Sutherland in 1928: "the principle is implicit that the three powers, executive, legislative, and judicial, shall be forever separate and distinct." [1] Others conceive of a balance between classes of society, each exercising a different function: "No power is to be attributed to either estate" (king, lords, or commons), said Hunton in 1643, "which directly, or by necessary consequence, destroys the liberty of the other." [2] Jonathan Swift took literally the word balance itself, saying that first there is the part which is held, together with the hands which hold it, and then the two scales with whatever is weighed therein, and so pictured the lords as a court of judicature holding the scales of king and people. [3] Blackstone and Dean Tucker talked of a balance between the abstract moral qualities necessary

---

[1] *The Federalist*, XLVII. Springer v. Philippine Islands, 277 U.S. Rep. 201 (1928).

[2] Philip Hunton, *A Treatise of Monarchie* (1643).

[3] Jonathan Swift, *A Discourse of the Contests and Discussions between the Nobles and the Commons in Athens and Rome* (1701).

in any constitution, the qualities of strength, wisdom, and goodness, never found in conjunction in the same person or group.[4] In all these expressions is something mechanical, something artificial; even thinking in terms of three, since three is the least number by which to build a balanced structure, is artificial—unless, indeed, it be mystical. For only by a certain willfulness of thought can one reduce classes or estates of society to three, and three only; or lump under the single word "executive" both the conduct of foreign affairs and the enforcement of a legislative act; or imagine that the Supreme Court, in every decision, acts in an exclusively judicial capacity.

It is the theory, then, of the balance between three equal estates or powers that I want to isolate and examine in this brief paper. In the actual arena of politics that theory has mostly been concerned with the governing power, with the relations between executive and legislative, not with the judiciary. Men who have loathed the idea of checks and balances have still believed in an independent judiciary. They have insisted, as did some of the Founding Fathers, that judges as judges "are not to be presumed to possess any peculiar knowledge of the mere policy of public measures." [5] But they have denied the validity of the theory of balance when its advocates extended it to the making and enforcement of law and policy. I omit therefore all but passing reference to judicial functions. One can believe in an independent judiciary, even a judiciary interpreting fundamental law, along with checks and balances, or without them.

The men who gathered at Philadelphia in May, 1787, believed in both. Most of them came intending to strike a balance, though they did not know what kind. For however hardheaded they were in seeking the national and individual security they knew the country needed, however practical in adapting colonial and state constitutional experience,[6] they still bathed willy-nilly in the stream of eighteenth-century thought. Arguments for balance were all about them, in pamphlet and treatise, in legal commentary, in reports of parliamentary debates, in encyclopedias, in classical works, in books on education, on morality, on philosophy, as well as in John

---

[4] Sir William Blackstone, *Commentaries on the Laws of England,* I (1765), 49–51; Josiah Tucker, *A Treatise concerning Civil Government* (1781), p. 206.

[5] Max Farrand, ed., *The Records of the Federal Convention of 1787,* II, 73; I, 98.

[6] Benjamin F. Wright, "The Origin of the Separation of Powers in America," *Economica,* XIII (1933), 169–85.

Adams's book—the whole of it a learned defense of balance—which they were all reading in the spring of 1787,[7] and in Madison's doctrinaire pronouncements on the convention floor. Not to call them theorists is to deny the fact; their practical plan was also a deliberate monument to a theory. Experience, reason, and authority alike seemed to proclaim its truth.

Though most of this vast literature in praise of balance was English, the origins of the theory were purely classical. First formulated by Aristotle's disciples, elaborated by the Stoics, woven into a philosophy of history by Polybius, and by him carried to Rome where Cicero embraced it, it thus had, in Addison's phrase, the authority of "the greatest philosopher, the most impartial historian, and the most consummate statesman of all antiquity"; [8] the "wisest men this world ever saw," added a fervent worshiper of the 1750s.[9] The classical theory I give in the curt words of Harrington, who tolerated without accepting it:

Government . . . is of three kinds, the government of one man, or of the better sort, or of the whole people; which by their more learned names are called monarchy, aristocracy, and democracy. These [the ancients] hold, through their proneness to degenerate, to be all evil . . . The corruption . . . of monarchy is called tyranny; that of aristocracy, oligarchy; and that of democracy, anarchy. But legislators, having found these three governments at the best to be naught, have invented another, consisting of a mixture of them all, which only is good.[10]

This was the theory advanced by Machiavelli to support his glorification of Rome, and it was the ancients and Machiavelli both that Bodin thought he had effectually squelched by pointing out, simply, that balance means anarchy.[11]

The classical notion first seriously entered English politics—whence in time the Philadelphia fathers were to take it—during the heated, profound constitutional discussions that preceded the out-

---

[7] John Adams, *A Defence of the Constitutions of Government of the United States of America* (1787). Farrand, *op. cit.*, III, 33.

[8] Joseph Addison, *The Freeholder, or Political Essays*, No. 51 (1716).

[9] "This, gentlemen, is your form of government, which the wisest men this world ever saw preferred to all others, and which you now live under; this is the government which your Saxon ancestors delivered down to you, and this the government which they enjoyed with very little alteration for about thirteen hundred years." *An Address to the Electors of England* (London, M. Cooper, 1756), p. 38.

[10] James Harrington, *Oceana*, Pt. I.

[11] Machiavelli, *Discourses upon the First Decade of Titus Livius*, Lib. I, Ch. II; also Sir Robert Filmer, *The Anarchy of a Limited or Mixed Monarchy* (1648).

break of the civil wars. It slipped in almost by accident. Under the late medieval and the Tudor constitution the king was absolute, but limited,[12] bound by the law of his judges or by the law made by him in parliament; his administrative acts he performed through his council. Men spoke of three estates of the realm, but the king stood above them, without master save God and his conscience. That free regal supremacy parliament challenged in James I's reign, and far more in the 1640s. Its nineteen propositions flatly demanded sovereignty, leaving to Charles I but the "shadow and empty name of king." Of the royal answer which Charles authorized to the propositions, Hyde tells us that the pertinent part was written, while the king was at York, by Sir John Colepepper, who, without realizing the full implications, accepted and copied what some bishops and lawyers had suggested to him.[13]

There being three kinds of government amongst men [so ran Sir John's unfortunate words], absolute monarchy, aristocracy, and democracy, and all these having their particular conveniences and inconveniences, the experience and wisdom of your ancestors hath so moulded this out of a mixture of these, as to give to this kingdom (as far as human prudence can provide) the conveniences of all three without the inconveniences of any one, as long as the balance hangs even between the three estates, and they run jointly on in their proper channel.

Colepepper's three estates were king, lords, and commons, the king only equal to, and not above the others. The three shared in legislation, which was supreme and unassailable by any court; the king had specified executive or administrative powers; the commons initiated money bills and impeached ministers who violated the law; "and the lords being trusted with a judicatory power, are an excellent screen and bank between the prince and people, to assist each against any incroachments of the other, and by just judgements to preserve that law which ought to be the rule of every one of the three." [14]

Hyde records that he at first refused to print the reply, since "in

12 See Professor McIlwain's description of the late medieval constitution on pp. 7–8.
13 *The Life of Edward, Earl of Clarendon . . . Written by Himself* (Oxford, 1759), pp. 130–32. Clarendon omitted this part in reprinting the answer in his history of the rebellion, and later, in *A Brief View and Survey of the dangerous and pernicious Errors to Church and State, in Mr. Hobbes's book, entitled Leviathan*, p. 54, he asserted that the doctrine of divided sovereignty had never been heard of in England until the rebellion, for the laws of England were most clear and positive against it.
14 *His Majesties Answer to the XIX Propositions* (Oxford, Leonard Litchfield, 1642; London, 1642).

truth the bishops make the third estate, the king being the head and sovereign of the whole," and only yielded to prevent ill-feeling among the king's advisers. Within the year appeared a pamphlet which turned Colepepper's remarks into a constitutional system which the king had violated.[15]

In the history of our theory, these loose words of Colepepper's have great significance. For at least sixty years they were quoted and invoked as King Charles's constitution.[16] On them as a compromise the monarchy was restored in 1660. In 1679, to express their constitutional stand in the Danby Case, the commons copied them verbatim in the journals of the house.[17] They were recalled to the convention parliament of 1689,[18] and however much Locke may have insisted that all government came from the people, there was nothing in the whole Revolution settlement but could stand as an affirmation and support of balance. In 1701, when was tacked to the Act of Settlement a clause providing for the complete divorce of executive and legislative, appeared a forthright statement of the beauty of the theory. Sir Humphrey Mackworth quoted Charles I, praised "the happy constitution of this government, which is the glory and happiness of England and the wonder or envy of all the world," and paraphrased Cicero:

The three several powers vested in the king, lords, and commons are like the three perfect conchords in musick, which being exactly tuned to one another upon proper instruments make admirable harmony; but if you stretch any one string beyond its proper pitch, you put all out of tune, and destroy the whole concert.[19]

Now if we disregard the conventions of the constitution, Mackworth's description of it in terms of equality and balance of parts was perfectly accurate, not only in 1701 but for forty years before

---

[15] [Henry Parker?], *A Political Catechism: or, Certain Questions concerning the Government of This Land, Answered in His Majesties Own Words: Taken out of His Answer to the 19 Propositions, pag. 17, 18, 19, 20; of the First Edition* (London, 1643).

[16] As, for instance, in Garroway's speech in 1679: "If they will break the late king's constitution, let not us." Anchitell Grey, *Debates of the House of Commons* (London, 1769), VII, 336.

[17] *Commons Journals*, IX, 633.

[18] *Proposals Humbly Offered to the Lords and Commons in the Present Convention, for Settling of the Government* (1689). Printed in *State tracts: being a farther collection of several choice treatises relating to the government from the year 1660 to 1689* (London, 1692), p. 455.

[19] [Humphrey Mackworth], *A Vindication of the Rights of the Commons of England* (London, 1701), p. 6.

and after. It was a far truer description than the High Church Tory doctrine: "Monarchy implies a soleship in government, and they who to monarchy would add the epithet of mixed, make but a contradiction *in adjecto,* if by mixed they mean a division among divers." [20] It was likewise truer than the extreme Whig position that since government came from and rested upon the consent of all, Parliament, representing the nation, should choose and hold responsible to itself great executive councils.[21] It was truer because a hereditary king *did* both assent to legislation and choose administrative officers responsible to him alone; a hereditary peerage *did* sit as a legislative body and as a court of last resort; an elected commons *did* both legislate and occasionally impeach. But it was most true only at those critical moments when, with executive and legislative at swords' points, the processes of government bogged down in chaos, as in 1680 and in 1701 itself. At other times it was so shaded as to lose its point by that convention of the constitution through which government officeholders and pensioners in parliament constituted a group, almost a government party, upon which ministers could rely. Well aware that an independent, unmanaged commons meant confusion, irresponsibility, and failure, ministers did the expedient thing; they ran it, if they could. Walpole, the greatest master of the arts of parliamentary management, was later to say that he believed in independency of parts of government, but not in too much independency.[22] That is not unlike Mr. Justice Holmes's remark that our own constitution did not establish "fields of black and white," but that each field "terminated in a penumbra shading gradually from one extreme to another." [23] But the English upholders of checks and balances would have none of such shadings. They were for the most part members of an opposition, Tories and discontented Whigs. They developed the argument of checks and balances as the most telling argument possible against the control of parliament by the crown's ministers. They excoriated ministerial practices—which must be considered, however they are

[20] [White Kennet], *A Letter from a Student at Oxford to a Friend in the Country, concerning the Approaching Parliament, in Vindication of His Majesty, the Church of England, and the University* (London, 1681).

[21] Henry Neville, *Plato Redivivus; or, A Dialogue concerning Government* (1681). Reprinted, 1763.

[22] [Sir Robert Walpole], *Some Reflections upon a Pamphlet* [by Joseph Addison] *Called the Old Whig* (London, 1719).

[23] Springer v. Philippine Islands, 277 U.S. Rep. 209.

interpreted,[24] as the most important convention of the constitution before the development of cabinet responsibility—as bribery, corruption, influence, the sinister arts of ambitious men; they demanded an independent parliament with no officeholders in it, and they summoned as justification those classical authors whose virtue and wisdom, in the Augustan age of English prose, none could deny.

These opposition tactics, this invocation of a mathematically perfect constitution which could be said to exist only if one discarded those practices which kept it going, continued in the eighteenth century. Under the Georges the argument for balance was used, again by a Tory opposition, against the Septennial Act; it was the chief theoretical justification for the Peerage Bill, on the ground that the royal power of creating peers infringed the independence of the lords; [25] by its aid a series of bribery bills, or bills designed to limit the number of government officials in the house, were introduced and sometimes passed; and in its name was waged against Walpole the opposition which finally destroyed him. If we could but return to that marvelous constitution devised by the wisdom of the past—so run the electioneering pamphlets—thwart the selfish aims of evil ministers, and attain again the perfect balance between free and equal powers, then would all troubles end. Exactly the same argument was used in the 1780s, and it, and not the movement for democracy, was the real genesis of parliamentary reform.

In the third and fourth decades of the century the theory commanded its widest assent. Begun as a face-saving compromise between Tudor theories of kingship and parliamentary sovereignty, continued as a compromise between the divine right of the Jacobite Tories and the sweeping demands of parliamentary Whigs, it lasted on when those earlier doctrines had died. By 1730 most men in

[24] W. S. Holdsworth, "The Conventions of the Eighteenth Century Constitution," *Iowa Law Review*, XVII (1932), 161–80.

[25] "From which we may reasonably infer, that whatsoever tends to cause a superior power in one part, either to control, or elude the effect of the other, is unnatural to the scheme and design of the fabrick of this government, and must bring it to decay, and in time hazard the desolution of it." From *Some Considerations Humbly Offer'd, Relating to the Peerage of Great Britain* (London, 1719), p. 9. See also for similar arguments: *Two Lists: Showing the Alterations That Have Been Made in the House of Commons, from the Beginning of the Reign of K. Henry VIII, to the End of That of King James I, and in the House of Peers, from the Accession of King James I to This Time* (London, 1719[?]). [Matthew Tindal], *A Defence of Our Present Happy Establishment and the Administration Vindicated . . . from Cato's Letters* (London, 1722).

England would have agreed that all governments, and not absolute monarchy alone, were ordained and approved by God. It was an age of rational reconciliation, and men tried to reconcile the theory of original compact with the doctrine of balance. Roger Acherley, a simple-minded and long-winded lawyer, showed that after the destruction of the Tower of Babel the people speaking the British language came to England, there met in a great assembly composed of the virtuous and propertied men, debated—he prints the debates themselves and the divisions—which form of government was best, and finally set up that mixed government which ever since designing monarchs had tried to destroy.[26] William Hay, Whig officeholder, humanitarian, and hunchback, improved upon earlier categories of the abstract functions of government: "it has been the practice of the wisest nations to divide them, esteeming it as the best security of their liberty to have one part of the supreme authority a cheque upon the other."[27] It was an age when history was popular, but history defined as example enforcing precept. The precept is that artificial, mechanical one: "In a compound machine," wrote Gregory Sharpe, chaplain to the Prince of Wales, "the several parts may have different powers and a different motion . . . take away one of the powers and the machine is destroyed. It is the same in mixed governments . . ." And history was simply an evaluation of past governments by the application of this one yardstick. "By attentively considering the different forms of government we shall discover the beauties of some, the deformities of others . . . admire the excellency of mixed government, such as is our own, and how to preserve the several parts of it in an equal poise, that one may not rise up and depress the other."[28] John Adams's method, in that book which was more famous in 1787 than now,

[26] Roger Acherley, *The Britannic Constitution; or, The Fundamental Form of Government in Britain* (London, 1727).

In 1730 the Board of Trade itself could describe the constitution of royal colonies as having been deliberately framed upon the British model, the governor representing the king, the council the house of lords, and the assembly the house of commons; "that every legislative act of theirs, like those of Great Britain, might pass a threefold approbation, and that each branch of their legislature subsisting upon an independent and distinct footing, might be reciprocally checks upon the other two." Calendar of State Papers, Colonial, 1730, §500.

[27] [William Hay], *An Essay on Civil Government: Treating Summarily of Its Necessity, Original, Dissolution, Forms, and Properties* (London, 1728), p. 60.

[28] [Gregory Sharpe], *A Short Dissertation upon That Species of Misgovernment Called an Oligarchy* (London, 1748).

was exactly the same. Such unhistorically minded historians, without going as far into the British past as did Acherley, found in the Anglo-Saxon constitution the golden age of balance. From the dictionary of the arts and sciences one learned that wherever the Goths came in Europe they set up a mixed government, depending upon a due poise and balance between king, nobles and people, but that everywhere save in England it had been driven out, and hardly the shadow of liberty remained.[29] Along with the appeal to history went the appeal to the classics. Interest in Cicero reached a peak in the third and fourth decades; Polybius was rediscovered; [30] and both were used, with Aristotle, to uphold balance.

The sagacious, penetrating Aristotle [wrote George Turnbull] saw that there was a form of government the world had not yet seen, which alone can stand firm and unshaken, and which when once rightly poised and fixed on its bases, will never totter—a government compounded of democracy, aristocracy, and monarchy, so as to make a perfect equilibrium.[31]

But greatest and most influential of all political theorists in these years was Bolingbroke, Walpole's evil genius. Of his philosophy the heart was simply: "it is by this mixture of . . . power, blended together in one system, and by these three estates ballancing one another, that our free constitution of government hath been preserved so long inviolate." [32] Through Bolingbroke's inspiration the freeholders of thirteen counties and twelve boroughs instructed their representatives in 1739 and 1740 to try to decrease ministerial influence over elections, and to restore the "independence of parliaments, without which the balance of our con-

[29] Article on "Government," *New and Complete Dictionary of Arts and Sciences. By a Society of Gentlemen* (1764).

[30] [Edward Spelman], *A Fragment out of the Sixth Book of Polybius, Containing a Dissertation upon Government . . . to Which Is Prefixed a Preface Wherein the System of Polybius Is Applied to the Government of England* (London, 1743). Also *A Parallel between the Roman and British Constitution; Comprehending Polibius's Curious Discourse of the Roman Senate; with a Copious Reference wherein His Principles Are Applied to Our Government. The Whole Calculated to Restore the True Spirit of Liberty, and to Explode Dependancy and Corruption* (London, 1747). An early use of Polybius to explain the British constitution was James Arderne, *The Kingdom of England the Best Commonwealth* (1660). There is a copy in the Newberry Library. It is mentioned by Ernst Klimowsky, *Die englische Gewaltenteilungslehre bis zu Montesquieu* (1927), p. 35.

[31] George Turnbull, *Observations upon Liberal Education* (London, 1742).

[32] [Bolingbroke, Henry St. John, 1st viscount], *A Dissertation upon Parties* (5th ed., London), 1739, p. 158.

stitution cannot subsist." [33] Montesquieu's great book when it appeared simply swelled this chorus of acclaim. He did not invent checks and balances; he was but the theory's elaborator, its refiner.

Twenty years later Blackstone's formidable approval bestowed even more pontifical blessing, and in 1771 the Swiss DeLolme wrote what John Adams called "the best defence of the political balance of three powers that ever·was written." [34] But by that time the critics of balance were sharpening their weapons, finding sounder, more historical interpretations of the constitution. The theory lingered on; it was used as a defense against radical democratic ideas; it appeared in parliamentary debates in the nineteenth century. As late as 1861 a treatise could describe the British constitution as the perfect mixture of monarchy, aristocracy, and democracy, and approvingly list the many checks and balances in it. [35] A few years later Bagehot's alarming book finally slew the theory in England.

The suggestion is worth making, if we do not push it too far, that the curve of acceptance of the theory of balanced government in England corresponds to the curve of acceptance of classical, system-building, *a priori* thought. For however much the government in the seventeenth and eighteenth centuries may have approximated a government of equal, balanced estates, the terms used to justify it were taken from the realm of mathematics and physics. In those terms, as pure *a priori* theory, it defeated earlier constitutional theories, attained fruition in the mid-eighteenth century, and succumbed in time to a view of government couched less in terms of abstract forces and devices than in human, social terms, and based upon a realistic examination of the present as a development out of the past.

But even its own adherents, when they were compelled to answer the damning criticism that a state of perfect balance meant a

[33] *Great-Britain's Memorial, Containing a Collection of the Instructions, Representations, of the Freeholders . . . to Their Representatives, for These Two Years Past* (London, 1741).

[34] Jean Louis DeLolme, *The Constitution of England, or, An Account of the English Government: in Which It Is Compared, both with the Republican Form of Government, and the Other Monarchies in Europe* (London, 1775; New York, 1792. The first French edition was published at Amsterdam, 1771).

[35] Henry, Lord Brougham, *The British Constitution: Its History, Structure, and Working* (London, 1861).

state of war, deserted the realm of mathematics for that of morality. In the beautifully poised government that was England's they argued that jealousy between separate powers was necessary to maintain stability and liberty, but that harmony among separate powers was necessary to avoid chaos. Which argument was used depended entirely upon the circumstances of the moment. But throughout the whole history of the theory the need for preserving a right understanding between king and people was emphasized. The three chords must sound in tune, the three powers pull together. For if they divide on a fundamental issue, as Hunton said in 1643, "it is a case beyond the possible provision of a mixed government . . . the appeal must be to the community, as if there were no government." Acherley, following the same line, maintained that there could be no fundamental issue dividing king and people. "The true interest of the nation and people was the plainest thing in the world; it was what everybody in Britain would find, or feel, and know to be right." And for that reason no judge was needed to decide whether there had been a breach of the fundamental constitution. But when it became increasingly clear to others of Acherley's time that the appeal to the moral sense in man was not always sufficient, they went a step further. They sought to eliminate immorality and selfishness from government. And that they thought possible by taking two steps: increasing the number of virtuous, independent, patriotic, propertied gentlemen in the house of commons; and ensuring by a right education of the heir to the throne that the chief patriot and first gentleman of England should be also the king. Then would be complete agreement upon the ends of government. Then would be no parties, which they called factions and the work of schemers. But king and people, representing the same virtues, the same class, would live happily as one. To that wild end the opposition which grouped itself around the Prince of Wales in the 1740s actually worked.

When one remembers that among the Prince of Wales's group was Bubb Dodington, most notorious of eighteenth-century place hunters, it is easy to see how appeals to balance came to be regarded merely as a political rallying cry:

These are they that talk of balance and counter-balance [wrote Thomas Pownall in 1752], of one power being constitutionally a check upon another; and that it is constitutionally the duty of these to pull different ways, even where there be no real matter of difference, yet to preserve the equilibrium of power. Or if they find with all their throat and lungs that they are not able to gain that influence, which they could wish to be at the head of, then the balance is destroyed, and the constitution is gone to wreck! *Obsecro populares, ferte misero atque innocenti auxilium*. Save my country, Heaven! Save the good old constitution, for I love the constitution of my country! This or idler cant will do, and be called Liberty.[36]

But Pownall, and other contemporary critics of balance, cut more deeply than mere personal invective. They understood the fundamental problem of government, how to reconcile liberty and authority, and for many of them liberty meant more precious things than it did to Bolingbroke's country squires. Every one of the fundamental tenets of balance they answered. If it was stability of government that the equilibrium of powers was meant to assure, they replied, as Harrington had done, that real stability comes from the proportioning of political power in a state to wealth. It is not checks and balances, but the fact that England's government rests squarely upon the consent of her propertied classes, from peer to yeoman, that makes her secure. If it was liberty that division of powers was meant to guarantee, they replied that the liberty of Englishmen does not come from any real or fancied conflict between executive and legislative, but from the law which the courts enforced, law with which no government would ever tamper, the great statutes of Magna Carta, Habeas Corpus, and the Bill of Rights, the common law which is "the soul which animates the body politic, the ligaments which bind together head and members, the act and deed of the body politic." [37] What liberty do you want that you have not already under the law, asked government pamphleteers of the opposition, unless it be liberty to rule in our stead?

The critics likewise attacked the mechanical quality of pro-balance thought. Theorizing of that sort, Bishop Butler warned the house of lords in 1741, was impracticable and dangerous; [38]

---

[36] Thomas Pownall, *Principles of Polity, Being the Grounds and Reasons of Civil Empire* (London, 1752), p. 14.

[37] *Parliamentary and Political Tracts Written by Sir Robert Atkins, Late One of the Judges of the Court of Common Pleas* (London, 1734), p. 190.

[38] Quoted by Mario Einaudi, "The British Background of Burke's Philosophy," *Political Science Quarterly*, XLIX (1934), 577–78. From Butler's sermon before the

and Bentham in 1776 called Blackstone's constitution exactly what it was, a mere mathematical symbol. They also denied the absurd use of history as example enforcing precept; [39] and by 1767 could describe the constitution as having continually changed, and as having conformed in every age to the level of culture attained.[40]

And finally the critics returned to another seventeenth-century doctrine, that the power lodged in the executive is only a trust when it is separated from the legislative, and all trusts, by their nature, imply accountability.[41] In 1770 Burke recognized and rather vaguely defined a new convention of the constitution, the convention of cabinet government which a century later Bagehot was finally to popularize. As Burke read history, every sort of government, unless it was to fall into hideous disorder, must have its administration correspondent to its legislature.[42] There are bound to be parties in a state, argued Burke. Set up, then, a party ministry in trust to the nation, with power to act efficiently, within limits defined by the law, responsible to the majority of the representatives of the people, and through them to the people themselves—that is Burke's great contribution to the art and practice of government.

Neither Pownall, nor Butler, nor Bentham, nor Burke was ever quoted at Philadelphia. Some members, like Franklin, would perhaps have agreed with them. But too few voices were raised in the convention, as too few in the eighteenth century, to offset the clear-cut, beautiful, unreal symbolism of government as an equipoise of equal powers.

---

house of lords, on Jan. 30, 1741, in *Fifteen Sermons Preached at the Rolls Chapel . . . To Which Are Added, Six Sermons Preached on Public Occasions* (4th ed., 1749).

39 *The Ancient and Modern Constitution of Government Stated and Compared, and Also Some Remarks on the Controversy concerning the Dependance of Members of Parliament on the Crown.* (London, J. Roberrts [sic], 1734).

40 Edward King, *An Essay on the English Constitution and Government* (London, 1767).

41 *The Judgment of Whole Kingdoms and Nations, concerning the Rights, Power, and Prerogative of Kings, and the Rights, Priviledges, and Properties of the People* (7th ed., London, 1713).

42 Edmund Burke, *Thoughts on the Cause of the Present Discontents* (1770).

European Doctrines and the Constitution ∞ R. M. MacIVER

WHATEVER may be the eruptive forces that precipitate the grand events of history, it can scarcely be denied that the particular contours of these events are molded by the thoughts of dominant minds. Underneath may lie the tensions and strains of the mass, but on every peak and crag are inscribed the insignia of the architect, the creative thinker. This holds as true of the American Revolution as of the French or of the Russian. It is as manifest in the more sober outlines of the Constitution as in the flaring upthrust of the Declaration of Independence.

In the political agitations that preceded the establishment of the Constitution the architectonic ideas were not indigenous but were derived from European, and above all from English, speculative thought. The thinkers who heralded the Revolution went back in particular to seventeenth-century England for the form and the idiom of their political philosophy. In America itself the speculative ground for this utterly unexpected event was unprepared. Neither the earlier theological preoccupations of the Puritan aristocracy nor such democratic revolts from them as were represented by Roger Williams had any relevance to the emergent issues. The older American tradition was decaying. The back country, to which the new immigrants, the ex-indentured men from Scotland, Ireland, and Germany were penetrating, was as yet politically mute. Among the leaders, in Charleston as in Boston, the Tory style was in the ascendant. There was nothing here from which to fashion the philosophy appropriate, indeed necessary, for the making of the new republic. Never in the history of the United States were the minds of men so exercised by argument over doctrines and theories of government as in the three decades of debate and contention that began about 1761. But the principles they proclaimed, the broad inevitable principles by which men justify alike their aspirations and their ambitions, were formulated in the England of a century before. For in that England, in the sequence of crises ending in the "Glorious Revolution," out of all the heresies and schisms of that time, there had emerged one distinctive mode of thinking, one "ideology" if you will, that proved notably congenial to the spirit of the new America. Of that mode of thinking the most adequate exponent was John Locke, and, curiously enough, Locke spoke in terms that were far more applicable to the American than to the English scene.

The seminal works of the age were English and French, those of Montesquieu, the physiocrats, and Rousseau on the one hand, and those of Locke, Harrington, Blackstone, Hume, Adam Smith, Algernon Sidney, and Tom Paine on the other. But Locke came nearest to the heart of the case. If an occasional criticism was passed on his plan of legislation for Carolina, as was done by John Adams—who did not accurately report it—it was only to show how "the most resplendent genius" may fail in practice.[1] The *Second Treatise on Government* was almost beyond criticism. How satisfying was Locke's persistent association of the ideas of liberty and property, with the unqualified corollary that no man could rightly be taxed without his own consent! How convenient for this undeveloped continent was his view of property, itself probably derived from his own acquaintance with American conditions, as that which a man appropriated by his labor from out the vast storehouse of nature! How well his simple concept of the "state of nature" served to turn men's thoughts from traditional notions of sovereignty, and how easy it was to see, with Benjamin Franklin, the same "state of nature" in the life of the American Indians! How comfortably did Locke's "law of nature," breathing quiet optimism and what Samuel Johnson of King's College spoke of as the "milder deism," fit in with the temper of an age that was retreating from a Calvinistic God to the God of nature, the invisible hand, the "legislator of the universe"! It is no wonder that Jefferson spoke of Locke as one of the three greatest men of all time, linking him with Newton and Bacon. The *ipsissima verba* of the *Second Treatise on Government* fell naturally from the lips of the fathers of the Constitution. These words seemed to express the very nature of things. "Do not every man's feelings," asked Franklin, "declare that his property is not to be taken from him without

[1] *Works of John Adams*, ed. by C. F. Adams, IV, 463–64.

his own consent?" [2] Add to Locke's teaching Montesquieu's more explicit doctrine of division of powers, inject into it some republican fervor, and you have the whole substance of the Virginia Bill of Rights, and indeed of all the preambles, manifestoes, and declarations of principle that followed.

I am not implying that the thinkers, publicists, and debaters of the constitution-making age merely echoed the doctrines of seventeenth-century England. They were theorists for a purpose and they took from these doctrines what was congenial to that purpose. English philosophy of the seventeenth century was the arsenal from which they drew the intellectual weapons they needed. Even Locke was treated in this way. Locke had made the legislature supreme over the executive and over the courts. But this aspect of Locke's theory the Americans finally rejected and in the rejection lay one essential difference between the emergent political system of America and that of England.

The pragmatic adaptation of European political ideas throughout the political developments converging on the Constitution is best revealed if we distinguish three stages of that process. In the first stage, beginning perhaps with the agitation over the Stamp Act, the main protest is in the name of fundamental law within the existing order, established by charter, by precedent, by the common law, by the series of acts beginning with Magna Carta which defined the principles of the British constitution. These principles, as the resolution of the Massachusetts house of representatives, inspired by Samuel Adams, stated in 1765, were "founded in the Law of God and of Nature" and were "the common rights of mankind." [3] But the appeal was for the vindication of rights regarded as already established within the Constitution. The nature of these rights had been set forth once for all by "the great Mr. Locke." They were summed up in his words that the legislature "cannot take from any man any part of his property without his own consent." "The position," declared Samuel Adams, "that taxation and representation are inseparable, is founded on the immutable laws of nature." [4]

[2] B. Franklin's marginal note on Ramsey, *Thoughts on the Origin and Nature of Government*, p. 27.

[3] Samuel Adams, *Writings*, I, 23–24.

[4] *Ibid.*, I, 175.

The ingeniously simple formulations of Locke were, however, two-edged. In his political philosophy, as in his epistemology, Locke always refrained from drawing the more radical conclusions implicit in his premises. He went so far and no further, never inquiring whether the road he followed did not lead far beyond his acceptable goals, beyond the doctrine of toleration and beyond the rights of freeholders. It was the spirit of Locke's political philosophy, and not its radical implications, that was so congenial to the thinkers and statesmen of America. A minority of radicals, like Samuel Adams, might draw the democratic conclusion that the ultimate sovereign is the people and that men owe no allegiance to laws they have not approved or to princes they have not set up. He interprets Locke in the terms of democratic individualism. "Mr. Locke, in his treatise on government . . . shows that express consent alone makes any one a member of any commonwealth." [5] But for the vast majority there was as yet no denial of a common allegiance nor on the other hand any readiness to accept the more radical implications of the "consent of the people." A few, like Patrick Henry and James Warren, were beginning to speak the complete language of the "rights of man," so much less circumspect than the Lockean language of "natural rights." The English republicans, particularly Algernon Sidney and Milton, were being read with new interest, but more for their views on liberty than for their republican sentiments. Benjamin Franklin had commended both for the education of the youth of Pennsylvania [6] and had given a special tribute to the "immortal *Discourses on Government* of Sidney, the British Brutus, the warm, the steady friend of liberty." [7] Harrington, who in his *Oceana* combined a republican philosophy with an aristocratic respect for landed property, was beginning to influence such men as John Adams and James Otis.[8] It is significant that Harrington ranks next to Locke among the English writers who had vogue in America. For Harrington political power went with land, and political leadership reposed with the landed proprietors. For Locke the preservation of property was the chief end of government. In its formative stage the

[5] *Ibid.*, II, 257–58.
[6] *Works*, II, 386–96.
[7] *Ibid.*, II, 295.
[8] Cf. T. Dwight, "Harrington and His Influence upon American Political Institutions," *Political Science Quarterly*, II (1887), 1–44.

movement that culminated in revolution was not a mass movement. Its philosophy was not by intention democratic. It had no
thought to subvert the economico-political *status quo*. The foundation of order was already set. The basis of protest was established
rights, and with John Adams and later with Alexander Hamilton
the appeal was from the acts of a parliament that overstepped its
bounds to the monarchy from which the original colonial charters
emanated.[9] This inherent conservatism of the first stage may be
illustrated by the attitude of the most cosmopolitan of American
thinkers, Benjamin Franklin. Although later in attacking the
order of the Cincinnati, he declared that he saw "more propriety,
because less hazard of mischief, in having hereditary professors of
mathematics" than in having hereditary legislators,[10] he nevertheless clung to the principle of a hereditary, though constitutional
monarchy, until the tide of revolution rendered it untenable. And
although in the revolutionary period he proclaimed that "the
franchise is the common right of freemen" his earlier view was that
those who had no landed property should have no vote in the affairs of government.[11]

As the rift with Great Britain widened into a chasm we enter
upon the second stage, which may be roughly identified as the
decade from 1772 to 1782. Now the doctrine of "natural rights"
becomes the indubitable ground of revolution and the necessary
foundation of a new order. The social contract doctrine takes on a
new amplitude. The consent of the people must mean that of the
people as a whole. The more radical note dominates. The Massachusetts delegates to the first Congress of 1774 are warned in New
York not to be too extreme for the milder temper of the Southern
delegates, and find that the South is prepared to go further than
themselves. A year later it is the young Southerner Jefferson who is
entrusted to state the American case, and in the most eloquent
language he proclaimed the rights of a people born free and equal.
Presently that language passed into the Virginia Bill of Rights and
into the Declaration of Independence. The principle of liberty was
released from the bracket of property. All power abides in and

---

9 Cf. *Novanglus* (Works of John Adams, IV, 99 ff.) and *The Farmer Refuted* (Works
of Alexander Hamilton, ed. J. C. Hamilton, II, 43–55).
10 *Works*, VI, 371. Cf. R. Eiselin, *Franklin's Political Theories*, pp. 79–80.
11 Cf. Eiselin, *loc. cit.*

derives from the people. Governments are not merely their trustees, they are also their servants.

Two contemporary books written by Englishmen had their effect at this juncture. It may seem curious that Blackstone's *Commentaries* was one of them. But Blackstone, jurist as he was, stated in the simplest and indeed the most naïve form the Lockean principle of inherent and indefeasible rights. Blackstone, whose work was very popular in England, was already being taught at William and Mary College. Burke in his Conciliation Speech of 1775 called attention to Blackstone's vogue in America. "I hear," he said, "that they have sold nearly as many of Blackstone's *Commentaries* in America as in England. General Gage marks out this disposition very particularly in a letter on your table." The other work was Tom Paine's *Common Sense,* published in America a few months before the Declaration of Independence. It is hardly conceivable that the iconoclastic passion of this manifesto would at any other time have deeply stirred the country. The time was exactly ripe. The old Whig appeals, from the parliament of England to the realm, from laws to royal charters, from executive encroachment to the constitutional monarchy, were ended with the fight at Lexington. And now came a pamphlet which branded monarchy as an abomination and inveighed against kings as the worst tyrants of the people. America was not only to be free, it was to be the one free land on earth, liberated from the oppressive traditions of the lands beyond the sea. This was the significance of Paine, that he proclaimed the end of the colonial attitude, and that he supplied the prophetic vision of a new Jerusalem on American soil, not the old Puritan vision but the dynamic myth of the one emancipated people, so that America might become the great "asylum for mankind."

As we pass into the third stage, wherein the issue was no longer the vindication of rights but the sure establishment of a greater state, there is again a very significant process of change in the atmosphere of thought. The change may be regarded as a mode of compromise between the dominant spirit of the first stage and that of the second, though there is a strong deflation of the more idealistic conception of democracy. Pragmatic aims are now more compelling than ultimate ideals. Nevertheless, theories of the state still play an important role. While it was the exigencies of the immediate situation, such as the need for compromise between the demands of the great states and those of the small states, that controlled the specific terms of the final covenant, yet men do not derive their practical expedients from sheer experience or from the mere light of nature. John Dickinson was demanding the impossible when he said at the Federal Convention: "Experience must be our only guide. Reason may mislead us." [12] Just as the Articles of Confederation and the state constitutions were heavily drawn upon to provide the formulas of the new document, so were the political theories of the time. Whether they are framing constitutions or pursuing their daily business, whether they are deemed to be demigods or to be more common clay, the thoughts of men run on the rails laid down in advance of action by their intellectual habits.

On the surface there was a greater doctrinal consensus in the second stage than in the third. The pragmatic test brought out the underlying differences. But the tide of effective opinion moved away from Paine and Jefferson in the direction represented by John Adams, who later wrote to none other than Jefferson that he had "never read reasoning more absurd, sophistry more gross . . . than the subtle labors of Helvetius and Rousseau to demonstrate the natural equality of mankind." It moved in the direction of Sherman and the Pinckneys and John Dickinson and Madison and Hamilton, who tempered Locke with the pessimism of Hobbes or with the skepticism of Hume. The doctrine that all men were "created equal" was no longer a self-evident truth, when the question had become one of its application, not to a whole people as a unity but to the social order and to individual men. It is a necessary *datum* of the nascent constitution, that "the people are the only legitimate fountain of power" [13] and that "federal and state governments are in fact but different agents and trustees of the people." [14] But the people are not to be construed as Rousseau's "people," the totality of component human beings expressing their sovereign will. There was besides the nice question whether the slaves should be counted as persons, or as three-fifths of persons, or as not persons at all. Liberty must reign, but it is Locke's "lib-

---

[12] James Madison, *Writings,* IV, 186.
[13] *The Federalist,* No. 49.
[14] *Ibid.,* No. 46.

erty," the liberty that is conjoined with property. The people must be sovereign, but in effect it is Locke's "people," the people with the stake of possessions, or even Burke's "people," the men of substance, discretion, and experience. The franchise must be universal, but the noxious growth of parties, otherwise "factions," must be avoided. The whole body of citizens must be the final arbiter of government, but under such conditions as to check what Alexander Hamilton called "the imprudence of democracy."

So in the constitution-framing stage the great problem of statesmanship is conceived as being the creation of such a balance between opposing interests or powers as will sustain the unity of the whole, protect each against all, and safeguard the established scheme of rights.[15] This was the problem to which the Constitution was the answer. There were statesmen of that age, some of its greatest figures, who thought—as Jefferson did on one count and Franklin on another—that the final problem of statesmanship was not properly set in these terms.[16] There are also worthy critics of our own day who agree with them. History does not decide between ideals. What history has decided is that, given the problem as the founders of the Constitution saw it, they solved it with eminent, and indeed unparalleled, success.

When the stream of history has once carved its channel we assume that it could have followed along no other path. But we can still raise at least this speculative question: What might have happened had such and such influences not been present? That there were other ways of stating and of solving the problem of the Constitution the debates of the time amply reveal. That the finally accepted way alike of stating and of solving it was influenced by the prevalent philosophies of government is equally clear. Even when we concede that these particular philosophies prevailed because they were in harmony with the attitudes or the interests of those who espoused them, their influence remains no less real.

Never before had the world seen an example of a balance of powers so elaborate and so consciously contrived as that provided in the Constitution. But the doctrine of balance had been pro-

[15] See, for example, *The Federalist*, No. 10 (Madison).

[16] Franklin likened the system of checks and balances to the putting of one horse before the cart and another behind—and whipping them both, the result being an arrest of motion or the dissolution of the cart. Cf. *Works of Thomas Paine*, Conway, ed., IV, 465.

claimed by various political thinkers, and particularly by those thinkers who, not only in the culminating stage but throughout the whole period of political ferment, were of most account in America. It was implicit in Locke, restraining the logic of his democratic ideas. A full generation before Locke it had been explicitly announced by Harrington as a primary condition of a stable state and embodied in his plan of an "equal commonwealth," his "empire of laws and not of men." Harrington was one of those detached and original thinkers who miss the tide of influence in their own time and place, to strike it again with greater effect in a later age. His ingenious and foresighted interest in the mechanism of representative government, his sense of the importance of land, and his combination of an aristocratic outlook with a zeal for republican institutions, made "the incomparable Harrington," as Otis called him, one of the most reputed authors of the constitution-making period.[17]

During this period the thinkers who had most effect were those who were at the same time liberalistic in policy and fundamentally conservative in outlook. It was precisely these thinkers who inclined to the principle of a balanced government. An example is Blackstone, who did not let his doctrine of indefeasible rights prevent him from finding an admirable proportion and balance in the British Constitution. Another work that was drawn on to the same effect was the *Essays* of David Hume. The studied moderation and the tempered skepticism of Hume were particularly attractive to Hamilton. It is significant that in the concluding paragraph of *The Federalist,* when Hamilton is seeking to sum up the whole matter, he has recourse to the "solid and ingenious Hume." "To balance a large state or society," he quotes from the *Essays,* "whether monarchical or republican, is a work of so great difficulty, that no human genius, however comprehensive, is able, by the mere dint of reason and reflection, to effect it. The judgments of many must unite in the work; experience must guide their labor; time must bring it to perfection." This was also the spirit of Hume's great friend, Adam Smith, himself an advocate of a federal system of government for the British Empire. His economic doctrine was *par excellence* a doctrine of the balance of interests, the counterpart and indeed the logical foundation of the principle

[17] Cf. H. F. Russell Smith, *Harrington and His Oceana.*

of the balance of powers. As such it appealed to Hamilton, who is recorded to have read the *Wealth of Nations* as soon as the first copies crossed the Atlantic.[18]

But none of these advocates of balance attained the authority of Montesquieu, "the oracle," says Madison, "who is always consulted and cited on this subject."[19] That the influence of Montesquieu was effective is evident not only from the definite embodiment in the Constitution, no less than in the earlier Bills of Rights, of his doctrine of the division of powers, but also from the frequent appeals made to his authority on other grounds. The ninth number of *The Federalist* is entirely devoted to meeting an attack on the republican principle, which professed to base itself on certain observations of Montesquieu, circulated "with great assiduity" by the opponents of the Constitution. Both Madison and Hamilton turn the tables on their critics by citing from that author a passage in which he dwells on the merits of a "confederate republic," a passage that Hamilton proclaims to be "a luminous abridgement of the principal arguments in favor of the Union."[20]

Nevertheless, the balanced state which Madison did so much to construct and Hamilton so much to defend had a character entirely different from that of the exemplars and models to which they pointed. The functional division of powers does not imply the constituent division of sovereignty itself. The latter had no real precedents.[21] It flouted an agelong tradition. It owed nothing to Locke or Harrington or even Montesquieu. Greatly influenced by European political philosophies as were the builders of the Republic, the fabric they constructed was in essentials, almost without their knowing it, profoundly new. That part of the ancient tradition of government that might have stood in the way they rejected almost without discussion. One of the ablest of the representatives at the Federal Convention, Rufus King of Massachusetts, expressed on one occasion his amazement that men were ready to sacrifice their substantial good to the "phantom of sovereignty." But it was only a phantom, vanishing before the face of necessity. They did not reason with it, they merely ignored it.

---

[18] Cf. C. G. Bowers, *Jefferson and Hamilton.*
[19] *The Federalist*, No. 47.
[20] *Ibid.*, No. 9. See also No. 43.
[21] Cf. S. Mogi, *The Problem of Federalism*, I, Ch. 1.

Therefore the political philosophy of the Constitution is a different thing from the political philosophies that moved its creators. In this respect they builded better than they knew, indeed better than the world yet knows.

Mercantilism : the Old English Pattern of a Controlled Economy ~ CONYERS READ

"MERCANTILISM" is a word borrowed by Adam Smith from France to designate the ideas prevalent in the political economy of the old regime. In time it applies roughly to the period between the end of the Middle Ages and the end of the eighteenth century; in place, to western Europe. It does not of course mean exactly the same thing at different times, or in different places at the same time.[1]

As distinguished from the period which preceded it, mercantilism approached the problems of political economy in terms of the nation as opposed to the municipality; as distinguished from the gospel of laissez faire which displaced it, it contemplated a controlled economy. That is about as far as we can go in the way of a definition generally applicable, though it is necessary to differentiate mercantilism from what Dicey has called collectivism, which is also national in its frame of reference and also advocates a controlled economy. The distinguishing feature here is that mercantilism advocated a controlled economy as a means of promoting the wealth and power of the state in the aggregate, whereas collectivism starts from the individual and undertakes to apply state control to promote the welfare and happiness of the individual. We might say that mercantilism exploited the individual to promote the power of the state, whereas collectivism exploits the power of the state in order to promote the welfare of the individual.

So much we can say and with approximate accuracy, whether we are speaking of the sixteenth or of the eighteenth century, and whether of England, of Germany, or of France. My concern is with England, for it can hardly be doubted that the economic thinking of our forefathers who wrote the Constitution was much more influenced by English than by continental conditions. I re-

[1] Much the best discussion of mercantilism as a whole is that by Eli Heckscher, *Mercantilism,* English trans. 2 vols. (London, 1935).

fer now not to the conscious theorizers who had read the writings of the Physiocrats and perhaps even the *Wealth of Nations*,[2] but to the all-pervasive climate of economic opinion which determined the standards of the average man.

It is important at the outset to recognize that while we may consider English mercantilism either as a pattern of economic thinking or as a policy of economic control or as a climate of economic opinion, it will not do to confuse one with the other. If therefore I confine my attention to economic policy, it will be understood that I am not unaware of the importance of other aspects of mercantilism, and that I am not intending to identify economic policy either with contemporaneous economic theory or with contemporaneous popular ideas about economic matters.

Yet even if one limit one's attention to economic policy, one is still faced with the difficulty of deciding just where to look for the authentic manifestations of it. The place to which one naturally turns first is to the statutes dealing with matters economic, statutes like the famous Act of Apprentices or the even more famous Navigation Acts. But the most cursory investigation reveals at once that laws often remain on the statute books centuries after they have ceased to be enforced and that even when they are enforced there is no uniformity about their enforcement. A law may be consistently applied, it may be consistently disregarded, or it may be sometimes applied and sometimes disregarded, or it may be applied in general but subject to dispensation in particular cases. One gets the impression, for example, from a study of Tudor legislation that laws were often made simply for the purpose of selling licenses to break them.[3] We can never assume that a law provides an accurate index to the economic policy of a government until we investigate the efforts on the part of the government to enforce it. As a matter of fact, economic legislation unrepealed on the English statute books presented a complete picture of a mercantilist economy long years after mercantilism was in fact a creed outworn.

---

[2] Notably, of course, Benjamin Franklin. For his relations with the Physiocrats and with Smith, cf. W. A. Wetzel, *Benjamin Franklin as an Economist.* "Johns Hopkins University Studies," XIII, 462 ff.

[3] This was notably true of the laws forbidding the export of unfinished cloth. Cf. on this subject Astrid Friis, *Alderman Cockayne's Project and the Cloth Trade* (Copenhagen, 1927), pp. 39 ff.

Nor is the administration of the law always conclusive. The executives of the government might approve of a law in principle which they found inexpedient to enforce in practice, or they might be guided by political partisanship, by religious bias, by economic interest. These considerations became increasingly important in England after the Revolution of 1688, when the power of the king gave way to the power of the cabinet and when cabinets rose and fell in response to the vicissitudes of party warfare. But it was in some measure true even before that. No one can read the records of the Parliament of 1621, so laboriously collected and so admirably edited by Professor Notestein and his co-adjutors,[4] without perceiving how widely at variance English politicians were even then upon some of the fundamental economic issues of the time.

And we must further consider the attitude of the courts of justice, the actual interpretation of the laws in judicial decisions. Nothing like adequate attention has been paid to this aspect of the matter, though it is clear enough that even in a country without a written constitution the application of the law is determined not only by the law as it is written or even as it is administered, but also by the law as it is interpreted in the courts. This also became increasingly important in the eighteenth century, when legislation in matters economic practically ceased and administration grew more and more languid. Then it was judge-made law which became the decisive factor in defining and enforcing economic policy.

Moreover, we must be careful always about using the term economic policy in the sense of any recognized underlying principle governing political action in economic matters. English political action has always been pragmatical, opportunist, designed to meet an immediate situation, not to conform to a definite program. Looking backward we can perhaps discover that the concrete acts in the aggregate form a consistent pattern and disclose a fairly consistent policy. But we must be careful not to assume that what we see in perspective was seen by the actors in the drama, nor that they were conscious of any guiding principle more profound than what they would themselves have called practical common sense.

[4] *Commons Debates, 1621,* ed. Wallace Notestein, Frances H. Relf, Hartley Simpson. 7 vols. (New Haven, 1935).

This much is clear to start with, that in the conception of a national economy and in the development of a national economic policy England was undoubtedly more precocious than the rest of Europe. The reasons for this are fairly obvious and need not detain us. And yet in England as in the rest of Europe the notion of a controlled economy antedated nationalism. There as elsewhere we have to look for the antecedents of a national economy to the municipal economy which preceded it. The concept of a national economy in England, in its earlier form, was in many respects simply an extension of the municipal concept to the national area. On that account there are elements in the earlier pattern which cannot be ignored if we are to comprehend the later one.

One of these was very definitely the fear of food scarcity. It is amazing to discover when one comes to examine municipal regulation of matters economic, how much of it was directed to the business of keeping up the quality and keeping down the price of food—particularly of those two staples, bread and beer. Speculation in food stuffs was not only frowned upon, it was definitely and severely punished. The engrosser, the regrater, and the forestaller, all of them manipulators of the grain market, were branded from one end of England to the other as the common enemies of mankind. Long after the towns had established a system of rigid protection for their industrial products, they insisted upon a free market for food stuffs. It is of course not surprising that they should have looked to their interests as consumers when their interests as producers were not in question. It is, however, rather surprising, in an England which was until the nineteenth century overwhelmingly agricultural, that the indifference of the towns to the interests of the agricultural producer should have been reflected as much as it was in the national economy. For it is apparent that the national policy toward food stuffs continued to be dominated by the consumer's interest until well past the middle of the seventeenth century—well past the time when English economic policy otherwise was pretty completely dominated by the producer's interest.[5]

It is, however, easy to overemphasize this aspect of the matter. In point of fact when the Tudors undertook to establish national

---

[5] D. G. Barnes, *The History of the Corn Laws* (London, 1930), Ch. I.

control in economic matters, they took definitely into account the agricultural as well as the industrial interests. Queen Elizabeth's Statute of Apprentices [6] which Professor Heckscher declares to have been the most ambitious attempt in the whole history of mercantilism to define in a single law a national economic policy,[7] favored agriculture at every turn. Even so it not only left to the towns the control of industry, but it tried to check the movement of the most important of all English industries, the manufacture of cloth, to the countryside.[8]

There was also another element in the earlier municipal economy which we must not lose sight of, for it was not absent from the minds of the Tudors and the early Stewarts though it faded quite away in the later days of mercantilism. That element was the rather definite subordination of what we should call the profit motive. The medieval community did not identify prosperity with material wealth. We may leave out of account purely ascetic considerations—that preoccupation with the world to come which underlay most medieval calculations and which always operated to discredit gainful occupations. The medieval man thought rather in terms of the group interest than of the individual interest. He thought in terms of a static society where there was only so much to go round and where you had to rob Peter to pay Paul. He thought not so much in terms of progress as in terms of security. He thought in terms of working for a living, therefore he condemned the money lender and the whole practice of lending money at interest. But he thought also in terms of getting a decent living by working. There was such a thing as a just price, there was such a thing as a fair wage, there was such a thing as the equitable distribution of economic opportunity so that each man should get his rightful share. To be sure, the municipal economists limited their attention to municipal interests and were quite merciless in their consideration of those beyond the town walls. But within their liberties the general welfare was the paramount consideration, and the objective of municipal regulation was to curb the individual acquisitiveness in the interests of the common

[6] 5⁰ Eliz. ch. 4, *Statutes of the Realm*, ed. A. Luders, *et al.*, IV, pp. 414 ff. The abbreviated versions of this important statute often leave out essential parts of it.

[7] Heckscher, *op. cit.*, I, 226.

[8] It did, however, recognize and make some provision for the "putting-out" system among the country weavers, for example in section XXV.

good. I do not mean that the medieval man did not seek his individual advantage; but I do mean, emphatically, that if he succeeded in raising his head very far above the common level of his
class, he had to justify his performance in terms of the common
good or be in danger of the judgment.[9]

The important point is not that medieval human nature was
less frail, but that its social and ethical standards were rather
clearer than they have since become—and that the mere accumulation of wealth did not enjoy the social approbation which it has
since acquired.

With the development of a money economy and the expansion
of trade, this state of things changed and with its change came a
gradual modification of social attitudes. Yet certainly a good deal
of the ethical and social content of the municipal economy was
transferred to the national economy and must be taken into account in any study of the earlier phases of mercantilism. It was
clearly the social argument which determined the attitude of the
Tudors and the early Stewarts toward the enclosure movement, it
was certainly the social argument which persistently opposed the
manipulation of the market in food stuffs and it was very definitely
the social argument which forced the clothiers to buy cloth from
the weavers when cloth was a drug on the market.[10]

It would be interesting if time served to follow the history of
mercantilism in terms of the gradual subordination of all other
considerations to the consideration of pecuniary wealth. As so
often happens the change came in fact before it was realized or
recognized or approved, and men paid lip service to the old ideals
long after they had ceased to be practical guides to conduct. A
great deal of the social literature of the sixteenth century took
the form of a protest against the greed, competition, and commercialism of the age, and the social reformers almost without
exception were calling for a rehabilitation of the old ethical and
social standards. Sir Thomas More's *Utopia* was much more medieval than modern in its essential attributes and the "very and

---

[9] Upon this subject in general, cf. R. H. Tawney, *Religion and the Rise of Capitalism* (London, 1926), as well as Prof. Tawney's earlier articles on the same subject in
Journal of Political Economy, XXXI (1923), 461–93, 637–74, 804–25.

[10] On the social aspects of the enclosure movement, R. H. Tawney, *The Agrarian
Problem in the Sixteenth Century* (London, 1912), particularly pp. 390 ff.; on the control of the cloth trade, Astrid Friis, *op. cit.*, pp. 26 ff.

true" commonwealths desired by Starkey and Crowley were after much the same pattern.[11] Other reformers followed later in the century, among them one of Elizabeth's own secretaries, Thomas Wilson.[12] They all sang much the same song—the swan song of the old order. Over half a century later we still get reverberations of it in Richard Baxter's *Christian Directory* and later still in Bunyan's *Pilgrim's Progress* and in his *Life and Death of Mr. Badman*. But Baxter's homiletics provoked little or no response from the wicked and perverse generation of Charles II, and Bunyan's popularity was rather due to the tales that he told than to the gospel that he preached. Already before the end of the sixteenth century a new code of morals was shaping itself to meet the requirements of a new conception of progress—a code of morals which made a virtue out of diligence in business and a great virtue out of business success. Professor Tawney has traced the gradual development and the ultimate triumph of this new pattern of morality so I need not dwell upon it. Our own Benjamin Franklin put the matter in a nut shell, though the expression was not original with him, in his "Honesty is the best policy." Nothing could be more characteristic of eighteenth-century English attitudes than this justification of moral rectitude in terms of business prosperity.[13]

It is to be noted to the credit of both the Tudors and the early Stewarts that they fought hard against the increasing commercialism of their times. English mercantilism as they applied it still retained a certain medieval flavor, still in some measure subordinated purely economic considerations to a larger social interest. But they had to fight an uphill fight. It became apparent as the sixteenth century gave place to the seventeenth that the policy of a controlled economy in the general welfare was becoming increasingly hard to impose. It called for an increasing amount of government oversight in all departments of economic life, and an increasingly elaborate administrative machine. In France later Colbert was able to develop a fairly efficient bureaucracy for the

[11] For More, cf. in particular R. W. Chambers, *Thomas More* (New York, 1935), pp. 125 ff.; for Starkey and Crowley, J. W. Allen, *A History of Political Thought in the Sixteenth Century* (London, 1928), pp. 138 ff.

[12] On the economic ideas of Thomas Wilson reference should be made to R. H. Tawney's brilliant introduction to *Wilson's Discourse on Usury* (London, 1927).

[13] The conventional eighteenth-century pattern of morality in England is well discussed in Norman Sykes, *Church and State in England in the Eighteenth Century* (Cambridge, Eng., 1934), pp. 257 ff.

purpose. But that was never possible in England. There more and more the whole burden of administration was shifted to the shoulders of the justices of the peace, who were neither trained to the business nor paid for doing it. They passed on as much of it as they could to subordinate officials no better qualified and no better paid. This meant that not only was the job badly done but it was done with constant reference to the economic interests of the class from which the J.P.s were recruited. It was that same class also which dominated the house of commons, that class moreover which to a considerable extent guided and determined articulate public opinion.[14] And so it was that when the early Stewarts came to loggerheads with their parliaments, they antagonized at the same time the very class upon which they had to depend for the execution of their policies. They made some attempt to build up independent agencies by transferring powers of government to private corporations or to individual monopolists. But here financial considerations intruded and what might have developed into an effective regulative device became more and more simply a money-raising expedient. The poverty of the early Stewarts colored their whole social program with a mercenary cast which robbed it of its popular appeal and gave the force of the moral argument to their opponents.

With the execution of Charles I the balance of power in the state passed definitely to parliament. It is true that monarchy was restored under Charles II, but restored on terms which if not expressed were implied. The Restoration marks the definite abandonment by the crown of any social and economic program, indeed of any program at all. Charles's personal popularity and his fine eye for the main chance prevented any serious trial of strength between crown and parliament during his reign, but after Charles's death his less engaging and less tactful brother brought the conflict to a head once more, and so preponderant was the strength of parliament that the issue was decided without a struggle. There-

[14] There is no first-rate book on the J.P.'s in the seventeenth century. S. & B. Webb, *English Local Government*, Pt. I, "The Parish and the County" (London, 1906), is excellent for the late seventeenth and the eighteenth century. Prof. E. P. Cheyney has a good account of the sixteenth-century J.P.'s in his *History of England from the Defeat of the Armada to the Death of Elizabeth*, 2 vols. (New York, 1914–26), II, 313–42.

after for better or worse the economic and social policy of England proceeded from parliament.

And parliament, as has been pointed out already, was drawn from the same class socially and economically as supplied the justices of the peace. We shall not be surprised, therefore, to discover that the British mercantilism of the late seventeenth and the eighteenth century was an economy controlled by the county and city magnates and that the national interest was identified with the interests of those particular groups.

As contrasted with the sixteenth-century version of mercantilism, the moral and social considerations which had tempered purely acquisitive impulses had largely passed away. The enclosure movement, which operated in general against the small landholder in favor of the large one, proceeded without further restraint at an accelerated pace until there was no more land left to enclose and until the yeomanry class in which the Tudors had taken so much pride had been practically exterminated. The insistence upon a fair price and a high standard of quality was abandoned, or where it still persisted, persisted simply as a fiscal expedient.[15] The gild regulations of industry within the towns were, if not removed, disregarded.[16] The state regulation of wages, originally designed to establish a direct relationship between earnings and the cost of living, was virtually ignored—in reality if not in form, and the wage earners were left to the unchartered mercies of the law of supply and demand. And all this happened, not by any change in the law, for the Statute of Apprentices remained on the statute books until 1814, but simply by a failure to enforce the law. It is quite apparent, if we examine the decisions in cases arising under that statute, that the judges generally favored the principle of freedom of contract as against the statutory restrictions, generally supported the right of a man to work at his chosen trade as against the limitations imposed by gild regulations or apprenticeship requirements.[17] In the eighteenth century

---

15 Heckscher, *op. cit.*, I, 255.

16 Stella Kramer, *The English Craft Gilds* (New York, 1927), pp. 139 ff.

17 R. H. Tawney takes this position in his introduction to *Wilson's Discourse on Usury*, Introduction, pp. 12, 13. His statement has been scrutinized critically by Donald O. Wagner in "Coke and the Rise of Economic Liberalism," *Economic History Review*, VI, No. 1 (1935), 30–44. The best study of the law reports on the subject is in

this attitude of the common law courts was immensely important because nothing was done by the administration or by the legislature either to direct or to define a consistent economic policy. The law as actually applied was simply the sum total of particular decisions under the old law, decisions rendered by judges who persisted in misreading Magna Carta and finding in a feudal document a bill of personal rights and liberties to Englishmen at large.

The consequence was that in matters agricultural and in matters industrial anything like a controlled economy was rapidly being abandoned for almost a century before Adam Smith's *Wealth of Nations*. So far as any effective governmental regulation was in question, the English official attitude was in fact laissez faire by the year 1700.

But if it was so in fact it was still not so in theory. The legal assumption still remained that economic control was the business of government. If government did not function in that capacity it still monopolized the field and was prepared to prevent any private functioning. The J.P.s might neglect to fix wages, but they would tolerate no preëmption of their prerogative by associations of wage earners. The workingman in eighteenth-century England found himself in a position in which he could neither get redress for his grievances from the government nor yet be permitted to organize in his own interests.[18]

Nothing perhaps illuminates more clearly the dominant interest in the English mercantilist policy of the eighteenth century than the official attitude toward the wage earners. As England became more and more deeply involved in foreign trade, her merchants and manufacturers became more and more aware of the importance of keeping down costs of production if they were to compete successfully in the continental markets. They succeeded in establishing the assumption that foreign trade was the life blood of England

---

Heckscher, *op. cit.*, I, pp. 304 ff. For decisions in the Courts of Quarter Sessions, there is not a great deal of material in print. E. G. Dowdell has made a good study of conditions in Middlesex in *A Hundred Years of Quarter Sessions* (Cambridge, Eng., 1932), pp. 137 ff. The subject is one which calls for careful research by a student of economic history who is learned in the law.

[18] J. L. and Barbara Hammond, *The Town Labourer* (London, 1917), pp. 112 ff.; *ibid.*, *The Skilled Labourer* (London, 1920), pp. 86, 157 ff., 205. S. & B. Webb, *History of Trade Unions*, pp. 52, 58. It is a striking fact that when the Statute of Apprentices came up for repeal in 1814, those who fought hardest against repeal were the wage earners. Cf. T. K. Derry, "The Repeal of the Apprenticeship Clauses of the Statute of Apprentices," *Economic History Review*, III, No. 1 (1931), 67–87.

and that the national interest could best be served by its encouragement. One important factor in production costs was wages. And therefore wages should be kept low. They even argued that if the wages paid were inadequate to meet the cost of living they might properly be supplemented out of public funds, as a kind of national subsidy for the promotion of the export trade. They justified long hours and impossible conditions of life for the laborer on the grounds that he was naturally a lazy fellow with evil propensities and that the only way to keep him at work was the threat of starvation, and the only way to keep him out of mischief was to leave him no leisure time for mischief.[19] There were a few economists even in the eighteenth century who realized that high wages meant greater efficiency, meant also greater buying power in the domestic market.[20] But no man regarded them. Those who directed policy had ceased to think of laborers as human beings, and they saw no national advantage in domestic trade. It did not increase wealth, it merely shifted it from English hand to hand.

Probably at no time in the whole history of England was the national attitude toward the laboring classes so heartless and inhuman as it was in the first half of the eighteenth century, at no time was the workingman so completely at the mercy of his employer, at no time were the interests engaged in exploiting him so completely in control of every possible avenue of escape for him. Church and state alike were in the hands of his masters. No wonder if he took to gin.[21] No wonder if he indulged in all the emotional orgies of revivalism. The wonder is that when the issue between democracy and privilege was joined in France at the end of the eighteenth century the English workingman, instead of taking up the cry for liberty, fraternity, and equality, shouted instead for church and king.

Most of what was written about English mercantilism, particularly in the seventeenth and eighteenth centuries, had to do with foreign and colonial trade and most of the legislation regarding it, particularly after 1660, had to do with trade regulation. It is I think apparent that England at large was from the middle of the

[19] On this subject in general, cf. the excellent study by Edgar S. Furniss, *The Position of the Laborer in a System of Nationalism* (Boston, 1920).

[20] Heckscher, *op. cit.*, II, 168.

[21] On gin and its effects, cf. Mrs. Eric George, *London Life in the Eighteenth Century* (New York, 1925), pp. 27-42.

sixteenth century onward becoming increasingly trade conscious. This was partly due to the actual increase in foreign trade. It was partly due also to the changing character of trading organizations. Down to the middle of the sixteenth century the merchant was a professional trader with a professional education and a professional status, and trade was a mystery analogous to all the other crafts or mysteries. The trading organizations were simply associations of professional traders, each one of whom operated with his own capital at his own risk. But the middle of the sixteenth century saw the beginning of the joint-stock companies which operated with a common stock and at a joint risk. At first the joint-stock company was more or less limited to professional traders, but when it became apparent, as it did very early, that shares in a joint-stock enterprise could be bought and sold without disturbance of the enterprise itself, then more and more foreign trade became a general investment opportunity, and more and more a financial interest in trade spread to every Englishman with money to invest. The climax of all this came of course in the South Sea Bubble of 1720, and the collapse of that bubble had some effect in discouraging the uninitiated from that type of investment.[22] Nevertheless the enormous expansion of joint-stock companies in the seventeenth and early eighteenth centuries certainly had a good deal to do with spreading a trading interest far beyond the limits of the professional trading class. Probably the so-called trade wars of the eighteenth century got called so not so much because trade was the paramount issue involved as because trading interest had become one of the articles of the English national faith and served as a cloak for other objectives in something like the way in which, two centuries earlier, the interest of the Protestant faith had covered the multitude of sins. It is one indication of the direction of English progress in social standards that between the sixteenth and the eighteenth centuries trade had displaced religion as the accepted shibboleth of English foreign policy.

Long after the principles of a controlled economy had been virtually abandoned in other areas of English economic life, they persisted in the field of trade. In the eyes of the earlier mercantil-

[22] On the development of the joint-stock company, cf. W. R. Scott, *The Constitution and Finance of English, Scottish, and Irish Joint Stock Companies*, 3 vols. (Cambridge, Eng., 1910–12), paticularly, for transferable shares, I, 443; for the effect of the South Sea Bubble, I, 438.

ists foreign trade was the only way in which the wealth of the nation could be increased, and since wealth was identified with the precious metals, the value of trade was measured in terms of its contribution to the national store of bullion. At the beginning, though Professor Viner has taught us to avoid generalities in this matter,[23] these so-called bullionists commanded the field. In a modified form they commanded it to the end. There were those who perceived that the effect of a large supply of bullion in the country was to enhance prices and so to drive the bullion out again for use in cheaper markets overseas. But this was a long view of the matter which made little or no impression upon current opinion. There were even those who had a truer perception of the real measures of wealth. But they again were mere academicians. Those who commanded the ear of the government were professional merchants less interested in a dispassionate analysis of the national interest than in an identification of the national interest with the particular interests they were engaged in serving. And those who opposed the government were no less disposed to identify self-seeking with the common weal. The fight against trading companies in the first quarter of the seventeenth century, for example, was probably based not so much upon a genuine zeal for greater freedom of trade as upon the jealous attitude of the outports toward London, where the monopolistic companies were generally centered.[24] The eighteenth-century fight for freer trade was at bottom a quarrel between country gentlemen and town industrialists—Tories vs. Whigs. And the issue over the French trade treaty of 1786 was in part at least an issue between the large-scale producers who no longer needed protection and the small-scale producers who still did.[25]

There were, besides, the interests of the English carrier, an element in the mercantilist economy which had much to do with dictating navigation laws and much to do indirectly with the breach between old England and the new England overseas. Space does

[23] Jacob Viner, "English Theories of Foreign Trade before Adam Smith," *Journal of Political Economy*, XXXVIII (1930), 249–301, 404–57.

[24] Astrid Friis, *op. cit.*, pp. 149 ff. Heckscher (*op. cit.*, I, 420, n. 85) believes that Miss Friis has overemphasized the importance of this conflict between London and the outports.

[25] Witt Bowden, *Industrial Society in England towards the End of the Eighteenth Century* (New York, 1925), pp. 181–90, 193, 205–7.

not serve to discuss this aspect of the question, though it should be observed that the interests of the English shipper were closely tied in with the interests of the English navy and with the whole problem of national defense. The Navigation Laws themselves, or at least the seventeenth-century version of them, were essentially war measures and their aims were accomplished when the Dutch competitor, by a combination of circumstances in which the Navigation Laws played a relatively small part, was driven from the field. England commanded the seas during most of the eighteenth century and had small need of legal protective devices to maintain her position. Her quarrels with her colonies belong rather in the category of domestical difficulties than of foreign trade. The restrictions she sought to impose upon New England were akin to those she sought to impose upon old Ireland. It was in both cases bad business and in both cases it led to disastrous results, but it must not blind our eyes to the fact that no part of English mercantilist policy was so successful in attaining its objective as that part which had to do with the control of overseas trade. Probably that is why mercantilism as a going concern persisted longest in the area of foreign trade. Yet even there, restraints were relaxed in fact long before they were relaxed in theory.

What strikes us most forcibly in any survey of English economic policy during the fifty years or so before the American Revolution is that there was no economic policy. The old laws remained. If they were not enforced they were not repealed, although they were shamelessly misinterpreted in the courts. The steady drift was toward greater and greater freedom of action in economic matters. But this received no official recognition, no legal endorsement. Statesmen were uneasily conscious that the old patterns of thought and action were no longer applicable, but they did nothing about it because they did not know what to do.

And then came Adam Smith to teach them that doing nothing was the best thing in the world to do.

I cannot pause to discuss the provenience of the *Wealth of Nations*. Certainly the hardheaded eighteenth-century business man was very little concerned about its provenience. For him it came pat upon the moment to define and justify an economic policy toward which he had been groping for over a century. And the best part of it all was that Smith's program seemed to bear a divine sanction. At least that is how the medieval economist would have phrased it. Smith himself, in an age of rationalism, preferred to speak of an Invisible Hand.

English and French Industrial History After 1540 in Relation to the Constitution ∿ JOHN U. NEF

OUR ancestors found this country rich in the mineral wealth necessary for the progress of industry. They found it peopled with Indians. As the Indians could not tell them how to exploit this wealth, they naturally turned back on occasion to the experience of the old Europe whence they had come.

One of many objectives of the Founding Fathers in preparing and recommending the adoption of the Constitution was to provide favorable conditions for the development of industry. This was partly a matter of self-interest. As Dr. Beard showed in 1913, a few of the leading delegates to the Convention were part-owners of textile mills and shipbuilding companies, while a much larger number, engaged as they were in trade and in the lending of money, stood to profit from an increase in the output of mines and factories.[1] The concern of the delegates over the future of American industry, in its infancy at the time of the Convention, was also concern for the future strength of the nation. For generations in Europe statesmen had regarded it as one of their duties to foster the birth of new industries and the expansion of old. The diversity of the private interests which influenced government policies and the conflict between different objectives which always confronted statesmen had prevented any statesman from devoting himself single-mindedly to encouraging industrial development; there had been great differences of opinion concerning the policies most likely to stimulate it; there had even been writers who thought their countries would be better off without it. But before the end of the eighteenth century there was pretty complete agreement, in America as well as in Europe, that the progress of industry, when not obtained artificially at the expense of the more basic occupation of agriculture, was bound

[1] C. A. Beard, *An Economic Interpretation of the Constitution* (New York, 1913). esp. pp. 40–42, and Chs. II and V generally.

to strengthen the state and to increase the material welfare of its people.[2] As early as 1774, Alexander Hamilton had written: "If . . . manufactures should once . . . take root among us, they will pave the way still more to the future grandeur and glory of America." [3] Americans in 1787 expected industry to develop rapidly, now that the artificial restrictions imposed by the British government on manufactures in the Colonies were no longer in force. "The time is not distant," Gouverneur Morris remarked at one of the meetings of the Federal Convention, "when this country will abound with mechanics and manufacturers . . ." [4]

In England and France, the two greatest powers of the eighteenth century, various policies designed to stimulate the growth of industry had been tried out. From English and French experience since the Reformation lessons could be drawn concerning the policies most likely to permit and foster such a growth. What could the industrial history of these two nations have taught the more learned delegates who assembled in Philadelphia in 1787? What could it have taught James Madison, James Wilson, and Alexander Hamilton, fresh from their study of history, law, and political economy? Madison and Wilson were among the few men chiefly responsible for the form the Constitution finally took, and Hamilton did as much as any man to bring about its ratification by the states.[5] Were the opinions which they might have formed from their knowledge of history likely to coincide with the private interests of wealthy textile manufacturers and financiers, like Robert Morris of Pennsylvania or Jacob Broom of Delaware, and of merchants, like Thomas Fitzsimons of Pennsylvania or John Langdon of New Hampshire?

The merchants, the financiers, and the manufacturers, as well as

---

2 Cf. the remarks on this matter by Alexander Hamilton in his *Report on Manufactures*, written in 1790 (A. H. Cole, ed., *Industrial and Commercial Correspondence of Alexander Hamilton* [Chicago, 1928], pp. 247 ff.) Even the French Physiocrats looked on industrial progress as desirable, provided it did not interfere with agriculture (cf. C. Gide and C. Rist, *Histoire des doctrines économiques* [4th ed., Paris, 1922], pp. 14–15). While Benjamin Franklin believed it was possible for a country to become "fond of manufactures beyond their real value," he felt that the United States would probably grow richer if they discouraged the importation of manufactured goods and thus fostered native industries (A. H. Smyth, *The Writings of Benjamin Franklin* [New York, 1905], I, 149; X, 122).

3 John C. Hamilton, ed., *The Works of Alexander Hamilton* (New York, 1851), II, 12.

4 Max Farrand, *Records of the Federal Convention* (New Haven, 1911), II, 202.

5 Cf. A. C. McLaughlin, *A Constitutional History of the United States* (New York, 1935), pp. 149–51.

the scholars, may have known that England's industrial leadership over the Continent in the use of labor-saving machinery, and in the per capita output of coal, metal wares, woolen cloth, and most manufactured goods, was no new thing. It was probably not until the thirties or forties of the nineteenth century that many historians and business men began to think England's supremacy had been produced by an "Industrial Revolution," which started after the accession of George III, in 1760.[6] As a matter of fact, this "revolution" only increased a lead in mining and heavy manufacturing that England had secured as the result of an earlier industrial expansion, which became rapid at the end of the reign of Henry VIII, after 1540, which was most remarkable in the reigns of Elizabeth and James I, from about 1575 to 1620, and which continued at a somewhat slower rate after the Civil War and the Revolution of 1688. The chief continental countries participated in this early industrial revolution much less than in the later one. In France, which became the mightiest political power on the Continent, the progress of mining between 1540 and 1740, and of almost all manufactures, except the artistic and luxury trades, was much less impressive than in England, especially between 1540 and 1640. In the reign of Henry VIII England had been industrially a backwater compared with nearly every continental country. By the Peace of Utrecht, in 1713, if not seventy-five years earlier, on the eve of the Civil War, she had become the foremost nation in Europe in mining and heavy manufacturing.[7]

How had she done it? This was a question that eighteenth-century mechanics, tradesmen, and financiers, economists, scientists, and even men of letters were asking themselves with increasing interest and increasing frequency. It was a question that Frenchmen were

[6] This idea did not become a commonplace among scholars until the eighties, after the publication of Toynbee's lectures, but it was expressed in an embryonic form long before Toynbee's time. The use of the word "revolution" in connection with industrial changes goes back at least to the beginning of the nineteenth century in France, and the phrase "industrial revolution" was common in French books of the twenties and thirties (Anna Bezanson, "The Early Use of the Term Industrial Revolution," *Quarterly Journal of Economics*, XXXVI [1922], 343–46). The first case I have found in which the phrase was used to suggest that the development of English industry had been phenomenally rapid as compared with continental, occurs in the early forties.

[7] Cf. J. U. Nef, "The Progress of Technology and the Growth of Large-Scale Industry in Great Britain, 1540–1640," *Economic History Review*, V (1934), 3–24; "A Comparison of Industrial Growth in France and England from 1540 to 1640," *Journal of Political Economy*, XLIV (1936), 289–317, 505–33, 643–66.

asking more often even than Englishmen, because they stood in greater need of an answer. The question first took on a compelling importance for them after the death of Louis XIV, in 1715, when they began to care less for the qualities of the age of the great monarch—good form, finish, and taste in the fine arts and in the art of living, reason and moderation in thought, high standards of moral conduct, combined with a belief in the church and in the divine right of kings—and began to care more for wealth, health, individual freedom, and the discovery of the secrets of the material world.

Echoes from discussions relating to the question must have been heard in America. Benjamin Franklin, who played an influential part in the Convention at his great age of eighty-one, had met ministers, *intendants,* and inspectors of manufactures, all of whom were much concerned in trying to overcome the economic superiority of the English. French merchants who came to America, like John Holker, were hardly less concerned. Holker's father had migrated from Lancashire to introduce English textile machinery into France, and had been made Inspector of Foreign Manufactures. The younger Holker was for six years, from 1778 to 1784, a business partner and associate of Robert Morris, who, as delegate to the Convention from Pennsylvania, played an important part in private negotiations. Holker also had close relations with Thomas Fitzsimons, and with the most influential of all the Pennsylvania delegates, James Wilson, the famous lawyer.[8] Wilson and Morris had been born abroad, and their interest in the question may have been enhanced by the direct knowledge of economic conditions in Great Britain which they had obtained in their early years. Delegates born in America, who had neither traveled abroad nor associated with foreign merchants at home, were not likely to escape the question if they read widely in French and English books. Various aspects of it were often mentioned not only by writers on industrial subjects like Gabrielle Jars, the French mining engineer, and Dean Tucker, who devoted an essay to "the Advantages and Disadvantages which respectively attend France and Great Britain with Regard to Trade," [9] but by great men of letters, like Voltaire, who were helping to mold European thought, and whose correspondence is full of

[8] From an unfinished thesis by Miss Marion Rice, "John Holker, French Man of Business in the American Revolution: an Economic Biography."

[9] *A Brief Essay on the Advantages and Disadvantages Which Respectively Attend France and Great Britain with Regard to Trade* (2d ed., London, 1750).

admiring comments about English scientific and mechanical discoveries.

To the question why had English industry developed more rapidly than French there are many answers which contain a measure of truth. In the eighteenth century many answers, not all of which contain even a measure of truth, were being given. Those who believed that the form of government and the policies of statesmen had an influence upon industrial progress could find important contrasts between the constitutional history of the two countries to help them in explaining the backwardness of France. Tucker, in an essay which was published in 1750, wrote that "The first Disadvantage . . . is the Government, which is arbitrary and despotick; and therefore such as a Merchant would not chuse to live under, if he knows the Sweets of Liberty in [England] . . . [where he] can go to Law with the Crown, as easily as with a private subject." [10] During the two previous centuries the English people, by a number of stages, had moved away from the absolute monarchy of Henry VII and Henry VIII, when the king had governed without having his prerogative seriously challenged, to the establishment and the strengthening of parliamentary government, and to a position where the crown was impotent in fundamental matters of policy without the support of the house of commons. Meanwhile in France the monarchy had continued to increase its power, at least from the accession of Henri IV in 1589 to the death of Louis XIV, and the representative assembly, the estates general, had not been summoned to meet since 1614. Tucker's opinion that an authoritarian government had handicapped France in her economic development was held by many Englishmen. It was coming to be shared by many Frenchmen, including some of the greatest men of the age. On what historical facts was it based?

In France the crown had used its authority to interfere increasingly with the freedom of industrial development. Thousands of decrees, edicts, ordonnances, *règlements,* and letters patent reenacted, elaborated, and extended medieval regulations and established new ones. As the powers of the provincial estates and *parlements* diminished during Louis XIV's long reign, the enactments of the king were made more and more effective. They were prepared, interpreted, and enforced by the central government, with

[10] Idem. The quotation is from the second, enlarged edition, pp. 23, 33.

the advice and help of an elaborate hierarchy of local officials appointed by the crown, especially the powerful *intendants* who governed the provinces, the *subdélégués* whom they appointed as their representatives in the *départements,* and the inspectors of manufactures, who were also to some extent subject to their authority.

As a result, at the beginning of the eighteenth century, the central government exercised control in varying degrees over all industrial enterprises, including those of the village craftsman who labored with his family in a humble cottage in parts of the kingdom remote from Paris. More and more master workmen everywhere, in some villages as well as in towns, were brought under the authority of the corporate gilds, whose number was increased by the crown and whose rules were subject in large measure to its approval. These rules generally limited the master to one or two apprentices, and thus hindered the growth of large enterprises. Royal enactments fixed the size and the quality of all kinds of cloth and leather goods, and even of soap and paper. Industrial products had generally to be marked in a specified way, and this caused trouble when the makers were illiterate. If any of the wares did not conform to all the regulations concerning them, the traders and merchants, who had put out the raw materials or partly finished goods to be worked on by craftsmen in their homes or at small water-driven mills along the streams, were not allowed to sell them. This obliged the traders and merchants to refuse to accept and pay for them when they were delivered at the warehouses.

Private persons with capital were seldom at liberty to start a new enterprise employing a dozen or more laborers without the permission of the central government. If a landlord, even in distant provinces, like the Comté de Foix in the shadow of the Pyrenees, wanted to mine within his lordship or to build a large forge for smelting ore, or if he proposed to lease his land for these purposes, he or his lessees had to seek a grant of letters patent, or some other sort of authorization, from the crown. This might be refused if the applicant could not prove, by ancient documents or by the testimony of old inhabitants, that an enterprise of the same kind had existed at the same place in earlier times. It might be refused if the new enterprise should conflict with one of the monopolies of mining in one or more provinces which the crown had been in the habit of granting for a term of years to rich noblemen and other persons, who sometimes claimed a special knowledge of the mineral arts and of the existence of minerals. It might also be refused if the new enterprise could be shown to jeopardize the future of some local mine or forge already in operation, or if there seemed to be no adequate market for the product.[11]

At the beginning of the eighteenth century nearly all the large industrial enterprises in metallurgy, cloth making, sugar refining, paper making, soap and glass making, were either royal manufactures or so-called privileged manufactures. Very few of them were owned directly by the crown and managed by its officials. But many had been started with the help of government capital, almost all with the help of government privileges, such as grants of land and exemptions from various taxes for the owners, managers, and workers. In return for such favors, the owners were bound to conform to the regulations of the governing authorities. These regulations were hardly less complicated than those enforced by the gilds. In many industries even the machinery used in workshops had to be approved of and marked by government agents. This sometimes led to absurd rules. The paper mills of Annonay, the largest in France when they were started early in Louis XV's reign, were subject to the control of the local *subdélégué*. He was stationed at Tournon, a little town on the right bank of the Rhône, facing the slope of Hermitage with its famous vineyards. Before the large wooden frames for paper making, fashioned at Annonay, could be installed in the factories there, they had to be carried to Tournon to be marked, a journey there and back of some forty miles along the precipitous paths of the Cévennes. As the frames were delicate, they were frequently broken. It cost several thousand francs in the money of the time to replace one of them.[12] In this way and in many other ways, the French regulations governing manufactures added to the expenses of production and hindered the growth of output.

While the control exercised by the central government over industry increased in France throughout the seventeenth and early

[11] These two paragraphs are based mainly on documents in various French *Archives départementales* and in the *Archives nationales* in Paris. Cf. Henri Hauser, "Les Pouvoirs publics et l'organisation du travail dans l'ancienne France," in *Travailleurs et marchands dans l'ancienne France* (Paris, 1920); P. Boissonnade, *Le Socialisme d'état* (Paris, 1927), and *Colbert* (Paris, 1932); E. F. Heckscher, *Mercantilism* (London, 1935), I, 137 ff.

[12] *Inventaire-sommaire des Archives départementales, Hérault,* série C, III (1887), 188.

eighteenth centuries, it diminished in England after the Civil War. It is true that during the century following the Reformation many attempts were made by the English crown to establish and extend its authority over manufacturing and even mining. Queen Elizabeth successfully challenged the Earl of Northumberland in the celebrated case of mines of 1566, when he claimed the ownership of a mine of argentiferous copper ore within his lands. As Dr. Read has remarked, the Tudors and early Stuarts made an effort to guard the social interest from exploitation at the hands of the profiteer and the capitalist, by statutes and proclamations designed to regulate industrial conditions.[13] An Act of 1555 aimed to prevent country weavers and clothmakers from keeping more than one or two looms. The Statute of Artificers of 1563 was enforced longer than any of the other industrial enactments. While it did not actually limit the number of apprentices a master could keep, it empowered the justices of the peace to fix wage rates and to enforce the obligation of a seven-year apprenticeship for all handicraft workers in existing industries.[14] Following the precedents set by continental princes, Elizabeth and her two Stuart successors established the right of the crown, through its agents and patentees, to license and control the new manufactures of saltpeter and gunpowder. Monopolies of the manufacture of glass, alum, and soap were granted to royal patentees.[15] Any project for state control that promised the crown a revenue independent of parliamentary grant was likely to find favor at court. By the reign of Charles I the coal trade had become of vital importance to the people of London, because coal had generally replaced wood as fuel. The king and some of his ministers toyed with the idea of making the trade a royal monopoly in the hands of a small group of projectors who offered to pay £50,000 or £60,000 annually for the privilege.[16]

But after the middle of the seventeenth century the power of the national government to control industrial life grew weaker. Even before the Civil War a decision given in 1566 in favor of the crown in the case of mines was interpreted to mean that all minerals,

---

[13] See above, pp. 66 ff.

[14] Cf. M. R. Gay, "Aspects of Elizabethan Apprenticeship," in E. F. Gay, *Facts and Factors in Economic History* (Cambridge, Mass., 1932), pp. 135–36, 142, 162–63.

[15] Cf. W. H. Price, *The English Patents of Monopoly* (Cambridge, Mass., 1906), *passim;* S. R. Gardiner, *History of England* (London, 1901), VIII, 71 ff., 284.

[16] J. U. Nef, *The Rise of the British Coal Industry* (London, 1932), II, 273 ff.

except those containing large quantities of precious metal, belonged not to the crown but to the private landlord, who was free to work or lease them as he chose. The Civil War put an end to the system of royal monopolies, and left the field of mining and manufacturing open to the private capitalist. New privately owned enterprises could be set up almost anywhere without the special permission of the state; mines and small factories were not subjected to any effective control by the government. Although the provisions under the Statute of Artificers which called for a seven-year apprenticeship retained some vitality until the middle of the eighteenth century,[17] most of the penal statutes had become a dead letter more than fifty years earlier. The laws remained on the statute books, but they were less and less effectively enforced. As one English writer put it in 1766, "the difference between us and France consists chiefly in this; that they take no less care in the execution of their laws, than in making them; we are remarkable for good laws, but are shamefully neglectful in their execution." [18]

If private enterprise was much more extensively regulated in France than in England, especially after the middle of the seventeenth century, it was also subjected to heavier financial burdens. The power of the French king to govern without a representative assembly made it easier to impose direct taxes on wealth. The *tailles,* the *capitation,* and the *dixième* (which eventually became the *vingtième*) lent themselves, as everyone knows, to great abuses. The clergy, the nobility, and most of the royal officials, when not exempted from paying them at the time they were first levied, managed to gain exemption before they had been long in force. But neither the French clergy nor the French nobility took much part in the development of large-scale industry during the two centuries following the Reformation. Their incomes were largely devoted to building, to caring for their parishioners, to adorning themselves and their followers with fine apparel, to ordering sumptuous repasts prepared by chefs who were sometimes ready—like the famous Vatel —to commit suicide rather than to serve an imperfect dish, to ornamenting their châteaux with carved railings and grills, beautiful

---

[17] I owe this information to Miss M. R. Gay, who has in hand an interesting thesis entitled "The Statute of Artificers with Special Reference to Apprenticeship Regulation."

[18] M. Postlethwayt, *The Universal Dictionary of Trade and Commerce* (3d ed. London, 1766), p. iii.

furniture, plate, tapestries, oil paintings, and sculptures which were the chief glory of the royal workshops. Most of the money to finance large industrial enterprises came from the mercantile classes. But the members of these classes who most frequently escaped from paying direct taxes were the crown officials and the owners of royal and privileged manufactures. They had an interest in maintaining the system from which they derived much of their income, and were not anxious to use their capital to set up new factories. The private merchant who was eager to develop enterprises outside the established system had frequently to bear, along with the peasant and the craftsman, a heavy load of direct taxes.

In England he was much better off. Before the Civil War the house of commons challenged the right of the crown to impose taxes without parliamentary consent, and during the late seventeenth and eighteenth centuries, the funds raised by taxation were usually obtained, not from taxes levied on income or personal property, but from a land tax, hearth and window taxes, and a great variety of indirect taxes and duties. These impositions left the fortunes of rich merchants largely intact; they did not greatly reduce the resources of the rising squirearchy, whose members were generally of mercantile origin and were more disposed than the French nobility to invest in large industrial ventures.

After the Restoration the wealth of many English merchant families was increased by the new opportunities they were offered to lend money to the government. In France private merchants were also becoming the creditors of the crown for much larger sums than in the past. But in France the creditors were less secure than in England against the risks of default and debasement. Between 1602 and 1740 the pound sterling lost only about a third, the *livre tournois* more than half, its value in terms of gold. At one time, in 1720, the *livre tournois* was worth less than a fourth as much in gold as in 1602.[19] The principle of maintaining a fixed gold standard for the national currency was more firmly established in England than it has ever been in France, partly as a result of the English recoinage of 1696, and the public discussions connected with it. The gold value of the English coins, which had recently fallen by about a fifth, was restored. Largely through the influence of John Locke

---

[19] A. Dieudonné, *Manuel de numismatique française*, II (1916), 340, 344, 350–51, 363; A. E. Feaveryear, *The Pound Sterling* (Oxford, 1931), p. 376.

(supported, it is said, by Newton) £3 17s. 10½d. an ounce came to be regarded as the magic and unalterable price for gold. Locke argued, as Alexander Hamilton was to argue during and after the Constitutional Convention concerning the repayment of the public debt, that the "public faith," the "establishment of the national character" as Professor McLaughlin has called it, was at stake.[20] The establishment of the English national character in 1696 did no harm to the financial and the landed interests, for rich men were given the opportunity to unload upon the exchequer all the bad money they held. They benefited in so far as they purchased bad money at a discount from those who were less fortunately placed to get rid of it,[21] and in so far as they were creditors of the state. The policies of the English government were encouraging the accumulation of capital by the persons most willing and able to invest it in private industrial ventures. The state took less money from them than in France; it gave back more.

Within France the mine owner and the manufacturer were handicapped in obtaining raw materials and in reaching markets by the great number of land and river tolls, a relic of feudalism, levied by local lords and towns on commodities passing through their territory, and also by the duties levied, in most cases by the crown, on interprovincial commerce. In spite of many attempts by statesmen to abolish the local tolls and to reform the public duties, little was accomplished to facilitate domestic trade. If the position of the trader was no worse in the eighteenth century than it had been at the Reformation, it was not conspicuously better. In 1701 commodities passing down the Loire from Roanne, where the river first became easily navigable, to Nantes, at the mouth, paid thirty separate local tolls; commodities passing down the Sâone and Rhône from Gray, in Franche-Comté, to Arles paid twenty-eight in 1786. Road tolls were hardly less common than river tolls. The producer in one province was frequently at several additional removes from the consumer in another on account of the public tolls. Dealers in commodities sent from Languedoc to Paris by the easiest route—the Rhône and the Sâone—had to pay, besides all the local land and river tolls, at least three interprovincial tolls, the *foraine*, which was levied on goods leaving Languedoc, and two *douanes* at

---

[20] Feaveryear, *op. cit.*, pp. 136–37; McLaughlin, *op. cit.*, p. 225.
[21] Feaveryear, *op. cit.*, pp. 128–29.

Valence and Lyons, before their shipments reached the boundary of the northern customs union, the *cinq grosses fermes,* where another duty was collected. The bill for tolls on a consignment of goods often greatly exceeded the bill for freight.[22] The effect was to hold back industrial concentration. Thus, in 1728 and again in 1738, we find the *subdélégué* at Tournon complaining that the expansion of the paper mills at Annonay was being prevented by the collection of the *foraine* and the *douane de Valence* on shipments of paper. These tolls, he pointed out, in effect subsidized the smaller and less efficient mills in neighboring provinces, as well as those in Switzerland and Germany.[23]

In contrast to France and other continental countries, England and Wales (and after 1707 the whole of Great Britain) offered the mine owner and manufacturer an area of almost complete free trade. Most of the medieval tolls levied by landlords on land and river traffic had disappeared before the Reformation.[24] The national government refrained from levying duties on domestic commerce, except in the case of the coastwise traffic in coal, which bore an increasingly heavy burden of impositions during the seventeenth and early eighteenth centuries.[25] These duties hindered the expansion of colliery enterprise near the coasts; but the domestic market was open without much interference to the mine owner elsewhere and to the factory owner everywhere. When Adam Smith compared the tolls levied in France and England, he remarked that the "freedom of interior commerce . . . is perhaps one of the principal causes of the prosperity of Great Britain; every great country being necessarily the best and most extensive market for the greater part of the productions of its own industry." [26] This was an opinion that his American readers were bound to share after their experience with impositions on interstate commerce under the Articles of Confederation.

Adam Smith could not regard English policy concerning foreign trade with the same satisfaction. England had been no more backward than France in laying tariffs upon imports and some exports; so economists were unable to find, in comparisons between the

[22] Cf. Heckscher, *op. cit.,* I, 78–109, esp. 94–95, 84, 86, 99–102, 103.

[23] *Inventaire-sommaire des Archives départementales, Hérault,* série C, III, 184–86.

[24] Cf. Heckscher, *op. cit.,* I, 46–56.

[25] Cf. Nef, *Rise of the British Coal Industry,* II, 268, 293–96, 305–15.

[26] *Wealth of Nations,* Bk. V, Ch. II, Pt. II, art. iv (Rogers ed., II, 499).

history of the two countries, support for a policy of international free trade, as they could for a policy of interprovincial free trade. It was possible to argue, as the free traders did, that England's prosperity had been secured in spite of tariffs. It was also possible to argue, as Alexander Hamilton did in America and as Friedrich List did in Germany, that tariffs were essential for the development of manufactures in industrially backward countries.

The lessons which could be most readily derived from French and English history seemed to be favorable to certain kinds of government interference with the freedom of economic enterprise, and unfavorable to other kinds. They were not clearly opposed to regulation of trade by the state, provided the regulations took the form of laying tariffs on imports and clearing away obstacles to the freedom of commerce within the country. They were opposed to the maintenance of industrial and commercial monopolies, and to a minute control over methods of manufacturing. But they seemed to be favorable to a government policy of encouraging inventors and scientists, and of bringing in skilled mechanics from foreign countries. Until after the death of Louis XIV, the English government did more than the French to stimulate technical improvements in mining and manufacturing. The system of granting patents for new inventions, as distinct from the granting of industrial monopolies, originated in England in Elizabeth's reign, and secured the support of parliament in the celebrated Statute of Monopolies of 1624.[27] During the late seventeenth and early eighteenth centuries, this system had done something to help English inventors to enjoy the fruits of their discoveries for a limited term of years.[28] At the same time the crown, especially after the Restoration, actively supported the study of experimental science, and encouraged scientists to devote attention to practical problems. Charles II and his ministers showed much interest in the proceedings of the Royal Society, which was incorporated in 1664, and which included among its members most of the great scientists of the age.

In France the Académie des Sciences was founded only two years after the incorporation of the Royal Society. But French thought, in

[27] E. W. Hulme, "The History of the Patent System," *Law Quarterly Review*, XII (1896), 144, 153–54; XVI (1900), 44; Price, *op. cit.*, p. 7; 21 Jac. I, cap. 3, secs. v, vi.

[28] There is some doubt as to whether the patent system actually helped the genuine inventor very much until after the Civil War (cf. Hulme, *op. cit.*, XII, 152; XVI, 53; Price, *op. cit.*, pp. 65–66).

its main currents, was still unfavorable to experimental science and technical improvement. Teaching and discussion were more dominated than in England by the scholastic philosophy. Alchemy and magic were taken more seriously. While statesmen like Richelieu sometimes saw the value of machinery designed to reduce labor, in practice they showed the inventor and the scientist little sympathy. When Richelieu had De Caus locked up as a madman for pestering him about the power of steam, he was reflecting the French distrust for the value of new forces, a distrust which persisted throughout the reign of Louis XIV. This distrust is to be found in the philosophy of Malebranche and the letters of Madame de Sévigné, as well as in the teachings of the Jesuits, who played a great part in educating the youth, and in the writings of Pascal and other Jansenists, whose books were widely read by the cultured nobility, as well as by the clergy. Statesmen of the French classical age were much more interested in the Académie Française, which Richelieu had fostered, in the Académie de Peinture et de Sculpture, founded by Le Brun in 1648, and in the French theater, than they were in the Académie des Sciences.

To many French writers of the eighteenth century, who were more materialistic in their thinking than their ancestors of the classical age, it seemed that their country had mistaken the ornaments for the substance of living. Impatient with his countrymen for their inability to understand Newton, Voltaire wrote in 1735, "In truth, we are the whipped cream of Europe." [29] For him, the grace, the precision, the sweetness, and the finesse of French culture could not make up entirely for what he called the more masculine virtues in which the English excelled.[30]

If, as seems to be the case, some eighteenth-century economists believed that England's industrial leadership over France could be explained mainly by the difference between the economic policies of the French and English governments, they were wrong. The study of constitutional history in England and France helps us to understand the more rapid growth of industry in England, but it should also put us on our guard against exaggerating the importance of government policies as an aid or a handicap to industrial

---

[29] Letter of Nov. 30, 1735, to Abbé d'Olivet (*Œuvres complètes de Voltaire* [Paris, 1880], XXXIII, 556).
[30] Letter of Nov. 11, 1738, to Abbé Le Blanc (*ibid.*, XXXV, 41).

expansion. The contrasts between industrial progress in the two countries were greatest before the triumph of parliamentary government in England, when the crown was attempting, with a measure of success, to regulate economic life along lines similar to those tried in France. After the Civil War, when government regulation diminished in England and increased in France, the contrasts were much less striking. England's industrial supremacy in the early eighteenth century had been gained as the result of a multitude of forces interacting upon each other. It was mainly the result of forces upon which government policies had little or no effect. The changes in English economic policies were more a result of the industrial expansion than a cause for it.[31]

Our inquiry into the possible influence of industrial history upon certain clauses in the Constitution is concerned, not with the relative importance of forces making for industrial progress, but with the opinions held in the eighteenth century about the rôle of government policies in that progress. It is true that, even in England, there were still writers, such as Postlethwayt, who argued that the enforcement of all kinds of rigid laws regulating the freedom of industrial enterprise was beneficial.[32] But by 1750, in France as well as in England, such views were less commonly held and less influential than they had been in the seventeenth century. A majority of writers had come to doubt the value of granting industrial monopolies, or of forcing mine owners and manufacturers to conform to a strict legal code. There was a disposition in France to exalt the English form of government and English economic policies, along with most things English.

These new views concerning the proper rôle for the state to play in economic life were strengthened by the history of the half century preceding the Constitutional Convention. This is the period when, it is still widely believed, the "Industrial Revolution" began in England. The "revolution" is supposed to have spread to the Continent later, after the United States Constitution had been working for some time. But we must push back the beginnings of rapid industrial change in France as well as in England farther than has been customary. Judged by the rate of increase in the volume of

[31] These conclusions are tentative. I hope to discuss the subject in some detail at a later date.

[32] Cf. Postlethwayt, *op. cit.*, p. iii.

industrial output and in the number of workpeople employed in mines and factories, the fifty years from 1735 to 1785 were possibly a period of even more rapid development in France than in England. The output of coal and probably of iron grew at a more rapid rate. While the output of cotton and woolen cloth probably grew more slowly, English machinery, English workmen, and English capital were being introduced in the textile industry, as in mining, metallurgy, paper and glass making, and nearly all other manufactures. France, in her turn, was borrowing technical skill from England, as England in the Elizabethan Age had borrowed from the leading continental countries. By the eve of the French Revolution several very large plants, each employing more than a thousand workmen and many millions of francs in capital, were in operation for mining coal at Anzin in the north, for metallurgy at Le Creusot in central France, and for making glass at Saint-Gobain in Picardy.[33] Establishments of this size were a novelty even in the second half of the eighteenth century. Mines and factories employing more than a hundred workmen were no novelty.[34] But the number of these increased very rapidly in France during the last fifty years of the *ancien régime*. By 1787 there were several score. While parts of the country were not touched by this remarkable industrial development, and while England remained in 1787 the most important industrial nation in Europe, her lead over France in the volume of output per capita from mines and manufactures was possibly less striking than it had been half a century before.[35]

The French industrial expansion was accompanied by some modification in the economic policies of the crown. During the eighteenth century many writers on economic subjects began to

[33] I owe this information about Saint-Gobain to Mr. Warren Scoville, who is at work on a history of the French glass-making industry.

[34] It is common, however, to exaggerate the number of such establishments in the reign of Louis XIV. Many of the "royal manufactures" employed most of the workmen in their own homes under the putting-out system.

[35] The argument in this paragraph is based on a study of MSS and printed materials too numerous to cite. I hope to return to the subject at a later date. It will be observed that I have not accepted the common opinion that industrial progress was more rapid in England than in France throughout the eighteenth century. This was doubtless true before 1735 or 1740 and after 1780 or 1785, but not, I think, during the intervening period. The remarkable progress of French industry after about 1735 perhaps explains why there were Englishmen like Postlethwayt, who believed in 1766 (erroneously, I feel sure, unless the statement is confined to the artistic and luxury industries) that "France has hitherto surpassed and out-rivalled all the world in their manufactures" (*op. cit.*, I, iii).

express the opinion that industrial enterprise was too much fettered by the government for the good of the country. We must not exaggerate the practical results obtained by this new movement in French thought. It was not strong enough to bring about, before 1789, any general suppression of the tolls imposed on the transport of raw materials and commodities within the country.[36] In spite of widespread opposition to the control exercised by the gilds over industry, which culminated in an edict of 1776, designed to throw all crafts and professions open to everyone, whether or not he had served an apprenticeship or joined a gild, the edict was withdrawn after the fall of Turgot. The gilds were reëstablished, and the corporate regime was even extended to certain crafts which had been free.[37] But there was a disposition on the part of public officials, in Paris and in the provinces, to disregard the old regulations, both of the gilds and of the central government, when they interfered with industrial production and the introduction of cheaper methods of mining and manufacturing.

We can see the process at work in Languedoc. Restrictions on the output of the chief textile enterprises there were withdrawn early in the eighteenth century, and each merchant or group of merchants was allowed to decide how much cloth should be produced for the market in the Levant.[38] The construction of large coal-burning factories for the manufacture of glass bottles was encouraged, even though this was clearly an infringement of the privileges of a closed craft, the gentlemen glassmakers, whose rights had been established by letters patent of 1436, and confirmed by subsequent letters patent of 1475, 1655, and 1727.[39] A decree of 1744 revoked the exclusive right to refine sugar in the province, which had been granted earlier to two successive companies of Montpellier merchants, and threw the industry open to anyone.[40]

Similar changes in policy may be observed in all provinces. The

[36] Heckscher, *op. cit.*, I, 85–87, 106–7.

[37] Cf. Henri Sée, *L'Évolution commerciale et industrielle de la France sous l'ancien régime* (Paris, 1925), pp. 194–99.

[38] *Archives départementales de l'Hérault*, C. 2949 (*Mémoire sur le commerce général de la province de Languedoc,* 1744).

[39] *Inventaire-sommaire des Archives départementales de l'Hérault*, série C, III, 384.

[40] *Archives départementales de l'Hérault*, C. 2698 (*Mémoire des intéressés à la raffinerie royale de Sete* and *Mémoire pour le Sieur Sabatier, propriétaire de la raffinerie de sucre, à Montpellier*). For transcripts of these documents, I am indebted to M. de Dainville, the chief archivist at Montpellier, and to his assistant, M. L. Maury.

manner of leasing coal mines throughout the realm was radically
changed by a decree of 1744.[41] In the past the crown had granted
widespread monopolies, often covering a number of provinces, to
various noblemen and others. Now concessions for starting new
collieries at particular places could be obtained by any persons
with sufficient capital. Traders, merchants, and landlords, whose
only passport was their financial resources, found it increasingly
easy to enter any industry.

At the same time, the burdens imposed by the financial policies
of the crown upon the resources of the private merchant were somewhat lightened. Industrial capital and the profits from industries
were largely relieved after 1725 from the obligation to pay the
vingtième. This impost became almost exclusively a tax on land.[42]
After 1740 the gold value of the *livre tournois* was maintained until
the Revolution, so that the risks to creditors of the crown from
debasement, if not from default, were diminished.

There was only one aspect of industrial life with which government officials concerned themselves more than in the past. Experience seemed to show in this case that government interference was
needed to promote prosperity. Ministers, *intendants, subdélégués,*
and inspectors of manufactures all worked to introduce new machinery, new kinds of furnaces, and new chemical processes into
manufacturing and mining.[43] The government advanced capital
more freely than in the past to help in the establishment of new
industrial processes. The immigration of foreign technicians and
capitalists was welcomed as never before. Although a patent system,
modeled on that of England, was not adopted until 1791, before
the Revolution much was done by the state to encourage the scientist and the inventor. Persons were no longer locked up as insane
when they sought support for their inventions; insane persons were
kept at liberty if they could help to introduce labor-saving machinery.

As the Revolution approached, men began to speculate about the

41 Cf. Marcel Rouff, *Les Mines de charbon en France* (Paris, 1922), Pt. I, Ch. VI, and
Pt. II.
42 Cf. A. Esmein, *Cours élémentaire d'histoire du droit français* (15th ed., Paris,
1925), pp. 550–51.
43 Cf. A. P. Wadsworth and J. de L. Mann, *The Cotton Trade and Industrial Lancashire* (Manchester, 1931), pp. 197–99.

causes for the growing industrial prosperity of France. Progressive-minded Frenchmen were seldom, if ever, satisfied with the progress that had been made, for England was still setting the pace in mining and heavy manufacturing. Many Frenchmen felt that if France were to overtake England as an industrial power, she must copy English economic policies in almost every respect. The changes in the relation of the government to economic life, introduced toward the close of the *ancien régime,* fell far short of such a goal, but they were sufficiently notable to be regarded sometimes as a cause for the expansion of industrial output. It is doubtful whether they had in fact as much to do with this expansion as the changes in English economic policies in the seventeenth century had had to do with England's industrial supremacy. But those delegates at Philadelphia who had kept up with recent French history could find in it new reasons for believing that the adoption of English economic policies was desirable for the industrial prosperity of the United States.

The Constitution seems to embody the lessons which were being derived in the late eighteenth century from French and English history by a majority of statesmen and writers on economic questions. There were no specific provisions for the setting up of government-operated mines and manufactures, for the granting of industrial monopolies, or for the direct regulation of industry by the state. There was, of course, the famous clause by which Congress received authority to regulate commerce.[44] In the eighteenth century the word "commerce" was often used in a much wider sense than is customary today, to cover nearly all branches of economic activity. It has been suggested that the Founding Fathers intended, by the commerce clause, to grant Congress power to formulate a policy for the national economy, a power which was to extend to manufactures, internal improvements, and the creation of corporations.[45] But in 1787 "commerce" was an ambiguous word. It was also used in its narrower, modern sense. Savary des Bruslons, in the 1742 edition of his *Dictionnaire universel de commerce,* which formed the model for at least one English dictionary on the same subject, de-

---

[44] Article I, sec. 8.

[45] Walton H. Hamilton and D. Adair, *The Power to Govern* (New York, 1937), *passim* and esp. pp. 119–20.

fined the word as "exchange, sale, purchase, traffic, or trade in merchandise." [46] The principal definition in most English eighteenth-century dictionaries was similar.[47] These definitions do not differ substantially from the first one in our American *Century Dictionary and Cyclopedia* of 1889: "Interchange of goods, merchandise, or property of any kind; trade; traffic. . . ."

If the delegates to the Constitutional Convention had wanted "commerce" to be understood in its broader sense, as covering industry or manufacturing, they could easily have made their meaning plain by adding one or the other of these words. From the beginning of the eighteenth century, if not earlier,[48] the word "industry" had been increasingly used, at least in France, in its modern sense of mining and manufacturing.[49] Thus we find the Duc de Saint Simon referring to Vauban's proposed tax "sur les terres . . . sur le commerce et l'industrie," and John Law writing in 1719 that the people of England and Holland are happy because "les terres sont bien cultivées, l'industrie et le commerce sont étendues." [50] In both passages industry and commerce are treated as separate phases of economic activity. Alexander Hamilton used the word industry a number of times with the same meaning in his *Report on Manufactures*,[51] and it is not likely that he discovered this usage during the two or three years which elapsed between the sittings of the Convention and the writing of that document. Such a usage was also known to Franklin.[52] Even if, as is possible, it was uncommon in English in 1787, by that time the word "manufactures" was frequently used in its modern sense. Madison spoke, at one of the early meetings in the Convention, of "the landed, the manufacturing," and "the commercial interests." Some of the delegates actually drafted a clause granting Congress power for "the promotion of

[46] I, Pt. II, 8. The full title of this work is *Dictionnaire universel de commerce, d'histoire naturelle, et des arts et métiers*. If the author had thought that "commerce" would inevitably be understood to include "arts et métiers," he would hardly have troubled to add these words.

[47] Cf. Hamilton and Adair, *op. cit.*, pp. 206–7.

[48] In a French ordinance of 1543, dealing with iron making, the word "industrie" is apparently used in the modern sense (*Archives nationales*, X¹ᴬ8614, fol. 22).

[49] Paul Harsin, "De quand date le mot 'Industrie'?" *Annales d'histoire économique et sociale*, No. 6 (1930), pp. 237–42.

[50] *Ibid.*, pp. 237, 240.

[51] For example, A. H. Cole, ed., *Industrial and Commercial Correspondence of Alexander Hamilton*, pp. 276–77.

[52] Smyth, ed., *The Writings of Benjamin Franklin*, I, 149.

agriculture, commerce, trades, and manufactures." [53] Like the clauses authorizing Congress to establish "public institutions" and to grant "charters of incorporation," it was not included in the Constitution.[54] The only clause which clearly gave the national government power to embark on business enterprise was the one providing for the establishment of post offices and post roads. When Franklin proposed to extend this clause to cover the cutting of canals, "where deemed necessary," his motion was defeated by a vote of eight states to three.[55]

We may perhaps conclude that a majority of the delegates were not anxious to establish government-owned or government-controlled industrial enterprises.[56] Nor is there any evidence in the debates that a majority wanted Congress to enact elaborate regulations for the conduct of mining and manufacturing, such as had been enforced in France. A majority were apparently in favor of the relative freedom of industrial enterprise which already existed in England, in spite of old statutes rusty for want of execution.

That a majority of the delegates favored the full repayment of the public debt is not open to doubt.[57] The financial clauses of the Constitution were bound to help wealthy persons to become still more wealthy. Against the danger of a government default, the payment of the nation's debts was made, by section 8 of Article I, the first objective of raising revenue, before the other two objectives, the "common defense" and the "general welfare." Revenue was to be raised mainly by duties, excises, and indirect taxes, which would fall less heavily on the financial and mercantile classes than would the "capitation or other direct tax," which the French king still levied, and which the Constitution expressly forbade.[58]

---

[53] Hamilton and Adair, *op. cit.*, pp. 109, 116.

[54] Cf. Farrand, *op. cit.*, II, 321–22, 325, 615, 616, and *passim*.

[55] *Ibid.*, pp. 615–16.

[56] It is true that two delegates, Mason and Gerry, refused to sign the Constitution, partly because they feared that the commerce clause might be interpreted as authorizing Congress to create monopolies and companies (Hamilton and Adair, *op. cit.*, pp. 118, 225). But this does not prove that a majority of the delegates intended that the clause should be interpreted in this way. James Wilson, who thought that the power to create mercantile (he did not say industrial) monopolies was included in the meaning of the commerce clause, did not believe that the clause gave the national government the power to cut canals. It was he who seconded Franklin's motion to add a specific phrase granting this power (Farrand, *op. cit.*, II, 615–16; cf. III, 463, 465).

[57] Cf. Beard, *op. cit.*, *passim*.

[58] ". . . unless in proportion to the census or enumeration herein before directed to be taken." (Article I, sec. 9).

Free trade within the United States was assured, and the basis
laid for the protection of American industries, by several clauses, in
sections 8, 9, and 10 of Article I, which granted Congress the power
to regulate foreign trade, and trade between the states, but prohibited the levying of taxes or duties, either by Congress or the
states, on interstate commerce.

Congress was given the authority, in section 8 of Article I, "to
promote the progress of science and useful arts, by securing for
limited times to authors and inventors the exclusive right to their
respective writings and discoveries."

How far a knowledge of English and French economic history
actually guided the Founding Fathers in drafting these economic
sections of the Constitution, is a question to which no precise answer can be given. The objectives of the delegates were numerous,
complex, and to some extent contradictory, like the motives behind
each objective. The future progress of industry was only one among
a number of aims which they had at heart. Economic considerations
generally were of less compelling importance in statecraft than
they were to become in the nineteenth century. It is probable that
the decision to confer upon Congress the power to regulate commerce was determined, less by economic considerations, than by the
belief that this power, exercised by the British parliament until
the Revolution, would strengthen the political authority of the
federal government.[59] It is probable that the widely felt need for
establishing the national credit, and the private interests of the delegates, as men of property,[60] played a greater part in determining the
nature of the clauses governing taxation and the payment of the
public debt, than the dimly perceived relationship between the
concentration of wealth and industrial prosperity. The fragmen-
tary records left us of the constitutional debates suggest that, when
the delegates talked about economic history, it was more often
American than European. We find, for example, in the debates
which resulted in the prohibition of taxes on commerce between
the states, no reference to the tolls levied on French interprovincial
trade, but several references to the duties recently levied by some

---

[59] Cf. A. C. McLaughlin, "The Background of American Federalism," *American
Political Science Review*, XII (1918), pp. 215–40.
[60] Cf. Beard, *op. cit., passim.*

states, under the Articles of Confederation, or interstate trade.[61]

American history was closer to the delegates than European, but, as Gouverneur Morris remarked in the Convention, it did "not savour much of real wisdom" "to draw from our short and scanty experience rules which are to operate through succeeding ages." [62] On economic questions, the lessons derived by the Founding Fathers from the more immediate experience of America were almost invariably reënforced, and on a few occasions even modified, by lessons derived from the experience of Europe since the Reformation. European precedents were often cited in the debates, and the economic thought of some of the most famous delegates was plainly influenced in important respects by English and, to a lesser extent, by French history. In commenting on the activities of European governments in regulating economic life, Franklin wrote as early as 1764: "At present most of the Edicts of Princes, Placaerts, Laws and Ordinances of Kingdoms and States for that purpose, prove political Blunders. The Advantages they produce not being *general* for the Commonwealth; but *particular,* to private Persons or Bodies in the State who procur'd them, and *at the Expense of the rest of the People.*" [63] Madison thought it should be the general rule among statesmen to leave "to the sagacity of individuals, and to the impulse of private interest, the application of industry and capital." But the industrial experience of prosperous European countries, and particularly the experience of Great Britain with the development of some branches of her textile manufacture in the late sixteenth and seventeenth centuries, had led him to believe it was necessary to foster the introduction of new manufactures, by liberal support of the government, or the aid of skilled immigrant workers, or both.[64] Some of the principal arguments in Hamilton's *Report on Manufactures* were supported by appeals to European, and especially to English, history. In dealing with public finance, he said it was "the prevailing opinion of the [English] men of business, and of the generality of the most sagacious theorists,"

---

[61] James Madison, *Journal of the Federal Convention* (E. H. Scott, ed., Chicago, 1898), I, 46–47; II, 622.

[62] Farrand, *op. cit.,* II, 126.

[63] Smyth, ed., *The Writings of Benjamin Franklin,* IV, 244.

[64] *Letters and Other Writings of James Madison* (Philadelphia, 1867), III, 42–43, 160, 653–54.

that the funding of the public debt in England, by helping to provide capital, had contributed to the extraordinary prosperity of "every species of [British] industry." A similar handling of the public debt of the United States, he suggested, would be likely to produce the same results.[65] In *The Federalist*,[66] he argued that the raising of revenue mainly by direct taxes was even less practicable in the United States than in England, and, as a justification for the financial sections of the Constitution, he pointed to the success of Great Britain in raising the greatest part of its national income by excises and duties on imports. Again, in the *Report on Manufactures*, Hamilton referred to the immense utility of the various societies organized in Great Britain for the encouragement of arts, manufactures, and commerce, and also to the protection afforded to industrial inventors in various European countries. He hoped that the federal government, in addition to fostering the patent system, would set up a commission "to induce the prosecution and introduction of useful discoveries, inventions, and improvements. . . ." [67] In advocating the creation of a Society for Establishing Useful Manufactures, he was undoubtedly influenced by the methods adopted by the French government during the last half century of the *ancien régime* of helping new industrial ventures by advancing capital.[68]

If some of the leading delegates to the Constitutional Convention were accustomed to turn to European experience as a guide to economic policy, it cannot be entirely accidental that the economic sections of the Constitution were written almost exactly as many students of English and French history in 1787 would have been disposed to write them. Whenever English or French industrial history was consulted by Americans, it seemed to justify the very policies which were favorable to the private material interests of the majority of the delegates at Philadelphia, and of the social classes which they represented. Thus the Convention could find in industrial history support for one of the most important innova-

[65] *Industrial and Commercial Correspondence of Alexander Hamilton*, p. 277; cf. pp. 274–79. The same argument concerning the rôle played by public credit in promoting manufactures, is contained in a communication of Hamilton to the house of representatives, Jan. 14, 1790 (John C. Hamilton, *The Works of Alexander Hamilton*, III, 5–6).

[66] Number XII.

[67] *Industrial and Commercial Correspondence*, pp. 294, 296, 319.

[68] *Ibid.*, p. 202; cf. pp. xxvii, 183–228.

tions of eighteenth-century thought, that by seeking one's own financial advantage in the market place one increased the general welfare, that in economic matters self-love and social were identical.

This belief found expression in the Constitution. In the nineteenth century, it came to be a more influential guide to private and public conduct in the United States than in any other country. It owed its origin partly to European industrial history before 1787.

The Concepts of Democracy and Liberty in the Eighteenth Century ⤳

GAETANO SALVEMINI

I

TODAY the word "democracy" evokes the concept of a political regime which grants equal rights to all citizens without discrimination of social classes. Such rights may be placed under two headings: (1) personal rights, i.e., life, property, freedom of occupation, the right of habeas corpus, and freedom of thought and of worship; and (2) political rights, i.e., freedom of speech, freedom of the press, freedom of association and of assembly, and the right of representation in central and local government.

The writers of the eighteenth century meant by "democracy" that form of government in which all the citizens, whatever their social station, met together in a general assembly and there made laws, gave the final decision on peace or war and on the most important affairs of the commonwealth, and appointed officials to deal with the minor matters of daily administration. Locke, to whom most of the liberal doctrines of the eighteenth century may be traced, defined democracy as that form of government in which "the majority having the whole power of the community naturally in them, may employ all that power in making laws for the community and execute those laws by officers of their own appointing." Analogous views are to be found in Burlamaqui, Montesquieu, Rousseau, John Adams, Madison, Jefferson, and all the other political writers of that age.

This concept of democracy had been transmitted by the Greek city-state to Roman political thought, and from classical antiquity to the Middle Ages and the Renaissance. To be sure, representative government had acquired in England, from the thirteenth to the seventeenth century, all the connotations which we associate with it today. But even in England the concept of democracy still remained the traditional one of those societies in which representative government was as yet nonexistent. The idea of sovereign powers personally exercised continued to have precedence in people's minds over the idea of representative government.

"Democracy" was also termed "pure," "perfect," or "simple" democracy, in order to keep it distinct from a democratic but representative regime. Jefferson called it a "republic" or a "pure republic," and called "government democratical but representative" the parliamentary regime based on universal suffrage. Madison gave "democracy," the common meaning and termed the representative system "republic"; thus the United States was a republic and not a "democracy." We today say "direct democracy" for the eighteenth-century "democracy."

It was a *communis opinio* that "democracy" was suited to small territories only. This doctrine is to be found in Burlamaqui, Montesquieu, D'Alembert, Rousseau, Price, Madison, Jefferson, and many others. "I doubt," Jefferson wrote, "if it would be practicable beyond the extent of a New England township." In fact, only in small communities would the citizens not be too numerous to participate in the sovereign assembly without rendering it unworkable. "The natural limit of a democracy," Madison wrote, "is that distance from the central point which will just permit the most remote citizens to assemble as often as the public functions demand, and will include no greater number than can join in these functions." For countries of moderate size representative monarchy was prescribed, while for a large territory a despotic monarchy was deemed suitable, unless the country was split up into small local units confederated for mutual defense. Such small local units might retain "democracy," thanks to their smallness, and thus international security and domestic "democracy" would be combined.

England and France in the eighteenth century were regarded as countries of moderate size to which a representative monarchy was best suited, while for colossal Russia a despotic monarchy was recommended.

In examining what type of representative regime would be more appropriate for their country, a group of Englishmen—the forerunners of the nineteenth-century radicals—on the eve of the French Revolution advocated universal suffrage, which was then termed "equal representation." John Wilkes in 1776 demanded in the house of commons "a bill for a just and equal Representation of the People of England in Parliament." John Cartwright adopted the idea of universal suffrage in the same year. The Duke of Richmond in 1780 introduced in the house of lords a bill "for declaring and restoring the natural, inalienable, and equal right of all the Commoners of Great Britain (infants, persons of insane minds, and criminals incapacitated by law only excepted) to vote in the election of their representatives in Parliament"; and in 1783 he repeated in an open letter that even "paupers and the lowest orders of the people" should have a vote. The Society for Promoting Constitutional Information, founded in 1780, organized a systematic campaign for universal suffrage.

But the influence of this movement was very limited. Richard Price, who was one of the moving spirits behind the Society for Promoting Constitutional Information, scorned the English electoral system of his day and advocated "complete representation," that is, "a body of Representatives, in appointing whom all the members of the commonwealth have voices." Yet he would have been content with a reform that conceded the franchise to a number of citizens no greater than that of those who enjoyed the privilege in his time, 200,000 persons in England and Wales out of a population of about 7,000,000, provided that the electors should be "independent persons, of all orders, in every part of the Kingdom." (A system of universal manhood suffrage would have enfranchised at least 1,800,000 citizens.) If it had been possible to obtain a reform of this kind, he would have been "less disposed to complain of the injustice done, by its inadequateness, to the greater part of the Kingdom, by depriving them of one of their natural and inalienable rights." If this was the way of thinking of a left-winger, it was natural that in the eyes of the Tories and of most of the Whigs the oligarchic constitution brought forth by the "Glorious Revolution" was the last word in perfection. "The divine right of kings had been supplanted by the divine right of freeholders."

In North America economic and social conditions were suited to a more democratic form of government than in old England. Yet the fact is well known that in all the North American states the franchise was based on property qualifications and that further safeguards for property were secured in the qualifications imposed on members of the legislatures and senates. Paine advocated "a large and equal representation." But he was also of the opinion that in North America "the sovereign power remained in the people . . . for the people in America are the foundation of power." In this opinion he was not embarrassed by the fact that "equal representation" was lacking in America. He was convinced that "the mercantile and manufacturing part of the nation" was its "great bulwark." From his mind the non-propertied man was absent. John Adams realized the existence of this man, but even when professing "revolutionary principles" he excluded him from the franchise.

As far as continental Europe is concerned, the distrust, not to say the contempt felt in France by men like Voltaire, Montesquieu, and D'Alembert toward the "dregs of the people," the "canaille," "the cobblers and the maidservants," "le bas peuple," is well known. All of them were disposed to repeat with the Swiss Burlamaqui that "if we consider the education of the vulgar, their application to labor, their ignorance and brutality, we must readily perceive that they are made to be governed, and not at all to govern others."

In respect to limited monarchy, which he deemed the best form of government, Montesquieu taught that "persons distinguished by their birth, riches, or honors" should not be "confounded with the common people" but that "the share they have in the legislature ought to be proportioned to their other advantages." Therefore the legislative power should consist of two chambers, one made up of a hereditary aristocracy and the other representing the people, it being well understood that "such as are in so mean a situation, as to be deemed to have no will of their own" should not be enfranchised. As regards the French monarchy, he was of the opinion that the king's powers should be limited solely by the privileges of the upper judiciary.

Turgot was convinced that no other class than that of proprietors, "the only one which is not bound by the need of subsistence to a particular labor, can be employed for the general needs of society."

The Swiss De Lolme explained that in England "the political rights of the people were inseparably connected with the right of property." With all this he considered the English electorate of the eighteenth century to be "the people of England."

If we turn to Italy, suffice it to remember that the poet Alfieri, who in 1777 wrote a booklet *On Tyranny* and whose tragedies overflow with tyrants who are killed by republicans, defined the people as the totality of "the citizens in more or less comfortable circumstances, who have their estates or trades, wives and children and relatives," and excluded from the people "the propertyless members of the vile herd, living from day to day, to whom all forms of government are a matter of indifference because they have nothing to lose." He insisted that the career should be left open to the talents, but—he was careful to explain—"on condition that the talents should at the same time possess some property."

During the second half of the eighteenth century, under Rousseau's influence, the principle of private ownership was widely discredited. The *Encyclopédie* of Diderot, in the article "Richesse," expressed the opinion that "to choose between wealth and poverty was to choose between vice and virtue." In the eyes of D'Argenson poverty was "the source of virtue." But even those left-wing French writers whom we today would regard as the forerunners of the socialists, had no respect for that "proletariat" which was to become the chosen people in the Marxian doctrine.

Diderot was of the opinion that "the progress of ideas is limited; it does not reach the suburbs; the people is too foolish; the multitude is always ignorant and stupid"; "the man of the people is the most stupid and wicked of men; to separate oneself from the people or to improve oneself, is the same thing."

Rousseau, no less than the others, disdained the "ignorant and contemptible multitude," "the brutalized mob loving bread more than liberty." He thought that democracy would be the best form of government because it was the least remote from the state of nature. But he admitted that democracy would be too perfect a form of government for humanity as it then existed: "Did there exist a nation of gods, their government would doubtless be democratical. . . . A true democracy has never existed and never will exist." A republic based on universal suffrage would, in his opinion, be the form of government least remote from direct democracy. But not even such a regime was practicable, because of the

corruption into which humanity had fallen as a result of civilization. For this reason he would have been satisfied if France had
had a parliamentary monarchy in which the franchise was restricted to "the middle order between the rich and the poor,"
"the soundest part of the nation." For Poland he did not even
propose the liberation of the serfs, and he did not spare his admiration for the aristocratic constitution of the Republic of Ge-
neva. The youth whom he had in mind when he wrote his *Émile*
must have belonged to a well-to-do family, which could afford the
luxury of hiring for their boy a tutor imbued with the pedagogical
doctrines of Rousseau.

Mably thought that "democracy" in Athens "debased itself"
when the workers acquired predominance in the government. He
invited his readers to admire the Author of Creation, who destined "the more numerous," "these dregs of humanity, to serve, so
to speak, only as ballast to the vessel of society." He warned the
lawgiver not to entrust to the worker "the deposit of sovereignty."

When Burke at the end of the eighteenth century expressed his
contempt toward "the swinish multitude," "the miserable sheep,"
he could have cited Rousseau and Mably among his authorities
against Price and Fox.

No wonder, therefore, if one of the most learned students of
French political literature of the eighteenth century did not know of
a single French writer of that century who demanded parliamentary
democracy based on universal suffrage. It was the United States who
made the first experiments in universal suffrage in the first half of
the nineteenth century. The United States is the youngest nation
but the oldest representative democracy in the world.

This line of thought will appear natural when one reflects that
in England the agricultural economic system had not yet been dis-
rupted by the Industrial Revolution and that in continental Europe and in the United States that revolution had barely begun.
The dominant political ideas were still those which had been
elaborated in the agricultural civilization of antiquity. There had
not yet clearly emerged a proletarian class, distinct on the one
hand from the independent artisans, tradesmen, and farmers, and
on the other hand from the mass of beggars and social refuse. In
modern industrial societies nobody would repeat with John Adams
that the poor man is "vicious, idle, ignorant," while the rich man

is "virtuous, laborious, learned." We have only to look around us to see masses of men who cannot find employment or who have been put out of business by causes beyond their control. In the agricultural society of the eighteenth century, population had not yet become superabundant, and the cultivable area had not yet been fully exploited. Thus the man without property was regarded as a social outcast. Addison had written at the beginning of the century: "Poverty and riches stand in our imagination in the place of guilt and innocence." What to Addison was a deplorable prejudice was a reasonable opinion to most eighteenth-century writers. They were not shocked by Montesquieu's pronouncement that "man is not poor because he has nothing, but because he does not work."

II

The concept of liberty was not so well defined as that of direct democracy or of representative government. Its meanings were many and varied from one writer to another—an affliction, for that matter, from which we still suffer today. Montesquieu observed that "there is no word that admits of more various significations, and has made more different impressions on the human mind, than that of Liberty":

Some have taken it for a faculty of deposing a person on whom they had conferred a tyrannical authority; others for the power of choosing a superior whom they are obliged to obey; others for the right of bearing arms and of being therefore enabled to use violence; others, in fine, for the privilege of being governed by a native of their own country, or by their own laws. A certain nation for a long time thought liberty consisted in the privilege of wearing a long beard. Some have annexed this name to one form of government exclusive of others: those who had a republican taste applied it to this species of polity; those who had enjoyed a monarchical government, gave it to monarchy. Thus they have all applied the name of liberty to the government most suitable to their own customs and inclinations.

Montesquieu mentioned some of these meanings merely in order to introduce into his treatise, as was his custom, relief spots for the benefit of the reader. What he defined as "the privilege of being governed by a native of their own country or by their own laws" is today called "national independence" or "self-determination."

The "power of choosing a superior whom they are obliged to obey" is today called the right to be represented in the lawmaking bodies. This is but one of those political rights which modern representative democracy grants to all citizens.

Richard Price used the word "liberty" in this meaning of the right of self-government: "Civil liberty is the power of a civil society or state to govern itself by its own discretion or by laws of its own making." From this definition he derived the right of the American colonies to revolt against the English government. The American Declaration of 1774 also stated that "the foundation of English liberty, and of all free governments, is a right in the people to participate in their legislative council." In that same year, 1774, Jefferson refused to admit that the electors of the British Isles should give law to the inhabitants of the United States: "Were this to be admitted, instead of being a free people . . . we should suddenly be found the slaves not of one but of one hundred and sixty thousand tyrants." Upon the same meaning of the word "liberty" the Society for Constitutional Information based its campaign for universal suffrage. This is why Rousseau wrote in his *Social Contract:* "The English people think it is free. It is mistaken. It is free only during the election of the members of parliament. As soon as the latter are elected, the English people is a slave, it is nothing." In writing these words, Rousseau had in mind only that meaning of the word liberty which made liberty and self-government interchangeable. And by the English people he meant not only those citizens who had no right to vote and therefore were permanently slaves, but also those who were enfranchised and who were free only at the moment when they were giving their vote.

De Lolme refused to attribute this meaning to the word liberty. According to him, it was "a play on words and nothing more" to say: "A man who contributes by his vote to the passing of a law, has himself made the law; in obeying it, he obeys himself—he therefore is free." The truth is that "when a law contrary to his intentions is enacted, he must nevertheless submit to it," which is not freedom. To have a share in establishing the law, is not to be free, but is "to enjoy a share of power" or to carry out an "act of government." Liberty is quite a different thing. It "consists in this, that every man, while he respects the persons of others and allows them quietly to enjoy the produce of their industry, be certain himself likewise to enjoy the produce of his own industry, and that his person be also secure." "To live in a state where the laws are equal for all and sure to be executed, is to be free." This liberty De Lolme called "private liberty or the liberty of the individual"; and explained that such liberty consisted of the right of property, the right of personal security, and the locomotive faculty. In other words, the private liberties of De Lolme were what we nowadays call personal rights, and what the French Constituent Assembly of 1789 termed "the rights of man." What we call political liberties and the French Constituent Assembly of 1789 termed "the rights of the citizen" were termed by De Lolme "general liberty."

The division between personal liberties and political liberties appears more clearly defined in the article "Liberty" in the *Encyclopaedia Britannica* of 1778–83. According to the author of this article, every Briton is endowed from birth with a number of rights and liberties or "personal immunities," which may be placed under three primary headings: "the right of personal security, the right of personal liberty, and the right of private property." In order to secure the actual enjoyment of such rights, there were in the English constitution "certain other auxiliary, subordinate rights of the subject, which served principally as barriers to protect and maintain inviolate the three great and primary rights of personal security, personal liberty, and private property." These auxiliary and subordinate rights which must buttress the primary and essential personal rights, were the political rights.

The difference that was more or less clearly felt between the essential liberties (personal) and the auxiliary liberties (political) explains why a man like Price could declare that, if he could imagine a perfect man becoming king, he, Price, would submit to his authority and not feel the need to demand political liberties. Even Rousseau was prepared to renounce political liberty on condition that absolute monarchy guaranteed the happiness of its subjects. He pledged himself to go and die of joy at the feet of Frederick the Second if Frederick succeeded in filling his country with a happy people. The writers of the Physiocratic School demanded economic liberty as one of the "natural" and essential personal rights; but the Physiocrat Le Trosne preferred the absolute French government to the English constitutional regime "because in France reforms changing the whole face of the country can be accomplished in the twinkling of an eye, while in England the very slightest reform can be frustrated by the hostility of parties." D'Argenson, who also was imbued with ideas which today would make him pass for a socialist, did not like deliberative assemblies: "The monarchical authority and the liberty of the people," he wrote, "are not enemies to each other and ought neither to combat nor to destroy each other." The ideal regime of the eighteenth century was enlightened despotism.

In the writings and in the political documents of that time, "life, liberty, and property" are found continually interlocked. According to Quesnay, the founder of the Physiocratic School, all natural rights are reduced to a single fundamental right: the right of property, which assumes three forms: (1) property in one's own person, or liberty; (2) personal movable property; and (3) landed property. These three kinds of property form an indissoluble whole. "Liberty and property," wrote Voltaire in the *Dictionnaire philosophique,* "is the great national cry of the English. It is certainly better than 'St. George and my right' or 'St. Denis and Montjoie' [the French national cry]. It is the cry of nature." For him the tyrannical regime differs from the free regime in this, that the tyrant "takes the property of his subjects and afterwards enlists them to go and take that of his neighbors." In De Felice's *Encyclopédie* we read: "Despoil a man of all his rights of property, and I defy you to find in him any vestiges of liberty; on the other hand, imagine a man who has been deprived of all kinds of liberty, and I challenge you to say that there remains to him in reality any right of property. . . . The amount of liberty which each man should be allowed to enjoy is always evident: it is given to us naturally by the right of property: as is the extent of his right of property, so should be the extent of his liberty." The *Encyclopaedia Britannica* of 1778–83 warned that the rights and liberties of the Britons were "highly necessary to be perfectly known and considered by every man of rank and property."

To be sure, there were among jurists and political writers two schools of thought. According to one of these schools, the right of property was one of those "natural rights" inherent in human nature and anterior to society which positive law must regard as inviolable. According to the other, the right of property, like political rights, was one of those "civil rights" which had been created after the emergence of society and were subject to the limitations which positive law might establish in the interest of society. But only the curate Meslier denied *in toto* the right of property, in a section of his work which remained unpublished until 1864. Rousseau described in glowing terms the state of nature in which men had not yet been corrupted by the institution of property, and painted in black colors the evil results produced by the introduction of property rights. But he also taught that, at the stage which humanity had reached in its development, society was as unavoidable to humanity as decrepitude to the individual and property had become an evil by means of which worse evils were prevented: "Human nature does not go backwards"; the destruction of the right of property would merely "substitute brigandage for corruption"; "the right of property is the most sacred of all the rights of the citizens." Émile was to be educated to respect the right of property, and therefore Rousseau assigned him a piece of land so that, by cultivating it, he would learn that property is the fruit of toil. According to Mably, "in the beginning, any law was vicious which tended to break the community of property. To the contrary, today any law will be wise which tends to remove from our passions any means or any pretext for wounding property-rights, even the slightest." Brissot, to whom may be traced the formula "Property is theft," which became the slogan of nineteenth-century socialists, never maintained that property should be abolished. He merely aimed at showing that theft should not be punished, like homicide, by the death penalty, since the thief violates only a "social" right, while the homicide violates a "natural" right.

The English radicals did not take a different view from the French *philosophes*. The Duke of Richmond, in maintaining that even "paupers and the lowest orders of the people" should have a vote, was careful to assure his friends that they would not have to fear falling "into all the confusion of a democratic republic" when a system of "equal representation" was established. "Education and knowledge generally attend property." Therefore, under a regime of universal suffrage, "those who possess them [education, knowledge, and property] ought to have weight and influence with the more ignorant. . . . Property will have its weight as it ever must have in all governments."

III

The doctrines concerning self-government, liberty, and property that were elaborated by the eighteenth-century liberal writers, have been defined by one of the most brilliant political writers of our day, Harold Laski, as "the philosophy of a business civilization." One can accept this label on condition that the idea of "big business" be expunged from our conception of that philosophy.

In the eighteenth century there did not yet exist a clear distinction between the concept of wealth and that of feudalism. The contrast between rich and poor was regarded as identical with that between nobility and commoners. Invectives against bankers had a substratum that was more political than social. The banker was not so much the dealer in money as he was the tax-farmer who grew fat at the expense of the taxpayers. The attacks on the general idea of property were at bottom attacks on that particular form of feudal property the weight of which was felt in the eighteenth century. The "people" to whom personal and political rights must be granted, were as a rule conceived of as consisting of those sections of the propertied classes who did not belong to the clergy, the nobility, and higher finance. The liberals of the eighteenth century were convinced that the unimpeded workings of economic forces would create a society of free and equal men, once the privileges of the clergy and the nobility were abolished. The "people"—that is, the middle classes—would be able to defend themselves against the return of ecclesiastical and feudal privileges and against the encroachments of absolutist bureaucracy and of the financiers encrusted upon despotic institutions. The representative regime, controlled by the landholding classes, among which the middle classes formed by this time the overwhelming majority, was the instrument by means of which the middle classes would be protected against the forces of the past and would create the new society.

The "man and citizen" of the eighteenth-century *philosophes* was a farmer, a tradesman, or a merchant who was secure in his economic independence but was not so powerful as to be able to threaten the economic independence of his neighbor. Those writers who demanded economic liberty and opposed the encroachments of government in the economic sphere, never dreamed that economic liberty might become the instrument with which the stronger might dispossess the weaker.

The *philosophes* attributed to the "magic of property," as Young called it, the capacity to produce miracles as soon as it was rendered fertile by free initiative and individual energies. An eminent authority on the eighteenth century, Leslie Stephen (*The English Utilitarians*, I, 134), has remarked that in that century "many of the most active prophets of the individualistic spirit were acting, and acting sincerely, in the name of humanity. . . . Possibly they expected too much from the simple removal of restrictions; but certainly they denounced the restrictions as unjust to all, not simply as hindrances to the wealth of the rich. Adam Smith's position is intelligible: it was, he thought, a proof of a providential order that each man, by helping himself, unintentionally helped his neighbors. The moral sense based upon sympathy was not opposed to, but justified, the economic principle that each man should first attend to his own interests."

The twentieth-century magnate who demands and gets high protective tariffs from the government, sets up monopolies, controls prices, bribes politicians and journalists to promote his peculiar interests in devious ways, and regards political rights and liberties as his right and liberty to utilize the machinery of representative democracy in order to wrest legislation that permits him to increase his property without limit at the expense of other people's property and to oust anyone who refuses to become a cog in the machine of big business—such a man would have been regarded in the eighteenth century as a caprice of nature, as a monster whom nobody, not even the most resolute upholder of private property and laissez faire, would have granted either political or economic liberty.

All the eighteenth-century *philosophes* regarded excessive wealth as a danger to be guarded against and to be suppressed where it existed. Voltaire, after glorifying free property, did not fail to observe that "it has happened in more kingdoms than one that the emancipated serf has attained such wealth by his skill and industry as has enabled him to occupy the station of his former master. The old noblesse have been degraded and the new have been only envied and despised." The fate of the countries in which "such usurpations" had occurred should be a warning and a lesson to others. It was necessary "to oppose the restrictions of laws to the cupidity and arrogance of upstart proprietors. . . . A good is never productive of evil but when it is carried to a culpable excess, in which case it completely ceases to be a good." Right-wing as well as left-wing liberals demanded legislation to combat great economic inequalities. The laissez faire of the eighteenth century is not the laissez faire of the big business man but the laissez faire of the small landowner, manufacturer, and merchant.

In the nineteenth and twentieth centuries, as the capitalist system has developed, the right-wing liberals have continued to repeat faithfully all the doctrines of the eighteenth century. Thus the concepts of liberty and property, which were worked out in the eighteenth century for the use of a society which supposedly should be formed of men more or less equal in wealth, have come to justify an economic and social system in which those words have acquired a context and are put to uses very diverse from those for which they were originally devised. On the other hand, the left-wing liberalism that was in the eighteenth century scarcely a small tributary of the broad right-wing liberal river, has grown broader and has become in its turn a vast river independent of the old one. The left-wing liberals are ever more vociferous and insistent in demanding that the right of property shall be expunged from the list of "natural," "inviolable, and inalienable rights and transferred to the list of those "civil" rights which society creates and which society may regulate, limit, suppress.

One who reads Mr. Hoover's book *Freedom,* may almost believe that Mr. Hoover is a right-wing *philosophe* of the eighteenth century, and projecting Mr. Hoover's doctrines against the economic and social background of our day, may find that they are perhaps a little outmoded and rather conservative. In the eighteenth century, however, novelty and revolution were expressed by those doctrines and not by those of the left wingers. The left wingers, in attacking private property, merely continued to breathe the air of absolute monarchy, in which the sovereign had unlimited power over the property of the citizens. They held out their hands to the upholders of monarchical-absolutist communism. On the contrary, the doctrine of the right-wing writers who refused the sovereign the power to alter the "natural" operation of economic laws and to interfere with individual initiative in the use of property, that doctrine in the eighteenth century acted as the true revolutionary force. In the twentieth century it acts for conservation.

The Appeal to Reason and the American Constitution ⟡ ROLAND BAINTON

THE Constitution was a product of the Age of Reason.[1] The term has three major meanings. Reason is a faculty of man; reason is a quality of the universe; reason is a temper in the conduct of human affairs. The first sense is basic for the Constitution, the second for the Bill of Rights, and the third for both.

Reason as a faculty of man lies behind the essential theory of the Constitution, which is government by consent, the federal theory of the consent of the states, the compact theory of the consent of the individuals. Each separate member of the body politic should acquiesce in the association. Now why should the voluntary assent of individuals be regarded as requisite? On the assumption that there is in man an inviolable something, call it reason, con-

[1] Reason is an elusive term and no comprehensive history of the concept is available. The article "Vernunft" in Rudolf Eisler's *Wörterbuch der philosophischen Begriffe* (Berlin, 1930) does not go far beyond a catena of definitions from the outstanding philosophers. The article "Ragione" in the *Enciclopedia italiana* is useful. The work of Allan J. M. Macdonald, *Authority and Reason in the Early Middle Ages* (London, 1933), shows that reason did not fare so badly as the handmaid of revelation. On the use of the word ratio in the Middle Ages, see G.-Ed. Demers, "Les Divers sens du mot 'Ratio' au moyen âge; autour d'un texte de Maître Ferrier de Catalogue" (1275), *Études d'histoire littéraire et doctrinale du XIIIᵉ siècle*, 1 Sér. I (1932), 105–39. (Publications de L'Institut d'études médiévales d'Ottawa). The various types of rationalism in the eighteenth century are analyzed by Arthur O. Lovejoy, "The Parallel of Deism and Classicism," *Modern Philology*, XXIX (1931–32), 281–99. On the concept of reason in modern philosophical systems, see Jean de la Harpe, "L'Idée de la raison dans les sciences et la philosophie contemporaine," *Recueil de travaux . . . Université de Neuchâtel*, XV (1930).

For the rôle of reason in law, see Otto Gierke, *Natural Law and the Theory of Society, 1500–1800*, translated by Ernest Barker (Cambridge, Eng., 1934), pp. 39, 235; and Giorgio del Vecchio, *Il concetto della natura e il principio del Diritto* (2d ed., Bologna, 1922). Paul Vinogradoff ("Reason and Conscience in Sixteenth-Century Jurisprudence," *Law Quarterly Review*, XXIV [1908], 273–384) points out that reason and conscience as normative principles in the application of law in England survived the collapse of the canon law. W. S. Holdsworth (*A History of English Law* [5th ed., 10 vols., London, 1931–32], II, 602–3) indicates, however, that the discontinuance of the canon law meant the separation of reason from nature. (Compare Hale's discussion of reason in application to law, *ibid.*, V, 482, 500–506). Charles McIlwain (*The High Court of Parliament* [New Haven, 1910], in the chapter on "The Fundamental Law") has many citations in which the law of reason takes the place of the law of nature.

science, or faith. The early sixteenth century preferred to talk of faith. This is something spiritual which can neither be created nor cut by the sword of the magistrate. The age of the religious wars spoke more of conscience. Here is the seat of man's integrity and if it be sapped his character will disintegrate. The eighteenth century appealed to reason. This, too, is inviolable by the civil sword, for "only light and evidence can work a change in men's opinions." [2]

The shift in terminology from the religious to the secular concept was aided by the spawning of sects with their rival claims to truth. For that reason Grotius, though a man of personal piety, sought a basis for government independent of religion. He found it in natural law, long associated with divine law, but pre-Christian in its origins.[3] The Stoics believed in the law of nature, the expression of the universal reason pervading the world and man. Grotius declared that this would be valid even if there were no God.[4] And Burlamaqui, who enjoyed a vogue in the colonies, asserted that natural law is evident to the mere light of reason and requires no revelation, because constant and independent of the caprice of the divine will.[5] Here, I suspect, we have the explana-

[2] "Four Letters on Toleration," *The Works of John Locke* (London, 1888), III, 6.

[3] The literature on natural law is very extensive. The best bibliography is in Charles Grove Haines, *The Revival of Natural Law Concepts* (Cambridge, Mass., 1930). The fusion of Stoic natural law with divine law in Hellenistic Judaism and in early Christianity is traced by Ernst Troeltsch, *The Social Teachings of the Christian Churches*, translated by Olive Wyon, 2 vols. (London, 1931). The development of the idea in Europe is covered by Otto Gierke, *Johannes Althusius und die Entwicklung der naturrechtlichen Staatstheorien*, "Untersuchungen zur deutschen Staats- und Rechtsgeschichte," VII (Breslau, 1880), and in his *Natural Law and the Theory of Society*, cited above. The American development is given by Benjamin Fletcher Wright, Jr., *American Interpretations of Natural Law* (Cambridge, Mass., 1931), who points out that until 1776 Americans identified natural law with the British constitution. Compare Charles F. Mullet, *"Fundamental Law and the American Revolution, 1770–1776,"* "Studies in History, Economics and Public Law," Columbia University, No. 385 (New York, 1933).

[4] Hugo Grotius, *De Iure Belli ac Pacis* (Paris, 1625), Prolegomena a 7 b: "Et haec quidem quae jam diximus, locum aliquem haberent etiamsi daremus, quod sine summo scelere dari nequit, non esse Deum." Otto Gierke (*Johannes Althusius,* p. 74) points out that Gabriel Biel said practically the same thing. This is significant because Biel belonged to the "Moderni," the late scholastics who sundered faith and reason. Locke owed much to Occam, the founder of the school.

[5] Jean Jacques Burlamaqui, *The Principles of Natural and Politic Law* (London, 1763; first English translation, London, 1748–52), p. 185: "If these laws were not a necessary consequence of the nature and constitution of man a very clear revelation would be necessary, but it is agreed that the law of nature is and ought to be known by the mere light of reason."

tion of the polite shelving at the federal convention of Franklin's plea for prayer. The framers were not averse to religion, but they resented the attack on the adequacy of the human understanding to operate unassisted in the area of natural law.[6]

The shift to reason in the eighteenth century was aided likewise by the decline of the doctrine of human depravity. The fall of Adam was believed by the followers of St. Augustine to have vitiated not only the moral but also the intellectual capacities of man. The Renaissance began to challenge this conception. One of the humanists declared that morally indeed Adam fell down, but intellectually he fell up, for he ate of the tree of knowledge and his eyes were opened.[7] The eighteenth century came to have great confidence in man's ability to understand and plan his world. Yet this confidence alone would scarcely explain the inviolability of individual reason had not the secularized concept trailed with it the aura of sanctity with which faith had been invested. This belief in something sacred in each person accounts for the voluntary character of all associations. Marriage is a social compact, not a family arrangement.[8] The church is a covenant of believers, not a community of those baptized in infancy,[9] and the state is likewise a voluntary society composed of those who yield certain alienable rights in order to safeguard the inalienable. Here is the root of government based on individual consent.

Nevertheless the framers entertained no extravagant notions of human reason and here, too, they were representative of their period, for it is the paradox of the century that the Age of Reason debased reason. At the outset exuberant and sobering currents were in conflict. Optimism attached itself to the method of Newton,[10] and men were naïve enough to suppose that even the truths

[6] Max Farrand, *The Records of the Federal Convention*, 3 vols. (New Haven, 1911), I, 451–52. Luther A. Weigle, *American Idealism*, "The Pageant of America" (New Haven, 1928), X, 124–25, shows that godlessness was not the cause of the omission. The Continental Congress observed daily prayer.

[7] Sebastian Castellio, "De Arte Dubitandi," *Per la Storia degli eretici italiani del secolo XVI in Europa;* testi raccolti da D. Cantimori e E. Feist, Reale Accademia d'Italia, "Studi e Documenti," VII (Roma, 1937), 367.

[8] John Locke, *Two Treatises on Civil Government*, II, Ch. VII, §78.

[9] John Locke, "Four Letters on Toleration," *Works*, III, 7.

[10] The optimistic strain is described by Ernst Cassirer, *Die Philosophie der Aufklärung* (Tübingen, 1932), in the chapter "Natur und Naturerkenntnis," but he shows how the line runs from Newton to Hume. The optimism is emphasized likewise by Carl L. Becker, *The Declaration of Independence* (New York, 1922).

of Christianity were demonstrable.[11] But many factors operated to demean the domain of reason. When man ate of the tree of knowledge and his eyes were opened, what did he behold? The appalling vastness of the universe of Copernicus and Galileo, before which the affrighted human atom recoiled [12] to take refuge in a homier and more manageable world.[13] The mood was reinforced by the revulsion against abstract theological speculation popularized by Erasmus,[14] and more markedly by the attempt of the Scottish school to salvage something from the onslaught of Hume by having recourse to common sense, to which reason was assimilated or subordinated. The Scotch signer of the Constitution, James Wilson, was contemptuous of philosophy. The theories of Locke, Berkeley, and Hume reminded him of My Lord Peter's brown loaf, which was one day mutton, the next beef, and the third plum pudding. Reason, he thought, should never be allowed to conflict with common sense. And what is common sense? It is that degree of reason which makes a man capable of managing his own affairs.[15] Wilson was not the only framer who entertained a moderate view of man's capacities.[16] Hence the constant search of the convention for checks and balances not only upon the departments of government, but upon the irrational tendencies of man. The almost religious concept of reason as an inviolable quality of

[11] The progressive disintegration of the attempt to demonstrate Christianity is illustrated in the documents collected by John M. Creed and John S. B. Smith, *Religious Thought in the Eighteenth Century Illustrated from Writers of the Period* (Cambridge, Eng., 1934).

[12] Blaise Pascal, *Pensées*, Ch. I. "Je vois ces effroyables espaces de l'univers qui m'enferment . . . comme un atome, et comme une ombre qui ne dure qu'un instant sans retour."

[13] Arthur O. Lovejoy (*The Great Chain of Being* [Cambridge, Mass., 1936], p. 122) discusses man's sense of his "inexpressible unimportance" before the "incalculable vastness" of the new astronomy. In the article " 'Pride' in Eighteenth-Century Thought," *Modern Language Notes*, XXXVI (1921), 31–37, he takes up the picture of man as the "Yahoo" and the "featherless human biped."

[14] The influence of Erasmus on the eighteenth century is shown by Werner Kaegi, "Erasmus im 18. Jahrhundert," *Gedenkschrift zum 400. Todestage des Erasmus von Rotterdam* (Basel, 1936), pp. 205–27.

[15] *The Works of James Wilson*, edited by James DeWitt Andrews, I (1896), 232–36.

[16] Franklin regarded the deadlock as a "melancholy proof of the imperfection of the human understanding" (Farrand, *op. cit.*, I, 451). Distrust of reason as a temper in human affairs is most marked in Hamilton, who was in the tradition of Hume (*ibid.*, I, 381). G. Morris said, "We must remember that the people never act from reason alone" (*ibid.*, I, 514), though he did think that a reasonable plan would commend itself to reasonable minds (*ibid.*, I, 529). Madison was alive to the corrupting influence of power (*ibid.*, I, 584).

man supported the theory of government by consent. The waning of the Age of Reason dictated restraint upon the contracting parties.

The second meaning of reason as a quality of the universe is basic for the Bill of Rights. For why should the reason, conscience, or faith of the individual man be respected as inviolable? To say that they cannot be created or cut by the sword of the magistrate does not settle the question. Why should society care whether they be either created or cut? The answer is that the reason in man corresponds to and is a part of the reason of the universe. To violate this principle in man is to transgress the universal law of life. This was again the old Stoic doctrine and had been potent enough to inspire intransigeance toward tyranny. One recalls the stalwart resistance of Paetus Thrasea to the despotism of Nero. Nevertheless, Stoicism did not develop a list of the rights of individual men. The explanation, I surmise, lies in the pantheistic diffusion of reason. Two steps were taken in the early sixteenth century toward a sharper demarcation. First the jurists set off man from the world by excluding the animals from the sphere of natural law.[17] The second and more decisive step was taken by a man of religion, when Martin Luther proclaimed the naked isolation of the individual soul before the face of that God who sitteth upon the circle of the earth to pass judgment upon the ways of men. Here is a principle of transcendence sufficient to set the individual man against society and to sustain him in his defiance. The Calvinist doctrine of election still further intensified the immediacy of each man's relation to the Supreme.[18] The classic American expression is found in the Biglow Papers:

> Ef you take a sword an' dror it,
> An' go stick a feller thru,
> Guv'ment aint to answer for it,
> God'll send the bill to you.

The finality of such sheer individualism is basic for the inalienable rights of man. Oddly enough by the time such rights had reached

---

[17] Otto Gierke, *Natural Law and the Theory of Society*, p. 233, note 22.
[18] Ernst Troeltsch, *Kultur der Gegenwart*, Teil 1, Abt. IV, 1, II Hälfte, pp. 577, 585. Hans Maier, *Die geistesgeschichtlichen Grundlagen der Konstitutionellen Theorie* (Tübingen, 1914), p. 22.

their maturest formulation, the religious overtone was waning, if not forgotten.[19]

[19] Georg Jellinek precipitated a lively controversy as to the origin of the rights of man in his *Die Erklärung der Menschen und Bürgerrechte* (1st ed., 1895, translated by Max Farrand, *The Declaration of the Rights of Man and of Citizens* [New York, 1901]). The discussion down to 1919 was summarized by his son in the preface to the third edition. Jellinek contended that the French declaration of 1789 was not derived from Rousseau, but from the American declarations, that the natural law tradition was inadequate to explain the source, that the real impetus came from the struggle for religious liberty, which he traced through the colonies to the Agreement of the People of 1647. Émile Doumergue ("Les Origines historiques de la déclaration des droits de l'homme et du citoyen," *Revue du droit public et de la science politique en France et à l'étranger*, XXI [1904], 673–733) drew the line forward from Calvin to the French declaration. David G. Ritchie (*Natural Rights* [London, 1903]) quite independently supported Jellinek as to the religious influence. J. Walter Jones ("Acquired and Guaranteed Rights," *Cambridge Legal Essays* [Cambridge, Eng., 1926], pp. 223–42) drew the line backward through the American colonies to the Agreement of the People of 1647.

Jellinek was criticized by Adalbert Wahl ("Zur Geschichte der Menschenrechte," *Hist. Zeitschrift*, CIII [1909], 79–85) on the ground that religious liberty was not conceived as a universal human right in the American colonies. Rationalism and individualism effected the change and these stem from Locke. But this still leaves the problem of the origins of Locke. Gustav Hägermann ("Die Erklärungen der Menschen und Bürgerrechte in den ersten amerikanischen Staatsverfassungen," *Hist. Studien*, LXXVIII [1910]) found the impetus for the American declarations in the economic situation and the source in the philosophy of the Enlightenment. Justus Hashagen ("Zur Entstehungsgeschichte der Nordamerikanischen Erklärungen der Menschenrechte," *Zeitschrift für die gesamte Staatswissenschaft*, LXXVIII [1924], 461–95) pointed to the incomplete attainment of religious liberty in the colonies. Men like George Mason and John Adams were more liberal as to civil than as to religious rights. The source of the rights of man is not American but European, and not religious but secular, in spite of Puritan elements in Locke. The root lies in natural law. Yet Hashagen recognized that the rights of man and natural law do not necessarily coincide. Gustav Adolf Salander ("Vom Werden der Menschenrechte; ein Beitrag zur modernen Verfassungsgeschichte unter Zugrundelegung der virginischen Erklärung der Rechte vom 12. Juni 1776," *Leipziger rechtswissenschaftliche Studien*, Leipziger Juristenfakultät, XIX [1926]) pointed out that Virginia, which made the first declaration of rights was dilatory as to religious liberty and the religious clause in the declaration of 1776 would have been more conservative had not Madison revised Mason. Otto Vossler ("Zur Erklärung der Menschenrechte," *Hist. Zeitschrift*, CXLII [1930], 516–45) found the source of the rights of man in English law, which was never sundered from the tradition of natural law. Roger Williams hindered, if anything, by severing the sacred and the secular so that the achievement of freedom in religion meant nothing for civil liberties.

The following discussions of Jellinek are interesting though not relevant to our immediate concern. James Sullivan ("The Antecedents of the Declaration of Independence," *Annual Report of the American Historical Association*, 1902, I, 67–81) went back to the Greeks, but he was discussing rather the origin of natural law than of the specific rights of men as individuals. Fritz Klövekorn ("Die Entstehung der Erklärung der Menschen- und Bürgerrechte," *Hist. Studien*, XC [1911]) supported Jellinek on the derivation of the French from the American. Robert Redslob (*Die Staatstheorien der französischen Nationalversammlung von 1789: ihre Grundlagen in der Staatslehre der Aufklärungszeit und in den englischen und amerikanischen Verfassungsgedanken* [Leipzig, 1912]) maintained that the French declaration owed some-

But the day was largely won. The framers of the Constitution did not quarrel with the content of the Bill of Rights. Some objected merely that the rights of individuals were the proper province of the states and not of the national government. Others brought forward the deeper criticism that fundamental rights cannot be secured by codification. Eternal law must be unwritten. A code, in the nature of the case, is positive law, the product of time and circumstance. James Wilson did not regard the American Constitution as fundamental law, rather it was municipal, or in medieval terminology, *ius civile*.[20] Roger Sherman referred to the "sublimity of nonsense and alarm" on the subject of a bill of rights which are "much too important to depend on mere paper protection." [21] For him the only guarantee was popular control over Congress. And John Dickinson said, "Trial by jury and the dependance of taxation upon representation, those cardinal stones of liberty, were not obtained by a bill of rights, or any other records, and have not and cannot be preserved by them. They and all other rights must be preserved by soundness of sense and honesty of heart. Compared with these what are a bill of rights, or any

thing to Rousseau because there was more of the sense of community than in the American declarations.

One observes that much of the criticism of Jellinek applies to the immediate American situation in 1776, when the lines of the previous three centuries were already interwoven and the original motives obscured. The critics themselves recognize the need of going back to Locke, but they do not undertake to analyze the struggles of the seventeenth century which he epitomized. Jellinek called attention to the fact that the first "native right" of the Agreement of the People in 1647 was "that matters of religion and the ways of God's worship are not at all entrusted by us to any human power, because therein we cannot remit or exceed a tittle of what our consciences dictate to be the mind of God without wilful sin." The point made by many that Calvinism was concerned not for universal religious freedom as a right of man, but for the recognition of Calvinism as the truth of God, does not invalidate the point that as a matter of fact Calvinism contributed mightily toward the recognition of an inalienable something in man, the more so because Calvinism did not sever religious and political life.

The best commentary on the whole controversy to my mind is that of Carl Schmitt (*Verfassungslehre* [München und Leipzig, 1928], pp. 158–59): "Dass die Religionsfreiheit das erste aller Grundrechte darstellt, ist also ohne Rücksicht auf die geschichtlichen Details der Entwicklung in einem systematischen Sinne unbedingt richtig. Denn damit ist das fundamentale Verteilungsprinzip aufgestellt: der Einzelne als solcher ist Träger eines absoluten Wertes und bleibt mit diesem Wert in seiner privaten Sphäre; seine private Freiheit ist infolgedessen etwas prinzipiell Unbegrenztes; der Staat ist nur ein Mittel und daher relativ, abgeleitet und in jeder seiner Befugnisse begrenzt und von Privaten kontrollierbar."

[20] *Works*, I, 94.

[21] Paul Leicester Ford, *Essays on the Constitution of the United States* (Brooklyn, 1892), pp. 218–21.

characters drawn upon paper or parchment, those frail remembrances?" [22] Here we are brought back to the first meaning of reason as a faculty of man. The eternal and universal reason of the world gives validity and inviolability to the reason in man, but the reason in man is the only guarantee that the reason in the world will be understood and obeyed in human affairs.

Once more, however, we are recalled to the sober picture of man's reason, so easily a prey to error and to passion. In almost the same breath with the above proclamation of "soundness of sense" Dickinson declared that by the "superior will of the people" he meant a "reasonable not a distracted will." But how preserve a reasonable will? The answer of the age was education. Here is the great faith of the century of reason in the enlightenment of the people. Jefferson was its prophet. "It is an axiom of my mind," said he, "that our liberty can never be safe but in the hands of the people themselves, and that, too, of people with a certain degree of instruction." [23]

We have already trenched upon the third meaning of reason as a temper in the conduct of human affairs, the round-table mood of matching mind with mind in the common quest for truth. It is the Socratic application of intelligence to life, Stoic equanimity and Christian forbearance. All these strains combined in Erasmus and again in Benjamin Franklin,[24] who was influenced alike by the Quakers and by the Enlightenment. Jefferson, too, spoke in similar vein. The Constitutional Convention elicited his admiration because "We are yet able to send our wise and good men together to talk over our form of government . . . with the same *sang-froid* as they would a subject of agriculture. The example we have given the world is single, that of changing our form of government under the authority of reason only, without bloodshed." [25] Had he lived later he would have realized that the discussion of agriculture can engender warmth, and had he been on the spot he would have known that the *sang* was not so *froid*. But

[22] Paul Leicester Ford, *Pamphlets on the Constitution of the United States* (Brooklyn, 1888), p. 186.

[23] *Writings of Thomas Jefferson*, XIX (Lib. ed., Washington, 1904), 24. Compare Roy J. Honeywell, *The Educational Work of Thomas Jefferson* (Cambridge, Mass., 1931).

[24] Gertrud Philippi, "Imperialistische und pazifizistische Strömungen in der Politik der Vereinigten Staaten von Amerika 1776–1815," *Heidelberger Abhandlungen z. mittleren u. neueren Geschichte*, XLV (1914).

[25] *Writings of Thomas Jefferson*, VII (Lib. ed., Washington, 1904), 73.

Franklin, on the floor of the convention when the deadlock came, commended the previous coolness and reminded his colleagues that they had been sent to consult, not to contend. In international relations Franklin rejoiced in the peace with England and hoped that mankind "as they call themselves reasonable creatures will have reason enough to settle their differences without cutting throats." Jefferson wondered whether the nations would not someday devise a "more rational umpire of differences than force," and Samuel Adams drafted a plan to invite Europe to compose national disputes "without the necessity of war . . . to the destruction of human happiness and the disgrace of human reason. . . ." [26]

This appeal is not popular today. One attack has come from those philosophies which rely on experience alone and eschew metaphysics. Unable, therefore, to arrive at universal principles of truth and right they regard every controversy as a clash of conjectures each of which has as much claim to be correct as the other, and the only arbitrament is a test of strength. If Locke is the parent of the bills of rights by his transmission of the mood of religious intransigeance, on the other hand by his empiricism he fathered the skepticism of Hume and the utilitarianism of Bentham. The only premise which gives point to the round-table method is the assumption of an ultimate and universal truth in some measure accessible to the mind of man. [27]

Even more fatal in our own day, because invested with a religious fervor, is the revolt of the Romantic movement against the individualism of the Enlightenment, with its universal reason diffused in every individual man. This atomism was swept out by the cult of the community, the *Volkgeist*, which, when identified with the state and personified in the ruler, banishes reason and tramples on the rights of man. [28]

[26] These and other passages are collected by Edwin D. Mead, *Washington, Jefferson and Franklin on War*. World Peace Foundation, Pamphlet Series III (May, 1913), 5.

[27] Morris Cohen protests against many varieties of contemporary irrationalism in *Reason and Nature* (New York, 1932), and Harold Laski points out that Duguit escaped the consequences of his denial of metaphysics only by inconsistency. "M. Duguit's Conception of the State," in *Modern Theories of Law* (London, 1933).

[28] Ernst Troeltsch ("The Ideas of Natural Law and Humanity in World Politics," App. 1 to Vol. 1 of Otto Gierke, *Natural Law and the Theory of Society*) in 1922 found the greatest difference between Germany and the Anglo-Saxon peoples in the survival of natural-law concepts among us and the disruption of that tradition by the Roman-

But if I break a lance for Minerva in her contemporary conflict with Mars and Dionysus, I would not be naïve. Reason, too, has her pitfalls. There was a touch of belligerency in the crusade against superstition which caused triumphant reason to extinguish fanaticism on the guillotine.[29] Seldom has a tone of aristocracy been lacking in the cult of reason. Locke based the power of the father over the child on the fact that the child was devoid of reason.[30] How easy to transfer that to the "little brown brother"! And reason is not above blindness and hypocrisy. The natural-law school taught that since war is a work of unreason, any nation which starts a war is necessarily bereft of reason.[31] They failed to foresee that since no nation ever starts a war, in every conflict each side would regard the other as a senseless brute to be treated like a wolf or a mad dog.[32] Well did Benjamin Franklin heed the stricture of a Quaker on his pride and add to his list of virtues to be emulated the quality of humility.

---

tic movement and the *Volkgeist* in Germany. A similar observation couched in quite different terms is made by Randolph Greenfield Adams, *The Political Ideas of the American Revolution* (Durham, N.C., 1922), p. 147.

[29] J. Peter and C. Poulet, "L'Église constitutionelle du Nord pendant la terreur," *Revue d'histoire ecclésiastique*, XV, 1 (1929), pp. 677–707.

[30] *Two Treatises on Civil Government*, II, §63.

[31] Emerich de Vattel, *Le Droit des gens ou principes de la loi universelle*, "The Classics of International Law," 3 vols. (Washington, D.C., 1916), Liv. III, §34, Vol. II, pp. 26–27.

[32] Much is made of these pitfalls in the rationalism of Jefferson by Otto Vossler, "Die amerikanischen Revolutionsideale im ihrem Verhältnis zu den europäischen," *Hist. Zeitschrift Beiheft*, XVII (1929), 132 ff.

The Puritan Background of the
First Amendment ∾ WILLIAM HALLER

THE crucial clause in the first provision of the American Bill of Rights as it appears in the First Amendment to the Constitution was, of course, that "Congress shall make no law respecting an establishment of religion, or prohibiting the free exercise thereof." This confirmed existing conditions by making religious liberty the law of the union, and from this, freedom of speech, freedom of the press, the rights of assembly and petition naturally followed.

It is important to note that the principle involved in this legalizing of the unprecedented situation which existed in the thirteen states appears not to have been questioned at the time or even discussed at any length. The Constitution in its primary form failed to affirm toleration not because its authors doubted the principle involved but because they took it for granted. The idea seems not to have occurred to them that one of the functions of the government of the United States might be to establish a church of the United States. As soon, however, as they saw that the affirmation of religious liberty was expedient for winning reluctant states to the union, they promptly affirmed it by amendment. Their object was union, and they found themselves in a situation where no union was possible which did not explicitly authorize the prevalent differences in religious faith and worship and hence in all thought and expression. Not to establish a church was not enough. The federal government must definitely establish toleration, must affirm by law the equal rights of citizens, denominations and states in respect to religion and must guarantee that each should be protected against all the others in the exercise of those rights. Toleration, thus established, did not spring from religious indifference. It sprang from political wisdom correctly recognizing and allowing for the prime religious conviction common to Americans and bred in them by the very nature of their religious experience. That conviction was that every citizen must be expected even on so momentous a concern as religion to have opinions and beliefs which might or might not be right, but which it was right for him to express and important for others to hear.

There is little I can say concerning the circumstances that directly led to the adoption of this provision in the Bill of Rights. There is also little that I could add to what has been written on the historic development of the doctrine of toleration.[1] I shall venture, rather, to offer some general suggestions concerning the causes for the condition of religious life in America which made toleration seem so natural a necessity to union. This condition, extraordinary at the time and of the utmost significance for the future of American civilization, arose from two intimately related causes in English life which came to their fullest fruition in America, namely the disruption of the historic church and the rise of Puritanism.

Religion, formerly the chief bond of union among the people of Europe, became in the England of the sixteenth century a principal occasion for disunion. Religion henceforth reflected not so much the common brotherhood of Englishmen with all Christians as their division upon various lines as Englishmen. The attempt to reform the English church which culminated in the great revolution of the seventeenth century achieved not the reform but the disruption of the church. The people flew apart into a host of communions, each professing to hold the one true faith; each excluding, even when not seeking to persecute, adherents of others; each struggling for existence if not for complete domination; and each torn by dissension within. Elizabeth supported the church and repressed its enemies, but only enough to maintain her own authority, not enough to restore the old order or forefend the anarchy to come. Every effort of her immediate successors to do more than she had done to reunite the people under the church served only to promote civil as well as religious disorder and to bring ruin on the state. Civil order was reëstablished only when in 1689 the state in effect abandoned responsibility for restoring religion to its former place and function in society. The government did not wholly abandon the church, but it acknowledged no responsibility greater than that of maintaining its own authority over all forms of religion. This it accomplished by compelling all to be not at one but at peace, proceeding only

[1] I refer especially to the recent work of R. H. Bainton, *Castellio: on the Coercion of Heretics* (New York, 1934), and of W. K. Jordan, *The Development of Religious Toleration in England,* 2 vols. (Cambridge, Mass., 1932, 1936).

against such as could plausibly be argued to be hostile to the political regime. Thus a measure of toleration was achieved in England by compromise, and toleration fostered national union while permitting religious disunion to crystallize quietly into the familiar pattern of our own times.

The adoption of the First Amendment signified the recognition in this country of a similar need in a situation brought on by the same causes, operating, however, on a simpler and broader scene and scale. From the point of view of one interested in the development of religious life, the settlement of North America by the English was an incident to the disruption of the historic English church, an incident rendered momentous by the nature and extent of the country. An enormous area was ready to be peopled by the religious minorities which sprang forward to remove themselves one after another into the wilderness. In England the diaspora of the church remained confined within definite social and physical limits. In America, they found a continent to deploy upon. Up to a point, the new society, or rather each particle into which the old society divided, reduplicated in little the religious pattern of the old, but with a difference of increasing significance. In each of the new communities, that is, some particular religious denomination was dominant. It had been there from the first settlement, which soon became in popular consciousness the year one, the apostolic age, of whatever the local faith might be. There was, however, no church common to all the new settlements, and the very idea of the church catholic, which never completely disappeared in England, became attenuated in America to nothing or practically nothing. In the typical American community, the local church, so often and so significantly called the first church, the denomination comprising the first families and the best people, might be Anglican in Virginia, but in Plymouth it was Separatist, in Massachusetts Bay Independent, in Pennsylvania Quaker, in Maryland even Roman Catholic, all enjoying in the country at large a quite unprecedented parity of prestige. Thus, freed from traditional checks, the religious divisions of the English people were leveled, yet at the same time perpetuated and fostered, by dispersion in this country. Even though old jealousies might survive here and there, Anglican Virginia could make good no claim to precedence over Puritan Massachusetts, and Pennsylvania, though Quaker, and Maryland, though Catholic, were under no compulsion to yield to either. Religion was from the start, and has continued in a measure to be, a local affair, representing differences and even conflicts between sectional cultures and interests, but not social or political inequalities.

The typical American community from the beginning also reflected the English pattern of inner division and dissent, again modified by the new conditions. The first church, the dominant communion, never comprised, never pretended to comprise, the whole society. Not all the passengers on the "Mayflower" itself were saints, and Governor Bradford in his chronicle had to begin early to record the strivings of the regenerate with the unregenerate at Plymouth. The members of the first church might deny political rights to the ungodly, might hope to convert them, might drive them out or persecute them, but they always had them on their hands. There was, of course, a good practical reason why this had to be. There was no way really to keep the ungodly out, and besides their presence was needed even in the godliest Utopia to help people the wilderness. Added to that was the fact that it was of the nature of American religious life to breed heterodoxy and disagreement within itself. Added too was the fact that the wilderness offered such a field for the flourishing of dissenters and minorities as had never been before. Someone once asked Hugh Peters what they did with such people in New England. He replied that they put them over the river. The ungodly, that is, had always the frontier, whither they might, to be sure, be pursued by the wrath of the godly or where they might be killed by the Indians, but where too they might set up new communities, prosper, perhaps trouble those they left behind and certainly engender fresh dissent among themselves and new exoduses to new lands of promise. Thus each new Jerusalem was always apt to be beset by a Jerusalem still newer. Like Massachusetts, every American community tended to raise up a Rhode Island, a Utah, on its borders, until the saints of the latter days spread to every corner of the continent.

The result of all this has been that American society from its inception was one in which there were churches, in a few instances for a short time churches established by local law, but never at any time in the historic sense the church. Every American religious communion has always had to maintain itself in the midst of competition, hostility, suspicion and indifference. Some when able to do so have resorted to persecution, some from conviction or weakness have not, but it must have been obvious early in our history that the forcible or legal imposition of any one church throughout the country could be accomplished, if at all, only at the expense of the others. What each had most to hope for, therefore, when it came time to form a political union, was the perpetuation of the anarchy to which each owed its present existence. Thanks to the disruption of the English church, thanks to the spacious hospitality of the unpeopled wilderness, religious freedom prevailed even before toleration was acknowledged as a sacred principle to be written into positive law. That it was written into the Bill of Rights gave evidence how completely the authors of that document were aware of the conditions and forces of American life.

But, though the people who settled this country did not bring the historic church with them, they did bring religion, and religion was to play a rôle of peculiar and great importance in the development of American civilization. What the founders of the national union did or did not do about religion was of utmost significance for the success of their enterprise. The assumptions concerning truth and human nature underlying the doctrine of religious liberty —namely that truth is most surely discovered when everybody is free to take part in the search for truth, and that it is at least equally as important for every man to think and speak as for some to think correctly and speak wisely—these notions now seem to most Americans axiomatic. Needless to say they have not been and are not now universally so regarded. They came to be so regarded in this country, where religion was of intimate and intense concern to so many, because of something most vital in the religion of the people itself, something which prevailed over all the divisions into which American religious life fell. Obviously, of course, religious toleration was not the result of reaction against religion as such, because the believers in some sort of religion have always been in the majority, and it was precisely they who had most to fear from any sort or degree of intolerance.

Now there can be no question that the type of religious feeling and behavior associated with Puritanism, regardless of denominational divisions, permeated the religious life of the American people. The specifically Puritan tradition of the age before the Puritan Revolution had its powerful seat in New England. The sects were Puritan in their provenience. Anglicanism in the colonies was not the high-flying Anglicanism of the Restoration, but the Calvinistic Low Church Anglicanism of the period before Laud. The libraries of Virginia, as has recently been shown, contained the same books of religious edification, and the pulpits undoubtedly often resounded with the same doctrines, as did those of New England.[2] All religious denominations, not excepting the Catholic, were deeply colored by American life, and American life was colored by Puritanism, as indeed the critics of Puritanism bitterly complain to this day.

If, then, we are to understand what it was in American religion as a whole which led directly to toleration, we must look to Puritanism itself. In making this statement, I am, of course, referring to Puritanism in its historic context, not to those aspects of Puritanism which, abstracted from their context, have been distorted into a convenient myth by critics of our contemporary society. Indeed, the attacks upon Puritanism of some present-day reformers have in them the same sort of emotionalized half-truth which characterized the attacks of Puritans against Anglicans in the seventeenth century. Historic Puritanism was a spiritual attitude, moral temper, and way of life preached in England after the accession of Elizabeth by men who, seeking to reform the church, were largely instrumental in revolutionizing English society and in founding a new society in America. They rationalized their zeal for reform in terms of theological doctrine, but they were reformers and preachers using the intellectual methods of their time rather than theologians and philosophers. Their enormous spiritual energy expressed itself best not in clear and consistent general ideas but in a prodigious quantity of popular discourse in the pulpit and the press, imaginative, emotive, provocative.[3] Logically absurd though the thinking in much of this literature may seem to the modern reader, psychologically, morally, it was supremely apposite to its own time. One has but to read that literature with some imagination in order to understand at least in part the reason why it appealed with such force to

[2] L. B. Wright, "The Purposeful Reading of Our Colonial Ancestors," *E.L.H., a Journal of Literary History*, IV (1937), 85–111, and "The 'Gentleman's Library' in Early Virginia," *Huntington Library Quarterly*, I, i (October, 1937), 3–61.

[3] For an account of Puritan literature in England with some reference to American beginnings, I would refer the reader to my forthcoming *Rise of Puritanism in Pulpit and Press, 1570–1643*, Columbia University Press.

the founders of our civilization, that is to say to people who were not very unlike ourselves. Reading thus, we can understand why toleration was the natural consequence of the prevalence of the Puritan spirit in American life.

The theory which supplied the formularies for Puritanism was the doctrine of predestination. Even though many, and in America probably most, Puritans deviated in some degree from orthodox Calvinism, their point of departure was still that doctrine of determinism, theologically conceived, which derives from St. Paul. The idea that man left to himself is utterly depraved and lost through primal sin and that God arbitrarily predetermines who shall be saved and who not is naturally abhorrent to minds colored by nineteenth-century humanitarianism. To common men in the seventeenth century it was not abhorrent but tremendously stimulating to morale, inspiring them, strange though this may seem, not to despair but to unbounded hope and self-confidence. If all men were equally deserving of damnation, then one man was as good as another and existing distinctions of rank, breeding, and wealth counted for nothing. If God alone knew who were the chosen and if he chose whom he would, again regardless of human distinctions, then one man had as good a chance as another. If the state of grace was evinced by faith in God, by emotional conviction that this was true, and if faith was evidenced not necessarily by righteousness but by struggle against unrighteousness and disbelief, by diligent pursuit of an honest calling and earnest effort to make the most of one's talents and opportunities, then any man could tell for himself whether he was likely to be saved or not. And if the triumphant outcome of his strivings was predetermined by divine will, then those who put themselves on the side of God need have no fear. Neither man nor devil could stop them from inheriting heaven, and if heaven, why not the earth? That is to say, if a man, moved by some preacher's eloquence, could identify himself emotionally with the elect, the doctrine of predestination opened for him a life of intense and strenuous activity and held forth the prospect of certain success. Now we must remember that the natural impulse of the preacher standing in the pulpit with the people before him, all the more when he preached hell-fire and damnation, was to make every one of his listeners desire to be not damned but saved, to make them identify themselves with the elect not the rejected. In the privacy of his study, he might be convinced that many, do what they would, were irrecoverably lost. In the pulpit, he must speak to the people as though every one of them had a chance to be saved if he would take it and make the most of it, as though it were a man's own fault if he were damned. And while the preacher stood speaking in the pulpit, he easily and they even more easily slipped into that heresy which everywhere beset Calvinistic dogma, namely that the grace of God sets not merely a few but all men free from the primal curse, equal in their opportunity to redeem themselves, in their title to all things in heaven and earth. The people were the saints. The damned were those who did not believe these things, those especially who denied the equality or repressed the freedom of the people. Among a people thus indoctrinated, blessed with such a theater for their activities as the American continent afforded, a policy of laissez faire in respect to religion was the only policy which government could safely pursue.

A factor, moreover, which made the preaching of such ideas particularly effective, a factor for which Puritanism was especially responsible, was the popularization of the Bible. The original Puritan reformers had not set out to disrupt the church, and it was long before they were anything but horrified at the thought that men should be left free to believe as they liked. Their wish was to revitalize the church, not to destroy it, and their dream was to erect through the church a theocratic Utopia. The argument for reform, however, the very plan and rule for the church and for the godly Utopia, was, they claimed, revealed to them in the sacred Scriptures. They turned for guidance away from tradition, established institutions, law, and custom, to a book. They did not, however, appreciate, what it is well for us to remember, the extraordinary character of that book. It is not a book of profound philosophical thought. It contains no body of political principles generally applicable to the erection and government of states. The penmen of the Holy Spirit were neither Platos nor Aristotles, but moralists and above everything else prophets and poets. They produced a literature second to none in imaginative richness and intensity, the unsurpassed expression of the spiritual life of a race of imaginative individualists, but a literature precisely lacking in the power of abstract thought or of lucid presentation of general ideas. If a law were to be found in pages so full of life, it had to be inferred from the metaphors and riddles in which—and not in syllogisms—the Holy Spirit generally preferred to speak. The original Puritan reformers, men learned in the traditional arts and sciences of their age, commanded a dialectic by which, it was thought, the general principles revealed in Scripture for man's guidance could certainly be understood and made plain. The Utopia they proposed to found on the word of God was to be a Utopia framed and guided by themselves as the experts and technicians of an infallible science. They reckoned, however, without understanding the nature of poetry, of the kind of poetry found in the Scriptures, or of the effect such poetry was likely to have on the popular mind. They failed, of course, to establish a new Jerusalem, even to maintain their monopoly as experts over the interpretation of the word of God. But the most important reason for their failure was that they succeeded so completely in making the people believe that in that poetic book was really to be found the answer to every mystery, the remedy for every iniquity, the surcease to every care, the substance of every hope in human life. The religious anarchy, which Elizabeth had found it expedient not to repress and which the American wilderness fostered, prevented the Puritan technicians from ever more than momentarily securing power to enforce theocracy by law, but it encouraged in every way their effort in pulpit and press to make everybody no matter how humble, ignorant, wrong-headed or dull read the Bible and try to understand it for himself as the very word of God. Thus the Scriptures, in the marvelous idiom devised by Tyndall and Coverdale and perfected by the makers of the Authorized Version of 1611, became the first universal classic printed in English in a form and at a price which put it within the reach of practically everybody, endorsed as no book has ever been before or since. People innocent of critical or historical perspective read it and saw in it not necessarily the particular doctrines or Utopian laws which this or that technician deduced from it. Without benefit of clergy, without the aid of scholastic logic, every man could find in the poetry of Scripture the mirror of his own thoughts and spiritual strivings, could talk, argue, preach and write about what he found there, could concoct his own Utopia by its aid.

No matter what dissension leaders make,
Where every private man may save a stake:

Rul'd by the Scripture and his own advice,
Each has a blind by-path to Paradise.

Thus the popularization of the sacred book enormously enhanced the forces of individualism in American life, and thereby
sealed the fate of the godly Utopia as well as of any other attempt
that might be made to interfere with the right of every man to read
and quote Scripture for his purpose. The theocrats of New England
continued for a time to check the individualism they had done so
much to provoke, but their fight was a rear-guard action of which
too much has been made. It is more important to bear in mind the
positive effect of Puritan spiritual energy on American culture than
to shudder over the dying extravagances of the short-lived and mori-
bund theocracy of Massachusetts. The preachers had to arouse
popular faith in Scriptures in order to prove their claims. The
popularization of reading in general, the stimulation of individual
spiritual and intellectual life, of self-help and the learning of things
useful here and now as well as hereafter, in a word popular education in the broadest sense, this became the prime objective even of
the preachers' efforts, and the godly Utopia retreated farther and
farther into the realm of things not realized. Puritanism was obviously not the sole cause for this development, but there can be no
doubt that it was a principal cause, or that in bringing it about so
swiftly and so generally Puritan New England took a leading part.
Massachusetts was founded under the personal leadership of Puritan intellectuals, preachers and men of learning, most of them educated at Cambridge and all of them fired with zeal for making the
word known to the people. By founding Harvard College immediately, and after Harvard other schools and colleges all over New
England, they and their successors initiated American education.
What the institutions they founded taught was not Calvinistic theology and theocratic politics, but the Bible and the classics, rhetoric,
oratory and forensic logic, mathematics, and moral and natural
philosophy.[4] From New England streamed preachers and school-
masters teaching men to believe they could be saved if they would
and bearing books, which they taught the people to read, to talk
and argue about, Bibles, spellers, dictionaries, readers, English

[4] For the importance of the Puritan intellectual caste in the founding of New
England, see S. E. Morison, *The Founding of Harvard College* (Cambridge, Mass.,
1935), and *The Puritan Pronaos* (New York, 1936).

literature. Regardless of religious divisions, this was what the people of all sections learned. Americans continued to go to different churches, but they all went to the same school, where they entered into the possession of a common language, a common literature, a common spiritual attitude. The most that a people thus divided and thus united could ask its new government to do in respect to religion was to let it alone, to make no law on the one hand establishing a religion, and on the other prohibiting the free exercise thereof. All they needed was to be allowed to get together and say what they would, even to complaining about their grievances, in other words, to continue as they had begun. That such freedom is likely ever to be justified by its results has never been better evidenced than by the work of the men who drafted the Constitution and the Bill of Rights.

James Madison in proposing the First Amendment might well have quoted the words in which the great Puritan poet had adjured parliament to set no check upon freedom of thought and discussion in England. "Consider," Milton had said, "what nation it is whereof ye are, and whereof ye are the governors: a nation not slow and dull, but of a quick, ingenious and piercing spirit; acute to invent, subtile and sinewy to discourse, not beneath the reach of any point the highest that human capacity can soar to." He might, if it had been necessary, have gone on quoting. "What should ye do then, should ye suppress all this flowery crop of knowledge and new light sprung up and yet springing daily?" The truth was that, except for the religious freedom which the new country made possible for those who fled to its shores, the occasion for forming a federal union affirming such liberty would never have come about. To have proposed any check to this liberty in 1789 would have been to render union impossible by denying the facts of American life. If Madison had quoted Milton again, he would have said, "Believe it . . . they who counsel ye to such a suppressing do as good as bid ye suppress yourselves." Madison did not need to quote Milton, but the words remain apt to this day.

Philosophical Differences between the Constitution and the Bill of Rights ⌁ HERBERT W. SCHNEIDER

I

TO ELIMINATE the arbitrary has always been a basic problem of moral and political philosophy. In our classical heritage two different types of solution to this problem have come down to us. The one, which in view of the present occasion I shall call the constitutional theory, comes to us from the Greek city-state. The Greeks called themselves freemen because they were members of free cities; and a free city was defined as one governed not by a person but by the laws or a constitution. Freedom was in this theory a collective quality; the state was free in so far as it was governed impersonally, by a universal structure of justice, not by particular acts of will. The arbitrary, the unjust, was ruled out by the very structure of the state. The culmination of this type of thought is Plato's *Republic* and the *Laws,* where the basic idea is that justice must be sought in the structure of the city (or the soul, for that matter), all rule being exercised by the philosopher and the philosopher being the least personal person possible, since his knowledge is a unified, mathematical system of pure form to the exclusion of the arbitrary and contingent aspects of experience.

Another type of theory arose apparently among those wandering teachers of virtue, or Sophists, who had no civic home and who looked upon the laws of states as mere conventions and as such arbitrary in the eyes of travelers who knew various polities. They as detached observers aimed to discover the universal principles of virtue, principles which even by these early Sophists were sometimes called *natural* laws, laws which reign not in man-made constitutions but in every man who can reason. As the city-states declined it became increasingly difficult to regard them as embodiments of reason, and philosophers, more foot-loose than ever, turned increasingly to nature as a pattern of government.

The Stoics fused (or confused) the two theories by teaching that nature is itself a city, a cosmopolis, and that all men are by nature citizens of a universal, impersonal order. In this order the exercise of self-government, that is, reliance on the integrity and independence of one's own will, became identified with living according to reason and nature.

This Stoic conception of individual self-government became embedded in Roman law. A man, simply by virtue of being a man, could make claims based on his *facultas,* his inherent power or personal dignity. Thus each man has a natural sphere of influence, so to speak, and can justly claim his "own." For the Roman the conception of justice as rendering to each his own did not beg the question, as it did for the Greek philosopher, since one's "own" in Roman law could be defined independently of any theory of distributive justice.

Among the Aristotelian scholastics, notably in St. Thomas Aquinas, a mixture of Platonic and Stoic doctrine was expressed in the doctrine that every rational animal as soon as he recognizes the "dictate of right reason" is *ipso facto* obliged to obey the dictate. In other words, according to this so-called intellectualist doctrine, moral obligation derives immediately from the knowledge of the rational good. Thus the medieval Aristotelians shifted the doctrine of individual moral responsibility from its Stoic basis of free will to its intellectual basis of the capacity of any rational animal to know the good.

Meanwhile, under Platonic inspiration, the Augustinians had revived the social or constitutional view of moral obligation. By Romanizing the Jewish and Christian tradition of the covenant relation Augustine arrived at his famous conception of the City of God, which like the Greek city-state was an exclusive community. Unified by the covenant of grace, the saints or elect form a mystic body, a society united by a contractual bond with one another and with God. For the Augustinians moral obligation was, therefore, defined in terms of voluntary and unconditional submission to the will of God. This will, which is the law of the City of God,[1] may

---

[1] Though the church is the best state, since its common good is God, the *civitas terrena,* whose common object of love is earthly power, is also a true community. Political states are to be identified with neither; they are defined by Augustine as peoples living in unity (*concordia*) under law and with a common interest. His conception of the *pactum societatis* is not that of a legal contract but of a natural bond.

be arbitrary from the point of view of human reason but obliges man none the less, since it is based on a voluntary covenant. Thus it is the command, not the reason, of God that obliges the human subject.

The conflict between these two theories of obligation became explicit when the Scotists, Ockhamites, and Calvinists pushed voluntarism to its logical extremes. This was the general situation when Grotius appeared upon the scene with his attempt to formulate a new jurisprudence. The confusion reigning in both law and theology is evident in his writings.

Grotius begins his *Prolegomena to the Right of War and Peace* by asserting that he intends to codify international law regardless of the theories of its origin, that is, "whether it proceed from nature or be instituted by divine commands or introduced by custom and tacit consent." [2] Then he defines natural law or right not in terms of its origin but of its purpose or utility, namely, the preservation of society,[3] but at the same time maintains that "utility is not the mother of right." [4] Then he remarks parenthetically that no other natural mode of men's obligating themselves can be imagined except contract, and that hence civil rights are derived from express or tacit promise. He appears to reconcile these various statements by the following amusing bit: "The mother of natural right is [not utility but] human nature [the desire for mutual society], and the mother of civil right is obligation by mutual consent, and since mutual consent derives its force from natural right, nature may be said to be the grandmother of civil right." [5] Then, apparently realizing that his metaphor is not an adequate argument, he adds immediately: "but natural law is reinforced by utility" and utility is the *occasion,* though not the ground, of civil law. Similarly God *adds* his commands to the dictates of natural law for the benefit of "weaker minds." [6] Then he departs still further from the intellectualist theory and maintains that right does not oblige *externally* unless it can use force. Hence, "many, individually weak, fearing oppression by those who were stronger, combined to establish ju-

---

See F. W. Loetscher, "St. Augustine's Conception of the State," *Church History,* IV (1935), 16–42.

[2] Section 1.
[3] Section 4.
[4] Section 16.
[5] *Ibid.*
[6] Section 13.

dicial authorities and to protect them by their common strength, so that those whom they could not resist singly, they might, united, control." [7] Having given this succinct statement of the social contract theory of obligation, he again retracts and says that law even without force is binding internally, "for justice brings serenity to the conscience." [8] And "though there were no utility to be expected from the observation of right, yet it would be wisdom and not folly, to obey the impulse of our nature." [9] Having thus appealed to the natural will to justice, he once more reverts to the intellectualist theory and asserts his intention to demonstrate a jurisprudence more permanent than that derived from will alone.[10] Thus throughout the *Prolegomena* Grotius oscillates between rival theories of right in his eagerness to bring to his support all the classic arguments for justice, whether they are mutually consistent or not. The same confusion reappears in the next chapter, but here it takes the form of distinguishing various kinds of law as though they had distinct functions and fields.[11]

These references to Grotius are sufficient evidence of the fact that by the seventeenth century the theories of right and obligation had become so complicated and confused that there was an obvious need for some new approach that would wipe the slate clean of all the classical polemics and give to jurisprudence a consistent, clear demonstration. Before I call attention to the great systems of the seventeenth and eighteenth centuries that made this attempt and

[7] Section 19.
[8] Section 20.
[9] Section 18.
[10] Section 31.

[11] In the most general sense, he begins, right is whatever is not injurious as a general practice to the society of rational creatures, or, which amounts to the same thing, whatever is not repugnant to the law of nature. In a second sense, right is a moral quality or faculty immediately attached to a person. This personal right comprehends the power we have over ourselves, which is called liberty, the power we have over children or slaves, the possession of property, and the power to demand payment of a debt (§5). In a third sense, and this Grotius derives from Aristotle, right is "lawful right," or the obligation to obey a precept not merely because it is just but because it is proper (§9). In contrast to this legal sense of right, Grotius then defines natural right in terms of "moral necessity," that is, a dictate of right reason which necessarily and of itself obliges rational nature and "therefore must be understood to be commanded by God" (§10). Hardly, however, has he given this orthodox Thomistic definition of the law of nature and God than he adds that this law is supplemented by *voluntary* law, both human and divine. The law of nature cannot be changed even by God himself, but voluntary laws, both divine revelation and human statutes, are subject to change. Lastly, he adds to his classification the laws of the divine covenants: the Mosaic law and the law of Christ.

failed, I must turn for a moment from the realm of philosophical speculation and recall the conflict and confusion which prevailed in the practical politics of the seventeenth century. I confine my remarks to England, because the Puritan Revolution constitutes the immediate background of our Bill of Rights.

II

The period of the Commonwealth and Cromwell brought into open conflict the various political theories that had found their way into Calvinism; particularly it revived in practical form the basic contrast between Greek republicanism and Roman Stoicism.[12] In general the English Presbyterians and the more conservative Puritans regarded the commonwealth as a contractual community governed impersonally by law. Their theocratic version of Platonism, in which the will of God is sovereign, turned out in practice to be nevertheless impersonal and legalistic, for the will of God was revealed in the word or law of God, and governments or magistrates were divine agents responsible to God and the people, under the terms of the covenant, for the administration of His law. It was therefore customary to regard the magistrate as in effect a party to the contract. The most conservative interpreted this to be merely a new name for the *feudus,* the feudal contract of personal subjection and protection. Cromwell was significantly Lord Protector. The more radically republican Puritans, on the other hand, looked upon the magistrate as little more than an agent of God's law, whose office is essentially an office of trust based on the covenant and revocable when the law is violated.[13] Even the subjects of law were

12 The foundations of constitutional philosophy in England were, of course, not wholly Puritan. They go back at least to the humanism of Sir Thomas Smith's *De Republica Anglorum,* written in 1565 and defending the courts of law (including parliament) as the essential structure of the constitution, and to Sir Edward Coke's defense of the common law against the prerogatives of James I. On the side of the assertion of individual rights English tradition goes back at least as far as Wycliff and the Lollards.

13 See J. W. Gough's discussion of Milton in his *The Social Contract, a Critical Study of Its Development* (Oxford, 1936), p. 95. Milton's Platonism led him at times to emphasize the authority of "wise men" rather than the structural principle of impartial law. Though he had a greater concern for liberty than the other Puritan leaders had, he shared their view of human corruption and their consequent repudiation of democratic principles. See especially his *The Ready and Easy Way to Establish a Free Commonwealth* (1660).

In general the reader is cautioned to distinguish sharply here between republicanism and democracy.

conceived impersonally as "interests" or "permanent fixed interests" rather than as individual citizens. And the ends of law were certainly conceived as the common good and the commonwealth, rather than as the protection of individual rights or liberties.[14]

The Presbyterian theory found its best expressions in Samuel Rutherford's *Lex Rex* (1644) and in Richard Baxter's *A Holy Commonwealth* (1659). The king is here conceived as a magistrate elected by the people to enforce the law, and parliament is regarded as essentially "the high court" of law. Neither the will of the people nor the power of the prince is sovereign, for both are subject to the word of God or law of nature, which has an objective existence and is the very constitution of the state. Breaches of this law or constitution on the part of either subjects or rulers must be punished, and parliament, as a court of law, has a moral duty to rebel against arbitrary rulers. The reign of impartial justice is the basic idea. Henry Parker, a lawyer, wrote in 1642,

> We had a maxime, and it was grounded upon Nature, and never till this Parliament withstood, that a community can have no private ends to mislead it, and make it injurious to it selfe, and no age will furnish us with one story of any Parliament freely elected, and held, that ever did injure a whole Kingdome, or exercise any tyranny, nor is there any possibility how it should. . . .
>
> Where the King and Parliament disagree . . . we must retire to ordinary justice. . . . The Law thinks it fit, that the King subscribe, rather than the Judge.[15]

And in the same tract he expresses his constitutionalist faith as follows:

> 'Twas spoken in honour of *Hen.* 7 That he governed his subjects by his Laws, his Laws, by his Lawyers, and (it might have been added) his subjects, Laws and Lawyers by advice of Parliament, by the regulation of that Court which gave life and birth to all Laws . . . for where . . . the Law is left to the interpretation of sworn upright Judges, and not violated by power; and where Parliaments superintend all . . . and . . . do the faithfull Offices of Umpirage, all things remain in such a harmony, as I shall recommend to all good Princes.[16]

[14] General Ireton in England, like John Winthrop in New England, explicitly asserted that right is civil right, not natural liberty. See Gough, pp. 86–90.

[15] Henry Parker, "Observations upon Some of His Majesties Late Answers and Expresses" (1642) in *Tracts on Liberty in the Puritan Revolution,* William Haller, ed. (New York, 1934), II, 188, 210.

[16] *Ibid.,* p. 208.

But hardly had this supposed reign of law been established than voices of protest were heard. The laws themselves were tyrannous, the lawyers corrupt, and the house of commons faithless to its trust. It was time to think of what parliament might and might not do.[17]

> Truly it is a sad thing, but too true, a plaine quiet-minded man in any place in England is just like a harmless sheep in a Thicket, can hardly move or stirre, but hee shall be strech'd, and loose his wooll.[18]

> Oh Englishmen! Where is your freedome? and what is become of your Liberties and Priviledges that you have been fighting for all this while . . . ?[19]

The pathetic nature of these cries by the Independents and the irony of the situation are revealed in Overton's "Remonstrance to Parliament," when he writes: "Wee must therefore pray you to make a Law against all kinds of Arbitrary Government."[20] Let parliament make a law against parliament! This is the basic paradox underlying all bills of rights.

Cromwell faced this issue in the course of a dramatic discussion in the army of the proposed new constitution and of the Levellers' *Agreement of the People,* wherein the popular grievances were summarized and remedies suggested. This discussion (preserved for us in *The Clarke Papers*) is truly a classic among political debates. Cromwell and Ireton defend themselves and parliament on the grounds of their contractual "engagements" or obligations.[21]

[17] See William Walwyn, "Englands Lamentable Slavery" (1645), in Haller, *op. cit.,* III, 313. Walwyn continues: "Shall not the Supreame Judicatory of the Common Wealth doe right? God forbid." (*Ibid.,* p. 315.) Similarly Richard Overton: "Yee were chosen to worke our deliverance, and to Estate us in naturall and just libertie agreeable to Reason and common equitie . . . we are the men of the present age, and ought to be absolutely free from all kindes of exorbitancies, molestations or Arbitrary Power, and you wee choose to free us from all without exception . . . we were full of confidence, that ye also would have dealt impartially on our behalf, and made us the most absolute free People in the world." ("A Remonstrance of Many Thousand Citizens" [1646], in Haller, *op. cit.,* III, 354–55.)

[18] Overton, "Remonstrance to Parliament," in Haller, *op. cit.,* III, 367.

[19] John Lilburne, "Englands Birth-right Justified" (1645), in Haller, *op. cit.,* III, 269.

[20] *Op. cit.* n. 18 *supra,* p. 358.

[21] They emphasize the dangers of proceeding by force instead of by justice and "treaty"; admitting that the security of the people is the supreme law, the army is bound in conscience by its agreements to serve parliament and even by its duties to the conquered king, for even "the Kinge is Kinge by contract," as Cromwell asserted, "and I shall say, as Christ said, 'Lett him that is without sin cast the first stone.'" (*The Clarke Papers, Selections from the Papers of William Clarke,* C. H. Firth, ed. [London, 1891], I, 368–69). And Ireton, a more legal mind, insisted that

The Levellers and Independents, on their side, unable to appeal to law or right in this contractual sense, talked vaguely of their "birth-right" either as Englishmen or as children of Adam; they appealed to their ancient liberties, their personal estates and property rights, to Magna Carta (the "charter of liberties"), and in general to the "grounds of common right, freedom, and safety." They were unable to account for the origin or nature of these rights, but they insisted: "These are our rights, and if wee have them nott, wee must get them the best way wee can." [22] Some thought parliament would be less arbitrary if all men regardless of property could elect its members; others thought that the root of the tyranny lay in the fact that the making and the execution of law were in the same hands, and they urged a separation of powers; [23] still others thought it useless to make parliament permanently just and trusted rather in formulating specific demands or "rights reserved to the people" and binding parliament by specific obligations or bills of "particular" rights.

It is often stated that the Levellers relied on the doctrine of natural rights, but the evidence is taken chiefly from the mouths of their enemies.[24] It is true that they were forced gradually to give up their vague appeal to constitutional and historical rights, since their opponents were on stronger ground constitutionally, but they seldom used the term "natural rights." Both sides, of course, appealed to the law of nature or natural right (in the singular), which was identical with an appeal to divine law or reason. Usually the Levellers seemed aware that they were arguing for civil liberties, not for natural rights. On the whole they appealed to the common law. "Common freedome," wrote Walwyn, "is every mans peculiar

"any man that makes a bargaine, and does finde afterwards 'tis for the worse, yett is bound to stand to itt." (*Ibid.*, p. 404.) The constitution must not be destroyed, and the authority of parliament must be respected. Parliament is rightly the representative only of those who have a "steady interest" in respecting law and property. Cromwell summed up the army's predicament: "Either they are a Parliament or noe Parliament. If they bee noe Parliament they are nothing, and wee are nothing likewise." (*Ibid.*, p. 369.)

22 *Ibid.*, p. 344.

23 John Lilburne, for example, in arguing for the separation of powers, wrote: "To me it is one of the most unjust things in the world, that the Law-makers should be the Law executors. . . . And therefore it were a great deal better for the Common-wealth, that all the executors of the Law should be such persons as doe not in the least belong to the Parliament." (*Op. cit.*, in Haller, III, 289.)

24 For example, Thomas Edwards's *Gangræna* (1646).

right so far as 'tis not prejudiciall to the Common." [25] And a "peculiar" right meant a personal privilege or "just liberty" and had
nothing to do with the "state of nature." [26] References to natural
rights are exceptional, and the accusations of their opponents, who
tried to convict the Levellers of antinomianism [27] and a belief in
preserving natural liberty and equality even in the civil state, are
scarcely justified.

Be this as it may, the debate made little progress. Both sides were
confused, and their premises were different. The arguments becoming abusive, Cromwell suggested a session of prayer and a waiting
upon God to speak to each. Thereupon both began quoting Scripture and speaking in the name of the Lord until the appeal to
revelation had to be given up in turn. After several days of fruitless
debate the council broke up, and after several years more of armed
conflict a military dictatorship put an end to an insoluble problem.

The Restoration put an end to the dictatorship, and the Glorious
Revolution of 1688 put an end to the Restoration. The Bill of
Rights of 1689 was the culmination of all this "agitation," and
though it was a solution in practice, it was intellectually a compromise. The Whigs took over the defense of the British constitution and secured the allegiance of the king to it on the basis of the
"original contract"; the Bill of Rights embodied some of the aims
of the Levellers. But the theoretical problem of the relation between
constitutional right and particular rights was as dark as ever.

III

The basic philosophical issue that emerged out of this conflict
may be stated as follows: Can right or law be defined as an institutional moral structure so that the general and permanent framework
or constitution of a state may be said to be either just or unjust,
rational or arbitrary? Or must the right be defined in terms of

[25] William Walwyn, "The Compassionate Samaritane" (1644), in Haller, *op. cit.*,
III, 67.

[26] Overton, to be sure, in a fit of rage spoke of "natural and legal freedoms and
rights," but that he was using this phrase rhetorically, not technically, is shown by
the fact that he speaks almost in the same breath of "natural, free commoners of
England." (See Haller, III, 377–78.)

[27] William Walwyn was probably an exception, for he seems to have been an
Antinomian, possibly even a Familist. See his tract, "The Power of Love," and others,
in Haller, *op. cit.*, Vol. III.

particular acts, which by their individual nature are just or arbitrary? In the case of England, this issue amounted in practice to the question of whether the sovereignty of parliament, that is, of the people's legislators, is *ipso facto* right, or whether even the law of the land may be arbitrary and hence require the people to "reserve" particular rights or liberties against its own representatives and laws. I have tried to show that the solution of this problem was difficult on the face of it because the two positions rested on two traditionally opposed theories of right and freedom, one based on impersonal reason, the other on personal will. It remains to point out how a few of the greatest philosophers of the seventeenth and eighteenth centuries tried to solve this basic problem.

Hobbes's solution is suggested in the very first sentence of his *Leviathan:* "Nature, the art whereby God hath made and governs the world, is by the *art* of man, as in many other things, so in this also imitated, that it can make an artificial animal." This artificial person or commonwealth is literally a public individual, formed by appointing a single person (or council) the authorized agent of all the actions of each member for the common security. Thus impartiality is given a personal embodiment in the sovereign. By definition, he can have no private interest, for he acts wholly in behalf of the commonwealth. It is also his interest to promote the public interest since his own power and security rest wholly on the collective power and security. For his subjects, or better, his "authors," have the natural liberty (though not the right) to destroy him when he threatens to destroy them. It follows that the only inalienable right of the citizen is the right not to harm or accuse himself. For, according to Hobbes, no man can be supposed to have contracted voluntarily to injure himself. All other liberty must be forfeited to the common agent or sovereign, since he must judge what may be necessary for the common security. This conception of the purely public person, without a private interest, is a clever theoretical solution of our problem, but obviously of little practical value, since Hobbes himself was unable to locate such a "mortal God." His theory is a secular mythology, designed to serve as a substitute for the theocracy of the Puritans.

James Harrington, like Hobbes a product of the Civil War, conceived a less contractual and mythical theory of commonwealth. His idea was so to construct the constitution that private interest and public interest would be identical, an idea that hypnotized social philosophy for more than a century. He would depersonalize law by distributing property or power in such a way that no particular interest could dominate. In other words, in a perfect republic the various classes and interests check and balance each other and thereby create a natural equilibrium that automatically does justice to each. By increasing the number of proprietors, by rotation of office and secret ballot, by separation of the deliberative and "prerogative" bodies, and other such constitutional devices, his "equal" or equilibrating commonwealth would enable each citizen in seeking his own interest to promote that of the whole. Harrington, like the other English republicans, was saturated with the ideas of Platonic republicanism, and he thought he had improved on the ancients chiefly in making his commonwealth immune from forces of corruption. In his republic might actually makes right, and hence there is no need for a bill of rights.

In many ways Spinoza's political ideas are closer to Harrington's than to Hobbes's. He, too, conceives political power as in last analysis a form of natural power, rather than like Hobbes of contractual obligation,[28] and rests his theory of political power on the observation that the government has as much power as it can command in fact, and that hence a democracy is "perfectly absolute dominion." [29] On the general assumption that the larger the number who enjoy political power the less the danger of arbitrary judgment, he argues that a democracy is most subject to reason and hence most free. There are two things, however, which by their nature are beyond the reach of even the most absolute political power, namely, piety and thought. Not being external acts they cannot be controlled externally. On this ground he regards personal religion, pure science, and private speech as free and inalienable natural rights (or powers).

---

[28] In his *The Social Contract* J. W. Gough makes the common mistake of attributing Spinoza's identification of natural law and natural power to Hobbes. Hobbes identified natural liberty and natural power and argued that man can have either liberty or peace, but not both. Natural right he defined as the claim of each to everything and hence the source of conflict; it is not limited to actual (natural) power. He used the term natural law, however, in the conventional moral sense, as the rule of equity and right reason, or, in his terms, the general theorems of utility. Spinoza, on the contrary, defined freedom as living according to reason either in the state of nature or the civil state, and regarded the state as a product of coöperation, rather than of contract, and hence completely subject to the reign of natural law.

[29] *Tractatus Politicus,* Ch. XI.

Samuel Pufendorf,[30] professor that he was, treats the problem in a pedantic manner. He suffers under many of the confusions that we have found in Grotius. On the whole he is inclined to agree with the voluntarists that natural law does not oblige of itself but needs behind it a "power of obligation." Hence we must either believe in God as the universal moral governor or agree with Hobbes and Spinoza that there are no obligations outside the commands of human government. But God's command must be executed either by physical necessity (as Hobbes and Spinoza maintained), in which case it is not voluntary obligation, or by persuasion based on prudence, which is also not obligation. God's supposed "power of obligation," therefore, remains a mystery in Pufendorf. Taking up Hobbes's concept of an artificial person and applying it to various corporate bodies, he distinguished between simple and compound persons, and the latter he divided into public and private. Any person, either simple or corporate, he called a "moral being" or bearer of right. These "moral beings" are "imposed" on the "supposed" state of nature. Thus he arrived at a pluralistic conception of corporate persons, in place of Hobbes's single Leviathan state, which opened the way for the doctrine of the real personality of corporations, both private and public. On the subject of property rights he agreed with Locke, to whom I now turn.

John Locke made a powerful hash of these seventeenth-century systems, on which political theory has fed ever since. I shall point out only two of his important innovations, since these two bear most directly on our problem. (1) He argued that subjection to another person does not constitute a true political obligation because disputes are certain to arise between the ruler and the subject and then there is no third party to serve as impartial judge. Hence men are still in the state of nature (that is, each man his own judge) until there is in addition to the sovereign power a "standing rule and common judge," [31] in other words, an impersonal legal order. This is his justification of Whig constitutionalism. (2) Men are inclined by nature to respect one another's persons and property. For property, provided it is "mixed" with one's *own* labor and personally used, is really an extension of one's person. Hence he

---

[30] His *De officio hominis et civis* was translated by Barbeyrac under the title, *Les Devoirs de l'homme et du citoyen*, which makes an interesting parallel to the French Declaration of 1789 entitled, *Les Droits de l'homme et du citoyen*.

[31] Two Treatises of Government, Bk. II, §91.

argued that personal rights exist antecedent to contract and may therefore be called natural rights, and that the political state is instituted to give security to property as well as to person, both of which are inalienable rights. After Locke it became a commonplace to regard the "reserved" rights of the people as natural and inalienable. Their preservation is the very end and function of government. Thus the social contract theory assumed its individualistic form and at the same time became hopelessly confused.

I need not elaborate the subsequent attempts to reconcile right and rights. During the eighteenth century these attempts became increasingly psychological mythologies. Montesquieu revived the classic doctrine of civic virtue or disinterestedness as the necessary moral basis of a republican constitution. This virtue, added to the separation of powers, was supposed to guarantee justice. Adam Smith and the Scottish Platonists appealed to the "disinterested spectator in the human breast." In general a moral sense or sentiment of sympathy was preached as a reconciliation of impersonal reason and unsocial passion. The culmination of this increasing psychological romanticism came with Rousseau and his doctrine of the General Will, which made it possible to "force men to be free." From Rousseau it is a short step to those idealists who, like T. H. Green, argued that the criminal has a "natural" and inalienable right to punishment. Fortunately for us our Constitution was framed before these enthusiasms of romanticism had secured a foothold here. The intellectual background of our Constitution and Bill of Rights [32] is essentially that of seventeenth-century England. John Adams was practically a reincarnation of Harrington and represents the one extreme of constitutionalism. Had we adopted his "scientific" frame of government, the depravity of human nature would have been so nicely checked and balanced by the institutions of government that we would have nothing to fear from the "insatiable and unlimited" "passions and desires of the majority of the representatives." Could he be here now he might be much gratified by the magnificent spectacle of checking and balancing which even our imperfect Constitution affords.

[32] The Virginia Declaration of Rights of 1776 and the state constitution are, of course, saturated with eighteenth-century ideas and resemble the French Declaration, which was directly influenced by them. But there are few traces of these distinctive traits in our federal Constitution and its amendments, which in contents and theory are nearer to 1689 than to 1776.

At the other extreme was Thomas Jefferson, who in his fear of the "tyranny of the legislatures" fought for the Bill of Rights as a "legal check" in the hands of the judiciary, which body, "if rendered independent and kept strictly to their own department merits great confidence for their learning and integrity." [33]

That these extremes were juxtaposed without being reconciled is evident from the argument of Alexander Hamilton, who in his eagerness to defend the Constitution appealed to both philosophies. He argued that bills of rights "have no application to constitutions professedly founded upon the power of the people, and executed by their immediate representatives and servants. Here, in strictness, the people surrender nothing." [34] But on the next page he writes: "The Constitution is itself, in every rational sense, and to every useful purpose, a bill of rights."

Possibly at some future celebration of the Constitution the truth may come out, but today, as one hundred and fifty years ago, the theory of duty and the doctrine of rights are still unreconciled.[35]

[33] Letter to James Madison, March 15, 1789.

[34] *The Federalist*, No. LXXXIV.

[35] See the article by James Truslow Adams, "Rights without Duties," in *The Yale Review*, XXIV, 237–50; also Charles W. Hendel, Jr., "The Meaning of Obligation," in *Contemporary Idealism in America*, Clifford Barrett, ed. (New York, 1932), pp. 237–95.

The Constitution and Its Influence upon American Thought

PART TWO

The Constitution and
Its Influence upon
American Thought

Historiography and the Constitution ⚬

CHARLES A. BEARD

EVERY discussion of the Constitution of the United States proceeds on some level of knowledge, thought, abstractness, and concreteness and it proceeds with reference to some conception or conceptions already in the minds of those who participate in it. Every discussion occurs at some time and in some place. Of necessity it is carried on by human beings, possessing and possessed by the characteristics of such creatures.

It is true that some historians once had the idea that they could emancipate themselves from these mundane considerations. They could, they seemed to think, discuss the Constitution on the one correct and indubitable level. They could, they seemed to imagine, emancipate themselves from the bonds of time and place. They could, they appeared to believe, free themselves from the parts, passions, and fallibilities of man. They could, they declared, write the history of the Constitution exactly as it had been (*wie es eigentlich gewesen ist*). In short, they could know the truth of the matter, secure the agreement of competence, and hence place their conclusions beyond debate, at least for adepts.

This thesis represents a consummation devotedly to be desired. But, to my mind, it is crypto-metaphysics. It does not correspond to any known experience in actual historiography. The sources available do not permit the achievement. Psychologically it is beyond our powers.

For saying this in other places, I have been called by a distinguished historian a sophist and defeatist, and by an eminent editor "a village atheist." But here I stand in this presence and declare that, with the best of will, I am unable to believe otherwise. I repeat, every discussion of the Constitution proceeds on some level of competence, with reference to some conception or conceptions; it is carried on by particular persons at a given moment and in a given place. It is not timeless, placeless, unearthly, omniscient.

It does not follow, however, as some would have it, that in surrendering the hope of bringing knowledge of the Constitution to the exactness of celestial mechanics, we can know nothing about it and attain no truth about it—no truth irrefragable in itself and important for life and practice. On the contrary, I maintain that only by surrendering pretensions to omniscience can we approach the borders of science itself. By cutting loose from crypto-metaphysics, we may acquire substantial knowledge, emancipate ourselves a little from bondage to time, place, personalities, and circumstances, and perhaps help to elevate the debates of practice above the passions of the party forum.

Although we cannot describe the making, development, or interpretation of the Constitution exactly as it has been, we can be reasonably sure of some things pertaining to this historical process. Certainly the formation, adoption, development, and interpretation of the Constitution must be considered as a phase of history. Any treatment of the constitutional process as separate from the conditioning and determining environment is arbitrary and does not correspond to the realities of the total situation. Any persistent quest for the utmost truth attainable about the Constitution leads us toward the very borders of history as actuality in its fullness. Any interpretation of the Constitution involves an interpretation of history in general, necessarily, in the nature of things.

What, then, is history as actuality, especially that political history in which the Constitution is immediately enmeshed? That is a fundamental question. The answer most satisfactory to me is the one formulated by Kurt Riezler: History is a manifestation of ideas and interests, evolving and involving in time. In political history, if not in all history, there are no ideas with which interests are not associated and there are no interests utterly devoid of ideas.

If this conception of history is true, and I believe it is, then it must control the treatment of any phase of political history, such as the formation, development, and interpretation of the Constitution, that is, any treatment which seeks the utmost truth available. Every treatment that deals with the Constitution or any aspect of it as mere idea or abstraction unrelated to associated interests is unreal, fails to correspond to history as actuality. Any work that deals with the Constitution as mere interests, and treats ideas as irrelevant, likewise fails in its conformity to history as actuality.

Yet, it is not given to historical scholarship to master the whole truth of the matter as it actually has been and is now. Every treatment of the subject, even in full consciousness of ideas and interests involved, is necessarily conditioned by personality, time, and circumstance. Are we not back then in that Serbonian bog of relativity and total impotence from which Riezler's conception of history promised to rescue us? Are we not mere victims of personal, temporal, and immediately surrounding pressures? I think not. If not permitted to climb Mount Olympus, we may perhaps stand a little bit outside ourselves and look at ourselves. That is one of the profound discoveries of modern psychology, especially social psychology.

When we look at ourselves with all the judicial calm we can command, we find that we fall into schools and groupings, despite the quirks and turns of personalities. We find also a certain correspondence between schools of thought and social groupings—a correspondence that is striking, if by no means exact. Although John Locke came close to this conception of our intellectual operations, not until our own time has it been set forth with great skill and detachment—in Karl Mannheim's *Ideology and Utopia*. In everyday language, it is by looking calmly at ourselves as well as others, by discovering the affiliation of personalities and ideas with interests, by recognizing frankly and with good humor that we stand somewhere—it is by doing this that we can approach, but never reach, that ideal of objectivity which the Ranke school claimed to have attained.

If this be true, and I believe that it is, the next task of scholarship in dealing with the Constitution is to discover how many and what schools of thought and groupings of interests have existed in the United States and now exist, and in what relation each historian stands to them. Pending a thorough inquiry into this subject, I venture to list two of them, subject to the correction and revision of fuller historical researches.

The first is what may be called for convenience the Federalist-Whig-Republican school. Its interests have been, in the main, commercial, industrial and financial, with an affiliation of the more prosperous farmers of the North. Its conception of the Constitution in respect of federal powers has been broad or narrow, according to its conception of interests temporarily affected, favorably or adversely.

The second school may be called for convenience Jeffersonian-Jacksonian-Democratic. Its interests were, originally, in the main agricultural, and to these were later added a large following of mechanics and industrial workers. Once committed to low tariffs permitting easy payment for farm produce in world exchange, it also won the allegiance of a large commercial wing engaged in importing and exporting goods and capital. In other words, it too has included a financial and commercial section and now draws upon industrialists largely dependent upon foreign business. This school took a narrow view of federal powers at the outset and has since taken the narrow or wide view with reference to pertinent interests.

If these conceptions of history and historiography are valid—that is, correspond to knowledge—then certain conclusions follow if we draw any conclusions at all.

If history as actuality is the evolution and involution of ideas and interests in time, then any history of the formation of the Constitution that pretends to represent actuality must show the configuration and tension of the economic interests prevailing in the period under consideration and present the relevant political ideas. A volume describing the economic interests is an economic interpretation, version, or exposition. A volume giving the political ideas is a political interpretation, version, or exposition. A general history of the formation of the Constitution which even approaches correspondence to actuality must combine both aspects with such fullness of treatment that their pertinence, their interrelated nature, and their deterministic aspects cannot be mistaken. Any other kind of written history pretending to cover the whole formation of the Constitution is false history, false in the sense that it is out of correspondence with the known actuality under review.

If history is an evolution and involution of ideas and interests in time, then any history of the development of the Constitution that corresponds to the known actuality of the development will repeat this process in dealing with the successive periods. It will, for example, associate statesmen with the economic interests with which they were associated in fact. Hamilton was a New York lawyer; Jefferson was a Virginia planter; Webster was affiliated with Northern merchants, industrialists, and financiers; Calhoun was affiliated with Southern planters; and so on through the entire list of events and personalities, down to the latest hour. Any realistic history of our constitutional development will constantly unite constitutional ideas with their relevant interests. Any history that does not fails to correspond to relevant actualities.

The same conceptions of history and historiography apply to the judicial, as well as to the political, branches of the federal government. Any realistic treatment of judicial interpretations of the Constitution will cover the ideas and interests of the judges who make the interpretations. For example, we read in the United States Reports that a justice rendered an opinion invalidating a minimum-wage law. We read in old court records that he was formerly of counsel for great corporations. We read in the reports of the American Bankers Association that, in addressing a branch of that society thirteen years before his opinion in the wage case, the learned justice said: "The business man in America today feels that he is doing business with a minion of government looking over his shoulder with an upraised arm and a threatening scowl. . . . Are we to go into a state of socialism, or are you men, and men like you, prepared to get out, take off your coats, and root for good old-fashioned Anglo-Saxon individualism?" We read in a dissenting opinion in the same wage case the words: "It is difficult to imagine any grounds other than our personal economic predilections for saying that the contract of employment is any the less an appropriate subject of legislation than are scores of others."

All such items of fact belong in any history of judicial interpretation that pretends to correspond to the known actualities of the judicial processes. Any other kind of history is unreal history, in the sense in which I have defined that kind of history. When a reference to such an affiliation of personalities, ideas, and interests is called indecent and is rejected, I can imagine no grounds other than personal economic predilections for performing that intellectual operation. Certainly the historian concerned with a search for the utmost truth in the premises and bound to cover all relevancies cannot approve that intellectual operation.

For the association of economic ideas with judicial interpretations of the Constitution we have authority higher than that of any remote historian. We have the authority of justices of the Supreme Court. Long ago, in the Lochner case, Justice Holmes said: "This case is decided upon an economic theory which a large part of the country does not entertain. . . . The Fourteenth

Amendment does not enact Mr. Herbert Spencer's *Social Statics.*"
In the Adkins case Chief Justice Taft intimated that the opinion of
the majority rested upon an economic theory and declared that it
was not the business of the Court to settle disputed problems in
political economy. Dissenting from the majority view in the New
York minimum-wage case, Justice Stone told his brethren that "The
Fourteenth Amendment has no more embedded in the Constitution our preference for some particular set of economic beliefs than
it has adopted, in the name of liberty, the system of theology which
we may happen to approve." Dissenting opinions are not law, to be
sure, but they are first-hand materials for the historian engaged in
tracing the affiliation of ideas and interests in constitutional development.

My conclusion is a kind of summation. Let me say again, as I
have said all along, economic interests are not the whole of history.
I have never said and do not now say that economic considerations
determine or explain all history. Let that be finally and clearly
understood and recognized. Yet it seems to me that there are elements of determinism in history. Otherwise the framers of the
Constitution could have set up a monarchy, founded a titled aristocracy, established a national church, abolished slavery, and voted
every adult citizen $250,000 in hard money with which to enjoy life.
The nature and degree of the determinism in history, it seems to me,
cannot be precisely disclosed and measured, but historians, if loyal
to truth, must recognize the reality of necessity in human affairs
(or, if you prefer, a high degree of probability). If this is not true,
then the historian must admit that anything can happen anywhere
on the earth for no reason whatever; for example, the American
republic can become a medieval monarchy over night.

If food, clothing, and shelter are necessities, if every human being
must live by his or her own labor or the labor of others, then it
follows that economic interests are among the deterministic features
of history. If the historian is true to the fullness of his own subject
matter and record, then, in my opinion, he must include economic
interests in any history of constitutional origins and development.
He must describe as fully and accurately as possible the economic
classes and interests of each period under review. He must state as
fully and accurately as possible the ideologies, economic theories,
and cultural values of the several classes and interests. In dealing

with individuals and groups, whether representatives, executives or judges, he must present their economic-group affiliations and the economic theories common to such affiliations. If the great object of government, as Madison said, is to protect the faculties for acquiring property and the principal task of legislation is that of regulating interfering economic interests, then the first and prime consideration of any realistic constitutional history is economic: whose property, what property, and what forms of regulation and protection? To repeat, this is not the whole of history, even constitutional history, but in my judgment to leave this out of written history, to make it a side issue instead of a central issue, is to write unreal and misleading history.

This conception, it seems to me, not only comports with the scientific spirit, but it has a profound meaning for the future of constitutional government as practice and for social living under the Constitution. It is, I venture to say, a method of approaching historical writing that leads to more generous judgments of humanity and promotes government by discussion as distinguished from government by force.

In the way of illustration let me ask two questions of those who represent here all sections of the country. When Frederick Jackson Turner and William E. Dodd discarded the idea that the struggle between the Union and the Confederacy was a conflict between persons possessing righteous ideas and others possessing unrighteous ideas, when they laid heavy emphasis on climate, soil, and economy as clues to differences of opinion and constitutional theory, were they not right as to historical facts? Did they not also tend to heal the breach between the two sections, contribute to a reunion of hearts and minds, and bring about a more rational discussion of old and new issues therewith connected? For me the answers are clear and final. They are in the affirmative.

Again, by the persistent association of ideas and interests in the historiography of the Constitution, do we not put men and women on guard against treating their own ideas as having the dogmatic force of divine revelation? Do we not aid mankind in emancipating itself from the idolatry of symbolism that is the essence of government by sheer force? By placing the ideas of schools and the structures of interests side by side and by refusing to recognize anyone as possessing a monopoly of divine revelation in matters constitutional, do we not soften the bitterness of conflict and open wider the door for understanding, mediation, and adjustment by the use of intelligence? For me the answers to these questions are also clear and final. They are in the affirmative.

The Path of Due Process of Law ⚚ WALTON H. HAMILTON

I

IN THE law the judgment of yesterday is the precedent of today. The words are set down in the reports and there they abide for all time, to be drawn upon now and then as "the opinion of the court" demands. The meaning is rooted in the case and the occasion—the exchange of views in executive session, the idiom of the day, the temper of the times, the preferences of the judges. Its specific reference and concrete meaning are inseparable from the record which called it into being; and, along with these, it gradually recedes into the mists of legal history. As in a continuous process judgment follows judgment into precedent, a doctrine is fashioned. Its raw material is a common sense which comes from without the law; its lines take on content from the prevailing opinion to which it is exposed; it is hammered into shape through a conflict of interests within a formidable procedure of litigation by unlike-minded jurists. As a product of a protracted intellectual process, it is a part of all that it has met. It is rare that a legal rule which rides high is the rule "originally laid down" in "the leading case"; and a doctrine on the make, like its human kin, usually exhibits scant respect for its humble beginnings.

In an era of constitutional law that flickers to a close, no doctrine has enjoyed greater prestige than "due process." It has come to be the symbol habitually invoked by private right, the barrier that guards the frontiers of business against the interference of the state, a sanction by which the judiciary reviews the work of the legislature. It has woven itself into the folkways of an industrial culture and called into being an august corpus of the law. Yet into an eminence that already shows signs of decay it has emerged out of an estate of little repute. The account of its coming up in the world is among the most dramatic of stories. It bristles with color and conflict, with surprise and paradox. A novelist who made ideas his characters would not—for fear of provoking disbelief—have dared to allow his imagination to contrive such a series of events.

Yet beneath the curious rhetoric of case and coincidence, of confused citation and vagrant judgment, the logic of events was always in command of a doctrine headed for parts unknown.

It all began quietly enough. The phrase "due process of law" is of ancient lineage. For a long time it had been an authoritative term for the established ways of justice. An injunction that "no person" shall "be deprived of life, liberty, or property without due process of law" had for decades reposed quietly within the Fifth Amendment. It served a necessary purpose in preventing arbitrary imprisonments, in forbidding seizures of possessions, in compelling resort to ordinary procedures, and in restraining public officials from acting without legal warrant. But in all the years that stretched away from the early days of the Constitution to the close of the Civil War, it was not an invitation to those who found Acts of Congress distasteful to appeal to the judiciary for relief. Save for an obiter dictum here and there—as by Mr. Chief Justice Taney in the Dred Scott Case [1]—the records of the United States Supreme Court are singularly unconcerned over what later became so mighty a matter. A like provision adorned with procedural concern the constitution of many a state. As the Civil War approached, a New York court declared that due process had to do with the substance of legislation; [2] and in litigious cause or congressional speech state acts which denied to freedmen of color the full privileges of citizenship were challenged as against due process of law. But such a demand for a substantive reading was casual and lacked authority. If there was a higher law in whose name legislation might be struck down by a court, it was elsewhere in the Constitution or in the great unchartered domain of natural rights. In reputable opinion due process of law was firmly fixed within the ancient domain of procedure.

It was the Civil War which disturbed the verbal calm. The course of events made the emancipation of the slaves a military and political necessity. The ways of thought again became receptive to the philosophy of Mr. Jefferson, and to the self-evident truths of the Declaration of Independence. The rights "to life, liberty, and the pursuit of happiness"—already inalienable within an order of nature—were written into the constitutions of several

---

[1] Dred Scott v. Sanford, 19 Howard 393 (1856).
[2] Wynehamer v. People, 13 N.Y. 378 (1856).

of the conquered Southern States. An injunction in perpetuity against slavery and involuntary servitude was made a part of the supreme law of the land, and a correlative amendment undertook to safeguard the rights of the newly enfranchised blacks. It began with the novel declaration that "all persons born or naturalized in the United States, and subject to the jurisdiction thereof, are citizens of the United States and of the state wherein they reside." Then, in words whose revolutionary character could be appreciated only by men of the age who had been steeped in an older political philosophy, it was provided that "no State shall make or enforce any law which shall abridge the privileges or immunities of citizens of the United States; nor shall any State deprive any person of life, liberty, or property without due process of law; nor deny to any person within its jurisdiction the equal protection of the laws." A number of other provisions, all relating to matters growing out of the late rebellion, were followed by a final section which granted, not to the courts, but "to the Congress," "power to enforce, by appropriate legislation, the provisions of this article." A little later the Constitution was made further to stipulate that "the right of citizens of the United States to vote shall not be denied or abridged by the United States or by any state on account of race, color, or previous condition of servitude." In occasion, ideology, and intent the Fourteenth Amendment seems clearly of a piece with the Thirteenth and the Fifteenth.

Yet high authority would dismiss context as irrelevance and would have construction accept "the plain and obvious meaning of the words." The bother is that the language is general and abstract. The clauses are filled with verbal symbols quite receptive to a content strong enough to possess them; not one single concretion is to be found to suggest interpretation or to point direction. The language is exposed to the greatest of all historical fallacies, which is to confuse event with intent and to read the exposition of a later age back into the pristine statement. The men who framed and ratified the amendment had only the dimmest knowledge of events to come; they had to explore its constitutional possibilities without benefit of the labors of jurists recently seated or not yet upon the bench; they had to set down general words in terms of the problems then current. For them the clauses lived with the breath of their own age. It is only by historical recon-

struction that the contemporary meaning of the Fourteenth Amendment is to be rediscovered. An understanding requires an appreciation of the crisis, the intellectual heritage and the expediencies out
of which it emerged. It demands even more an oblivion to the gloss
of a later day which lies thick upon the text.[3] It is easy enough from
the vantage point of what came of it all to look back over our shoulders and to give order and purpose to the course of judicial events.
But in 1868—and decreasingly in the years to come—the immediate
past was more insistent than the distant future. The folk of the time
had to meet events head-on.

II

If words are in want of definition, the proper appeal is to the law.
And it was hardly half a decade after the amendment had been
adopted before the meaning of its high-sounding phrases became
the concern of the United States Supreme Court. Due process
made its judicial entry with the fanfare of trumpets and in the
livery of a strange master. The men who had taken part in the
late rebellion had been disenfranchised; the reconstruction program of the Black Republican Congress was in full swing; and in
the states which had made up the Confederacy, the legislatures
had fallen into the hands of freedmen of color and carpetbaggers.
A flood of reckless legislation ensued; some marked by social vision, some savoring strongly of privilege and corruption, all
anathema to the white aristocracy which before the war had been
in the saddle. The old South had lost in war and at the polls. But
someone within its defeated ranks had the vague idea that an
appeal to the courts might yet save the situation. Whose idea it
was is lost to history. But an adage was current—"Leave it to God
and Mr. Campbell"—and presently the Hon. John Archibald
Campbell [4] was putting his ex-judicial mind to a difficult problem.

---

[3] An understanding of the Constitution in the making rests upon a genetic account
of its doctrines. Yet the paraphernalia of learning is set against such an inquiry. Few
bodies of material are as adequately indexed as the law reports; but the headings are
abstract concepts, verbal symbols, and legalisms. Records are not reported, and dates
and occasions are swept away as of no account. Entries are set down as if the law
were universal and unchanging; and holdings from a miscellany of times and jurisdictions are brought together to spell out a doctrine. The ghost of theology is still
at large; and inconsistencies are leveled beneath the skills of the system-builder.

[4] John Archibald Campbell was born in 1811 and died in 1889. He became a justice
of the United States Supreme Court in 1853 and resigned in 1861, when his state,
Alabama, left the Union. Upon his judicial appointment he freed his slaves. In the

Who chose the particular statute which in single combat was to stand for hundreds of its kind has escaped the record. But whether choice fell to an unknown, to Mr. Campbell, or to a group, a more strategic selection could not have been made. An act of the legislature of Louisiana had granted to a corporation of seventeen persons for a period of twenty-five years an exclusive franchise in respect to the slaughtering of animals for meat in the parish of New Orleans and the two next adjacent. In giving effect to the act a citizen has been enjoined from the sale of his land for a rival slaughterhouse; a like interdict had been laid upon a boatload of cattle headed for market by an unorthodox route; butchers who for years had done their deadly work were no longer free to follow their trade; and the local public was forced to have commerce with a monopoly or turn vegetarian. Here were, ready at hand, causes as perfect as if they had been fashioned for the oncoming judicial ordeal.[5] They offered all the raw materials which a popular legal crusade demanded; they gave opportunity to all the symbols by which the emotions are stirred and the judge-within-the-man is moved. American institutions were being flaunted; a monopoly, odious at law and to the people, had been given a legislative blessing; the laborer had been denied his Biblical doom and God-given right to work. The enemy was an octopus of a corporation; the cause was the cause of the workingman; the rights at stake were the rights of man. The requisite stuff of persuasion was there; there was need only to chisel it into a compelling legal argument.

The situation clearly invited a challenge of the statute in the name of the higher law. But to Mr. Campbell no ready-made formula was at hand. He had daringly to blaze a new trail; and a number of briefs which are rather successive drafts of the same argument than complementary lines of reasoning attest the arduous progress of his labor.[6] It is impossible for the lawyer of today,

<hr>

Dred Scott Case he concurred in the judgment of the court in a separate opinion. After the war he resumed the practice of law and frequently argued constitutional cases before the court of which he had once been a member.

[5] The suits were consolidated and in the reports appear as *The Slaughter House Cases,* 16 Wallace 36 (1873).

[6] Except for edited excerpts in the law reports, the briefs have not been published. They are, however, a part of the official record of the case. It seems unnecessary in the pages that follow to tag every reference with a citation to brief and page. The reasons are recited over and over again, and anywhere the reader turns he will chance upon statements of a kind with those quoted here.

with a head full of the things that came later, to appraise the quality of his performance, and even the historian with his art of re-creation can form no certain judgment.[7] In his briefs there is nothing of clean-cut concept, of rule of law chiseled with neatness and precision, of sweep of syllogism to its inevitable therefore. They are clothed in a rhetoric alien to the legal persuasion of today. But history is here—its pages are filled with the conditions of the working classes in America, in England and Scotland, in France and Prussia. Learning is here—there is hardly a page not adorned with its apt quotation from some writer on government, jurisprudence, economics, or philosophy. Authority is here—citations of cases are alternated with statements from Turgot and Guizot; Buckle and de Tocqueville; Hallam, Macaulay, and G. C. Lewis; Mr. Jefferson and Adam Smith; John C. Calhoun, Mr. Justice Curtis, and Cooley on *Constitutional Limitations*. A sentence from the *Wealth of Nations* which makes of a man's right to his trade both a liberty and a property was copied from the brief into a dissenting opinion and to this day goes resounding down the law reports. Even the arts have their dialectical due in an occasional line of poetry or a rhymed couplet of a Negro minstrel.

The books were at hand—and a skill in their use—to serve the cause of the butchers. The task was to mold a medley of materials into a legal entity. Mr. Campbell had only foresight—not the hindsight of a later generation. His endeavor is marked, not with the delicate articulation of the codifier, but by the daring of the adventurer and the fumbling of the pioneer. His strategy had the audacity of an ex-member pleading before his old court, of an ex-rebel confronting his victorious enemies. He abandoned the older parts of the Constitution, whose well-litigated clauses did not point his way, and took his stand upon an article which as yet had drawn forth no judicial utterance. He decided to add another to the many paradoxes with which the history of legal doctrine is strewn. The Fourteenth Amendment was intended to secure the rights of the recently emancipated blacks against their former

[7] The account of the argument in the official report, 16 Wallace 36, is scrappy; the more regimented lines in 21 L. Ed. 394, attest an editorial hand of a later date. A jurist before whom he pleaded regarded it as among the most original and profound of constitutional arguments. A distinguished teacher of the law characterized it to me as "such a brief as a clerk would draw."

masters. The ink upon the fresh constitutional entry was hardly dry; yet he proposed to use the self-same article to guard the rights of the Southern whites against the political power of the newly liberated Negroes.

In spite of a wandering style that jumps from Illinois to Norway and takes the distance from Scotch thralldom to Southern slavery in a stride, the substance of his contention is clear and its focus never lost. His oral argument before the Supreme Court was an exposition of the unity of the Thirteenth and Fourteenth Amendments; and the great objective of which they are instruments is the theme of all the briefs. All over the Western world, and almost within a century, a revolution had taken place in the status of the workingman. In France thralls had been eased of their ancient dues; in Prussia serfs had become their own masters; everywhere the feudal ties which had bound vassal to lord had been loosed. Even in the United States of before the war there had been slaves, freedmen, and free-born citizens and "the state might and did make large differences in the positions of men in the social and political system." The Thirteenth Amendment ended not only slavery but involuntary servitude in every degree and form; it made forever unlawful throughout the whole land a servitude for a year, for an hour, or even for an occasion. A master could no longer command a servant to dance, to frolic, or to make merry before him.

But the impulse of a mighty revolution was not spent in a single enactment. In the Fourteenth Amendment all ranks were leveled, all marks and perquisites of social status were obliterated. All classes, whatever had been their previous conditions, were made a single people. "The law of citizenship became as broad as the law of freedom"; and every person became the equal of every other person before the legislature and at law. In respect to "conscience, speech, publication, security, occupation, freedom, and whatever else is essential to liberty or is proper as an attribute of citizenship," every man became equal to every other man. The amendment—a political as well as a social revolution—"brought the federal government into immediate contact with every person and gave to every citizen a claim upon its protecting power." The natural rights of men, "life, liberty, property, protection, privilege, and immunity"—their reiterated beat falls upon page after page—are "the sacred inheritance of the people." The Fourteenth Amendment "was designed to afford a permanent and powerful guarantee to them." They are to be recognized as "the assured estate of the population"; the mandate to the states is, not "to abridge or destroy," but "to maintain and preserve them." In respect to these rights, inalienable and indefeasible, the federal government becomes every man's guardian.

With such a philosophic start it was easy to get down to constitutional concretions. Although the reasons are not neatly tooled, the substance of the argument is repeated again and again with cumulative effect. The Fourteenth Amendment created a national citizenship, fitted it out with "privileges and immunities," and placed this heritage from times of old beyond the power of the state government. These privileges and immunities are nothing other than the natural rights of man. Among these rights—quoting Mr. Jefferson and the new constitution of Louisiana—are "life, liberty, and the pursuit of happiness." It is—in an argument helped along by Turgot, Adam Smith, and Mr. Campbell's own common sense—impossible for a man to sustain life, to enjoy liberty and to pursue happiness if denied the chance to work. Man "has a right to labor for himself and not at the will or under the constraint of another." Moreover, a man's right in his own labor is not only a liberty but a property as well. As "a natural right of person" it is a liberty; in "its results or the expectation of results" it is a property—the only property of substance the working man possesses. It follows that he has a natural right to dispose of his service—note the quiet appearance of a term which later made a mighty sound— by "freedom of contract." An argument so surely upon its way was not to be halted here; and, with strokes so deft that the transition is unobtrusive, Mr. Campbell converts an abstract right to work into the worker's vested interest in his occupation. Every trade must—in an order of nature to which the Constitution has come into accord—be open to all who choose to take its chances; and "no kind of occupation, employment or trade can be imposed upon" the workingman "or prohibited to him so as to avoid election on his part." Here, then, in tangible and specific terms is a constitutional right, a privilege and an immunity of citizenship, a liberty and a property, a claim to the equal protection of the laws, which the national government must under solemn mandate maintain against a state legislature gone astray.

And, having given concretion to his absolutes, with telling strokes the attorney drove the argument home. He had no quarrel with the state in its exercise of the police power; its right to promote by legislation "salubrity, security, and order" is not challenged; but the statute on trial is not a health measure. Instead "the recitals of concern for the general welfare," the "delusive and deceitful promises of public good," the "expression of an unusual benevolence for the domestic comfort or the sanitary care of a neglected community" are sheer pretense. The statute emerges from "no proper legislative procedure"; it serves no motive—note the usage of the time—"of the public utility." On the contrary its one characteristic, its sole import, is to create a private corporation and to grant to a favored group of seventeen the exclusive privilege of an ordinary occupation. The ordinance was a return to the age of feudalism; it had created a banality in favor of a single firm; Louisiana had, in defiance of the federal Constitution, become "enthralled ground." There is at issue not one jot or tittle of regulation by the state which those who are pressing the suits wish to avoid. Instead a monopoly—under the ban of the common law, intolerable in a democracy, forbidden by the Fourteenth Amendment—has been created at the expense of men who have made "an ancient trade the business of their lives." The Louisiana statute abridges the privileges and immunities of citizens of the United States; it denies to persons life, liberty, and property without due process of law; it takes from them the equal protection of the laws. Liberty and property were before there was law. The rights of man, which belong to the order of nature, are above "the chartered rights" of a corporation. The cause is that of the workingman, of the community, and of the Constitution.

It was a powerful—even if not quite successful—appeal. In the decision all the justices who spoke for the court or in dissent addressed themselves to Mr. Campbell's argument. At its judicial début four out of nine were converted to a novel constitutional doctrine and the majority of five found it hard going to contrive a dialectical answer. Chance got in its deft stroke and shaped the course of constitutional events by a single vote. As Mr. ex-Justice Campbell, the Southerner, argued for national sovereignty, Mr.

Justice Miller, the Northerner, denied it.[8] As the native of Georgia argued that all citizens were one people in an indivisible union, the unionist from Iowa refused to curb the authority of the states. As the ex-Confederate asserted that whites and blacks were equal before the Constitution, the abolitionist on the bench refused to erase the color line. There was, according to the court, a citizenship of the United States, but Mr. Justice Miller neglected to remove it from the realm of the abstract, to define its terms or to endow it with substantive rights. The Fourteenth was an addendum to the Thirteenth Amendment; it had been designed to make secure the rights of the blacks. But white men, though industrious artisans, were without benefit of its coverage. The legislature had passed the statute as a health measure, and with the act of a sovereign state the Court would not interfere.[9]

It was, however, only as a judgment to go at that. Mr. Justice Field boldly spread upon the record a powerful dissent.[10] The court, like lost sheep, had gone astray; he with three of his colleagues—especially he—was sound in a just-discovered faith. There was a citizenship of the United States, whose privileges and immunities had by the Constitution been put beyond the reach of the state, and that citizenship knew neither race nor color. The rhetoric was the rhetoric of Field, but the ideas were visible imports from the Campbell briefs. A milder echo of the same argument reappeared as the opinion of Mr. Justice Bradley.[11] In the midst of a paragraph toward the end—as if it were a passing thought—he set it down that a possible mandate with which to curb the power of

[8] Samuel Freeman Miller was born in 1816 and died in 1890. At the age of thirty-one he deserted the vagaries of medical practice for the more comfortable certainties of Blackstone's *Commentaries*. The intellectual climate of his native Kentucky was too severe for his abolitionist sentiments, so he moved over into Iowa. He was lifted from the obscurity of country practice to the highest bench in the land by his fellow Kentuckian Abraham Lincoln in 1862. He remained on the bench until his death.

[9] *The Slaughter House Cases,* 16 Wallace 36 (1873), p. 57.

[10] *Ibid.,* p. 83. Stephen Johnson Field was born in 1816 and died in 1899. As a war measure a new circuit was created on the Pacific coast "to save California to the Union"; Field was appointed to the Supreme Court in 1863, and served until his retirement in 1897. He was of all the members most insistent upon reading substance into due process; and what he often said in dissent eventually came to be "the opinion of the court."

[11] *Ibid.,* p. 111. Joseph P. Bradley was born in 1813 and died in 1892. He had been an ardent unionist; was appointed to the Supreme Court by Ulysses S. Grant in 1870 and remained a member until his death.

the legislature might be found in "due process of law." So the cause was lost. The "privileges and immunities of citizenship" disappeared from constitutional law—and we hear little more of it until its ghost returns after sixty-five years to serve a cause of tax avoidance of the vintage of 1935.[12]

But the loss of a cause is not the loss of a doctrine. Fate, attended by coincidence and paradox, was on the job to pull a trick more audacious than a story-teller would dare to invent. The butchers, still intent upon following the ox to the shambles, had lost their case but not their persistence. The good citizens of the state, with suffrage restored, presently reclaimed the legislature. By statute the monopoly was stripped of its franchise and the butchers were again free to follow their trade. This time it was the Crescent City Company which refused to accept the voice of the people and girded itself for judicial combat. As the situation demanded, the two combatants exchanged positions, legal weapons, and arguments. The monopoly hurled at the Court the Campbell brief done up in fresh verbiage. Since privileges and immunities had failed to prevail, under the thin veil of the reputable doctrine of obligation of contract, the familiar arguments were recited as a denial of liberty and property without due process of law. Counsel for the other side, perhaps a little shamefacedly, went to Washington with pleas for the supremacy of the police power, ably buttressed by the judgment of the United States Supreme Court in the Slaughter House Cases.

It was with no unity of feeling that the Court welcomed the return of the prodigal case. Mr. Justice Miller and his erstwhile colleagues must have felt a trifle embarrassed; and their brethren, Field and Bradley, JJ., could hardly restrain the thought, "Oh Lord, Thou hath delivered mine enemy into mine hands." The cause which in the Slaughter House Cases Mr. Justice Miller had sustained and the doctrine he had used in its support were now in collision. He had to desert the cause of reconstruction and renounce a legislative grant he had pronounced valid—or he had to recant a neatly woven constitutional argument. In the emergency he did not hesitate; he forsook secular cause and political concern and valiantly made a stand upon his dialectic. In his "the opinion

[12] Colgate v. Harvey, 296 U.S. 404 (1935).

of the court" he took many pages to say in substance, "The legislature has given and the legislature has taken away; blessed be the
name of the legislature." [13]

Had Field and Bradley, JJ., been ordinary men, a period might
then have been written to "due process" as it had been to "privileges and immunities." Had they been content to join Miller, J.,
and the majority of the Court, or to concur without opinion, the
attempt to fuse substance into the Fourteenth Amendment might
not have survived this second and more ignominious defeat. The
result was to them admirable; but they could not allow their joy
at the discomfort of Mr. Justice Miller to blind them to the acuteness of their own plight. As the power of the state was vaulted
aloft, they hit upon a telling—even if outrageous—strategy. As they
viewed with an inward dialectical joy the loss of all its exclusive
privileges by the Crescent City Company, so the call was for a
separate concurring opinion. In this, with superb audacity, they
argued, not that the charter had been rightfully taken away, but
that it had never been lawfully granted; not that the second act of
the Louisiana legislature was valid, but that the first act had all
these years been invalid.[14] Miller, J., had for the Court argued the
Crescent City Case; Field and Bradley, JJ., in certainty and a dissenting concurrence, reargued and redecided the Slaughter House
Cases. The unusual occasion was seized; the peculiar turn of
events was capitalized for a little more than it was rightfully
worth. And, under the signatures of two eminent jurists, the doctrine of due process was set down in the law reports as an alternative reading to the police power.

After two decisive defeats, the Fourteenth Amendment came
quietly into constitutional law. The pomp and circumstance which
had attended the previous causes was absent. A municipal ordinance in California had made a pretty verbal display to the effect
that laundries carried on in brick buildings were within the law;
but if they were housed in wooden structures, the authorities must
be satisfied that the chance of fire was not a hazard to public safety.
In obvious intent and in administration it said that the trade was

[13] Butchers' Union Slaughter-House v. Crescent City Live-Stock Landing Co., 111
U.S. 746 (1884).
[14] For the concurring opinion of Mr. Justice Field, see *ibid.*, p. 754, and of Mr.
Justice Bradley, *ibid.*, p. 760. In Mr. Justice Bradley's dissent, Harlan and Woods, JJ.,
joined.

open to the whites but that Orientals were to be subjected to the closest scrutiny before admission to so exclusive a club. Yick Wo, denied the right to work at his chosen trade, essayed judicial combat, had syllogisms broken in his behalf, and came away with the signal victory of the highest court in the land. His right to his trade was as good as that of any other man.[15] The victory was scored, not by a recently emancipated black, not by a Southern white whose pride in race did not forbid the use of the Negro's legal protection, but by a yellow man from China. Against the arbitrary act of the state, "equal protection of the laws" came into constitutional law where "privileges and immunities" and "due process" had been denied admission. And the new doctrine had been accepted by the Court without a single vote in dissent.

The breath of life had been breathed into the Fourteenth Amendment. The right to work at one's chosen occupation had at last become a part of the supreme law of the land. The substance to which "equal protection" gave a verbal home could pass on by contagion into a liberty and a property fortified by "due process." Eighteen years had passed since the amendment was adopted and fourteen since Mr. Campbell had blazed the path for a novel doctrine. But at last, in 1886, even against the action of the state, the rights of man had been accorded the protection of the Constitution.

III

Yet long before this decision another course of events was under way. The Campbell arguments were much too useful to be left to butchers, bakers, and laundry workers. At the bar, and at least before the bench, we find them presently clad in the livery of an alien master. In his briefs—with all their concern for the liberties of the workingman—ex-Justice Campbell could not leave the word "property" alone. He made the right to work a property; and somewhat abstractly, on his own and within quotation marks, he declared the idea that property derives from the state to be the most revolutionary of notions; for, "if the state creates, the state can destroy." As with the individual, so with the nation-on-the-make, no clean-cut line was to be drawn; liberty was the liberty to acquire property. To Mr. Justice Field, rounding out his decades

15 Yick Wo v. Hopkins, 118 U.S. 356 (1886).

on the high judicial bench, liberty and property came to be a single word with a constant shift of accent to the right. In the Crescent City Case the familiar dialectic contrived as a plea for liberty appeared in the service of corporate privilege. And, long before Yick Wo won his legal tilt against Hopkins and California, attorneys for corporations as plaintiffs in error were presenting in brief and oration a round of exquisite variations on a theme of Campbell.

Although lawyers were admonished for pleading reasons that had been rejected, the recitation went on. In the challenge to the regulation of grain elevators, to the railway legislation of Granger days, to legislative attempts to abate or to subdue the trade in alcoholic beverages, the theme was omnipresent. It was always put forward as a defense of the frontiers of business enterprise against legislative attack. If invariably it fell before the police powers of the state, it acquired momentum and an enhancing repute in the opinions in dissent. As the decade of the eighties moved along, general admissions that legislation must meet the standards of due process were wrung from the Court, while it was still loath to apply the doctrine in the instant case. It was, however, not until the nineties that the personnel of the bench became radical enough to give effect to novel doctrine. Then, by judicial surgery, the Interstate Commerce Act was stripped of its sting and the Sherman Anti-Trust Act limited to an innocuous domain. Although the first real program of national regulation was rendered impotent rather than declared invalid, and the Fourteenth Amendment was not called into service, a judicial opinion had come to prevail in which a due process, fitted out with substance, might by the Court be thrown as a buttress about corporate interest.

The first decisive commitments came—if not off stage—at least in the realm of dicta. In arguing a case of tax avoidance for a railway company, Mr. Roscoe Conkling attempted to use a humble confession to advance the cause of his client. He hinted that the Fourteenth Amendment was the result of a conspiracy between politicians and industrialists; and admitted that, in Congressional committee, the word "person" had been chosen instead of "citizen" to extend the protection of the due process clause to the corporation. His prestige at the bar was at its height; he had refused the high office then held by Mr. Chief Justice Waite and the hardly less honored seat then occupied by Mr. Justice Blatchford. He quoted at some length from the minutes of the Congressional committee; and although the record had not been published and he did not produce it, his remarks made quite an impression. They left no decisive imprint in the reports; for although the Court found it easy to listen to elaborate constitutional argument, it found it difficult to resolve the issue. As the months passed without result, a motion to dismiss was allowed on the ground that the question had become moot, and the issue was left in abeyance.[16] It was long afterward that the minutes of the committee were made available and it was discovered that Conkling had taken excerpts from their context, tempered entries to his cause and reshaped quotations to serve his argumentative purpose.

But decades before historical research was to reveal a deliberate indulgence in historical error, his confidential knowledge had had its effect.[17] Four years later, in 1886, an attorney for the same railroad, in another case of tax avoidance, proposed to argue the same issue. He was stopped by Mr. Chief Justice Waite, who announced that the Court was prepared to admit, without argument, that a corporation was a person within the intendment of the equal protection clause.[18] Again a case, elaborately argued on constitutional grounds, was disposed of without recourse to constitutional doctrine; and the elevation of the corporation to the protective eminence of a person remained a dictum. But the dictum was set down in the reports; and, oblivious to its lack of authority, it began presently to assert its claim as a holding.

The eighties gave way to the more receptive attitude of the nineties. Courts must await their causes; and from the play of minds upon issues which are potential the law takes its course. A simple case from Minnesota concerned with the regulation of railroad rates touched off a conflict of values and quickened the germs of doctrine into life. A state commission, acting in pursuance of

[16] San Mateo County v. Southern Pacific R.R., 116 U.S. 138. The case was argued Dec. 19, 20, 21, 1882; as the passage of time brought no decision, a motion to dismiss was eventually made on Dec. 17, 1885, and allowed four days later. It is of note that the official record is so barren of the issue in controversy that there is no mention of Conkling's name, and only the attorneys appearing on the motion to dismiss are listed.

[17] Howard Jay Graham, "The Conspiracy Theory of the Fourteenth Amendment," *Yale Law Journal*, XLVII (1938), 371.

[18] Santa Clara County v. Southern Pacific R.R. Co., 118 U.S. 394 (1886), p. 396. The point had been voluminously argued in briefs submitted by counsel.

statute, had fixed rates for milk moving within the boundaries of the commonwealth. No notice had been given, no hearing held, no opportunity accorded for the presentation of evidence. A railroad company, denied an opportunity to present witnesses, regarded the act of the commission as "unjust, unreasonable, and confiscatory" and appealed to the judiciary. To minds steeped in the requisites of criminal process such behavior was most irregular, and the majority of the Court chose to find a procedural issue.[19] The Act deprived "the Company of its right to a judicial investigation, by due process of law, under the forms and with the machinery provided by the wisdom of successive ages for the investigation judicially of the truth of a matter in controversy." It "substitutes as an absolute finality the action of the Railroad Commission" which "cannot be regarded as clothed with judicial function or possessing the machinery of a court of justice." As a result —with an easy transition from procedure to substance—if "without a judicial investigation" the company "is deprived of the power of charging reasonable rates," it is "deprived of the lawful use of its property and thus, in substance and effect, of the property itself." Thus the ancient right of access to the court, with little bother as to what is a proper cause of action, is used to proclaim a judicial overlordship over what had up to the moment been set down as the province of the legislature.

The self-assumed task of the Court did not go unchallenged. The presence of opinions, other than that "of the court," indicates a still unformed state of mind. As Mr. Justice Blatchford for five members of the Court stated the issue, its answer is reasonable enough. But in the impact of the law upon the state of facts, there were other ways of putting the question. In a concurring opinion, Mr. Justice Miller writes down a series of propositions which are a primer of the division of labor between legislature and judiciary in respect to public regulation.[20] There is "an ultimate remedy . . . especially in the courts of the United States" against "a tariff of rates" set down "arbitrarily and without regard to justice . . . so unreasonable as practically to destroy the value of property," whether established by legislation or commission. This "is a

---

[19] Chicago, Milwaukee and St. Paul Ry. Co. v. Minnesota, 134 U.S. 118 (1890). The opinion of the Court was delivered by Mr. Justice Blatchford; but the line of argument bears the craftsmanship of Mr. Justice Brewer.

[20] *Ibid.*, p. 459.

denial of due process of law in a proceeding which takes the property of the Company." And, going beyond the decision which ordered the cause remanded "for further proceedings not inconsistent with the opinion of this court," he declared that "if this"— that is, his own—"be a just construction of the Statute of Minnesota, it is for that reason void." Eighteen hundred and ninety is a far cry from 1873, and in the intervening years Mr. Justice Miller had drifted far across the line which he himself drew.

It is likewise curious to discover Mr. Justice Bradley in dissent just as due process comes into its own. But, in putting the question before the Court in his own way, he remains true to—even if not quite consistent with—his ancient faith. His attack is substantive, not procedural.[21] The regulation of railroad rates is a legislative, not a judicial, prerogative; it involves "considerations of policy as well as of remuneration." "The state might build its own railroads if it saw fit," for it has "a duty" to provide "means of intercommunication between one part of its territory and another." This duty is devolved upon the legislature, and if "it commissions private parties, whether corporations or individuals, to the performance, it is its prerogative to fix the fares and freights" for "such transportation." The chartered rights of carriers are not above the state. The Court has confused the issue and treated the present case "as if the constitutional prohibition was that no state shall take private property for public use without just compensation—and as if it were our duty to judge of that compensation." The Act was not struck down, but chartered rights were moving into the succession; and the brew of nullity, in the name of due process, was in the pot. Campbell was dead; Bradley stood fast; Miller came over; and Field, eternally right, marched with the marching doctrine.

Another six years passed. A number of significant causes came and went, stamped with the attitude of the changing bench. But not until 1897—and then only through a reaching out toward issues that need not have been raised—did an opportunity come for a better fitting of due process to the current temper of the Court. A Louisiana statute had prescribed a regulation of insurance companies within the state; the officials had attempted to bring under its penal provisions a firm which had contracted for marine in-

---

[21] *Ibid.*, p. 461. In his dissent Gray and Lamar, JJ., concurred.

surance upon shipments of cotton with a New York company. It
seems to have been admitted by all concerned that the contracts
had been made in New York and that in the instant case the only
matter of local concern was the notices sent of shipments upon
which the insurance was to take effect. It was easy enough for the
Court to waive so incidental a part of the transaction out from
under the Act. That done, the decision of the case demanded no
more than the simple comment that an act of Louisiana had no
application to a matter beyond the jurisdiction of the state. It
might even have been declared null and void as an interference
with commerce among the several states. But so obvious a disposition was not for the new blood within the Court. Mr. Justice Peckham, a fresh recruit, had the zeal of the reformer and a faith in the
enlightened opinion of his own day untroubled by doubt. The
holding depends upon the way the question is put; and he chose—
with the consent of his brethren—to view the Act as a "real" interference with "the liberty of the defendants to place insurance on
property of their own" where they pleased. Thus the issue became
larger, more general, and more significant than the unresolved
query in the litigation. As thus stated no question of the right of
the Court to review the matter was raised by any of the nine justices. That hurdle had been got over by a succession of rhetorical yieldings in a number of important cases—helped along by the
high vault in the Minnesota milk rate case. As formulated by the
spokesman for the Court, business privilege was squarely opposed
to state regulation with "due process of law" as the arbiter.[22]

It is idle to argue that he went out of his way to do it; for, to the
individualistic mind of Mr. Justice Peckham, his was the only way.
It was a superb opportunity to bring the orthodoxy of classical
economics into the higher law and he was not going to allow it to
pass. In a rhetoric which is strangely familiar the dissent of yesterday becomes the opinion of the Court. He quotes Mr. Justice Bradley in the Crescent City Case as if he had been the spokesman for
the Court; and the familiar arguments, even the illustrations of the
Campbell brief, are repeated. The "inalienable rights" of the
Declaration of Independence; the pursuit of happiness; the right
of the butcher, the baker, and the candlestick-maker are all there.
As Peckham quotes Bradley, who paraphrases Campbell—thus pil-

[22] Allgeyer v. Louisiana, 165 U.S. 578 (1897).

ing a superfluous Ossa upon a Pelion of dicta—"I hold that the
liberty of pursuit—the right to follow any of the ordinary callings
of life—is one of the privileges of a citizen of the United States."
Although the path of his argument is beset with questions, his
faith in the efficacy of free contract to take care of all the affairs of
business rises above all bother over relevance. The privileges and
immunities of citizenship may be outmoded, but there is a constitutional successor. A nimble sentence may be made to travel a long
doctrinal way; its hurried words may overcome formidable obstacles where the argument at a leisurely pace would break down.
Thus, "it is true that these remarks are made in regard to questions
of monopoly, but they well describe the rights which are covered
by the word 'liberty,' as contained in the Fourteenth Amendment." The "privilege" quoted is that of "pursuing an ordinary
calling or trade"; but—without setting down a period or evoking
a therefore—smoothly he glides along through "the acquiring,
holding, and selling" of "property" to "the right to make all
proper contracts in relation thereto." Thus, in the name of due
process of law, freedom of contract is thrown up as a fence about
the domain of business enterprise against the incursions of the
state. And no one on the high bench said to the contrary.

In the Allgeyer case "the police power" remained in the background. The cause had little concern with human rights; a trio of
judicial bows acknowledged an abstract authority to regulate; and
judicial silence prevented a conflict between an upstart due process
and the more venerable doctrine. Again the next year a head-on
collision was avoided when—with Brewer and Peckham, JJ., in
dissent—a statute of Utah establishing an eight-hour day in smelt-
ers and underground mines won the imprimatur of the Court; [23]
and it was only in 1905 that due process first won in a clean-cut
combat with the police power. A statute of New York had limited
the hours of employees in bakeshops to ten in any one day or sixty
in any one week; and, because of his lack of workaday respect for
the Act, the People of New York were at odds with a certain Mr.
Lochner. The judgment of the Supreme Court—one of the habit-
ual five to four variety—was again delivered by the learned jurist
and sound economist, Mr. Justice Peckham.[24] He had only to

[23] Holden v. Hardy, 169 U.S. 366 (1898).
[24] Lochner v. New York, 198 U.S. 45 (1905).

elaborate his former argument, now fortified by the official citation of *Allgeyer* v. *Louisiana.* Freedom of contract, in respect to
trade or employment, was an aspect of the liberty and property
which a state might not abridge without due process of law. The
challenge of the police power was met by a formidable parade of
personal and common-sense opinion that the hours of bakers had
little or no relation to the public health.

Again the distinguished jurist made the question before the
Court far broader than the issue which the case presented. If such
an act were allowed to stand, "a printer, a tinsmith, a locksmith, a
carpenter, a cabinetmaker, a dry-goods clerk, a bank's, a lawyer's,
or a physician's clerk"—in inelegant verbal parade—would "all come
under the power of the legislature." In fact "no trade, no occupation, no mode of earning one's living, could escape this all-per-
vading power." Since "there is no contention that bakers as a class
are not equal in intelligence and capacity to men in other trades"
or are "not able to assert their rights and care for themselves," the
real question is the general use of "the protecting arm of the
state" to interfere with "the independence of judgment and of
action" among men of every occupation. "Statutes of the nature of
that under review, limiting the hours in which grown and intelligent men may labor to earn their living, are meddlesome interference with the rights of the individual." And, since such "interference on the part of the legislatures of the several states with the
ordinary trades and occupations of the people" seemed "to be on
the increase," it was time to call a halt. The opinion of the Court
was intended to be an apostolic letter to the many legislatures in
the land, appointing limits to their police power and laying a ban
upon social legislation.

So it might have become but for the dissent. Mr. Justice Harlan
objected that the question of the relation of hours to health was
one of fact; that as reasonable men, members of the legislature
were entitled to their opinion; and that "there are few, if any,
questions in political economy about which entire certainty may
be predicated." With him White and Day, JJ., concurred. A
youngster of sixty-four, newly come to the Court, seized his chance
and scribbled the most famous dissent in all legal history. Mr.
Justice Holmes insisted that "general propositions do not decide
concrete cases." He accused the Court of interpolating economic

doctrine, insisted that "a constitution is not intended to embody a particular economic theory, whether of paternalism and the organic relation of the citizen to the state or of laissez faire"; and protested against freezing the law into "Mr. Herbert Spencer's *Social Statics.*" It is common for latter-day liberals to set this down as the first blast of the trumpet in behalf of a social oversight of human rights; but the historian is more likely to view it as a lance worthily broken in behalf of an ancient cause now in retreat. But the four dissenters saw as clearly as the five—who, by the virtue of being one more, were the Court—that the challenged act might be "the first installment of a general regulation of the hours of work"; and they wished to keep the way open. It was probably too late for Harlan, J., or even for Holmes, J., to argue that in such matters the legislature was the sole and exclusive judge and that the Court had no rightful power of review; at least such an argument was not attempted. The all-but-equal vote led to an even balance of doctrines. Neither the police power nor due process was to be preferred; in an even-handed formula, liberty and property are to be set against public policy; as case follows case, these concepts are to be filled with the values of life, a balance is to be struck, and a judgment rendered. An engaging number of rules for the game of review have come and gone; the decisions of the Court have with the circumstances, its personnel, and the temper of the times swung now toward one side, now toward the other. But the balance of values recorded in *Lochner* v. *the People of New York* has endured as the judicial formula for the ultimate judgment upon legislation designed to promote the public interest.

Thus a collusion of occasions and persons, causes and ideas, shaped the course of doctrinal events. It was quite untouched by conspiracy, unless it be of the gods or of that Providence which is said to preside over American institutions. A constitutional doctrine contrived to protect the natural rights of men against corporate monopoly was little by little commuted into a formula for safeguarding the domain of business against the regulatory power of the state. The chartered privileges of the corporation became rights which could be pleaded in equity and at law against the government which created them. In a litigious procedure in which private right was balanced against the general good, the ultimate word was given to the judiciary. A last ironic note attends the closing story; the words of the doctrine of due process remain true to their democratic origin; it is only the substance which has come to serve a strange master. But such an antithesis of language and content is "of the nature of things." For in respect to the public control of business, the Constitution of the United States dates, not from 1787, nor from 1868, but from 1905.

IV

All of this has to do with the rhetoric of the coming of due process. The account has as its narrow concern a sequence of judicial events; it is drawn from the official records of a single court; in all its detail it can be supported by the sanctions of exact documentation. But the larger story of the making of the doctrine lies elsewhere; in the development of industrialism, in the changing state of opinion, in the assembly of ideas from far and near into a principle of law, in urges within an economic order that could not be judicially denied. A part of that history has been written; distinguished scholars have garnered from legal literature the germs of the doctrine and have shown how the catholic concept of due process offered a home to notions of natural rights. But if the raw material has been exhibited and the verbal history of the doctrine written, the impulses within the social order—in particular, economic interest and legal persuasion—have not been accorded their part in the drama. Here off stage are the forces which give life to abstractions. The records of the Court reflect only in a series of passing shadows their tumultuous vitality. And the history of due process is far more than the judicial record it has left.

A shift from rhetoric to logic, from recorded doctrine to compelling impulse, is an engaging hazard. It is an inquiry into a series of "if's," many of which escaped actuality by the narrowest of margins. If in the Slaughter House Cases, the Campbell argument had commanded just one vote more, what difference would it have made? We would doubtless by now possess an august corpus on the privileges and immunities of citizenship, and the entries under due process would be correspondingly thin. But would the hypothetical domain be a great and humane code concerned with the rights of man? Or would the corporation, which became a person, just as easily have passed into the protected position of a citizen of the United States? And, in such an event, would the only change be that all that is now written down as liberty and property would be entered as the privileges of citizenship?

Or was the logic of the commitment inevitable—and the specific legal doctrine by which business enterprise sought immunity from regulation a mere rhetorical device? Due process was fashioned from the most respectable ideological stuff of the later nineteenth century. The ideas out of which it was shaped were in full accord with the dominant thought of the age. They were an aspect of common sense, a standard of economic orthodoxy, a test of straight thinking and sound opinion. In the domain of thought their general attitude was omnipresent. In philosophy it was individualism, in government laissez faire, in economics the natural law of supply and demand, in law the freedom of contract. The system of thought had possessed every other discipline; it had in many a domain reshaped the law to its teachings. A respect for the obligations of contract had been set down in the Constitution in 1787; the "ancient maxim" *caveat emptor* had become dominant in the law of sales by the forties; an individual responsibility for industrial accidents was definitely established in torts shortly after the middle of the century. An impact that had been irresistible elsewhere should surely have won its way into constitutional law. Its coming seemed inevitable; the constitutional concept which it made its domicile was a mere matter of doctrinal accident. Words on parchment could not be adamant before so powerful a thrust; privileges and immunities, due process, equal protection, were all available; and, had there been no Fourteenth Amendment, "the obligations" might have been made to encompass "the freedom" of contract; or as a last resort, a vague "natural rights" as a higher law might have been found to permeate the whole Constitution.

The wonder is, not that laissez faire made its entrance, but that it found so insecure a lodgment within the Constitution. Ex-Justice Campbell had a superb case, his strategy was adroit, he suited his arguments to a state of mind which it took a civil war to produce— yet he could not quite command a majority of the Court. It was nearly twenty years before even as a dictum the protection of the Fourteenth Amendment was accorded to a corporation and it was nearly twenty more before the first installment in a program of social legislation was struck down by the Court. Even when it was at last accorded constitutional standing, its victories were often obtained by the narrow margin of five to four. Its triumph did not come until half a decade after the turn of the century, when it had ceased to be common sense, when legislators were forsaking its precepts, and when in philosophy, economics, and government it was on the way out. Even then its victory was inconclusive; it could never claim the faith of the full bench, and it had to share its sovereignty with the antithetical doctrine of the police power.

Freedom of contract took up its abode within "due process of law" too late for easy and secure lodgment. Its legal insecurity may rest upon personnel; a change of a justice here and there would have affected mightily the course of judicial events. It seems strange that so many jurists stood steadfast against the seductions of laissez faire; history, political science, and economics can boast no such record. Or it may be due to the older and established doctrine that the state might intervene with regulation to promote public safety, public health, public morals, and public welfare—against which the cause of the independence of the business system could achieve only a partial success. Or does the whole story, in irony, paradox, and compromise, derive from the innate conservatism of the law—a rock of ages which even the untamed strength of laissez faire could move but could not blast?

Minority Rule and the Constitutional Tradition ⤙ MAX LERNER

I

"LAW," Aaron Burr once remarked, "is that which is boldly asserted and plausibly maintained."[1] I prefer this insight, crude as it may seem, to much of the wisdom of the whole array of schools of legal philosophy.[2] Burr must have had an uncanny prescience about the development of American constitutional law. Into the increasingly bold assertion of judicial supremacy—the history of the judicial power—I do not propose to enter here.[3] It has been explored a good deal recently and is a matter of record in the annals of the court. That record is one of tortuous maneuverings and bold *faits accomplis* in the field of governmental practice. The men who have guided the destinies of the judicial power, from Alexander Hamilton and John Marshall to Chief Justice Hughes in our own day, have been masters of the art of political manipulation and anything but novices in the technique of presenting the enemy with the completed actuality of a decision.

I am not one of those who regard the bold assertion of judicial supremacy as an act of usurpation.[4] It is a truism, of course, that the power of judicial supremacy over the whole governmental process is nowhere to be found expressly granted in the constitutional document. It is a body of inferences, a system of "givens" and "therefors," an intellectual construction. But it has by this

[1] Quoted in Nelles and King, "Contempt by Publication in the United States," *Columbia Law Review* (1928), XXVIII, 401, 428.

[2] I say this, of course, while recognizing that Burr's remark represents in itself a school of legal philosophy—something that would correspond to a cross between the American realists and the glorification of the survivor contained in some of the German jurists. But while we may formalize Burr's remark thus, Burr himself did not.

[3] This is dealt with in Lerner, "The Supreme Court and American Capitalism," *Yale Law Journal* (1933), XLII, 668.

[4] The theme of usurpation, either in assertion or denial, is the grand underlying theme of most of the recent literature on the Supreme Court. Thus also the theme of exploitation has been used as the grand theme of much of the recent literature on capitalism. But the abstract question of legalism would seem to have as little to do with political power realities as the abstract question of social justice with economic power realities. In either case they are usable primarily as evocative myths.

time become accepted as a living institution, and I have too much respect for any part of an organic going concern to think that it can be exorcised out of existence by legalistic discussions of whether it was actually intended. The judicial power has by this time *written itself* into the Constitution by court interpretation and prescriptive right, just as much as if it were clearly granted in the document. In short, it is a colossal gloss upon a text not given, a gloss with which we must deal as we would with any political actuality.

It is time that American thought on the Constitution moved away from the question of original intent, away from *whether* the men in the Constitutional Convention intended judicial review, to the question of *how* judicial supremacy has been built up and maintains itself in what is presumably a democracy. To move from the *whether* to the *how* is, perhaps, always a step forward—from what can be only subjectively guessed at to what can be objectively observed, from theology to science, from polemics to history. What can be said of intent with respect to judicial review although it will undoubtedly prove eternally interesting, is actually rather little, and that little is uncertain. One may balance the warily expressed desires of the framers against the clear aversion of the people at the time and get nowhere.[5] What can be said of the logic of the way in which the judicial power has been built up is clearer—that it is the natural outcome of the necessity for maintaining the rule of a capitalist minority under the forms of a democracy. Judicial review has not flowed merely from the will-to-power of individual justices, but has been the convenient channel through which the driving forces of a developing business enterprise have found expression and achieved victory.

Let us, however, turn to the last half of Aaron Burr's definition. "Law is that which is boldly asserted *and plausibly maintained*." Bold assertion is pursued in the realm of political action and economic pressure. Plausible maintenance proceeds in the realm of symbols, interest structures, and idea systems. The aggressions of the judicial power cannot be understood unless we see them as part of the attempt to maintain the existing power structures in our

---

[5] Paraphrasing Lord Justice Buckley in Hanau v. Ehrlich (1911), 2 K. B. 1056, 1069, one may say that it is a century and a quarter too late to apply our own minds independently to the task of determining whether judicial review was intended by the Constitution.

peculiar form of capitalist democracy. But the defenses of the judicial power are also formidable. Every going institution seeks to build a triple line of defense. First, there is the area of *symbols,* or what Professor Elliott calls "social myths" [6] and Thurman Arnold calls now "symbols" and now "folklore." [7] The realm of symbols is most often an unconscious realm; when they have become too articulate their spell is broken. I have sought to examine elsewhere in a paper the interrelated symbols that the Constitution and the Supreme Court have built up in the mind of the common man, and especially the symbolism of the divine right of judges.[8] Secondly, there are *interest structures,* the pulls and thrusts of class relations that make various groups defend the judicial power and that have made the Supreme Court defend those groups; these interest structures are generally unconscious and operate best on the level of unconsciousness, but in times of tension they tend increasingly to become articulate. In between these two there is the third area—that of *formal apologetics*—the ideology by which the judicial power has operated and has been defended. Thus we have, in a triple defense ring around the judicial power, symbolic structures, interest structures, and idea structures. It is with the relation of the last two that I am here principally concerned.

II

The Court's own *apologia* for its power—what may be called the "official" theory of the judicial function—is well known, but I shall take the liberty of recapitulating it. It runs somewhat as follows: We have a fundamental law, in the form of a written constitution, overriding legislative enactments that are not in harmony with it. We have a federal system, in which powers must be divided between the states and the central government; and a system of separated powers, in which the lines must be drawn between the departments of the government, and the encroachments of one upon the others avoided. We have thus in two respects a system that would result in chaos or tyranny unless there were a final arbiter. We have, moreover, the danger that men in power

---

[6] See his paper, "The Constitution as the American Social Myth," pp. 209 ff.
[7] See Arnold, *Symbols of Government* (1935) and *Folklore of Capitalism* (1937).
[8] See Lerner, "Constitution and Court as Symbols," *Yale Law Journal* (1937), XLVI, 1290.

will aggrandize their power at the expense of other men, and invade their rights; we have a people safe from such invasion only under the protection of the Constitution. We have finally a judicial body, deliberately placed above politics and beyond partisan control, and empowered to assure for us a government of laws and not of men. The fund of knowledge and principles to which this body appeals is to be found in the Anglo-American common law, the precedents of constitutional law, and a "higher law" resident in the "genius of Republican institutions."

In its way this official theory is something of a masterpiece. It is, to be sure, a mosaic pieced together from diverse materials: the Federalist Papers, court decisions and dicta, commentaries by scholars like Kent and Cooley, classic speeches like those of Webster; but, while it is a mosaic, it is a thing of beauty nevertheless, neat, logical, close-fitting, comprehensive—so long as you grant its premises.

Let me set out some of those premises, generally unexpressed.[9] The official theory assumes that a fundamental law must be superior to all legislative enactments, despite the example of the English system, where the line of constitutional growth lies in parliamentary enactment rather than judicial construction. It assumes that other departments of the government may not be as capable as the judiciary of the task of constitutional construction —assumes, that is, a fund of exclusive and inspired knowledge of the law on the part of the judges. It assumes that the binding obligation of a litigant at law to accept the court's construction of a statute is binding as well upon Congress. It assumes on the part of the executive and the legislature an imperialistic thirst for power and expansion, and despite Justice Stone's agonizing cry *de profundis* in the Butler Case ("the only check upon our own exercise of power is our own sense of self-restraint") [10]—despite this cry, the official theory makes no similar assumption about the stake the judges have in their own power. It assumes that all government is dangerous, and thus adopts a negativist attitude toward governmental powers. It assumes that the legal aspects of a governmental problem can be separated and abstracted from its real as-

---

[9] I am indebted here to some extent to Edward S. Corwin's acute article, "Judicial Review," *Encyclopedia of the Social Sciences*, VIII (1937), 457.

[10] United States v. Butler, 297 U.S. 1, 79 (1936) (dissenting opinion).

pects. It assumes, in short, a closed Constitution in a malignant universe, instead of an open instrument of government in a changing and challenging world.

I have spoken thus far of the formal ideology of the judicial power. But an ideology is not merely a series of linked propositions drawn from related premises. It sometimes draws its greatest strength from allies—ideas in this case not directly within the official *apologia* of the Court's power, but imbedded in the popular mind and strengthening the acceptance of that power. I want to pick four of them for brief discussion—the doctrine of limited governmental powers, the doctrine of the sanctity of property, the doctrine of federalism, and the doctrine of minority rights.

The Constitution was born in a century obsessed with the notion of limited powers, a century overhung by the shadows of Locke and Rousseau. Conservative thought clung to the rights of minorities against the tyranny of the majority; and radical theory, such as that of Jefferson and the great European rationalists, took the form of belief in the perfectibility of man and the malignancy of government. But the pattern of the century contained a curious inner contradiction in its thought. Its prevailing economic policy was mercantilistic, with all the close and comprehensive controls that the mercantilist state exercised over economic life, and with all its resulting concentration of authority.[11] Its prevailing political thought, however, was atomistic, with its emphasis on individual liberties and governmental dangers. The men who framed the Constitution and ran the government that it created were caught in this contradiction. Their conservative economic interests dictated a strong central mercantilist government; the prevailing political ideas of the time, fortifying their fear of democracy, made them place that government of expanded powers in an intellectual framework of limited powers. Hence, to a large extent, the confusion of the constitutional debates. The interesting fact is that judicial ideology still clings to this doctrine even in a world where to act on it would be grotesquely tragic, and where the popular impulse is to abandon it.

When we pass to the doctrine of the sanctity of property, we find that the sense of property has assumed a variety of forms in our his-

[11] For the mercantilist character of the economic thought of the era of the Constitution, see Hamilton and Adair, *The Power to Govern* (1937), 103–44.

tory, but always the protection and support it has accorded to the judicial power has been a continuing factor in the Court's life. American life has pushed forward along a variety of trails—farm, frontier, and factory; plantation and city; trade route, logging camp, mining town and real-estate boom; corporation and coöperative. But through all these the common base-line has been a persistent and pervasive sense of property. It first took the form of the land mysticism and land hunger of physiocratic thought, deeply resident in the whole movement of colonial land settlement, and from which Jefferson eventually drew much of his support; then the sense of vested rights and the deep sense of contractual obligation, to which Marshall gave doctrinal expression in his "contract decisions," [12] and which, using and twisting somewhat Sir Henry Sumner Maine's terminology,[13] provided a new sort of status for an age of capitalism; then the sense of property individualism, born of the movements for European liberation, blessed with the approval of Protestant capitalism,[14] flourishing in the wilderness of the American frontier, turned into laissez faire by the conditions of a reckless and exploitative capitalism; and finally, when individualism could no longer thrive as an idea because it had been extinguished as a fact in economic life, the clinging to the profit system and the cash nexus as bulwarks against social anarchy and the destruction of the social fabric. This sense of property, even when its widespread social base has been so largely destroyed in the age of absentee ownership, is still a powerful ally for the judicial power.

When we turn to the theory of federalism and states rights, we are dealing with a powerful intellectual and sentimental force that the Supreme Court has at times had to fight and more latterly has been calling to its aid. We are all acquainted with the kinds of arguments which, like ghosts, are continually looming up in the world of ideas, which rule us from the past by their wraith-like being, although we are aware they no longer represent actualities. The idea of free opportunity under capitalism is one, and it lingers on even in a world dominated by monopoly. In the political realm

[12] See Isaacs, "John Marshall on Contracts—a Study in Early American Juristic Theory," *Virginia Law Review*, VII (1921), 413.

[13] I am referring, of course, to his famous distinction between status and contract. See Maine, *Ancient Law* (6th ed., 1876), p. 170.

[14] See Tawney, *Religion and the Rise of Capitalism* (1926) (following Weber); and apropos of the Weber-Tawney thesis, see Laski, *The Rise of European Liberalism* (Eng. ed., 1936), pp. 29–34.

the most potent and assertive American ghost is still federalism.[15] Most of its former functions have been stripped from it; it haunts a nation in which every force drives toward centralization, both economic and political. But when I call it a ghost, I do not mean it is no longer a fact to be reckoned with. The strength of a ghost, it must be remembered, rests in its capacity to get itself believed; and that, in turn, depends more than anything on our own needs and fears. And the fear of over-centralization, of the wiping out of the traditional political and cultural landmarks of the states, is a very real fear, especially in the light of what the fascist dictatorships have done to federalism.[16] And it is a fear which the Supreme Court, as witness the AAA case,[17] has not been averse to exploring and exploiting.

It may be said of the doctrine of minority rights and individual liberties that recent events have given them or seemed to give them even greater meaning than they once possessed. This tradition of minority rights has always been an important source of strength for judicial supremacy. The doctrine of vested rights,[18] the sanctity of contract and liberty of contract,[19] the doctrine of due process of law—all have drawn upon this tradition. In fact, most of the Court's decisions invalidating legislation hostile to property might be interpreted as proceeding from its zeal for minority rights, rather than from any untoward zeal for business interests. Nevertheless, as long as a strong rationalization for capitalist power existed in economic

[15] Lest this be interpreted as an attempt to depreciate the value of the federal principle, I want to say that I value our regional cultures highly. But one must not confuse such personal valuations with the stream of tendency. And while I believe that an element of the federative principle will always remain in American political history, I must recognize that the strength of federalism lies in the past and not in the future. The corporation has not obliterated federalism in political theory, but it has done so in economic fact. I have found much of interest on federalism in Dicey, *Introduction to the Law of the Constitution* (8th ed., 1915), especially the introduction to this edition; Friedrich, *Constitutional Government and Politics* (1937), Ch. 12; McMahon, "Federation," *Encyclopedia of the Social Sciences*, VI, 172.

[16] For a moving account of the German experience, witten by a German liberal of the old school to whom the federative principle meant much, see Mendelssohn-Bartholdy, *The War and German Society* (1937).

[17] United States v. Butler, 297 U.S. 1 (1936).

[18] Edward S. Corwin's articles on vested rights are, of course, well known. I have sought to treat the subject in my article, "Vested Interests" (1937), *Encyclopedia of the Social Sciences*, XV, 240.

[19] See Hamilton, "Freedom of Contract" (1937), *Encyclopedia of the Social Sciences*, VI, 450. See also Laski, *op. cit. supra* note 14, 237–64, where he treats of the liberalism of the Supreme Court majorities and concludes that it serves only to clothe the business interests that they guard.

thought and opinion, the civil liberties and minority rights argument was secondary. Now, however, two things are happening to push it to the fore. One is the decline of laissez faire, both in practice and in thought. The second is the spread of fascism in Europe and the fear of it in America. The first has made the businessman and the judges turn increasingly to the rhetoric of civil liberties; the second has made the liberals and the middle classes more ready to accept the Court's guardianship of civil liberties, even if it means a measure of judicial control over economic policy.[20]

About civil liberties and minority rights and the liberals I shall have more to say later. But I want to pause here for a moment to survey the meaning of these four ideological allies of the judicial power. All four, viewed historically, have their roots in majority movements, and have played a great and even revolutionary rôle in the history of the Western world.[21] And all four have been turned to the uses of minority rule as parts of the constitutional tradition. Take, first, the idea of a government of limited powers. The notion of a higher law; the idea of natural rights of individuals, which adhere to them independently of government and even in despite of government, and which must be protected against government; the necessity of disobedience to a government that violated these rights —these had once been living parts of a revolutionary movement that swept western Europe from the parliamentary champions of the struggle against the Tudors and Stuarts to the philosophers of the French Revolution. They were majority movements, aimed at limiting the powers of minority governments of the dying classes. They rationalized the actual movement toward parliamentarism in England and toward middle-class democracy in France. But in taking them over, judicial review turned them to quite different uses— to defeat parliamentary supremacy and hedge democracy around with severe limitations—in short, to the uses of minority rule. And the same may be said of that property sense which has been part of the American democratic experience, of the democratic localism that underlies federalism and states rights, and of the democratic

[20] During the public controversy in 1937 over President Roosevelt's court reorganization plan, many liberals who had earlier been critical of the Court's decisions came to its defense, motivated largely by the fear that "packing" the Court or weakening its prestige would remove the principal guarantee of civil liberties.
[21] See Laski, *op. cit. supra,* note 14.

movements that generated the doctrines of civil liberties and minority rights. All have been twisted out of their original context, and turned to the uses of minority rule.

III

I want now to examine more closely what I mean by three concepts I have been using—democracy (or majority will), minority rule, and minority rights. The relation between these three is central to an understanding of the ideology of the judicial power.

Scratch a fervent believer in judicial supremacy, and like as not you will find someone with a bitterness about democracy. The two are as close as skin and skeleton. When I speak of *democracy* here, I want to distinguish it sharply from *liberalism*. There is no greater confusion in the layman's mind today than the tendency to identify the two. American history has been the scene of a protracted struggle between democratic and anti-democratic forces.[22] Anti-democracy started as aristocratic thought, with emphasis on a neo-Greek élite. Alexander Hamilton, heartbroken because the new American state could not be a monarchy with George Washington as king and himself as kingmaker, sublimated his monarchical passion in a dream of America as an aristocracy of property. And a whole school followed him. But it soon became clear that in a country where a revolutionary war had been fought to achieve democracy, an aristocratic body of thought could not form the base of any party successful at the polls. The collapse of the Federalist Party proved it.

A shift was made, therefore, to liberalism; and so powerful an aid did liberalism become to the anti-democratic forces that even conservatism grew shamefaced and, in order to survive, had to don the garments of liberalism. In the South alone, in the period of tension preceding the Civil War, slavery as an economic base caused aristocratic theory to linger on, and the spokesmen for the slav-

[22] The sharpest delineation that I know of this struggle in American history is to be found in Parrington's three-volume work, *Main Currents in American Thought* (1927–30). Parrington stood on the shoulders of J. Allen Smith, whose two books, *The Growth and Decadence of Constitutional Government* (1900) and *The Spirit of American Government* (1907), are not as well known as they deserve to be. Latterly the work of the Marxist historians has begun to realize the implications for American history of this struggle between democratic and anti-democratic forces.

ocracy defended it as an élite that had reëstablished a Greek republic among the roses and cotton bolls below the Mason-Dixon line.[23]
But the Civil War proved by blood and iron that aristocratic theory
was, like slavery, an unnecessary survival from archaic times. The
northern financial oligarchy that rose to unchallenged political
power out of the Civil War spoke thereafter in the name of an
orthodox, if slightly cynical, liberalism. And it has continued to
do so.

Let us be clear about it; minority-rights liberalism (which becomes in practice minority-rule liberalism) furnishes the only reasoned defense of the capitalist power that we have in America. This
liberalism has three facets: a defense of individual civil liberties
against society, a defense of minority rights (including both human
and property rights) against the possible tyranny of the government,
and a belief in rationalism and in the final triumph of the idea. In
the course of the liberal revolutions in Europe, democratic forces
were unleashed which sought to carry the implications of the
libertarian movements to their logical conclusion not only for the
middle class but for the underlying population as well, not only for
political but for economic freedom and equality. These forces are
what I shall call the "democratic impetus" or the "democratic
thrust." They began to loom as the great threat to the privileged
position of the middle classes. Fortunately for those classes, they
could find in the armory of liberalism the intellectual weapons they
needed for fighting the democratic threat. The basis of democracy
is that the majority will shall prevail; its premise is that the common
man can fashion his own political destiny, and that government
must consist of representative institutions to carry the majority will
into execution. To this, liberalism has opposed the proposition that
the freedom and rights of the individual and the minority were
more sacred than the will of the majority. In that lies the essential
distinction between liberalism and democracy.

In their fear of majority will the propertied groups have depicted
the democratic mass movements in the darkest colors of extremism.

---

[23] I do not mean to say here that the Athenian republic was a slavocracy in the
sense in which the American South was. The recent researches of Zimmern and others
have shown that the slave base of Athenian society was by no means as rigorous as
had been previously believed. See Westermann, "Ancient Slavery" (1937), *Encyclopedia of the Social Sciences*, XIV, 74–77. But it did furnish a convenient *apologia* for
the classical-minded defenders of the Southern economic system.

They have called the Jeffersonians "Jacobins," the Jacksonians "Locofocos," the Abolitionists "Niggerlovers," the agrarian radicals "Populists," the trade unionists "Reds" and "Bolsheviks." The democratic forces in turn have responded by calling the propertied groups "monarchists," "plutocrats," "economic royalists." The two barrages of epithets have enlivened American politics, but failed to illuminate them. But behind the battle of the epithets there has been a very real struggle between the thrust of majority will, ever present in a nation whose collective life has been based on democratic premises, and the counter-thrust of minority rule.

This has been the basic paradox of American life—the necessity we have been under of squaring majority will with minority rule—that is, democratic forms with capitalist power. It has made us, in one sense, politically speaking, a nation of hypocrites. But it has also spurred our wits and sharpened the edge of our political inventiveness. Out of it have emerged our peculiar institution of judicial supremacy and that whole idea structure of the defense of judicial supremacy which I have outlined.

The mistake we are all too ready to make is to pose an antithesis between the Constitution as such and the democratic impulse, an antithesis that does not exist. We have been led into this error partly by the excellent work of Charles Beard and his school in proving that the Constitution represented the property interests of the minority.[24] That is true enough. But we must also remember that the Constitution, without the accretion of judicial review, could (whatever its origins) have become an instrument of the majority will. The whole animus behind it, despite the system of checks and balances, was a flexible one. It was meant, as has recently been pointed out with great effectiveness by Professor Hamilton [25] and Professor Corwin,[26] to adapt itself to the changes and chances of the national life. It is significant that the majority groups, who were first rather sullen about it and then accepted it after affixing to it a bill of rights guaranteeing individual liberties, finally became enthusiastic about it. It is well known that Jeffersonians as well as

[24] I refer, of course, to his *Economic Interpretation of the Constitution* (2d ed., 1935). I do not mean that Mr. Beard has himself fallen into the error of posing an antithesis between the Constitution and the democratic impulse, but that the emphasis in his early work lent credence to that error.

[25] Hamilton and Adair, *The Power to Govern* (1937).

[26] Corwin, "The Constitution as Instrument and Symbol," *American Political Science Review*, XXX (1936), 1071.

Hamiltonians and Marshallians vied in their praise of the Constitution.[27] What they differed about was the judicial power. The real antithesis is between the democratic impulse and the judicial power.[28] And with Jefferson and the so-called Revolution of 1800, which saw the triumph of Jeffersonianism, began that series of democratic thrusts, upsurges of the majority will, that has enlivened and vitalized American history. In Jefferson and Jackson—notably in the Bank War and the Dorr Rebellion—in Lincoln, to an extent in Cleveland, in the Populist movement and Bryan, in Theodore Roosevelt and Woodrow Wilson, in Eugene Debs, in Franklin Roosevelt and the New Deal, and in John L. Lewis and the C.I.O., we have had repetitions of that democratic thrust at the seats of minority power. It became the task of the propertied minority to ward off those thrusts. And they have been thus far enabled to do it through the instrument of judicial supremacy, the ideology that surrounds and defends it, and especially the ideology of liberalism.

In two senses judicial supremacy has smoothed the way for minority rule. In one specific instance after another, measures of policy which the majority has desired have been invalidated by the courts. If the people of Georgia wanted to undo a corrupt grant of land,[29] or the people of New York wanted an eight-hour working day in bakery shops,[30] or the people of Oklahoma wanted to restrict the number of ice plants,[31] their wishes were so much dry stubble to be trod under foot by the minority will of the Court.

But there is an even deeper sense in which the Supreme Court has acted as the final barricade against the assaults of democratic majorities. We must remember that the process of the triumph of the democratic majority is a long and tedious process, as majority leaders from Jefferson to Franklin Roosevelt have discovered. It is a process of seeking to displace the enemy from one position after another. There is a vast inertia of the party system, with an auton-

[27] For the best statement of this development, see Schechter, "The Early History of the Tradition of the Constitution," *American Political Science Review,* IX (1915), 707.

[28] Louis B. Boudin has brought out with the greatest sharpness the distinction between the Constitution, as embodying the democratic experience of the past and democratic potentialities for the future, and judicial supremacy as an instrument of minority power. See Boudin, *Government by Judiciary* (1932), and especially Boudin, "The United States Constitution 150 Years Later," *New Masses,* September 21, 1937.

[29] Fletcher v. Peck, 6 Cranch 87 (U.S. 1810).

[30] Lochner v. New York, 198 U.S. 45 (1905).

[31] New State Ice Co. v. Liebmann, 285 U.S. 262 (1932).

omous force of its own even after popular sentiment has changed; there is the political apathy of the masses, the tendency they have of forgetting to remember. There is the pressure of special interests, blocking up committees, arranging filibusters. There is the control that the vested interests exercise over our newspapers and our very patterns of thinking. And there is, finally, the effective weapon the propertied minority has in withdrawing capital from investment and thus paralyzing the economic process. And after all these positions have been captured, the anti-democratic forces retreat to their last barricade—judicial review. There, behind the safe earthworks of natural law, due process, minority rights, the judges can in the plenitude of their virtue and sincerity veto and outlaw the basic social program of the majority.

IV

The democratic forces of the country have known, in intervals of lucidity, what they were up against and what they were fighting. But in addition to all the difficulties of mustering the necessary big electoral battalions, they have become increasingly confused recently. And their confusion has risen from the fact that the rationalizations that are used to explain and defend the Supreme Court power are the rationalizations that flow from the premises of liberalism—that minority rule uses the theory of minority rights, and manages somehow to equate the two.

Minority rule has recently had to work very subtly to defeat majority will. There was a time, in Alexander Hamilton's day, when the anti-democratic theorists could say frankly, when confronted with the accusation that they had defeated the people's will: "Your people, Sir, is a great beast." [32] Or they could speak more gravely, as did Fisher Ames, of "a government of the wise, the rich and the good," [33] as if all three were coterminous. Later they had to convert the Bill of Rights and the Fourteenth Amendment, the heart of the protection of minority rights, from a charter of liberties to a charter of property protection. The task, as is well known,

[32] Henry Adams, *History of the United States during the Administration of Jefferson,* I (1930), 85.
[33] Ames's writings are the classic repository of anti-democratic comment. "Our country," he wrote in 1803, "is too big for union, too sordid for patriotism, too democratic for liberty." *Ibid.,* I, 83. And George Cabot, another high Federalist, wrote in 1804, "We are democratic altogether; and I hold democracy in its natural operation to be the government of the worst." *Ibid.,* II, 165.

was a difficult one, and involved two major intellectual somersaults
—twisting due process of law from a procedural meaning to a substantive meaning, and endowing the corporation with all the attributes of human personality. But, while the task was well done, it
was done with a certain cynicism that is particularly apparent in
the political commentaries between the Civil War and the World
War, as well as in the court decisions of that period. Now, however,
in the midst of world tensions in which democracy has taken on a
new meaning and a new prestige for us, it is necessary to be more
subtle in defense of minority rule. The new defense is, therefore,
not only a plea for minority rights, powerfully evocative in itself in
these days, but a new interpretation of majority will as well.

That interpretation is to be found in its most finished form not
in the Supreme Court decisions, in all of which it is implicit, nor
even in scholarly commentary, but in two popular commentators,
Mr. Walter Lippmann and Miss Dorothy Thompson. It is significant that Mr. Lippmann embodies it in his book, *The Good Society*,[34] which is an attack on economic planning, the most dangerous threat to the economic power of the minority. It is even more
significant that Miss Thompson's theory, which is the more sharply
delineated, is to be found best in a series of three articles which
form a critique [35] of Mr. Roosevelt's Roanoke Island speech.

The new theory (I use Miss Thompson's articles as a model) re-
interprets the democratic principle so that it becomes something
quite different from the naked principle of majority will. First, not
only must minorities be protected from majorities, but majorities
must even be protected from themselves.[36] Second, if true democracy does operate in terms of majority will, it is not the will of a
numerical majority, but a very different conception.[37] Third, the

---

[34] (1938). I have made an attempt to analyze the argument of this book and point
out some of its implication in "Lippmann Agonistes" (Nov. 27, 1937), *The Nation*,
CXLV, 589.

[35] Thompson, "The President's Political Philosophy," N. Y. *Herald-Tribune*, Aug.
23, 1937, p. 15, col. 7; Aug. 25, 1937, p. 17, col. 7; Aug. 27, 1937, p. 15, col. 7.

[36] "But the converse of oligarchic rule is not rule by an unchecked majority, for
there can be an oligarchy of the majority as well as of the minority. The converse
of minority rule is the restoration in this country of genuine popular constitutional
government, of government by law, to which not only minorities but majorities and
bureaucracies, Congresses and the government itself, must give obedience." *Ibid.*,
Aug. 23, 1937, p. 15, col. 8.

[37] "For the American tradition conceives of democracy not as something which
functions periodically, in the form of ratifying or rejecting plebiscites, but as something which functions continually; which derives authority, not from the majority,

notion of numerical majorities really smells of fascism.[38] And having arrived at that position, one falls back in fright on minority rights, even if it involves scrapping the TVA, the Wagner Act, the Securities Exchange Commission and the Labor Relations Board.

When we say that majorities must be protected from themselves, the premise is the anti-democratic one—that the common man may be good material for being ruled but that he has no capacity for governing.[39] When we go on to talk of "true" democracy, as distinguished from majority will, what are we saying? We are saying that democracy is nothing so vulgar and demagogic as a counting of heads, but that there is a "real" national will, as distinguished from the one that expresses itself at the polls. That real national will is somehow a trusteeship [40] of the minority. For the few know what is

---

but from the whole people . . . and which avows that every individual is invested with certain natural rights, which not even a majority of 99 per cent can divest him of. . . .

"The parents of American democracy never advocated mass rule or the will of the majority as the final and sole authority." *Ibid.*, Aug. 25, 1937, p. 17, cols. 7, 8.

[38] "The important thing about the president's conception of government—of the unchecked reign of the majority expressed in the form of a blanket mandate—is that it is not incompatible with dictatorship but does, indeed, furnish the philosophical justification for modern dictatorships which have conquered the state by democratic means." *Ibid.*, Aug. 23, 1937, p. 15, col. 7.

"The conception that the majority's ratification of any executive program is the final expression of the democratic principle is, therefore, a revolutionary idea. Its adoption will inevitably lead to a change in the spirit and the form of American government. . . . The appeal to that principle is what Machiavelli recommended to his prince. The German socialists taught it to Hitler. And Aristotle was familiar with it, in the fourth century before Christ. It is revolutionary, but it is not liberal. It is, I believe, deeply reactionary." *Ibid.*, Aug. 25, 1937, p. 17, col. 8.

[39] This conception of the common man is embodied in the anti-democratic philosophy of Nietzsche and other German romantics; it deeply influenced the thought of Carlyle, Ruskin, and other English writers of the nineteenth century. See Brinton, *English Political Thought in the Nineteenth Century* (1933); Lippincott, *Victorian Critics of Democracy* (1938). It has also found expression in such contemporary writers as Wyndham Lewis, *The Art of Being Ruled* (1926); Mencken, *Notes on Democracy* (1926).

[40] There is an interesting parallel between this notion of political trusteeship by the minority for the majority, and the notion of economic trusteeship by the propertied minority for the propertyless majority. It is worth noting that the minorities and majorities are roughly the same in the two instances. Economic realism has made Americans increasingly skeptical of the notion of trusteeship in the economic realm, and cautious in accepting the claim, voiced most articulately once by George F. Baer of anthracite fame, that God had granted the captains of industry their wealth to hold in trust for the welfare of the masses. They have not yet applied a similar acidity to the parallel claims in the political realm. Ultimately, of course, the concept has been extended—notably by Henry Sumner Maine—to the fabric of society itself. Maine held that all civilization was a trust held by the few for the many. See Smellie, "Sir Henry Maine," *Economica*, VIII (1928), 64.

to the interest of the many better than the many know themselves. This whole conception of the national will as something transcending numbers and having no traffic with the felt desires of the day is an essentially mystical conception.

It has always been the rôle of reactionary thought to retreat to a mystical conception of the body politic, as witness Burke, de Maistre, Adam Müller and the French Catholic school.[41] For mystical notions enable you to escape from the fact of the naked majority will. And conservative minority groups have always regarded the majority as unsavory, as meaningless by the very fact of numbers, strident and mechanical like the clashing of weapons through which the primitive Germanic tribes indicated their assent by the greatest noise.[42] What is novel is the fact that all this is now said—and believed—in the name of liberalism. And yet not so novel if we consider the extent to which the ingredients of liberal thinking—that is, minority rule thinking—have entered into the traditional defense of the judicial power under the Constitution.

What has happened, of course, cannot be blamed on the Constitution. What has happened is that there has been built in America an extra-democratic structure of economic reality which dare not operate through the democratic machinery; for the democratic machinery is too easily turned into an instrument for leveling economic privilege. When this extra-democratic structure of economic reality (I use it as an academic phrase for the structure of corporate power), when this is challenged, and a successful attempt is made to take our democratic theory literally and nakedly, how far will the corporate groups allow this attempt to go? To my mind, this is the most important question that the Constitution faces in the calculable future, and it faces it more dangerously than it has confronted any problem since the Civil War. Does the economic interest of the corporate groups so far outweigh their sense of commonwealth as to make them ready either to keep their minority rule or scrap the whole democratic framework? My own conviction is that this is their attitude, and that they will insist on one or the

[41] For an interesting study of liberal Catholicism that sought to mitigate the rigors of de Maistre and Chateaubriand through the writings of Lammenais, Ozanam, Donoso Cortes and Bishop Ketteler, see Götz Briefs, "The Dispute Between Catholicism and Liberalism in the Early Decades of Capitalism," *Social Research*, IV (1937), 91.

[42] See Konopczynski, "Minority Rights" (1937), *Encyclopedia of the Social Sciences*, X, 525.

other of these alternatives. When the corporation cannot win its fight against democracy by economic means, it may call in military and political means and become (if I may give the term a twist) the corporative state.

If this is so, the new attack on the majority principle, represented by Miss Thompson and Mr. Lippmann, takes on a disquieting importance. A counter-thrust against a successful labor government, for example, will look for a theory to attach itself to. Here is a theory ready-made. The naked majority principle, Miss Thompson tells us, is really fascist; it is part of a totalitarian state. I find a readiness in surprisingly intelligent quarters to accept this paradox. If that readiness spreads, corporate power will not lack those intellectual garments which it needs to stave off a socialized democracy —intellectual garments which the liberals are now spinning just as assiduously as the Parcae once spun other fateful garments.

The Constitution as the American Social Myth ⌒ W. Y. ELLIOTT

THE expression "social myth" like other terms in the title that I have used for this essay needs defining and I shall make the attempt. But it never has fallen so strangely or alarmingly on the ears of historians as it used to upon the hearing of my brethren among the political scientists of a generation ago. Even Charles Beard would have hesitated to make play with it, and if he had, would have applied it in a bad sense.

No doubt fascism and communism have helped to bring this about. But what I may call the psychiatric cast of thought in the social sciences is even more important. A new generation of these social scientists has arisen which is inclined to view all cultural manifestations with the unhallowed detachment of what may be lumped together and called the Freudian tradition. The psychiatrists of politics like to pull men and movements to pieces, as if they were clocks with wheels, or patients under the most cruel of all dissecting scalpels, that of psychoanalysis. This attitude helps amazingly to buttress the ego of the "debunker" who so obligingly shows us "what fools these mortals be"—nay, have been and ever will be.

I do not come before you as one who would apply the term *myth* simply to one more adventure in exploding the usual firecrackers about judicial review *pour épater les bourgeois*. Let the sophists like T. R. Powell take their pleasure in reminding us that "a switch in time saves nine." I am not bent on debunking, but on that more difficult thing—understanding the peculiar fact that is the American Constitution. For, it is a *fact* even though a myth. I am even prepared to say myths are necessary, though some are better than others. I should like if possible to do justice to Edmund Burke's profound insight into what he called "prejudices," even more than to the Mephistophelian promptings of Georges Sorel or his disciples Robert Michels and Pareto. And I believe it necessary to go back even beyond Plato for our understanding of social mythology; back to the Bible and to such cultural anthropology as throws real light on the religions and the laws of the Egyptians, Hindoos, Chinese, and so forth.

Ancient polities, in such light as anthropology and history can throw upon them, seem to have had an almost uniform characteristic that gets too little notice from political theorists: the combination of king with high priest, that characterized early Greek society, recurs in various forms in most primitive stages of civilized peoples. The connection between, for example, the Pharaoh and the priesthood in Egypt was so intimate as to give a theocratic cast to that government. This may be taken as an archetypal form of primitive polity. The incorporation of the state religion in a myth served to buttress political power and to sanctify authority—for example, the mystery religions of the Greeks, their connection with local divinities; and the Pharaonic embodiment of the immortality of the Egyptians in the person of the ruler (compare the Mikado in modern Japan).

Laws become the enunciation of God to Moses, the Law Giver on Sinai; or the Roman Twelve Tables, equally god-given; or the codes of Manu and Hammurabi. The story is the same; as it is, for that matter, in the Golden Book of the Mormons, in our own times.

This primitivism reappears in theories like those of the divine right of kings in much later history and is today being given a definite form, comparable to that of the Roman *divus Caesar,* in the "leader principle"—characteristic of the fascist systems.

In a broad sense all mythology is social mythology; I dare say, even political mythology. For mythology aims at shaping a whole *way* of life. To the word "mythology" orthodox Christian doctrine has assigned a pagan (and hence untrue) connotation which is but another mark of how our whole Western thought bears the impress of our own religious mythology. A glance at Roget's Thesaurus is more instructive in some ways than a study of the encyclopedias on this point. The word is listed under "untruth," and is linked with "chimerical," "fabulous," "heathen," (or "bosh," "moonshine," "all-my-eye"), and so forth; with a pantheon that includes everything from Greek gods to Beelzebub and Mumbo Jumbo. But mythology in its scientific sense merely means the presentation of the ultimate speculations of metaphysics, including cosmology, in a coherent system of symbols which are invested with a *religious* emotion. Myths are a method of cultural (and in that

sense *ethical*) instruction, to make viable the whole range of speculative religious thought, particularly moral thought, to the vulgar.
In the form of folklore the vulgar has helped to shape the myth. In
the epic, which I ask you to note as the shaping myth of every great
culture, the bardic tradition is at many levels, some folk, some individual. Thurman Arnold puts into folklore many of the con-
trivances of the priestcraft in his work on *The Folklore of Capitalism*. Myths are produced by both priests and folk. The highest
mysteries of the priestcraft must be mediated by a theogony that
can be effective as symbols to the people. Popular pressure for emotional satisfaction produces idolatry. (Compare the strong tendency
toward Maryolatry in certain levels of Roman Catholicism, and
Henry Adams's unforgettable chapter in *The Education* on the
Dynamo and the Virgin.) Something of the same tendency has been
at work in investing judges with their peculiar American majesty.

Symbols are therefore the proper vehicle for myth-making. But
symbols are themselves not myths, though they are often treated as
such (compare Lerner, Arnold, and Corwin). A myth is *an epic
collection of symbols* into which rationalized theology has already
entered. Some of these symbols seem to be necessarily personalized
into gods or demigods—always in human form, often pitted against
monsters or angels, created by human imagination (Pantheon,
Olympus, or Valhalla; Labors of Hercules, Loves of Zeus). I shall
call these "personification symbols." Another set of symbols is
more abstract in reference, though using more concretely things of
ordinary life—such as the swastika, the cross, the caste marks, the
horns of Satan, the cloven hoof, the three-forked crossroads of
Hecate, the falcon of Osiris, and so forth. Ordinarily the latter symbols are concentrated representations of the central meaning of a
whole epic. Edward Sapir has called "condensation symbols" something which is a little different from this symbolism. Not to borrow
his word, I want to call these symbols "epic symbols."

All these symbols, as used by mythology, have a storied reference.
They are not, as Mr. Arnold makes them in his interesting little
book on the *Symbols of Government,* just about any dramatic feature of a culture, including slogans and stereotypes of every order.
I agree, as Professor Arnold does, with Whitehead's emphasis on
the dramatization implied in symbols. But though Whitehead
put it "It seems that mankind must be always masquerading,"

the important thing, as he notes, is not merely heightened self-dramatization—"the object of symbolism is the enhancement of the importance of what is symbolized" (*Symbolism,* page 63). Ordinarily, symbols are *associated* by means of legends, and give rise to rallying cries or slogans. But the true symbol gains its meaning through presenting a sense datum or image as charged with the whole emotional background of its own mythology. It both simplifies and emotionalizes loyalties by pointing to an epic way of life, and by arousing religious or heroic loyalties.

Primitive and even early civilized societies so linked religion with law that the law givers were also the prophets: state and church are one. Socrates is put to death on the charge of corrupting the Athenian youth by undermining the state religion. Yet, the same Plato who draws the magnificent tragedy of the *Apology* and the *Phaedo,* would in his own latest work on politics, *The Laws,* advocate the death penalty for those who undermined the religion of his state. It seems fatally necessary that the sophist in Socrates should make fun of the low level of godhood represented in Homer: Zeus always gallivanting around and sometimes without the decency even of a cloud. But it is to build a better myth—a more noble or "royal lie" like that of the Republic and the Myth of Er—that Plato's Socrates must first destroy the unworthy myths.

This is the function of theology—including political theology—to destroy only to rebuild. It is the difference between Socrates and the Sophists. Prejudice makes it inevitable that those who initiate new things should rouse the fears and the wrath of the fundamentalists. Revolutions in religious mythology are often as painful as in political. There is a sound instinct in human societies to cling to the old until the new is more than born. Let T. R. Powell and our sophists perform their useful work of ridicule and criticism. The American people remain a nation of "constitution worshippers," as Maury Maverick said the other day. There is even a proper Greek myth to symbolize this natural conservative hatred of radical critics: Kronos *ate* his children, who on being disgorged, dethroned their parent. That is perhaps the sort of mythology most stressed by Burke (the eating of the children) as against the revolutionary overturning of Thomas Paine and the French Revolution. The former is the function of prejudice and of fundamentalism; the latter (disgorging the indigestible stones that turned into the newer gods, Zeus *et al.*) is the function of revolutionary and creative times. Myths hold societies together; so they make martyrs, by their birth and death. That is the meaning of social revolutions—the overturning of a whole value system and the classes which embody it. But healthy societies transform their myths by a process of altering the meaning of the symbols to fit new needs. Only a great shift like the Reformation produces the violent wrench of general revolution. The church's hold was supplanted by that of the mercantilist and absolute state, under a monarchy which triumphed at once over feudalism and the religious claim to temporal sovereignty.

As the effects of western European development made themselves felt in the always greater separation of church and state, the simpler theories of divine right (whether by ordination of the vicar of God, or by descent from the gods or Adam's first born) had to give way to newer myths that would at once symbolize and rationalize the authority of temporal power. A religious myth is, in so far as it has ethical and political implications, always a social myth. But a political myth with the broadest social implications need not be religious in the sense of being otherworldly. It may substitute a religion of state, as Hobbes did in his "mortal god," *The Leviathan,* for the otherworldly Pantheon. Such a social mythology rationalizes the folklore of accepted laws and customs, and finds a basis in some view of man in nature, without theistic implications. Fundamentally that is the nature of the whole "social contract" theorizing—whether it derive from the Sophists' view of Hobbes or the Stoic view of Locke as to a state of nature. This type of social mythology is less emotionally attached to symbols, and more rationalistic. It is like scholasticism, in this respect, and is in fact the proper though late and crossbred fruit of scholasticism. But it must have a dogma on which to operate, taken as an act of faith. That is the concept of nature. And if it is to be viable historically it must develop an adequate symbolism. Hobbes's Leviathan really produces *divus Caesar* on the Roman model—the "leader" (Duce or Führer) of modern fascism. "Destiny" is the god who produces the great leader, though Hobbes tries to introduce the original compact as the Caesars strove for popular acceptance (retaining the S.P.Q.R.) and as their modern counterparts appeal to plebiscites.

This effort to invoke acceptance by the individual as part of a contract is a startling new factor, product of the Reformation maybe, but certainly influenced by feudal conceptions of allegiance. It is developed by Locke and deified by Rousseau under the mystic conception of a *moi commun* possessed of a *volonté générale*. The individual must be bound by his own free will (contract). That is the beginning of the long reign of the ethics of individualism in European, and particularly in American, thinking.

That the social-contract construction rests upon assumptions taken as a matter of faith (though not theistic faith) there can be small doubt for anyone who troubles to examine the views of nature (physical, social and individual) on which each contract theory is based. Each is, in the sense that I have defined, a social myth, necessarily political in that the focal point for assessing all social values is political authority. Law must justify authority in terms of a whole way of life acceptable to the individual conscience.

It would be a mistake to suppose, therefore, that any political system can escape the necessity of living upon a basic social myth. Plato's own formulation in the *Republic* was in terms of what he called a noble or a "royal" lie. That is, all the citizens were to be taught that men were born gold, silver, or the baser metals to correspond to the class struggle of his society, though he was very careful not to adopt the hereditary caste basis that would close a career to the talented. There is no social contract here. The individual is to be indoctrinated. He is a part of the organic state.

To sum up the meaning of social myths for politics: every system of government has required the rationalization of a system of fundamental beliefs as to the ethical basis of authority into a political way of life. These beliefs themselves rest on a quasi-religious faith not subject to further examination, but serving as a jumping off point for subsequent doctrinal development. A social myth may, therefore, be defined as a system of beliefs about a whole political way of life which can be symbolically represented, and at the same time rationally developed. My point has been that symbols are always part of a more or less coherent social myth. Symbols, therefore, must be found for all myths. As Whitehead says in his remarkable little book on *Symbolism*, "You abolish the etiquette of a royal court, but at official receptions you ceremonially shake the hand of the Governor of your state. Just as the feudal doctrine of a subordination of classes, reaching up to the ultimate overlord, requires its symbolism; so does the doctrine of human equality require its symbolism" (page 62).

But symbols are not the strong point of rationalized social myths. In the history of the social-contract theory, Hobbes chose as his own what I have called an epic symbolism, the figure of *The Leviathan,* "that mortal god," unfortunately headed in his frontispiece with the head of Charles I, but lately laid on the block; Locke uses the figure of man in a state of nature (later to be translated into a "noble savage"). Locke's development of the social contract offered no richer symbolism than the notion of the commonwealth with appropriate organs (executive, legislative, and federative powers); but the concept of private property itself comes nearest to being Locke's master symbol—a freehold, almost epic in character.[1] For Locke's whole way of thinking of the trinity of life, liberty, and property, the greatest of these was property. It symbolized freedom and all the limitations on governmental power. Rousseau pushed the symbol of the social contract into the hypostasizing of a general will, produced by a *moi commun* created in turn by *man's acting together in a small community* under a social contract. He personified his symbol.

Various derivative symbols could be drawn from the primary myths imposed by these forms of social-contract theory, such as, for example, in Hobbes, the crowned sovereign as the bearer of the whole authority of society; for Locke, revolution as an answer to the usurpation of power by rulers; and for Rousseau, a sort of deification of popular will, which reached its apogee in the French Revolution, though with the curious perversion—from Rousseau's point of view—of being a representative will embodied in the national assembly.

It is characteristic of all these approaches to the problem of authority under the social-contract theory that they derive from assumptions about human nature which are treated as articles of faith, though each pretends to a scientific (theological) rationalization. Each is aimed at the justification of the ways of the state toward man in terms of these fundamental presuppositions as to a way of political life. For Hobbes, law and order are ends in themselves;

[1] The irony of this symbolism, used to defend a squirearchy which had been raised on the back of the enclosure movements, no more appeared to Locke than does its modern use to others.

for Locke, life, liberty, and property; for Rousseau, the harmony of a community will, through which alone freedom can be understood in political society.

In so far as the English constitution has been symbolized in the crown, it has had to develop in accordance with a theology rather more like that of Locke than of either Hobbes or Rousseau. The emphasis placed upon the procedural protections of civil liberty has been erected in England into a basic element in the political myth.

Rejecting alike the divine right of kings (Sir Robert Filmer for the Stuarts), or the lawful nature of all-sufficient power (Hobbes), and the operation of the unchecked majority principle (Rousseau), there is in England the tendency toward the supremacy of the house of commons, by no means complete so long as the house of lords and the crown retain their present powers. This trend emphasizes in Locke's thinking the *majority principle* rather than those *limits* on legislative supremacy on which he equally insists, to wit the law of nature, the necessity of settled procedure rather than arbitrary rules (due process of law), and the protection of private property. Parliamentary supremacy has, with the broadening of the suffrage to universality among adults, tended toward a democracy limited only by its own traditions.

In the United States, the evolution of our social mythology has emphasized the limiting factors in Locke's doctrine rather than the majority principle, though our whole history has been something of a conflict between the two. Stated in another way, this can be put in terms of *Hamilton* v. *Jefferson,* or *Marshall* v. *Jackson,* etc.— that is, by the use of what I have called the personification symbols of our myth.

The Declaration of Independence was almost pure Locke, as has often been observed. In it the doctrine of inalienable rights was reconciled with the right of revolution. It was Jefferson's hand that shaped this application of Locke's philosophy to our revolutionary purposes, though it is significant that he mentions the pursuit of happiness rather than the property of Locke's immortal trinity. He does, however, pledge our "lives" and our "fortunes" as well as our "sacred honor," and he showed throughout his own career a certain reverence for the Whig side of Locke's doctrine—to wit, the necessity of some stake in the community, usually landholding, as the basis of a political share in government through the suffrage.

"Why should Locke have been chosen to this end?" Carl Becker has pretty adequately told that story. He did not try, and of course I am not trying, to write down our history in terms of purely literary influences. Locke suited the revolting colonists because he had taken the elements of their folklore of a political myth—that is, Magna Carta, the apotheosis of the common law protection of civil liberties (though not quite in Coke's manner), the Bill of Rights, and their feelings developed about them, and given these elements a sort of theological rationalization fit to justify another revolution. But his emphasis on limits of governmental power suited a distrustful pioneer society.

It remained for the development of the American constitutions, both in the states and in the federal government, to give a new twist to Locke's social contract theory. These documents in many instances *placed limits upon the majority principle itself by bills of rights, that is, admonitions to the legislature which aimed at preventing the abuse of private rights.* In several cases they went further and treated certain aspects of the constitutions as "fundamental" in Cromwell's sense, "somewhat fundamental, like Magna Carta." Provisions for limiting the amendment of the constitutions in these respects occurred in a few constitutions in a more formal manner, for example, Delaware, Maryland, Massachusetts, New Hampshire, and so forth.[2]

2 Provision for *amendment* in original state constitutions: A. By the people—through special convention and referendum, (a) Massachusetts; (b) New Hampshire (1784 and 1792). Must be adopted by a two-thirds majority of voters; cf. Connecticut. B. By the legislature, (a) Delaware, a five-sevenths majority of the assembly—seven members of the legislative council. (b) Maryland, "that this form of government and the Declaration of Rights, and no part thereof shall be altered, changed or abolished, unless a bill so to alter, change or abolish the same shall pass the General Assembly, and be published at least three months before a new election, and shall be confirmed by the General Assembly after a new election of delegates, in the first session after such new election." i. e.: Simple majority vote of two successive legislatures. (c) South Carolina Constitution of 1790—as in Maryland, except that successive legislatures must pass by a *two-thirds majority.* (d) Georgia Constitution of 1798—almost exact counterpart of 1790 one of South Carolina. (e) Delaware Constitution of 1792—a two-thirds majority vote of each house of one legislature (with Governor's approval), publication of proposal for popular consideration, and a three-fourths majority vote of each branch of the next legislature. C. By the legislature and the people, (a) Connecticut Constitution of 1818 most interesting: "originated the plebiscital method which was destined soon to meet with general application throughout the States" (Oberholtzer). "It was the New England system of a popular vote upon constitutions

From this idea of the Bill of Rights as the perfect statement of the protection of liberties comes, of course, the constitutional negativism (as Professor Corwin calls it) rooted in Locke's version of the social-contract myth. The federal Constitution gave this evolution, however, a further development by incorporating alongside a somewhat disjointed Bill of Individual Rights (sections 9 and 10 of Article 1, and the first eight amendments) the whole federal principle of states rights (amendments Nine and Ten), and a further limitation of constitutional amendment to extraordinary majorities even as respects the rights of person and property (section 5). That is to say, the federal Constitution in many cases put beyond the reach of the majority principle not only the rights of states but the rights of individuals. It erected a separation of powers (Montesquieu through Blackstone) much more genuine than that of Locke, and it incorporated an instrument which was to reduce the supreme legislature of Locke's thinking (and Jefferson's) to the "creature of the Constitution." That instrument was, of course, the Supreme Court of the United States, through which the doctrine of judicial review developed. The notion of a "fundamental law," traced—and I dare say occasionally misused—by my colleague McIlwain, was a precious heritage for the men of law. The inscription of our Harvard Law School Library, Langdell Hall, runs in Coke's quotation from Bracton, "Non sub homine, sed sub deo et lege." Its true translation should read, according to the Law School, "Not under man, but under God and the lawyers."

Again the elements of folklore and of popular experience enter along with Montesquieu, Blackstone and the rest. Colonial experience has been adequately ransacked for precedents. But the Fed-

---

or parts of constitutions, received from conventions, grafted on to the Maryland scheme of amendment by legislature, which was generally coming into vogue in the South." It runs as follows: "Whenever a majority of the house of representatives shall deem it necessary to alter or amend this Constitution, they may propose such alterations and amendments, which proposed amendments shall be continued to the next General Assembly and be published . . . and if two-thirds of each house at the next session of said Assembly, shall approve the amendments . . . said amendments shall . . . be transmitted . . . to each town . . . and if it shall appear . . . that a majority of the electors present shall have approved . . . the same shall be valid." This is a combination of an unusual majority and a bare majority. Massachusetts Constitution of 1820—a two-thirds vote of two successive legislatures, and a majority of the voters. Maine Constitution of 1819 had similar provisions. D. No provision for amendment in original constitutions of (a) New Jersey, (b) New York, (c) North Carolina, (d) Virginia. E. Pennsylvania and Vermont Constitutions provided for recommendations for amendment from a council of censors.

eralist papers served to theologize all these solutions in a way suitable for a basic body of later scholastic dogma.

This engine, judicial review, Marshall turned against Jefferson and the states righters. But he also erected judicial supremacy into a commanding position to define the economic and social contents of the national mythology. Ironically enough, it was Taney who did the real damage in the Dred Scott decision. The subsequent history of the "the Constitution" becomes inextricably identified in American thinking with the oracle which symbolizes the Constitution, that is the Supreme Court. The myth of natural rights, protected against government itself, lent the Court its color of impartial arbiter of the system. It is not too much to say that our social myth as a nation has been grounded upon those fundamental beliefs incorporated in the Constitution, not alone in the Preamble, but in the separation of powers, the limitations on legislative power (Article 1, sections 9 and 10), the phrase concerning the supreme law of the land, and the amendments further limiting both federal and state powers.

Lawyers, who have been our rulers for most of our national history, identify the Constitution with what the judges say it is. This accounts for the unique feature of judicial review. The Supreme Court has tended to become the "epic symbol" of the whole myth. John Marshall and the "nine old men" also substitute as personification symbols for the voice of the Founding Fathers. This rule by lawyers, through the Court, has roots entirely natural to our system. None but lawyers can understand its complex structure. Lawyers were the natural protectors of the wealthy, that is, of those who saw the sources of power in exploiting and organizing our resources, man power, and public utilities. Lawyers run business men in public relations and often in policies. Lawyers love litigation. To them it is the ideal means of determining social policies, negative though it be in its implications.

It goes without saying that the rôle of the Supreme Court as the theological expounder of our legal scholasticism, developed from this basic theology, did not go uncriticized or unchallenged.[3] The

---

[3] Senator William H. Crawford (1811): "Many of the various constructions given to the Constitution are the result of the belief that it is absolutely perfect! It has become so extremely fashionable to eulogize the Constitution whether the object of eulogy is the extension or contraction of the powers of the government, that when its eulogium is pronounced I feel an involuntary apprehension of mischief."

unique virtue of the American social myth, from the point of view
of liberal thought, was that it contained within itself a basic protection of skepticism as to all matters, including the Constitution itself, and a protection of the rights of utterance of that skepticism.
Teachers' oaths and similar modern developments run into this
aspect of the Constitution in a manner showing the ambiguity of
the attempt to force compulsions of this type upon public education, and indeed upon all education. Critics necessarily developed
within the system itself. The doctrine of the Court's monopoly of
the rôle of sole expounder of the Constitution was quite late in being accepted. Marshall was willing, when Chase was under fire, to
exchange it for security against impeachment. Jackson's views as
to the coördinate power of the three departments of government
in interpreting the Constitution even today find some defenders
(compare Professor Corwin's views on this point).

But the personification symbols of our national mythology developed apace. The "Founding Fathers" offered the convenient
Pantheon in which divergent views of orthodoxy might be reconciled. Every myth must have such flexibility. Aided by this degree of
free play in its theology Jackson himself apostrophized the Constitution (Farewell Address, 1837) as no longer an experiment. I need,
certainly for this audience, only to point to signposts for historians
in the evolution of this fundamentalism: The important signposts
are the alternative theologies of the Constitution such as those
given by Calhoun, Jackson, and Lincoln; the struggle over constitutional interpretations leading to the Civil War, and the triumph
of the "Union" doctrine. Then come the subsequent identification
of the Constitution with the supremacy of the federal government
and the alternative extensions of judicial usurpation through the
Fourteenth Amendment, occurring notably at the end of the nineteenth century—a path sufficiently blazed by Charles Beard and by
a host of others.

The modern period produces a struggle over the contents of the
myth, as is always the case when its main outlines have been accepted. Theodore Roosevelt and Wilson each introduced a new
element into the doctrine. Roosevelt emphasized once more in the
Progressive movement the necessity of bringing the Constitution
back to the people, with Locke's rights of revolution implicit in the

initiative, referendum, and recall, including the recall of judicial decisions, and so forth; Wilson insisted upon the expansion of positive federal powers, through majority rule, in a way presaging the New Deal. The War gave a powerful impetus to the Wilsonian interpretation, but the post-war period witnessed a relapse into "normalcy" in the field of constitutional interpretation as well as in other social trends. The sacredness of the fundamental dogma during this period allowed protest only on account of the decisions in the Child Labor Cases, along with some other rumblings within the labor movement at the Court's extraordinary differentiation between labor aspects of restraint of trade and other applications of the Sherman and Clayton acts.

On the whole, however, the period is marked by the tremendous increase in compulsory courses in the Constitution, backed by the patriotic societies, American Legion, Daughters of the Revolution, and so forth, and in interpretation of Americanism in terms of loyalty to the Court's pronouncements.

A certain amount of discredit of such patriotic encouragement of this form of the social myth attached to the failure of the Hoover administration to continue the more abundant life in the version of the 1920s. It was significant, however, that the mythology held sufficient strength to deter the New Deal from a frontal attack on the institution of judicial review until no alternative seemed left, if its whole program was not to be disastrously censored by the aristocracy of the robe. The significant struggle between the "Liberty League" view of our Constitution and that advocated by many academic critics and politicians reached its apogee in the struggle over the so-called "reform" of the judiciary in 1937.

The lines drawn in this contest showed conclusively the strength of the American social mythology of the Constitution and the success of the long tradition sedulously encouraged by the Bar Association and allied groups in identifying the Constitution with the Court. Many of those who felt critical of the Court's policies hesitated to back Mr. Roosevelt's program for "swamping" the Court, and resented its implications. The backwash against this attempt has gone far to create a weakening of prestige in the administration, even though the attempt succeeded for the time being in putting such pressure on the Court as to make it seem in the

recent cases to have altered its attitude toward New Deal legislation. Resignations have now begun to accomplish what the effort
to increase the number of judges was aimed at.

Undoubtedly the Court's part in the American tradition as the
oracle of the Constitution is not beyond challenge. The great bulk
of opinion among the detached students, as opposed to the practitioners of constitutional law, has condemned the usurpation of
power by the Court at each successive turn. "Due process of law"
was not transformed without a challenge into putting the final
judgment as to the reasonableness of laws in the courts; nor was
the later revival of the Tenth Amendment to hamstring the federal
powers, nor the new and dangerous use of a judicial veto on any
delegation of legislative power to the executive not considered
seemly by the judges. Proposals to make law more secure by speed-
ing up the final word of the Supreme Court look toward advisory
opinions. Much legal as well as lay opinion would back a requirement of some extraordinary majority of the Court to declare laws
unconstitutional. The Court's decisions and the Court itself can be
reached through the amending power. Indeed, alternative methods of putting pressure upon it appeared to be within the legal
possibilities of the Constitution itself (congressional power over
the whole of appellate jurisdiction, increasing the size of court,
and so forth). Its main strength would seem to have to lie in the
tradition that has been built up about this social mythology. To
preserve that strength it yields to pressure, if the election returns
go against its views. The present chief justice appears to view his
functions in terms of the statesmanship of a constitutional monarch with a veto—to be used only if it does not seem too dangerous.

It becomes imperative that a revaluation of social mythology
and of our national symbolism should be made at this time. The
lines generated by the struggle over the Court bill were somewhat falsely drawn on account of Mr. Roosevelt's strategy. Many
people who would have supported an attempt to amend the Constitution, or even an attempt to require an extraordinary majority
of the Supreme Court to declare laws unconstitutional, did not
feel able to support this badly veiled threat to the independence
of the judiciary. This would seem to indicate that the Court had
established itself as a valuable organ in the view of a command-

ing majority of the American people. Our federal structure needs an umpire. So long as it plays that rôle, and not the rôle of censor of social policy, it is safe. But federal jurisdictional problems permit court censorship, as the Canadian and Australian experience would show, even if we did not have our own. We need a tradition of the judicial function like that of Justice Holmes—ably carried on today by Mr. Justice Stone—that is, one which imposes upon the judges the honest and not merely the professed respect for the co-ordinate branches of government and their motives. What is required is judicial self-restraint, as opposed to the maxim too long honored: *boni judicis ampliare jurisdictionem.*

The real questions as to the nature of our Constitution itself include a recurrence to those fundamentals which Locke laid down as basic to a government under law that would preserve both a sense of community and a true liberty. The Constitution as a document always takes the form of the entire social mythology of the nation. We badly need to find new epic symbols for property relationships less subject to dispute than the perversions sometimes made of Locke's doctrine in the defense of private property by the propounders of "the American way." The conception of the State as a "partner" in industry may well be the new form of American doctrine, since it would seem most nearly to symbolize the existing procedures for regulation and for participation in the economic life of the country on which there is general agreement. Public interest must be conceived in more positive terms than the unstable equilibrium that is no more than a resultant of special interest pressures.

The larger question is the possibility of survival for the American social myth itself: a limited government, with restrictions on majorities, fares badly in times when the drift toward organic nationalism seems all to be in the direction of a managed economy. How much skepticism can be tolerated in a period of new faiths that really clash? This is a problem of greater and more permanent import. Will it be possible to retain a form which places such emphasis on negative restraints on power through checks and balances—the federal principle, judicial review, etc.—in times when the national security and domestic tranquillity, that is, so-called social security, both seem to indicate a concentration of powers for planning that can accomplish results without the possibilities of stalemate and indefinite delays? This question will not be answered by the success or failure of the New Deal in retaining its hold on the electorate. The contagion of a form of organization called the corporative state is spreading to England, though it as yet is unacknowledged there, and is skillfully cloaked in a re-armament program, operating under the demand for a wartime economy. The conception of a "general staff" type of governmental organization is becoming universalized as planning is forced more and more upon the economies which are insulated from the effects of autocratic adjustments. Can the government of the United States successfully resist this universal drift? What concessions must we make in changing the contents of our political forms if we are to transform our social myth into a workable, modern faith? Whitehead, once more, has put all this very beautifully:

As a community changes, all such rules and canons require revision in the light of reason. The object to be obtained has two aspects; one is the subordination of the community to the individuals composing it, and the other is the subordination of the individuals to the community. Free men obey the rules which they themselves have made. Such rules will be found in general to impose on society behavior in reference to a symbolism which is taken to refer to the ultimate purposes for which the society exists.

It is the first step in sociological wisdom, to recognize that the major advances in civilization are processes which all but wreck the societies in which they occur:—like unto an arrow in the hand of a child. The art of free society consists first in the maintenance of the symbolic code; and secondly in fearlessness of revision, to secure that the code serves those purposes which satisfy an enlightened reason. Those societies which cannot combine reverence to their symbols with freedom of revision, must ultimately decay either from anarchy, or from the slow atrophy of a life stifled by useless shadows.[4]

[4] Whitehead, *Symbolism: Its Meaning and Effect*, p. 88.

Constitutional History and the Higher Law ⟡ HENRY STEELE COMMAGER

"SHOULD an act of parliament be against any of his natural laws, which are immutably true, their declaration would be contrary to eternal truth, equity and justice, and consequently void." [1] . . . "There are eternal principles of justice which no government has a right to disregard. . . . Some acts, although not expressly forbidden, may be against the plain and obvious dictates of reason." [2] . . . "It is conceded . . . that there are certain limitations upon this power, not prescribed in express terms by any constitutional provision, but inherent in the subject itself, which attend its exercise under all circumstances and which are as inflexible and absolute in their restraints as if directly imposed in the most positive of words." [3] . . . "It is true that no one has a vested right in any particular rule of common law, but it is also true that the legislative power of a state can only be exerted in subordination to the fundamental principles of right and justice which the guaranty of due process in the Fourteenth Amendment is intended to preserve." [4]

Here are four *obiter dicta*. The first is from James Otis's famous argument against parliamentary tyranny in 1764, the second from Justice Green's opinion in the Tennessee bank case of 1831, the third from the great Cooley's ruling on the nature of a public purpose in 1870, the fourth from Chief Justice Taft's defense of the use of the injunction in labor disputes in 1921. Approximately half a century separates each of these four dicta; the philosophy, even the language, is the same. Nor would it be difficult to discover similar expressions of juristic philosophy for every decade of our history; [5] such an exercise is scarcely necessary to emphasize what

[1] James Otis, *Rights of the British Colonies Asserted and Proved*, p. 70.
[2] Bank of State v. Cooper, 2 Yerg. (Tenn.) 599.
[3] People v. Salem, 20 Mich. 452.
[4] Truax v. Corrigan, 257 U.S. 312.
[5] Writing in 1894 Judge Dillon pointed out that "Rules regulating civil conduct may . . . be imported by the tribunals, when necessary for the purposes of actual de-

these brief excerpts illustrate, that is the persistence of the doctrine of the higher law—a persistence all the more remarkable in that the philosophy which justifies it has been repudiated now for three-quarters of a century.[6]

It is as dangerous, perhaps, and as gratuitous, for the historian to suggest a definition of the higher law as for the courts to attempt a definition of due process or the police power, and we would have irreproachable precedent for evading the task. Yet we may submit a characterization. We may suggest that higher law is that body of law which is grounded in the nature of man and finds its inspiration and derives its authority from *a priori* or intuitive rather than experimental facts. Such a law was natural, inevitable indeed, in the eighteenth century. It fitted a universe ruled, it might be supposed, by reason, and susceptible to understanding. It was the logical expression of the philosophy of the Enlightenment, and served well as the Constitution for the heavenly city of the eighteenth-century philosophers.[7] It is superfluous here to observe, what has been observed so often and so learnedly, that it served, too, the purpose of Americans in their struggle with the mother country

cisions of causes, from the field of morality. Such rules, however, become invested with the quality of law only when and to the extent that the judges authenticate or adopt, or set upon them the *imprimatur* of the State,—that is, recognize and enforce them by their judgments. . . . It is a mistake to suppose that this process has ceased. In consequence of modern inventions, aggregations of capital, and changed social conditions, I am inclined to think that at no previous period has this method of legal growth and change been in more constant and active operation than at the present time." John F. Dillon, *The Laws and Jurisprudence of England and America* (Boston, 1894), p. 5. For examples and discussion of higher law pronouncements from state and federal bench, see C. G. Haines, *Revival of Natural Law Concepts* (Cambridge, 1930), and *The American Doctrine of Judicial Review* (New York, 1914); Benjamin F. Wright, *American Interpretations of Natural Law* (Cambridge, 1931); J. R. Commons, *Legal Foundations of Capitalism* (New York, 1924); John Dickinson, *Administrative Justice and the Supremacy of the Law in the United States* (Cambridge, 1927); Edouard Lambert, *Le Gouvernement des juges et la lutte contre la législation sociale aux États-Unis* (Paris, 1921); Louis Boudin, *Government by Judiciary*, 2 vols. (New York, 1932); E. S. Corwin, "A Basic Doctrine of American Constitutional Law," *Michigan Law Review*, XII, 247, and "The Doctrine of Due Process of Law before the Civil War," *Harvard Law Review*, XXIV, 366, 460; John Dickinson, "The Law behind the Law," *Columbia Law Review*, XXIX, 113; C. G. Haines, "Implied Limitations on Legislatures," *Texas Law Review*, II, 269; and "Law of Nature in State and Federal Decisions," *Yale Law Journal*, XXV, 617; and Louis Boudin, "Anarchic Element in the Notion of a Higher Law," *New York University Law Quarterly*, VIII, 1.

6 "To defend a doctrine of natural rights today requires either insensibility to the world's progress or else considerable courage in the face of it." Morris Cohen, "Jus Naturale Redivivum," *Philosophical Review*, XXV, 761.

7 See Carl Becker's masterly *Heavenly City of the Eighteenth Century Philosophers* (New Haven, 1932).

and in their effort to construct a political system grounded on reason [8]—superfluous to recall Jefferson's appeal in the Declaration to self-evident truths and to the laws of Nature and Nature's God, or John Adams's faith in rights "rooted in the constitution of the intellectual and moral world," or the youthful Hamilton's joyous assurance that "the sacred rights of mankind are . . . written as with a sunbeam in the whole volume of human nature, by the hand of Divinity itself, and can never be erased or obscured by mortal power." [9]

This concept of law, which was to Americans the common sense of the matter, implied if it did not implacably require that law was a science, that it followed a fixed and regular course, that it was the same yesterday, today, and forever. The principles of law were like the axioms of Euclid, nor did they appeal with any less compelling force to the understanding of right-minded men. This attitude toward law, like the concept of higher law itself, is a tenacious one. It persists today in what Dean Pound has called mechanical jurisprudence,[10] Professor Cohen the phonographic theory of the law; [11] it persists in the decisions of the courts and the lucubrations of the bar,[12] and few things are more suggestive than the

---

[8] See especially C. F. Mullett, *Fundamental Law and the American Revolution* (New York, 1933); B. F. Wright, *op. cit.;* R. G. Adams, *Political Ideas of the American Revolution* (Durham, 1912); A. C. McLaughlin, *Courts, Constitutions and Parties,* Ch. 1 (Chicago, 1912).

[9] Quoted in C. E. Merriam, *American Political Theories,* p. 48.

[10] Pound, "Mechanical Jurisprudence," *Columbia Law Review,* VIII, 605. The great John Austin referred to "the childish fiction employed by our judges that judiciary or common law is not made by them, but is a miraculous something made by nobody, existing, I suppose, from eternity and merely declared from time to time by the judges." *Lectures on Jurisprudence* (4th ed.), p. 655.

[11] Morris R. Cohen, "Legal Theories and Social Science," New York State Bar Association, *Proceedings,* XXXVIII, 177.

[12] "The judges make no laws, they establish no policy, they never enter into the domain of public action. They do not govern." Justice Brewer, in *The Movement of Coercion* (1893), quoted in Dickinson, "Law behind the Law," *Columbia Law Review,* XXIX, 113, 115; and in South Carolina v. U.S., 199 U.S. 437 at 448. Justice Brewer said, "The Constitution is a written instrument. As such its meaning does not alter. That which it meant when adopted it means now." "Any intimation that the Constitution is flexible, even in response to the police power, is unsound. . . . That a state may not impair the obligations of a contract or that a person can not be deprived of his property without due process of law, are principles fundamental, and if the Legislature, in response to public clamor for an experimental social reform, may break down these constitutional guaranties . . . all guaranties of the Constitution . . . may be exchanged, modified, or totally eliminated." Judge Van Orsdel, in Adkins v. Children's Hospital, quoted in Boudin, *Government by Judiciary,* II, 551. "The provisions of the Constitution seem so direct and definite as to need no reinforcing words and to leave no other inquiry than, Does the statute under review come within their prohibition? . . . By

cavalier and even contemptuous manner in which masterly analysis of this phonographic theory was dismissed by members of the Bar Association of New York.[13] We have here to recognize what Justice Holmes called the illusion of certainty,[14] and that it is an essential part of the concept of natural law.

Americans, having discovered the usefulness of natural law, elaborated it, and having justified its application by success, protected that success by transforming natural into constitutional law: the state and federal constitutions. And in so far as natural law had found refuge in written law, there was little reason to invoke it; it was automatically invoked whenever the constitution was invoked, and this was the logic of Marshall in the Marbury case.[15] There were, to be sure, occasions when judges of state and federal courts found it desirable to suggest natural law limitations distinct from and superior to even written constitutions,[16] but the impressive thing is the paucity of such occasions in the first half century of our history.[17]

Not indeed until the rise of transcendentalism in the 1840s did the doctrine of the higher law become again significant, and then it was applied more realistically, more radically, and more honestly,

---

the Fifth Amendment no person can be deprived of property without due process of law. The prohibitions need no strengthening comment. They are as absolute as axioms." Dissenting opinion of Justice McKenna, in Block v. Hirsh, 256 U.S. 135. And as recently as 1937, we may read, "It is urged that the question involved should now receive fresh consideration . . . because of the 'economic conditions which have supervened,' but the meaning of the Constitution does not change with the ebb and flow of economic events." Justice Sutherland, in West Coast Hotel Co. v. Parrish, 75th Cong. 1st Sess. Sen. Doc. No. 46, p. 10.

[13] See discussion of Professor Cohen's address, in *Proceedings* New York State Bar Association, XXXVIII, 177.

[14] "Perhaps one of the reasons why judges do not like to discuss questions of policy, or to put decisions in terms upon their views as lawmakers, is that the moment you leave the path of merely logical deduction you lose the illusion of certainty which makes legal reasoning seem like mathematics. But the certainty is only an illusion nevertheless." *Collected Legal Papers*, p. 126. See also "The Path of the Law," *ibid.*, p. 167, and W. N. Hohfeld, "Fundamental Legal Conceptions as Applied to Judicial Reasoning," *Yale Law Journal*, XXVI, 711.

[15] 1 Cranch 137.

[16] See, for example, the early case of Calder v. Bull, 3 Dallas 386 and the much later case of Wynehamer v. The People, 13 N.Y. 378, and other cases discussed in E. S. Corwin, "Doctrine of Due Process before the Civil War," *Harvard Law Review*, XXIV, 366, and "Extension of Judicial Review in New York State, 1783–1905," *Michigan Law Review*, XV, 281, and Rosenthal, "Massachusetts Acts and Resolves Declared Unconstitutional by the Supreme Court of Massachusetts," *Massachusetts Law Quarterly*, I, 301.

[17] Corwin, Haines, and Wright are all agreed on this point.

than at any other time in our history.[18] Judges such as Marshall, Chase, Story, or Kent, and their successors, were always under compulsion to circumscribe their interpretation of the higher law by written constitutions, precedents, and juridical philosophy; this left some room for intuition, but only in limited fields. Emerson, Channing, Parker, Sumner, Phillips, and Garrison were embarrassed by no such considerations. They recognized readily enough that the higher law was intuitive, recognized it even where they made concessions to the skepticism of men by substantiating facts of intuition with facts of experimental observation. And they applied the higher law not only to the institution of slavery—the most familiar application—but to all human institutions: church, state, property, the family, and not the least of these was property.[19] They challenged society to show, before the bar of reason, its title to the accepted order of things.[20]

It was not difficult for philosophers to do this, only courageous, for consistency demanded the philosophical conclusion but did not require its practical application. Men breathed still the intellectual atmosphere of the Enlightenment, lived in a universe guided by reason and guarded by a beneficent providence, cherished faith in virtue and in the ultimate authority of justice and morality. The appeal to the higher law was valid; it was inevitable. And it was made on behalf of human rights rather than of property rights.

It was, to be sure, a matter of emphasis. The Revolutionary Fathers had invoked the higher law on behalf of life and liberty as well as of property, but did not assume or even suspect the existence of any conflict; the transcendentalists discovered a basic conflict between liberty and property, and invoked the higher law on behalf of the former.[21] Justice Shaw had already defined the police

---

[18] H. S. Commager, *Theodore Parker* (Boston, 1936), *passim*.

[19] See, for example, Parker's sermons on "The Mercantile Classes," "The Perishing Classes," "The Dangerous Classes," and "The Moral Dangers Incident to Prosperity," in *Works* (Centenary ed.), Vol. X.

[20] Emerson's "New England Reformers" is still the best account of this.

[21] See for example Parker's sermon on "The Function of Conscience in Relation to the Laws of Men," *Works*, Vol. XI: "The law of God has eminent domain everywhere, over the private passions of Oliver and Charles, the special interests of Carthage and Rome, over all official business, all precedents, all human statutes, over all the conventional affairs of one man or of mankind. My own conscience is to declare that law to me, yours to you, and is before all private passions or public interests, the decision of majorities and a world full of precedents." For a fuller discussion, see Commager, *op. cit.*, Ch. X, "Slavery and the Higher Law."

power,[22] but the possibilities of the police power for the regulation
or even destruction of property devoted to antisocial or immoral
uses was not apprehended. So transcendentalism, instead of formulating a socio-legal philosophy which would have permitted the
state, in the exercise of its police power, to strike down slavery,
intemperance, immorality, and the inequitable accumulation of
wealth, encouraged instead a highly individualistic and personal
repudiation of evil. It was a natural attitude, for transcendentalism
is necessarily individualistic, but the failure of the transcendental
reformers to socialize their conscience or to develop a legal instrument with which to implement their higher law concepts was significant. Had they been able to formulate a rationale for the identification of the individual conscience with the social conscience,
had they been able, in short, to socialize the higher law, it is probable that much of the later conflict between due process and police
power would have been avoided. It is probable, indeed, that the
courts might have been forced to recognize the consonance of higher
law and police power instead of arraying the two in opposition.

The world of reason, the universe of law, was shattered by the
doctrine of evolution; the kingdom of law gave way to the principalities of laws, the law of nature to the laws of men. Transcendentalism was abandoned for experimentalism, idealism for prag-
matism. Science, theology, politics, education, economics even, all
accommodated themselves to the new philosophy, all recognized
the evolutionary and pragmatic character of their data. Yet the
doctrine of natural law, repudiated in all the sciences and in most
of the social sciences, found refuge in jurisprudence, or, at least, in
the courts. It found not only refuge here, it found implementation.

This, the third chapter in the history of the higher law in America, begins properly with the due process clause of the Fourteenth
Amendment. That clause was not a new one in our Constitution,
but it was new as a limitation upon states, and the meaning which
was read into it was new. That property rights constituted one of
the sacred trinity of natural rights was not a discovery of either
Justice Field or Justice Brewer; the fact had been observed by the
Fathers and adumbrated by the courts on numerous occasions. It
was the singular achievement of the courts in the last half century
to broaden immensely the concept of property, to read property

[22] Commonwealth v. Alger, 7 Cushing 53 (Massachusetts Reports).

into the concept of liberty, and to apply extra-constitutional guarantees to both by interpreting due process as an implied limitation upon legislative action.[23]

This is a thrice-told tale. But what must be emphasized is that the court, in interpreting due process, police power, property, liberty, reasonable, fair return, public interest, public purpose, and so forth, has been engaged not only in legislation but in superlegislation.[24] The function of the courts, in importing higher law doctrine into the Constitution, has been constitutional rather than legislative merely, and it may be said that since the 1880s the Supreme Court has sat as a continuous constitutional convention. For the laws which the Court has formulated are in very fact higher laws. They have not only legislative but constitutional validity. They are not subject to repeal, except through the most laborious and uncertain process, by ordinary political action.[25]

What we have to consider, then, is a body of legislation and of constitutional provisions formulated by the courts with the particular purpose of protecting property against legislative restrictions or exactions. It would be superfluous to recall particular examples of such higher law legislation; it may be suggested that wherever the due process clause has been given substantive rather than merely procedural significance, and wherever police power has been challenged to show its credentials, such judicial legislation has occurred.[26] It may be suggested more specifically that every attempt by the judiciary to discover what property is clothed with

[23] Haines, *Revival of Natural Law Concepts.* See also Ray Brown, "Due Process, Police Power, and the Supreme Court," *Harvard Law Review,* XL, 943.

[24] "The chief law-makers in our country may be and often are, the judges, because they are the final seat of authority. Every time they interpret contract, property, vested rights, due process, liberty, they necessarily enact into law parts of a system of social philosophy; and since such interpretation is fundamental, they give direction to all law-making." Theodore Roosevelt, Message to Congress, Dec. 8, 1908. "The Court in addition to the proper use of its judicial function has improperly set itself up as a third House of the Congress—a superlegislature, as one of the Justices has called it. . . ." F. D. Roosevelt, Address on Reorganization of the Federal Judiciary, March 9, 1937. "Denying that they are applying anything but the express terms of written constitutions the justices of higher courts in the United States have in effect created a superconstitution, a superior law which in certain respects is regarded as unchangeable by the people themselves." Haines, *Revival of Natural Law Concepts,* p. 227.

[25] The failure of President Roosevelt's effort to reform the federal judiciary in 1937 is evidence enough on this point.

[26] Note Judge Story's reference to the due process clause of the Fifth Amendment: "This clause in effect affirms the right of trial according to the process and proceedings of the common law." *Commentaries on the Constitution,* sec. 1789. The literature on this subject is immense. See especially, R. L. Mott, *Due Process of Law: an Historical*

a public interest,[27] what action constitutes a public purpose,[28] what occupations or what conditions are of a nature to justify state regulation,[29] what constitutes liberty in the economic order,[30] and what may be a reasonable and what a confiscatory return on investment,[31] is higher law legislation.

And this judicial higher law, like all higher law, is intuitive and transcendental; Dean Pound characterized it more bluntly as "purely personal and arbitrary." [32] For, as Professor Corwin has

---

and *Analytical Treatise* (Indianapolis, 1926); L. P. McGehee, *Due Process of Law under the Federal Constitution* (Northport, Long Island, 1906); E. Freund, *The Police Power, Public Policy, and Constitutional Rights* (Chicago, 1904); C. E. Hughes, *The Supreme Court of the United States* (New York, 1928); H. E. Willis, "Due Process of Law under the U.S. Constitution," *University of Pennsylvania Law Review*, LXX, 331; C. M. Hough, "Due Process of Law—Today," *Harvard Law Review*, XXXII, 218.

[27] Munn v. Illinois, 94 U.S. 113. But see Taft's opinion in Wolff Packing Co. v. Kansas Court of Industrial Relations, 262 U.S. 522, Holmes's dissent in Tyson v. Banton, 273 U.S. 418, Brandeis's dissent in New State Ice Company v. Liebmann, 285 U.S. 262, and the admirable discussion in W. Hamilton, "Affectation with a Public Interest," *Yale Law Journal*, XXXIX, 1104.

[28] By 1880 the courts had arrived at the position, announced by Judge Cooley in his *Constitutional Limitations*, that it is for the courts to determine what is a public purpose. The leading case is Loan Association v. Topeka, 20 Wallace 655. But note Judge Clifford's dissent, and the modification of the doctrine in Green v. Frazier, 253 U.S. 233. "A careful reading of the numerous cases in which this doctrine has been announced impels the conclusion that none of them progressed very far in the direction of finding constitutional basis for the doctrine either in express provisions or reasonable implication." McBain, "Taxation for a Private Purpose," *Political Science Quarterly*, XXIX, 185. See also illuminating study of the subject in F. Goodnow, *Social Reform and the Constitution*, Ch. 7.

[29] The cases are too numerous to list, but see *in re* Jacobs, 98 New York 98; Holden v. Hardy, 169 U.S. 366; Lochner v. New York, 198 U.S. 45; Adkins v. Children's Hospital, 261 U.S. 525; and any wage or hour or factory law cases.

[30] See Pound, "Liberty of Contract," *Yale Law Journal*, XXIII, 472. Most important labor cases involve a consideration of the nature and meaning of "liberty" in the Fourteenth Amendment. H. R. Seager, "Attitude of American Courts toward Restrictive Labor Legislation," *Political Science Quarterly*, XIX, 589; T. R. Powell, "The Judiciality of Minimum Wage Legislation," *Harvard Law Review*, XXXIX, 545.

[31] In Munn v. Illinois this question was resigned to the legislative branch, but by the end of the following decade the Court had beat a retreat from this dangerous position, and the requirement of judicial review, e. g., judicial determination, was clear by 1889. Chicago, Milwaukee and St. Paul R.R. Co., v. Minnesota, 134 U.S. 418. See H. Hull, "Reasonable Rates," *Michigan Law Review*, XV, 478; R. Brown, "Due Process of Law, Police Power and the Supreme Court," *Harvard Law Review*, XL, 943; and D. Richberg, "Value—by Judicial Fiat," *Harvard Law Review*, XL, 567.

[32] "Common Law and Legislation," *Harvard Law Review*, XXI, 383, at 393. John Dickinson has put it well: "The body of considerations which chance to operate on a judge or court at the moment of bringing a new rule of law into existence may properly be regarded as the determining factor in the creation of law. The theory of the 'higher law' . . . is nothing but a persistent assumption that these considerations must themselves take the form of, or at least be conceived as constituting, jural law." "The Law behind the Law," *Columbia Law Review*, XXIX, 307.

recently observed, "in relation to constitutional law . . . the constitutional document has become hardly more than a formal point of reference. For most of the Court's excursions in the constitutional sphere the constitutional document is little more than a taking-off ground; the journey out and back occurs in a far different medium of selected precedents, speculative views regarding the nature of the Constitution and the purposes designed to be served by it, and unstated judicial preferences." [33]

These views and preferences are conditioned, to be sure, by precedents, but the choice of precedents is almost limitless,[34] and recent decisions and dissents have revealed that judges rarely find themselves embarrassed by the absence of precedents that appear controlling on either side of an issue.[35] The question, indeed, is not one of precedents, but of the choice of precedents, and what conditions this choice is what Mr. Holmes has called the "inarticulate major premise." [36] Whenever the court is called upon to determine whether mining is a hazardous occupation,[37] whether labor in a bakeshop is fatiguing,[38] whether warehouses,[39] slaughterhouses,[40] insurance,[41] banks,[42] ice plants,[43] employment agencies,[44] theaters,[45] are businesses clothed with a public interest, whether women are physiologically different from men,[46] whether the decision of a

[33] "Standpoint in Constitutional Law," *Boston University Law Review*, XVII, 513.

[34] There is an illuminating discussion of this in E. C. Corwin, *Twilight of the Supreme Court* (New Haven, 1934), Ch. 3.

[35] Many of the New Deal decisions have taken the form of elaborate debates between liberal and conservative members of the Court. Note Justice Harlan's frank statement in Monongahela Bridge Co. v. U.S., 216 U.S. 177, at 195: "The courts have rarely, if ever, felt themselves so restrained by technical rules that they could not find some remedy consistent with the law, for acts . . . that violated natural justice or were hostile to the fundamental principles devised for the protection of the essential rights of property."

[36] Lochner v. New York, 198 U.S. 45, at 74. See also "The Path of the Law," *Collected Legal Papers*, p. 167. "I think that the judges themselves have failed adequately to recognize their duty of weighing considerations of social advantage. The duty is inevitable, and the result of the often proclaimed judicial aversion to deal with such considerations is simply to leave the very ground and foundation of judgments inarticulate, and often unconscious."

[37] Holden v. Hardy, 106 U.S. 366.   [38] Lochner v. New York, 198 U.S. 45.

[39] Munn v. Illinois, 94 U.S. 113.   [40] Slaughter House Cases, 16 Wallace 36.

[41] German Alliance Insurance Co. v. Lewis, 233 U.S. 389.

[42] Noble State Bank v. Haskell, 219 U.S. 110.

[43] New State Ice Co. v. Liebmann, 285 U.S. 262.

[44] Adams v. Tanner, 244 U.S. 590 and Ribnik v. McBride, 277 U.S. 350.

[45] Tyson v. Banton, 273 U.S. 418.

[46] Muller v. Oregon, 208 U.S. 412 and Adkins v. Children's Hospital, 261 U.S. 525.

commission conforms to due process,[47] whether a minimum wage [48] or a limitation upon hours [49] or a prohibition of a yellow-dog contract [50] constitutes deprivation of property without due process, whether education,[51] or the distribution of seed,[52] or the amelioration of the lot of the blind [53] are public purposes—whenever the Court is called upon to decide any of these questions, it makes a choice of precedents and invokes the higher law to validate the choice.

The character of that choice becomes more apparent if we note some of the alternatives among which the Court has chosen. Why, for example, has the Court permitted a liberal interpretation of due process where state control over personal rights was at stake, but insisted upon a narrow and traditional interpretation where regulation of property was involved? [54] Why has the Court chosen to read a broad interpretation into the word property, but a narrow interpretation into the phrase property clothed with a public in-

---

[47] C. M. and St. P.R.R. Co. v. Minn., 134 U.S. 418, and Smyth v. Ames, 169 U.S. 466.

[48] Adkins v. Children's Hospital, 261 U.S. 525: Morehead v. N.Y. ex. rel. Tipaldo, 298 U.S. 587; West Coast Hotel Co. v. Parrish (March 29, 1937), U.S. 75th Cong. 1 Sess. Sen. Doc. No. 46.

[49] Bunting v. Oregon, 243 U.S. 426, and *supra*, note 37, 38.

[50] Hitchman Coal and Coke Co. v. Mitchell, 245 U.S. 229.

[51] The Supreme Court of Missouri invalidated a law providing for progressive inheritance tax for purposes of scholarships at the State University. "Paternalism," said the Court, "is an assumption by the government of a quasi-fatherly relation to the citizen and his family, involving excessive governmental regulation of the private affairs and business methods and interests of the people . . . and is pernicious in its tendencies. . . . Paternalism is a plant which should receive no nourishment upon the soil of Missouri." State v. Switzler, 143 Missouri 287.

[52] State v. Osawkee Township, 14 Kansas 418, invalidating a state law providing for the free distribution of seed to farmers.

[53] Lucas Co. v. State, 75 Ohio 114, invalidating a county ordinance providing for allowances to indigent blind. "If the power of the legislature to confer an annuity upon any class of needy citizens is admitted upon the ground that its tendency will be to prevent them from becoming a public charge," said the court, "innumerable cases may clamor for similar bounties, . . . and it is doubted that any line could be drawn short of an equal distribution of property."

[54] See for example Spies v. Illinois, 123 U.S. 131, Brooks v. Missouri, 124 U.S. 394, and, above all, Hurtado v. Calif., 110 U.S. 516. In his dissent in Maxwell v. Dow, Justice Harlan said, "If due process of law, required by the Fourteenth Amendment, does not allow a state to take private property without just compensation, but does allow the life and liberty of the citizen to be taken in a mode that is repugnant to the settled usages and modes of proceeding authorized at the time the constitution was adopted . . . it would seem that the protection of private property is of more consequence than the protection of the life and liberty of the citizen." 176 U.S. 581, at 614. And Holmes, in his dissent in the Frank case, expressed the same idea even more bluntly: "We see no reason for a less liberal rule in a matter of life and death." Frank v. Magnum, 237 U.S. 309. See also J. R. Commons, *Legal Foundations of Capitalism*, pp. 341 ff.

terest? [55] Why has it seen fit to sustain uniformity of railroad rates in intrastate as well as interstate commerce as a proper instrument for regulation,[56] but rejected protection of the right of railway labor to organize as an improper extension of the commerce power? [57] Why has it recognized the concept of public purpose and public interest with reference to the advantageous exploitation of natural resources,[58] but not with respect to the advantageous conservation of human resources? [59] Why has it imported the rule of reason into the Sherman Act with respect to industry [60] but ignored it with reference to labor? [61] The questions could be multiplied almost indefinitely, but these will suffice for illustration. In no instance was the answer inescapably determined by the words of the Constitution and by precedents. In every instance the answer was given on the basis of considerations of higher law imported into the Constitution by the judges themselves.

We come here, at long last, to the business of the constitutional historian. In so far as our constitutional history, especially since the Fourteenth Amendment, is judicial legislation inspired by higher law, his business is to trace that legislation and analyze that law. The historian certainly cannot be content with recording the conclusions of the Court, as if they were self-explanatory. Conclusions may be sufficient for the professional lawyer and are—if we may trust the casebooks—sufficient for constitutional law, but the historian can no more read constitutional history through decisions

[55] The best analysis of the relation of the judiciary to the protection of property is to be found in R. Ely's masterly *Property and Contract in Their Relation to the Distribution of Wealth,* 2 vols. (New York, 1914). Commons, *Legal Foundations of Capitalism,* and Goodnow, *Social Reform and the Constitution,* are scarcely less valuable. See also, A. T. Hadley, "The Constitutional Position of Property in America," *The Independent,* April 18, 1908; J. Orton, "Confusion of Property with Privilege," *Independent,* Aug. 19 and Aug. 26, 1909; and Kales, "Due Process, the Inarticulate Major Premise, and the Adamson Act," *Yale Law Journal,* XXVI, 519.

[56] R.R. Commission of Wisconsin v. C.B. & Q. R.R. Co., 257 U.S. 563.

[57] Adair v. U.S., 208 U.S. 161.

[58] See the thoughtful remarks in Goodnow, *Social Reform and the Constitution,* pp. 325 ff., and citations.

[59] It is unnecessary here to recapitulate the long history of judicial review of wage and hour, tenement house and factory inspection and compensation legislation. Ives v. South Buffalo, 201 N.Y. 271 and Adkins v. Children's Hospital, 261 U.S. 525, are typical.

[60] Standard Oil Co. of N.J. v. U.S., 221 U.S. 1.

[61] I imply that a "rule of reason" for labor would have resulted in a different decision in Duplex Printing Press Co. v. Deering, 254 U.S. 443, and in Bedford Cut Stone Co. v. Journeymen Stonecutters, 274 U.S. 37, both involving some phase of the secondary boycott.

than he can read political history through statutes. He is required to discover the philosophical and temperamental bases of judicial legislation, required, particularly, to discover the nature of the higher-law concepts which control so many of the more important decisions.

We live under governments whose limits are set by courts,[62] and with reference to intuitive ideas that find expression in the slippery phrases of due process, police power, liberty, public purpose, and so forth. Nor are these limits negative merely; the application of limitations is a positive act. Yet we lack appreciation of the nature of these intuitive concepts, and we lack a codification of legislation inspired by them. We confess that the judiciary is a constitutional convention, but we have not inquired into its membership, credentials, purposes, or achievements; we confess that it is a legislative chamber, but we do not know what laws it has made. We have not even analyzed the psychology of popular acquiescence in the higher law, though it constitutes obviously a basic paradox in our political system. How does it happen that democracy not only tolerates but encourages the application by courts of higher law restrictions upon itself? Hamilton, who approved of judicial review, pointed out that abuse of this power, if it ever occurred, would be speedily rebuked by impeachment; [63] how does it happen that the sanction of impeachment, as a weapon of democracy, has never been effectively invoked to restrain judicial abuse of power? An elective rather than an appointive judiciary held promise of articulating the courts to democracy; can it be shown that elective judges have been less eager to apply higher law limitations upon democratic processes than have appointive judges? [64]

[62] "We are governed by our judges and not by our legislatures. . . . It is our judges who formulate our public policies and our basic laws." Bruce, *The American Judge* (New York, 1924), pp. 6, 8. On judicial government, see also Brooks Adams, *The Theory of Social Revolutions* (New York, 1914), Cardozo, *Nature of the Judicial Process* (New Haven, 1921), Holmes, *The Common Law*, pp. 34 ff.

[63] *The Federalist*, No. 81. "It may in the last place be observed that the supposed danger of judiciary encroachments on the legislative authority, . . . is in reality a phantom. Particular misconstructions and contraventions of the will of the legislature may now and then happen; but they can never be so extensive as to amount to an inconvenience, or in any sensible degree to affect the order of the political system. . . . And the inference is greatly fortified by the consideration of the important constitutional check which the power of instituting impeachments in one part of the legislative body and of determining them in another, would give to that body upon the members of the judicial department. This is alone a complete security. . . ."

[64] Dean Frank Sommer of the New York University School of Law has investigated

The fact is that a certain divinity has hedged the Court and its cabalistic oracles, until it has come to seem almost blasphemous for historians to suggest that the Court is a political institution or that jurisprudence is sociological, though deans of law schools may, apparently, make these observations with impunity.[65] The historian has no hesitation in investigating the mechanism of the legislative or executive departments or the history of tariff or land or banking legislation, but he has avoided a realistic consideration of the mechanism of the judiciary or the history of judicial legislation. He abandons Plutarch and embraces Boswell or even Strachey as a model for political biography, but he has scarcely attempted to write biographies of judges, and when he does he dons his most somber robes.[66] He assumes cheerfully enough the rôle of social or economic or intellectual historian where the executive or legislative departments are concerned, but does not willingly confess the same technique applicable to the study of courts.

Yet the character of the modern higher law, subjective as it is, is no more elusive than the character of Jeffersonian democracy or Manifest Destiny or other concepts which the historian has managed to pin down and survey. Certainly it is subject to investigation and susceptible to interpretation. We cannot discover with finality just how and why the Court imported into the Constitution higher-law doctrines of laissez-faire capitalism, any more than we can discover with finality just how American business embraced Spencerian philosophy. But we can achieve an awareness of the fact and we can perhaps illuminate the process.

"The very considerations which judges so rarely mention," said Justice Holmes, in his memorable study of the common law, "and always with an apology, are the secret roots from which the law draws all the juices of life. I mean, of course, considerations of what is expedient to the community concerned. Every important principle which is developed by litigation is in fact and at bottom the

---

this subject and concludes that elective judges are, on the whole, no more responsive to democratic opinion than are appointive judges.

65 Pound, "Scope and Purpose of Sociological Jurisprudence," *Harvard Law Review,* XXIV, 591; XXV, 140, 489. See also his *Law and Morals* (Chapel Hill, 1926) and *Interpretations of Legal History* (New York, 1923).

66 See, for example, the reverent approach of Beveridge in his biography of *Marshall* or of Trimble in his recent *Waite.* Only Silas Bent, *Justice Oliver Wendell Holmes* (New York, 1932) and Mason, *Brandeis and the Modern State* (Princeton, 1933) escape the taint.

result of more or less definitely understood views of public policy; most generally, to be sure, under our practice and traditions, the unconscious result of instinctive preferences and inarticulate convictions, but none the less traceable to views of public policy in the last analysis." [67] What Judge Holmes had in mind was in part, and only in part, the intellectual climate in which judges lived and wrote. Thus it is easy to discover the judicial reaction to the philosophy of laissez faire, easy to remark, as Holmes himself remarked in the most hackneyed of his asides, that judges wrote into the Constitution Herbert Spencer's *Social Statics*.[68] We need not subscribe to Mr. Dooley's conclusion that the Supreme Court follows the election returns in order to appreciate the fact that courts cannot be insensitive to public opinion or fail to reflect it; [69] a comparison of the New York [70] and the Washington minimum-wage decisions,[71] the Schechter [72] and the Jones and Laughlin [73] cases, illuminates this generalization. Nor is it an original observation that judicial opinions are often political as well as constitutional. We know that *Marbury* v. *Madison* was concerned with something more than the right of Marbury to his job,[74] that *Cohens* v. *Virginia* squinted toward state rights,[75] that *Scott* v. *Sandford* was designed to allay sectional antipathies,[76] that the Milligan case was a declaration against political radicalism [77] and the Pollock decision was directed against the rising tide of socialism,[78] and we may suspect that recent

[67] *The Common Law*, pp. 35–36. See also, dissenting opinion in Vegelahn v. Guntner, 167 Mass. 92: "The true grounds of decisions are considerations of policy and of social advantage, and it is vain to suppose that solutions can be attained merely by logic and the general propositions of law which nobody disputes," and perspicacious observations in "The Path of the Law," *Collected Legal Papers:* "I think that the judges themselves have failed to recognize their duty of weighing considerations of social advantage. . . . I cannot but believe that if the training of lawyers led them habitually to consider more definitely and explicitly the social advantage on which the rule they lay down must be justified, they sometimes would hesitate where now they are confident, and see that really they were taking sides upon debatable and often burning questions." p. 184.

[68] Lochner v. N.Y., 198 U.S. 45.

[69] See, for comparison, A. V. Dicey, *Lectures on the Relation between Law and Public Opinion in England during the Nineteenth Century* (New York, 1905), esp. pp. 361 ff.

[70] Morehead v. N.Y. ex. rel. Tipaldo, 298 U.S. 587.

[71] West Coast Hotel Co. v. Parrish (March 29, 1937), U.S. 75th Cong. 1st Sess. Sen. Doc. No. 46.

[72] Schechter Poultry Corp. v. U.S., 295 U.S. 495.

[73] National Labor Relations Board v. Jones & Laughlin Steel Corp. (April 12, 1937), U.S. 75th Cong. 1st Sess. Sen. Doc. No. 51.

[74] 1 Cranch 137.   [75] 6 Wheaton 264.   [76] 19 Howard 393.

[77] 4 Wallace 2.   [78] 158 U.S. 601.

decisions on New Deal legislation were not announced in a judicial void nor uninfluenced by the threat of judicial reform.

But it is equally obvious that the intellectual air which judges have breathed is conditioned; every judicial invalidation of a legislative act proves that the air of the court room is not the same as the air of the legislative chamber. It is not sufficient, then, that we discover the explanation for *Chicago, Milwaukee and St. Paul* v. *Minnesota*[79] or *Smythe* v. *Ames*[80] or *in re Jacobs*[81] or *Lochner* v. *New York*[82] or *People* v. *Williams*[83] or *Adair* v. *United States*[84] or *Ives* v. *South Buffalo*[85] or *Hitchman Coal Co.* v. *Mitchell*[86] or *Hammer* v. *Dagenhart*[87] or *Adkins* v. *Children's Hospital*[88] and scores of similar decisions in general ideas of laissez faire. Legislators who voted affirmatively for the acts invalidated by these decisions were equally exposed to ideas of laissez faire, and rejected them.

The historian has to recognize that in tracing the formulation and application of the higher law he is concerned with a body of philosophy which has been cherished especially by the judiciary. For, as Dean Pound has observed, "We must admit the divergence between legal thought . . . and economic and sociological thought. . . . Hence we have not merely to ask, what is the legal idea of justice? It is of no less moment to know why this idea differs from the economic and sociological idea of justice. We have to ask, why did the legal idea come to be what it is, and why does it so persistently remain such?"[89]

But there is a preliminary observation which must be made if we are to understand why the judicial differs from the political atmosphere, even in a democracy. We must realize that the law, like other faiths, lives by symbols,[90] and that two symbols most passionately cherished are those of reason and of consistency.[91] We demand of

---

[79] 134 U.S. 418.   [80] 169 U.S. 466   [81] 98 N.Y. 98.
[82] 198 U.S. 45.   [83] 189 N.Y. 131.   [84] 208 U.S. 161.
[85] 201 N.Y. 271.   [86] 245 U.S. 229.
[87] 247 U.S. 251.   [88] 261 U.S. 525.
[89] "The End of Law as Developed in Legal Rules and Doctrines," *Harvard Law Review*, XXVII, 195, at 198.
[90] T. Arnold, *Symbols of Government* (New Haven, 1935), esp. pp. 49 ff. and 67 ff.
[91] "The truth is," wrote Holmes, "that the law is always approaching and never reaching consistency. It is forever adopting new principles from life at one end, and it always retains old ones from history at the other. . . . It will become entirely consistent only when it ceases to grow." *Common Law*, p. 36. Arnold has some shrewd comments on the necessity of the appearance of consistency, *Symbols of Government*, p. 49.

law that it should be both philosophy and science, and we call it jurisprudence; [92] we sternly require of judges that they justify their pronouncements upon more than opportunistic grounds. And it follows from this popular image of the law as a science that we demand consistency; it is indeed a common observation that certainty in law is more important than justice.[93]

We expect our judges, then, to be both scientific and consistent, but we do not expect our legislators to be either scientific or consistent, and we have rejected a statesman who tried to be an engineer and have embraced enthusiastically one who avowed the opportunistic policy of the football quarterback.

Now there is nothing either scientific or consistent about the higher law, in actual experience; and the words due process, reasonable, and liberty have no precision. Yet when judges fall back upon the higher law, they appear to be conforming to the ideal of a law of nature, and thus satisfy the demand for reason and consistency in law.[94] Actually judicial higher law, as we have seen, is moral law, and when judges invoke it they speak as the conscience of political society.[95] But moral attitudes are determined, in large part, by intellectual inheritance and environment, and the moral attitudes of judges, as expressed in the higher law, reflect an individual or a professional philosophy of life. "The words of the Constitution," as Professor Frankfurter has recently said, "leave the individual justice free, if they do not compel him, to gather meaning not from reading the Constitution but from reading life. . . . The process of constitutional interpretation compels the translation of policy into judgment, and the controlling conceptions of justices are their 'idealized political picture' of the existing social order. Only the conscious recognition of the nature of this exercise

[92] T. Arnold, "Apologia for Jurisprudence," *Yale Law Journal*, XLIX, 729.

[93] Even Justice Holmes subscribed to this doctrine. See "The Path of the Law," *Collected Legal Papers*.

[94] See T. Arnold, *Symbols of Government*, Ch. 3, "The Mystery of Jurisprudence."

[95] "We must begin by ourselves understanding that the constitutional provisions which are contained in our bill of rights in the state and federal constitutions are moral principles, as weighty in moral authority and as vital to the safety of society as any that have ever been promulgated, not even excepting the golden rule. After that we must teach the people. We must make them understand that constitutional rights are moral rights, and . . . that they must never try any experiments which will imperil those moral rights." *Report* of Special Committee . . . to Consider the Question of an Amendment to the Constitution of the State of New York Empowering the Legislature to Enact a Workmen's Compensation Law, p. 17.

of the judicial process will protect policy from being narrowly construed as the reflex of discredited assumptions or the abstract formulation of unconscious bias." [96]

In the last analysis, then, history, in so far as it takes cognizance of the legislative character of higher law pronouncements, comes back to judicial inheritance and environment, and to judges individually and collectively. Judges are in society, but insulated from it. They are students and scholars, but concerned daily with practical problems of the most complex and urgent nature. They are recruited from and servants of a capitalist economy, but barred from personal participation in that economy. They are part of a democratic political system, but aloof from it. Their function is to pronounce law as immutable justice and to interpret the law as the will of the sovereign. Needless to remark, they cannot meet these contradictory specifications, perform these contradictory functions. But what determines the choices which are made?

We may suggest here a few of the more obvious factors which require consideration: the rôle of the bar, and of arguments of counsel; the nature of professional training; the influence of the great commentators and text-writers; and the character of the judges themselves. We must begin with the bar, rather than the bench, and this not only because our jurists are trained first to professional life, but because the interaction of bar and bench is continuous. Most of our justices have been recruited from the bar; it is not inconceivable that the tendency of the bar, in the last half century, to become an adjunct to corporate business, has had some influence upon the judicial view of economic questions. Nor can we ignore the fact that the psychology of the bar is transferred, imperceptibly, to the bench; that partisanship cannot become impartiality overnight, or alertness to technicalities become sublimated to anxiety for principles.[97]

Mr. Gustavus Myers is the only historian of the Court who has attempted to discover, in a realistic way, the professional training and interests of the members of the highest bench,[98] but even Mr. Myers has failed to appreciate the influence of the bar on the bench

[96] "The Supreme Court," *Encyclopaedia of the Social Sciences* (1937 ed.), VIII, 479–80.

[97] See M. Cohen, "Legal Theories and Social Science," New York State Bar Assoc. *Proceedings*, XXXVIII, 192 ff.

[98] Gustavus Myers, *History of the Supreme Court* (Chicago, 1918).

through arguments of counsel, and historians have largely ignored this factor, until it might be supposed that judicial information was acquired by inspiration.[99] We are reminded, to be sure, of the impassioned appeal of Webster in the Dartmouth case, the eloquent argument of Pinkney in the McCulloch case, the surprising gesture of Conkling in the San Mateo case, the perfervid demagoguery of Choate in the Pollock case, and the famous Brandeis brief in the Muller case, but these exceptional instances have been noted rather for their dramatic qualities than for their constitutional significance. Yet the economic and sociological complexities of modern cases make the Court in large measure dependent upon the facts and briefs presented by counsel.[100] There is, of course, the important reservation that the choice which judges make from opposing briefs will depend in part upon the prepossessions of the judges themselves. Yet it is not quite true, as Mr. Justice Sutherland acrimoniously remarked of the minimum wage legislation, that "the elucidation of that question cannot be aided by counting heads." [101] Quantitative as well as qualitative considerations do weigh with judges, and it is well to recall Mr. Justice Cardozo's recent observation, apropos social security legislation, that "it is too late today for the argument to be heard with tolerance that in a crisis so extreme the use of moneys of the nation to relieve the unemployed . . . is a use for any purpose narrower than the promotion of the general welfare." [102] However much, or little, confidence judges may place in counsel, it remains true that they are dependent upon counsel for facts; when the history of constitutional decisions is written without reference to this source of information, it is written in a vacuum.

Equally important is a consideration of the professional training and equipment of judges. It may be observed, for example, that one explanation for the popularity of the higher law in the early years of the Republic was that no other law was available; lacking collections of cases, precedents, judges were forced to fall back upon

[99] Cardozo, *Nature of the Judicial Process, passim;* E. S. Robinson, *Law and the Lawyers* (New York, 1935); C. A. Beard, "Little Alice Looks at the Constitution," in *Jefferson, Corporations, and the Constitution* (Washington, 1936).

[100] Frankfurter, "Hours of Labor and Realism in Constitutional Law," *Harvard Law Review,* XXIX, 371.

[101] Adkins v. Children's Hospital, 261 U.S. 525.

[102] C. C. Steward Machine Co. v. Davis, 57 Supreme Court Reporter, 883.

their own conceptions of law.[103] The reason has disappeared, but the habit has continued. Or, to look to modern conditions, it is suggestive that deans of law schools and editors of law journals complain with monotonous regularity of the inadequacy of the teaching of constitutional law and history; it is no less significant that until recently, and except in a very few schools, the economic and sociological aspects of jurisprudence have been neglected. For every Brandeis familiar with economics, for every Holmes versed in literature, for every Cardozo learned in philosophy, there are a dozen judges who regard such learning as esoteric if not irrelevant.

Nor has the decisive influence of great expounders of the law upon our constitutional system been appreciated by the historian. The most recent, and best, constitutional history of the United States [104] does not think it necessary to mention Judge Cooley or his constitutional limitations, though the author once edited Cooley's own *Principles of Constitutional Law in the United States.*[105] We lack almost entirely studies of bar associations, law schools, the great teachers and text-writers of the past whose teachings have molded American judicial thought from the days of Wilson and Story and Kent to those of Gray and Thayer, Cooley and Dillon.[106]

Finally, we come to the judges themselves. If law is fixed and immutable, and if the function of judges is *jus dicere* only, and *jus dare* belongs to God,[107] then there is logic in judicial anonymity. But few now subscribe to this phonographic theory of the law, and the opposition to the appointment of Mr. Brandeis or of Mr. Black to the highest court indicates that the rôle of the judges in making law is acknowledged.[108] Yet we know shockingly little about our

[103] When Kent became Chancellor of New York State, in 1814, he was able to say, "For the nine years I was in that office (court of equity) there was not a single decision, opinion, or dictum of either of my predecessors . . . from 1777 to 1814 cited to me or even suggested." Quoted, Pound, "Judge Story and the Making of American Law," *American Law Review*, XLVIII, 676, at 683. See also J. Goebel, "The Courts and the Law in Colonial New York," *History of the State of New York*, Vol. III.

[104] A. C. McLaughlin, *Constitutional History of the United States* (New York, 1935).

[105] *The General Principles of Constitutional Law*, 1880, ed. 1898.

[106] See comments by Pound, *American Law Review*, XLVIII, 676. Three of these teachers are subjects of old-fashioned Memoirs, but there is no critical analysis of the contribution of any one of them.

[107] Otis, *Rights of the British Colonies*, p. 70.

[108] See C. G. Haines, "General Observations on the Effects of Personal, Political and Economic Influences in the Decisions of Judges," *Illinois Law Review*, XVII, 96, and G. Everson, "Human Element in Justice," *Journal of Criminal Law*, X, 98 ff.

judges. Of some four score judges who have sat upon the Supreme Court we have biographies of perhaps a dozen,[109] and acceptable biographies of half that number. If we look to the state courts, the situation is even more scandalous. Kent, Shaw, Gibson, Ruffin, Doe, Cooley, Dillon, Clarke, to mention only some of the more eminent, all want biographies. Nor can it be alleged that those studies vouchsafed us illuminate the rôle of the judges in reading higher law into the Constitution. The parts played by Marshall, Taney, Field, Lamar, Harlan, Brandeis, and Holmes have been, after a fashion, revealed, but constitutional biography, like constitutional history, has evaded the crucial question of the nature of the judicial process and the creation and re-creation of the higher law.

If much of this is obvious, we can find refuge in Justice Holmes's observation that "we need education in the obvious more than investigation of the obscure." [110] I have suggested that the higher law is intuitive, personal law, and that it persists down to the present. Used originally as a substitute for written law, it came to be embodied in written law, but continued an independent existence. In the hands of the mid-century reformers it became a weapon on behalf of human and against property rights, but the individualist approach of the transcendentalists prevented at this time the formulation of a higher-law concept of police power that would command the approval of the courts and commend itself to society. With the Fourteenth Amendment began a new and increasingly important chapter in the history of the higher law. Largely through interpretation of due process, higher law was imported into the Constitution, and generally as a limitation upon legislative control of property. This interpretation, taken collectively, constituted judicial legislation and constitution-making upon subjects of utmost importance; and the character of the new legislative and constitutional provisions was determined by the judicial view of the nature of society, the function of government, the relative importance of personal and property rights, and similar considerations. We can discover, more particularly, the nature of that legislation by an inquiry into those factors which have conditioned it: the symbolic

[109] There are biographies, some excellent, some passable, a few wretched, of Jay, Iredell, Marshall, Story, McLean, Taney, Curtis, Miller, Field, Chase, Waite, Lamar, Holmes, Brandeis, Harlan, Taft, Cardozo. Only those of Jay, Marshall, and Taney can be called definitive.

[110] "Law and the Court," *Collected Legal Papers*, p. 292.

rôle played by judges and courts, public opinion, political considerations, the judicial climate of opinion, the influence of the bar, of
professional training and scholarship, and the character and career
of the judges themselves. When we have achieved a codification of
natural law and an appreciation of the nature of the judicial process, we shall be in a position to record our constitutional history in
more realistic terms.

Constitutional Democracy: a Nineteenth-Century Faith ∾ RALPH HENRY GABRIEL

THE group of anxious men who assembled at Philadelphia in 1787 to frame a constitution for the new United States had almost universally that confidence in human reason which stemmed from Newton's scientific achievements of the century before, and back of that from the triumphs of the classical philosophers. Americans were interested in the individual man. Democracy is the appropriate political expression of the atomistic social emphasis, yet many of the framers had a healthy skepticism of democracy. To some it suggested the triumph of mediocrity, and to others the substitution of the rule of passion for that of reason. But the United States was committed to the principle of democracy by the logic of the Revolution, and, as a consequence, the framers established their government in frank Lockean style upon the consent of the governed. In the framing of their great document they were both rationalists and empiricists. When they were done, they rightly looked upon themselves as initiating a great experiment in popular government.

Fifty years passed. When Americans of the new generation met to celebrate the fiftieth anniversary of their constitution, they remarked that the experimental period had passed. The demonstration of the efficacy of popular sovereignty had been made. Under it the United States had become an important nation. The fears of the fathers concerning democracy had not been justified by later events, and with Andrew Jackson the common man, now skilled in the political art, had come to power.

Americans of the middle period lived in a climate of opinion different from that of the Founding Fathers. Eighteenth-century Deism, charged with causing the excesses of the French Revolution, had long since been driven underground. Tom Paine, returning as an old man to America, had found the doors of respectability closed and had gone to a lonely death. Evangelical Protestantism was covering the nation like a rising tide and reached its apogee in the middle decade of the nineteenth century. The popular symbol of social stability for this generation was not, as in our day, the Constitution of the United States or the Supreme Court, but was rather the village church, whose spire pointed significantly heavenward. "Civilization," remarked Emerson, "depends on morality." And it was the almost universal belief of his generation that morality rests upon religion. But Emerson was disgusted with the anthropomorphism of the conventional Christianity of his day and was dissatisfied with the pale negations of Unitarianism. He announced his transcendentalism in a little book entitled *Nature,* published in 1836, the year before the fiftieth anniversary of the Constitution. Four years later, an inconspicuous citizen, named George Sidney Camp, wrote a small volume which he called *Democracy,* and which Harper and Brothers thought expressed so well the mood of the age that they published it in their Family Library and later brought out a second edition. "Faith," said Camp, "is as necessary to the republican as to the Christian, and the fundamental characteristic of both." [1] "We are born believing," added Emerson. "A man bears beliefs as a tree bears apples." [2] Faith is the clue to the understanding of the democracy of the middle period.

Among these Americans the word "democracy" took on two different but interrelated connotations; it had both a realistic and a romantic meaning. Realistic democracy was a behavior pattern which included caucuses and logrolling, the struggle for office among individuals, and the sparring for advantage among sections or pressure groups. Romantic democracy was a cluster of ideas which made up a national faith and which, though unrecognized as such, had the power of a state religion. Some of these ideas were as old as classical Greece and others were as new as the American nation. But, though most of the ideas were old and were borrowed, the configuration of the cluster was unique.

A secular national religion, such as the communism of Lenin's Russia or the national socialism of contemporary Germany, must meet certain basic psychological needs of the people who profess it. Among a disunited people it must emphasize the group and its solidarity. To a depressed people or to one suffering from a sense of

[1] Quoted in Warfel, Gabriel, and Williams, *The American Mind* (1937), p. 436.
[2] *Works* (Riverside ed., 1883), VI, 195.

inferiority it must give that illusion of superiority which springs from the doctrine that the nation has a great mission to perform in the world. To an anxious people, fearful of the future, a national religion must give a sense of security. In the America of the middle period, unity was a primary problem. Those transportation facilities which bind a nation together could not keep pace with the rapid westward advance of the frontier. Climatic differences had created a social problem which threatened the United States with division along sectional lines. The United States faced the menace of separatism. A lesser mid-nineteenth-century American need was for some defense against a sense of inferiority to Europe. This became acute in the middle period because in that age Americans were sensing their intellectual and their national power at a time when foreign travelers, some of them of the prominence of Dickens, were coming in increasing numbers and were returning to the Old World to write frequently unjust and almost universally offensive books. In such a scene Ralph Waldo Emerson threw off the robes of a Unitarian clergyman. He announced in 1836 the cosmic philosophy upon which his transcendentalism was founded. He proclaimed in 1837 in his famous Phi Beta Kappa address at Harvard College the American declaration of intellectual independence. "We have listened too long to the courtly muses of Europe," he said to the young scholars before him. "We will walk on our own feet; we will work with our own hands; we will speak our own minds." [3] From that day Emerson became the Isaiah of that democratic faith which was at that very moment taking form spontaneously among the American people.

The foundation of this democratic faith was a frank supernaturalism derived from Christianity. The twentieth-century student is often astonished at the extent to which supernaturalism permeated American thought of the nineteenth century. The basic postulate of the democratic faith affirmed that God, the creator of man, has also created a moral law for his government and has endowed him with a conscience with which to apprehend it. Underneath and supporting human society, as the basic rock supports the hills, is a moral order which is the abiding place of the eternal principles of truth and righteousness. The reiteration of this doctrine of the moral order runs through mid-nineteenth-century social and

[3] *Works* (Riverside ed., 1883), I, 113–14.

political thought like the rhythm of the drums through the forest scene of O'Neill's *Emperor Jones*. "There are principles of abstract justice which the creator of all things has impressed on the mind of his creature man," said John Marshall in 1823 in an opinion from the bench, "and which are admitted to regulate, in a great degree, the rights of civilized nations." [4] "In ascending to the great principles upon which all society rests," added Justice Joseph Story in 1828, "it must be admitted that there are some which are of eternal obligation, and arise from our common dependence upon our Creator. Among these are the duty to do justice, to love mercy, and to walk humbly before God." [5] "There is a higher law," proclaimed William Ellery Channing long before Seward's famous speech in the Senate, "even Virtue, Rectitude, the Voice of Conscience, the Will of God." [6] "The moral law," said Emerson in 1836, "lies at the center of nature and radiates to the circumference." [7]

To trace the origin or the history of this doctrine of a higher or fundamental law is not our present task, for to do so would be to examine one of the more important strands of thought in Western civilization. Suffice it to say that in the United States in the middle years of the nineteenth century the existence of a moral order which was not the creation of man but which served as the final guide for his behavior was almost universally assumed among thinking persons. For Christians the moral law was the will of God; for the small company of articulate free thinkers it was the natural law of eighteenth-century Deism. Mr. Justice Story in his *Commentaries on the Constitution* succeeded in phrasing the doctrine in terms which would be acceptable both to those who still found their guide in reason and to those who looked for direction to the Scriptures. "The rights of conscience," said he, "are given by God, and cannot be encroached upon by human authority, without criminal disobedience of the precepts of natural, as well as of revealed, religion." [8] Before the moral law all men stood on a footing of equality; from it they derived equal rights. Among the latter was the right to the private ownership of property.

The universal acceptance of the doctrine of the moral order sug-

---

[4] Johnson and Graham's Lessee v. William M'Intosh & Wheaton, pp. 543, 572.
[5] *Miscellaneous Writings* (1835), p. 74.
[6] *Works* (11th ed.), II, 40.
[7] *Works* (Centenary ed.), I, 41–42.
[8] *Commentaries on the Constitution of the United States* (1876).

gests that it had uses in the culture of the time. American skies were darkened during the middle period by a storm which gathered momentum and increased in intensity with the passing years. The controversy over human slavery put the realistic democracy of American political institutions to the test of the hurricane. Anger mounted on either side, and, long before the final break occurred, passion threatened to replace reason in the councils of the nation. Garrison in the North and Yancey in the South early advocated breaking the ties which bound the sections together. Americans turned to the Constitution as the fundamental law of the land for those common agreements between the contending parties without which debate is impossible. But this instrument appeared to fail them. Instead of resolving the dispute, the Constitution became the very center of controversy as the sections divided on the question of its origin and of its nature. Webster for the North affirmed that the document drawn up at Philadelphia was the supreme law for a nation; Calhoun for the South replied that it was no more than a compact among sovereign states. The positions were at opposite poles and were irreconcilable; yet faith in constitutionalism was not shaken. Even after the final break the Confederacy did not abandon constitutionalism. The event suggests that the American faith in constitutional democracy did not have its ultimate origin in the constitution which established it. Emerson in 1854 sought to explain the paradox. "Whenever a man," said he, "has come to this state of mind, that there is no church for him but his believing prayer, no Constitution but his dealing well and justly with his neighbor; no liberty but his invincible will to do right, then certain aids and allies will promptly appear; for the constitution of the Universe is on his side." [9] The doctrine of the moral order was, in effect, a doctrine of cosmic constitutionalism. The body of natural and of moral law was the fixed and unchangeable constitution of the world. The fundamental law of the Republic was thought to be but a man-made imitation of a divine archetype. When it failed to provide those common agreements necessary to rational debate, recourse must be had to those unwritten and eternal principles which, in the universal belief of Americans, made society possible. Emerson, in appealing to the "constitution of the Universe," was discussing the Fugitive Slave Law to which he was opposed. Southern

[9] *Works* (Centenary ed.), XI, 236.

proponents of the peculiar institution, despairing of the Federal
Constitution, were at the same time founding their defense of slavery upon the same moral law. "Negroes are not free," said George
Fitzhugh, "because God and nature, and the general good, and
their own good, intended them for slaves." [10] The doctrine of the
moral order was here providing those agreements which by functioning as the foundation of logical discussion made it possible for
the democratic process to continue. Because Americans believed
that fixed laws and eternal principles underlay society, they believed in written constitutions. But these, after all, were experiments, as the delegates at Philadelphia had suggested. If constitutions should fail, as the Federal Constitution failed in 1861, they
should be reconstructed, as the Confederates tried to do, in accordance with unfolding human experience and with new light on the
nature of the moral order.

The arguments of Emerson and of Fitzhugh sound strange in our
post-Versailles world in which the prestige of Christianity has declined and naturalistic philosophies have captured the social dis-
ciplines. The absolutism of the nineteenth century which expressed
itself in the theory of the moral law is out of fashion in our America.
Faith in the eternal character of right and wrong is in retreat before
the advance of the pragmatic ethics of expediency. But the retreat
has not yet ended and, while it continues, modern Americans are
confused. The bitter fruit of their confusion is a sense of intellectual and of social insecurity. Our age is witnessing many attempts
of individuals and of groups to escape from the malaise of insecurity, but nothing in America is more pathetic or, perhaps, more
menacing than the efforts of those who would set up the Constitution as a fetish and worship it in the spirit of the tribe which prays
to idols of its own making. There was no Constitution-worship
before Sumter fell. The Webster-Calhoun debate prevented it and
the doctrine of the moral order made it unnecessary. That article of faith gave to mid-nineteenth-century Americans that mental
peace and that sense of security which comes to the man who feels
that he has planted his feet upon the eternal rock.

The second doctrine of the democratic faith of the middle period
was that of the free individual. It contained a theory of liberty and
of the relation of the individual to the state which he ultimately

[10] *Cannibals All* (1857), p. 116.

governed. The doctrine was derived from that of the moral order. The path which led from the one to the other was a philosophy of progress. This philosophy affirmed that the advance of civilization is measured by the progress of men in apprehending and in translating into individual and social action the eternal principles which comprise the moral law. The advance of civilization, in other words, is the progress of virtue. "Nothing can be plainer," remarked William C. Jarvis, counselor at law, in 1820, "than that the barbarian in the desert requires the restraint of a more powerful arm than the individuals whose passions and propensities are under the eternal restraint of moral and religious sentiments." [11] "Civilization," added Frederick Grimke quaintly some thirty-six years later, "is that state in which the higher part of our nature is made to predominate over the lower." [12] Out of this concept that the civilized man is the virtuous man and this hopeful philosophy that mankind is on the march toward a better world came the nineteenth-century theory of liberty. As men become more nearly perfect in obedience to the fundamental moral law, as they develop what Irving Babbitt used to call the "inner check," they need less the external control of man-made laws. "Hence," insisted Emerson, following Jefferson, "the less government the better. . . . The antidote to the abuse of formal government is the growth of influence of private character, the growth of the Individual. . . . To educate the wise man the State exists, and with the appearance of the wise man the State expires." [13]

Henry Thoreau, Emerson's Concord friend, carried this reasoning to its logical conclusion. The man who has achieved moral maturity, he thought, should reject imperfect laws made by stupid majorities and should accept the higher law which is disclosed by his conscience as the sole guide and regulator of his life. In particular, he should practice civil disobedience when the state embarks upon an immoral policy. The fiery Thoreau emphasized his point by going to jail rather than pay a Massachusetts poll tax which he assumed would be spent to further iniquitous policies. That such extremism was rare in nineteenth-century America, however, was illustrated by Emerson's anxious visit to his friend behind the

[11] *Republican* (1820), p. 56.
[12] *Nature and Tendency of Free Institutions* (1856), p. 1.
[13] *Works* (Centenary ed.), III, 215–16.

bars. "Henry," asked the great transcendentalist, "why are you here?" "Waldo," replied the jailbird, "why are you not here?" Emerson, the hardheaded Yankee farmer, thought such extremism in the nineteenth century would defeat its own ends. "We think our civilization is near its meridian," Emerson remarked, "but we are only yet at the cock-crowing and the morning star. In our barbarous society the influence of character is in its infancy." [14] But before Emerson, as before Thoreau, shone the ideal of liberty as the ultimate goal, of liberty not as a means to an end but as an end in itself. "Liberty," said Emerson, "is an accurate index, in men and nations, of general progress." [15] He was the greatest of the preachers of the democratic faith. He traveled from end to end of America preaching his gospel of self-reliant individualism. He moved the young men of the middle period as no other figure of the age. He opened doors for them which enabled them to escape from the stuffy confines of evangelical Protestantism into a glorious out-of-doors. He filled the disciples of the democratic faith with the hope of a better and freer world in the creation of which they would have a share.

It has commonly been said that the exaltation of the individual and the apotheosis of liberty of the mid-nineteenth century was the natural result of certain economic and social factors. A relatively small population was scattered over a vast area. Capitalistic enterprise had not developed beyond the stage in which its most important figure was the individual entrepreneur. Inevitably in such a social scene the focus of attention must be upon the individual. The conquest of a wilderness in the West and the attempt to establish a new industrialism in the East put a premium upon individual initiative and hence on individual liberty. Important as were these factors, there was another of equal, if not greater, significance for the doctrine of liberty. Down to the very eve of the fall of Sumter, Americans of the middle period enjoyed a sense of security rarely to be duplicated in modern history. Not only were there no dangerous potential enemies beyond the national frontiers holding the threat of invasion over the citizens of the Republic, but Americans marched in triumph into the capital of Mexico and dictated the terms of a profitable peace. An ocean guarded the eastern cities

14 *Works* (Centenary ed.), III, 216–17.
15 *Ibid.*, XI, 229.

against attack from Europe. The opportunities of the frontier, moreover, offered to every able-bodied man the possibility of personal economic security. The doctrine of the moral law gave to the men of the middle period a sense of stability and of security in a world of change. The American philosophy of liberty had its seventeenth- and eighteenth-century origins in protests against established orders. It was then primarily a means to an end. In the middle of the nineteenth century, when it reached its maturity with the belief that liberty is an end in itself, it rested squarely upon a universal sense of security. When the traditional foundations of a culture crumble, as we are seeing them do today and in the Western world crazed by nationalism, when government by law gives way to government by irresponsible force, the preoccupation with liberty as an end in itself is replaced by a new search for security, mental, social, economic, and even physical. In the middle period, however, when Americans felt safe, they could afford to enjoy their doctrine of the free individual.

The third doctrine of the democratic faith was that of the mission of America. It was a mid-nineteenth-century version of those myths of unique origin and of unique destiny so common in tribal tradition. Liberty, according to a widely accepted version of American mythology, had been established by deity in an empty western continent so that, freed from the burden of European tradition, it might flourish and become an inspiration to the world.

> O God, beneath thy guiding hand
> Our exiled fathers crossed the sea . . .

sang Leonard Bacon in 1833.[16] George Bancroft, historian, saw the hand of the Omnipotent in the founding of the Republic. As late as 1866 Samuel Kirkland Lothrop, addressing a great Boston meeting upon the anniversary of the Declaration of Independence, proclaimed again the supernaturalistic interpretation of the origin of American democracy. "God in the hour of its utmost need," he declared, "gave . . . liberty an opportunity to plant itself on this new continent and strike its roots so deep that no despotic power could tear them up." [17] The doctrine of mission was merely an extension of that origin. "Standing where we now do," prophesied

[16] "The Nation," a hymn (1833).
[17] *Oration,* delivered in Boston, July 4, 1866.

A. A. Bennet, addressing his neighbors of the New York frontier on the national anniversary of 1827, "we may look forward to the period when the spark kindled in America shall spread and spread, till the whole earth be illumined by its light." [18] "Already," added Justice Story in 1828, "has the age caught the spirit of our institutions." [19] Whitman distilled a folk belief into deathless verse.

Sail, sail thy best ship of Democracy
of Value is thy freight . . .
Thou holdst not the venture of thyself alone, nor of the Western continent alone . . .
With thee time voyages in trust, the antecedent nations sink or swim with thee,
Theirs, theirs as much as thine, the destination port triumphant.[20]

What was the significance of this doctrine of origin and of destiny? It provided the formula which expressed that sense of superiority that an in-group normally feels with respect to outgroups. It was the American way of saying: We are the Greeks; the rest of the world is made up of barbarians. As an expression of the American tribal ethnocentrism it assisted in that subtle osmosis by which a federation of particularist states was transformed into a united nation. But it did more even than strengthen and glorify the nation. It provided for American democracy, with its emphasis upon diversity, a philosophy of unity. And this doctrine of the destiny of America held up before the humble democrat, whose drab world rarely extended beyond the main street of his village, a romantic vision in which he could see his inconspicuous efforts after righteousness invested with a world significance.

If Emerson was the prophet and Whitman the poet of the democratic faith, Herman Melville, ex-whaler, was its savage critic. Putting his thought for the most part into allegory but permitting himself at times direct, barbed thrusts, he assailed every doctrine of the ruling creed of his age. How do you know, he asked the Christians in effect, that God has created a moral order? God is past finding out. To the most urgent questions of men God answers nothing. If

[18] *Oration*, delivered at Avon, N.Y., July 4, 1827, printed by Bemis, Morse, and Ward, Canandaigua, N.Y.
[19] *Miscellaneous Writings* (1835), p. 86.
[20] "As a Strong Bird on Pinions Free," Commencement Poem, Dartmouth College, June 26, 1872.

religion offers no security, thought Melville, neither does science, for science is but a lightship whose rays illuminate a circle in the darkness. It is man's incomprehensible fate that his days are set in mystery and that the essence of his life is hazard. Melville thought that the fundamental delusion in his age was that absolutism which held both religion and science in an iron grip and which was the foundation of the democratic faith. Out of this absolutism came the doctrine of the moral law, the belief in progress, and the gospel of liberty as an end in itself. Phantasms all, thought Melville. Melville rejected eternals. Each age, he taught, is new. Each age has its good and its evil and to the end of time neither will conquer the other. He assailed in particular the belief in progress. "There are many who erewhile believed that the age of pikes and javelins was passed," he said in *Mardi* in 1849, "that after a heady and blustering youth . . . [the world] was at last settling down into a serene old age; and that the Indian summer, first discovered in your land [of America], sovereign kings! was the hazy vapour emitted from its tranquil pipe. But it has not so proved. The world's peaces are but truces. Long absent, at last the red comets have returned. And return they must, though their periods be ages. And should [the world] endure till mountain melt into mountain, and all the isles form one tableland; yet would it but expand the old battle-plain." [21] Turning to the doctrine of the mission of America to spread democracy throughout the world, Melville declared that the fate of the American Republic must be the same as that of its Roman predecessor. Democracy, thought the author of *Moby Dick,* is but a moment in history, not the end toward which all history runs. Yet Melville was not a pessimist, his critics to the contrary notwithstanding. Evil, he insisted, is both unconquerable and unconquering. A man can and must save his soul by fighting the evils of his day as Ahab on the deck of the "Pequod" pursued Moby Dick, well knowing that, though the chase must end in the defeat of the captain, yet it would not be a triumph for the white whale. If a man would be an individualist, taught Melville, if he would be free, let him stop running with the Christians to the Everlasting Arms, let him cease deluding himself with Emerson that the constitution of the universe is on his side. Melville in the middle years of the nineteenth century pitched overboard every one of the philosophies of

[21] *Mardi* (Standard ed., 1922), pp. 244–45.

individualism which dominated his age. Then the intellectuals of an era which proclaimed the ideal of liberty as an end in itself cast him out. His generation condemned Melville to nearly a score of years of living death as an outdoor clerk at the New York Customs House. He was defeated but he did not surrender. In *Billy Budd*, completed three months before his death in 1891, he challenged brilliantly and for the last time the democratic faith of America. Melville's was a troubled spirit which in coming to earth opened the door upon the wrong century.

PART THREE

*Repercussions of the
Constitution outside
the United States*

The Constitutional Cult in the Early Nineteenth Century ∽ GEOFFREY BRUUN

On a souvent attribué notre révolution à celle d'Amérique: celle-ci eut, en effet, beaucoup d'influence sur la Révolution française, mais elle la dut moins à ce qu'on fit alors aux États-Unis qu'à ce qu'on pensait au même moment en France. . . . Les Américains semblaient ne faire qu'exécuter ce que nos écrivains avaient conçu: ils donnaient la substance de la réalité à ce que nous étions en train de rever.[1]

TO APPRAISE the influence which the Constitution of the United States exercised on the political thought and practice of revolutionary Europe is a perplexing assignment. During the years from 1789 to 1815, European thought on constitutional matters was dominated by the revolutionary experiments of the French, and the French, in so far as they responded to American influences at all, received those influences on two quite disparate planes. On what may be called the official plane, the governments of France and the United States understood each other reasonably well, influenced each other very little, and treated each other with a distrust which often verged on hostility. On the intellectual plane, the two peoples misunderstood each other enthusiastically, and admired each other with a fervor which ranks among the great international flirtations of history.[2] It was on this secondary and sentimental level that the force of the American example made its principal contribution to the revolutionary ideology, but the influence thus exerted remained in very large measure the influence of an illusion. There is so little evidence that Frenchmen sought to achieve a critical comprehension of the American experiment,[3] there are such insignificant traces of direct practical borrowing from American sources, that the student is moved to

---

[1] Alexis de Tocqueville, *Œuvres complètes*, 9 vols. (Paris, 1864–67), IV, 215. From *L'Ancien Régime et la révolution*, Bk. III, Ch. I.

[2] B. Faÿ, *L'Esprit révolutionnaire en France et aux États-Unis à la fin du XVIIIe siècle* (Paris, 1925), p. 318.

[3] As a symptom of this indifference to the pragmatic value of the American experiment, it may be noted that nowhere in the general *cahiers* of 1789 is there a specific reference to America. See B. F. Hyslop, *A Guide to the General Cahiers of 1789* (New York, 1936), p. 77.

wonder how European theorists could so long postpone a study of
the facts, while paying lip service to the fiction that the United
States had sprung forth like Pallas, armed and undefiled. The explanation of their obsession, and of their indifference to pragmatic
tests, is to be found, of course, in the ideological mood of the reformers themselves. The rôle played by the American myth in the
political thought of the age was part of a larger intellectual drama,
the drama of what may be called the rise and decline of the constitutional cult. To the exponents of this cult the search for the super-
lative seemed more important than the pursuit of comparisons. Not
until the French revolutionary ideology had lost much of its fascination did Europeans address themselves seriously to the critical and
somewhat disillusioning task of appraising democracy in America.

In the field of jurisprudence, as the late Mr. Justice Holmes
pointed out in one of his illuminating essays, the search for absolute standards is a romantic gesture.

> It is not enough for the knight of romance that you agree that his
> lady is a very nice girl—if you do not admit that she is the best that God
> ever made or will make, you must fight. There is in all men a demand
> for the superlative, so much so that the poor devil who has no other way
> of reaching it attains it by getting drunk. It seems to me that this demand
> is at the bottom of the philosopher's effort to prove that truth is absolute
> and of the jurist's search for criteria of universal validity which he col-
> lects under the head of natural law.[4]

The juristic quest for criteria of universal validity attained
what is perhaps its most typical expression in the constitutional
acts of the French Revolution. It is easy to forget, as one reads
these formal documents, in how large a measure they were exer-
cises of the romantic imagination. The student of today, who
wishes an explanation of the constitutional cult, will no longer
find it in the letter of the statutes. The clue lies in a lost mood, the
mood which invested the Declaration of the Rights of Man with
such thrilling certitude for the ardent spirits of the revolutionary
age. The generation which reached maturity in 1789 suddenly
found the arid and inhuman terms of legal phraseology suffused
with poetic glamour, and it requires a considerable degree of romantic fervor to make legislation lyrical. That the early revolu-

---

[4] O. W. Holmes, *Collected Legal Papers* (New York, 1920), p. 310.

tionaries achieved this fervor even the sober Wordsworth has tes-
tified in his dirge for that bright dawn:

> Oh, times,
> In which the meagre, stale, forbidding ways
> Of custom, law, and statute, took at once
> The attraction of a country in romance.[5]

The most notable charter of this country in romance, and the
purest reflection of that golden hour which was the honeymoon
of politics and philosophy, is the republican constitution of 1793.
Therein may be found, enshrined in its most doctrinaire form, the
dogma that "forgetfulness of, or contempt for, the natural rights
of man are the sole causes of the unhappiness of mankind. . . ."[6]
The Jacobin committee, which drafted this sanguine document in
nine days, was suspicious of anything which squinted at federalism,
and noted with regret that the Constitution of the United States
betrayed this defect. The doctrinaire Saint-Just even ventured to
doubt whether the United States could be considered a true republic at all, with federal elements hindering the free, uniform,
and unanimous expression of the general will. "Some day," he
prophesied, "—and may it be far distant—one state [there] will take
up arms against another."[7] So these young Solons drafted a constitution for a French Republic, One and Indivisible; but it proved
inexpedient, in the midst of the revolutionary turmoil, to expose
their lofty conceptions to the test of application.

By 1795 there were signs that the vision splendid was yielding
to the light of common day. In the constitution of the Directory
the Rights of Man are supplemented by nine paragraphs on the
duties of the citizen, duties which (it was hoped) would likewise
prove to be "inscribed by nature in every heart."[8] But it is the
Constitution of 1799, which followed the *coup d'état* of Brumaire,
that ended the more idealistic phase of the revolution in France.
There the Rights of Man disappear, along with much of the ideology which had sanctioned them, and the instrument which legal-

---

[5] "The French Revolution, as It Appeared to Enthusiasts at Its Commencement,"
Poetical Works of William Wordsworth (Oxford ed., London, 1923), p. 208.

[6] L. Duguit and H. Monnier, eds., *Acte constitutionnel of June 24, 1793. Les Constitutions et les principales lois de la France depuis 1789* (5th ed., Paris, 1932), p. 66.

[7] L. A. de Saint-Just, *Œuvres complètes,* C. Vellay, ed., 2 vols. (Paris, 1908), I, 456.

[8] Duguit and Monnier, *op. cit.,* p. 80.

ized the Consular régime reads for what it was, a severe and pertinent contract between the government and the people.[9]

All the Napoleonic constitutions are realistic documents obedient to the new pragmatic mood. They do not theorize about the best form of government or the perfectibility of man, they define the duties of the administrators and lay down rules of action. When, in deference to the waning constitutional cult, they incorporate echoes of the current generalities—such phrases as "sovereignty resides in the universality of the citizens" or "the welfare of all is the first law"—the statements strike an incongruous note, as if a general should preface his plan of campaign with the announcement that the aim of military strategy is to win battles. In all the sister states where the French example and French influence predominated, the methods of administration reflect this decisive pragmatic bent after 1800. So forthright are the organic articles promulgated for the vassal republics or kingdoms, so matter-of-factly do they specify the functions of the administrators and the annual contribution in men and money which the subject state must provide, that the librarian may well ponder whether to list them under constitutional law or international treaties. It is this realistic spirit, this savage empiricism, no less than their disregard of democratic principles, that makes the Napoleonic statutes the apocryphal canons of the constitutional cult. They are the proof that after 1800 France suffered a change of inspiration and of mood, a change which Bonaparte defined with his usual laconic accuracy when he stated that the romance of the revolution was over.

For Frenchmen the romance of the revolution might be over, but the imperial adventure provided a gratifying and spectacular substitute. For German patriots, denied an equivalent sense of manifest destiny, the era of the French imperium was a period of heartsickness and humiliation. The German nation was not physician enough to make itself whole, but its spokesmen learned, during the intellectual war of liberation which preceded the *Freiheitskriege,* to develop effective antidotes against the "poison of French ideas." They saw that the primal flaw in the logic of the ideologists sprang from their faith in human perfectibility. The orators and pamphleteers of the early revolution had never tired of

[9] Duguit and Monnier, *op. cit.,* pp. 118–29.

insisting that once man was given laws which accorded with his reason and his heart he would cease forthwith to be unhappy or corrupt. But this notion of redemption by statute satisfied German moralists as little as a papal indulgence had satisfied Luther. "Nature," Novalis protested, "should not be expounded as a state of immobility but as a strenuous progression towards morality." [10] It would be difficult to sum up more tersely the ethical conflict which then divided the French and the German schools of thought.

A second tenet of the revolutionary creed against which the Germans revolted was the claim that truly rational institutions would be found to possess universal validity. As the resentment against the French hegemony deepened, German patriots fortified themselves with the reminder that nations are, after all, unique and unassimilable organisms which must be permitted to bear their fruit after their own fashion and in the fullness of time: that, as Herder phrased it, "a nationality is a plant of nature." [11] The ideal of society as a *système d'analyse* was yielding to the organic concept of nations and institutions as living products of an evolutionary process. By 1815 the universal and apocalyptic elements of the revolutionary faith had been systematically discredited in Germany, but in repudiating them German thinkers had found it necessary to dissolve the premises upon which the constitutional cult had rested.

In England, likewise, especially after 1793, the *a priori* tenets of the revolutionary philosophy encountered a climate of opinion increasingly hostile to their pretensions. If, at first thought, it seems inconsistent that the English, who had endorsed the Bill of Rights of 1689, should distrust the Declaration of the Rights of Man of 1789, the answer appears to be that Englishmen objected to the Declaration, not because of its principles, but because those principles were taken logically. Though British political theorists have seldom failed to discover attractive principles at need, the electorate in general has remained triumphantly obtuse to the fascination of abstract reasoning, and British legislators in particular have never displayed much enthusiasm for the idea that the public

[10] E. Spenlé, *Novalis: essai sur l'idéalisme romantique en Allemagne* (Paris, 1904), p. 216.

[11] R. R. Ergang, *Herder and the Foundations of German Nationalism*, "Columbia University Studies in History, Economics, and Public Law," No. 341 (New York, 1931), p. 95.

welfare can be promoted by pure logical deductions. No doubt, after 1793, French ideas would have become suspect in England in any case, as the notions of a regicide people with whom Great Britain was at war. But even if conditions had remained favorable for the infiltration of French doctrines, English political reformers would still have found the dogma of human perfectibility, deduced from the fiction of natural rights, little suited to their use, especially when they had at hand the (to them) more plausible philosophy of utilitarianism.

The year 1815 may be taken as marking the close of the apostolic era of the constitutional cult. By that date the glittering generalities of 1793 had been tarnished and devitalized. The revolutionaries had committed the logical error of linking their program for representative government to a system of natural philosophy with which it had not the remotest deducible connection. The assumption that nature held in reserve the facsimile of a perfect society, a formula which the genius of the legislator might reveal, was an argument which could be invoked with equal plausibility to defend any type of government. Leading thinkers of the Enlightenment had cited it to support their preference for benevolent secular despotism, and Pius VII invoked it with similar assurance when he promulgated an organic statute for the Papal States in 1816:

We have felt from the first [runs the preamble to this papal ordinance], that unity and uniformity ought to form the basic principles of every political institution. Without them it is difficult to assure the stability of the government and the happiness of the peoples. The more nearly a government approximates that unified system which God has established in the natural order and in the sublime edifice of religion, the more justly it may flatter itself that it has approached perfection.[12]

For the disillusioned rationalists there was, perhaps, a touch of irony in the fact that this papal constitution was the only edict of the Restoration era to affirm with such unshaken serenity the existence of an immutable basis for human institutions.

Disabused of their illimitable hopes, the ideologists might have been expected to turn at this point to a more pragmatic philosophy

---

[12] P. A. Dufau, J. B. Duvergier, and J. Guadet, eds., *Collection des constitutions, chartes, et lois fondamentales de l'Europe et des deux Amériques*, 6 vols. (Paris, 1821–23), IV, 391.

of political reform. A majority of their contemporaries came to terms with reality and some were even reconciled to it. But many enthusiasts preferred to cling to their dissolving dream, that dream which lies like a field of magnetic force at the threshold of the nineteenth century and has distorted the reckoning of so many observers. Had the liberal theorists applied a pragmatic yardstick, they might have modified their enthusiasm for the French constitution of 1893, have given more weight to the consideration that it never functioned, and have recalled that it received only half as many votes from the French electors as the Napoleonic Acts.[13] They might likewise have recollected, when extolling in the Spanish constitution of 1812 its bold assertion of popular sovereignty,[14] that this constitution never was, and, it is safe to say, never would have been ratified by a majority of the Spanish people. Further application of the pragmatic test might have suggested that the most intelligent constitutional contracts of the revolutionary age were the Swiss Act of Mediation which Bonaparte edited in 1803, and the charter which Louis XVIII granted to France in 1814, both of them sober but successful contributions to politics as the art of the possible. But the idealists were not primarily interested in men as the compromising creatures which they so often demonstrated they were, but with mankind as it ought to be.

It would be an interesting exercise, if time permitted, to compare the revolutionary constitutions venerated by the liberal idealists with the charters granted by the monarchs of the Restoration Era. More constitutions were promulgated in Europe in the twenty years which followed 1815 than in the forty years preceding that date.[15] Some of them, those of Württemberg, Bavaria, and Baden, for instance, though issued in the bleak years of reaction 1818 and 1819, were in operation for the remainder of the century, and must have possessed more contractual virtues than the textbooks commonly suggest. It might be interesting, too, to reconsider the surprisingly liberal constitution which Alexander I granted to Russian Poland after 1815, and to decide to what degree

[13] M. Deslandres, *Histoire constitutionelle de la France de 1789 à 1870,* 2 vols. (Paris, 1932), I, 290, 444, 524.
[14] Dufau, Duvergier and Guadet, *op. cit.,* V, 85.
[15] The estimate is based upon the texts reproduced by K. H. L. Pölitz, ed., *Die europäischen Verfassungen seit dem Jahre 1789 bis auf die neueste Zeit,* 4 vols. (Leipzig, 1832–33).

the Poles themselves were responsible for its failure. The hardy legend that Alexander had become a renegade to all liberal principles by 1820 might also be checked by a reconsideration of the Russian charter completed in that year. As early as 1805 Alexander had corresponded with Thomas Jefferson in his desire to learn how the Constitution of the United States functioned; [16] and although it is difficult to find any direct borrowing from American sources in the abortive Russian charter of 1820, the charter itself is of interest as the first constitutional attempt of a European ruler to unite the federal and monarchical principles. [17]

But a revaluation of the constitutional progress achieved during the Restoration Era lies outside the limits of this paper. In concluding, it may be noted that the faith in a democratic Utopia, generated by the Revolution, continued after 1815 to warp the judgment of political idealists on American, no less than on European, issues. It is significant that the first visitors who attempted a critical and objective study of democracy in the United States were not members of the more radical schools of political thought. Harriet Martineau, with her Whig predilections, appreciated the republican simplicity of manners but was alert to the defects of American society, especially the evils of slavery. Alexis de Tocqueville, whose *De la démocratie en Amérique,* published between 1835 and 1840, was the most profound analysis of the American experiment which had yet appeared, came to these shores as a critic, not as an admirer, of democracy.

To De Tocqueville may also be granted the credit for first clearly diagnosing the religious and romantic character of the revolutionary faith. His judgment, formulated in *L'Ancien Régime et la révolution,* may be taken as an epitaph on the constitutional cult and the hopes of a romantic generation. [18] He saw that the king-

[16] A. E. Berg, ed., *The Writings of Thomas Jefferson,* 20 vols. in 10 (Washington, D.C., 1907), XI, 101–6.

[17] The text and a criticism of the charter may be found in G. Vernadsky, *La Charte constitutionnelle de l'empire russe de l'an 1820* (Paris, 1933). On the question of American influence see pp. 164–67.

[18] Alexis de Tocqueville, *Œuvres complètes,* 9 vols. (Paris, 1864–67), IV, *L'Ancien Régime et la révolution,* Bk. I, Ch. III, Bk. III, Ch. I. D. M. Mirsky has recently paid tribute to the universality of the revolutionary mood in his penetrating observations on the Decembrists (who likewise, and characteristically, studied the Constitution of the United States with more ardor than understanding). "The fact is," Mirsky notes, "that the Decembrists were not a party, or a sect; they were a generation." D. M. Mirsky, "The Decembrists," *Slavonic Review,* IV (1925), 400.

dom which the doctrinaires had conceived was not of this world, and he understood why these knights-errant of humanity found it so difficult to accept the verdict of experience that in politics the best is the enemy of the good. Somewhere, they persuaded themselves, in renascent Hellas, or in America, they would yet discover the land between dawn and sunrise which they were pledged to seek, and they refused their allegiance to the sober statesmanship which brought a measure of peace to Europe after 1815. For they saw too clearly—they always saw too clearly on a nearer view—and they have impressed their verdict on posterity, that the restoration settlement was a shameless, political *mariage de convenance,* contracted in disillusionment above the grave of a dream.

The Holy Roman Empire versus the United States: Patterns for Constitution-Making in Central Europe ⚓ ROBERT C. BINKLEY

FOR sixteen years, from 1790 to 1806, while the United States was beginning its one hundred and fifty years under its Constitution, the Holy Roman Empire was ending the one hundred and fifty years of its political life as organized in the Peace of Westphalia. While the United States was living under its Constitution, the area that had lived under the shadow of the Holy Roman Empire experienced eight different political systems, proposed or operative. In this area, as in the area of the United States, there was a fundamental problem of maintaining a federative society, balancing unity with diversity, and protecting security. But this area was unlike the United States and more like the world in its variety of languages and historical particularisms. In fact, sixteen of the thirty-two political languages of the world are spoken in the Central European area.

These eight Central European systems were: sixteen years of the old Empire, eight years of Napoleon, thirty-three years of the Metternich system, two years of revolution in 1848–49, the reform movement of the early 1860s, the Bismarck system, the *Mitteleuropa* projects of Friedrich Naumann during the World War, and the triumph of Wilsonian principles at the Paris Peace Conference.

Throughout this sequence of eight political structures, the elements of two contrasting patterns can be traced: that of the native tradition and constitution of the Holy Roman Empire on the one hand, and that of the imported pattern of the United States of America on the other. In the setting up of the Metternich system the influence of America was nil; in 1848 it was very high; in 1863, because of the Civil War, it was low again; and in 1918 with Wilson it was again high. It was characteristic of the pattern of the Holy Roman Empire that it always tended to hold Central Europe together; of the American pattern, that it tended to break it to pieces.

What were the essential characteristics of these two great political formations? Commentators disagreed over both of them. Some held that the Holy Roman Empire was a very much limited monarchy; others, that it was a peculiar republic of princes. Some held that the United States Constitution was the supreme law of the land; others, that it was a compact between states. But whichever theory of structure was adopted, for the analysis either of the Empire or of the United States, the differences between the two systems were comprehensive and systematic.

These differences are summarized in three particulars: the Empire was based on hierarchy, the United States on equality; the Empire, on an unbroken fabric of law from top to bottom, the United States, on concurrent or superimposed systems of law; the Empire operated upon states, the United States operated upon individuals. These contrasting features of the two constitutions are systematically interrelated.

The American principle of equality, as contrasted with the Empire principle of hierarchy, is shown in three distinctive ways. First, American citizens were equal. No titles of nobility were permitted them; they were directly active as citizens of the federal government, and the federal government operated directly upon them. The subjects of the Holy Roman Empire, on the other hand, were not only ranked in orders of nobility, but were divided into two main classes: the few hundreds who were immediately members of the Empire, and the remaining millions whose membership in the Empire was only indirect, through their own princes or the lords of their lands. Second, the American states as such were equal. In the Empire, on the contrary, nine of the two hundred immediate princes were designated as electors, with special rights and duties. Not only did they elect the Emperor, but they constituted a separate house in the imperial diet. They were the "Great Powers" of the Empire system. In each of the circles into which the Empire was divided, certain princes were ranked as leading princes with special rights and duties. Some of these exercised a kind of regional hegemony. Finally, the constitutional principle of America was republican, that of the Empire monarchic.

These three differences, taken together, led into another significant distinction. Every American citizen had a dual capacity, as a citizen of his own state on the one hand, of the United States on the other. The subject of the Empire, whose membership was through his prince, did not have such a dual capacity. But every prince of the Empire, as a monarch, was a member not only of the Empire, but also of the community of European monarchs. By the Treaty of Westphalia he had a right to transact in international politics, to make treaties and alliances, to declare war and to make peace, provided only that he did not direct his diplomacy against the Empire. The American states, on the contrary, were excluded from foreign policy activity. The politics of the Empire were consequently inextricably interwoven with European international politics; in America there developed a tradition of isolation—a tradition that could not have been sustained if each American state had possessed and utilized a right of diplomatic negotiation abroad. Moreover, among the princes of the Empire most of the more important ones possessed lands outside the Empire. Their dual capacity as members of the Empire and as rulers of other lands tended further to merge Empire politics with international politics. In the United States, the lands not organized in the states were held by the federal government, and their defense against foreign encroachment was a federal function.

This political situation is related to the juristic distinction that was second principal difference between the two patterns: namely, that the system of law in the Empire was an unbroken continuity from international law through public constitutional law to private law; while the system of law in the United States was divided into separate spheres and levels of law.

The constitution of the Empire was unwritten, and was compounded of usages, traditions, charters, laws, and international treaties. The Constitution of the United States was a written document, in a class by itself. It was so far from being fitted into the framework of international law that the federal government, though it screened the states in international relations, lacked the power to compel them to make reparation for international wrongs. The princely or inheritance settlements in the Empire were carried through all the levels of jurisprudence; they were private law contracts between great families, enacted as law in the diets of their lands and carried up for imperial ratification. Some succession provisions were even made the subject of international treaties, notably the Pragmatic Sanction of 1723. As in all Old Regime systems, private property rights and political rights were indistinguishable. America had the simple private-law institution of chattel slavery, while the varied and complex relations to which we give the name "serfdom" were found in the Empire. Finally, the American system set the legal sphere of the states apart from that of the federal government in such a way that very little connection between them existed until 1868. But the Holy Roman Empire offered to every subject of every prince protection of his right to due process of law at the hands of his prince. This was the most signal evidence of the continuity of the fabric of law in the system of the Holy Roman Empire.

Although the greater princes of the Empire all obtained before the end of the eighteenth century the privilege of *non appellando*, that is, the right to keep their own subjects from appealing to imperial courts, there was one class of complaint to which the privilege of *non appellando* never extended, and that was "denial of justice." Any German subject who had been denied due process of law by his own prince could appeal to the Empire. Thus, in 1737, the Elector of Cologne was called to order by the Imperial Court when he failed to respect the privileges of Münster in a homicide trial; in 1738 a subject of the Elector of Brandenburg successfully appealed to the Imperial Court for an order asking the Elector, who was king in Prussia, to give the case a new trial. In the same year the court issued a writ against the Duke of Holstein, who was king in Denmark, on behalf of a man who was imprisoned without trial. In none of these cases would an American federal court have heard an appeal against action of a state until after the adoption of the Fourteenth Amendment.

What protection did the American Constitution give the private-law rights of its citizens against the states? When Chisholm sued the state of Georgia and the Supreme Court took jurisdiction, the immediate reaction was the Eleventh Amendment, closing the federal courts to suits brought against a state government. The American Constitution did indeed forbid states the right to pass *ex post facto* laws, bills of attainder, or acts impairing the obligations of contract; but it was not until 1868, when the Fourteenth Amendment was adopted, that the American citizen had the right to due process of law protected against the states by federal law.

When it came to executing the laws or the decisions of courts, with perfect consistency the Empire operated through the princes or immediate members; the American government operated on the individual citizens. This was the third major distinction between the two systems.

What if a princely government should refuse to execute the law of the Empire? In such a case, another prince would get an imperial mandate to invade his domains and compel obedience by armed force. With perfect consistency the Empire acted not only through but upon its member princes and their states.

In the American system, on the contrary, there was absolutely no provision for the use of federal armed force against a member state, nor for giving to one state a commission to invade another state in order to punish its government.

It is often said that the Empire in its last 150 years was in-effective, as if all this fabric of law was on paper only. But here was a community that maintained the separate existence of two or three hundred small principalities settled in the midst of greater states, and maintained them intact for 150 years. It could not have been force and arbitrary violence that secured this amazing result; it must have been law. The very success of the system in maintaining collective security for a century and a half became later a theme of disparaging criticism.

The structure of the Empire, its hierarchy or powers, held to-gether in a comprehensive fabric of law, and, operating upon in-dividuals only indirectly, may have possessed values that historians have forgotten. And among those values was its supreme symbol —the emperor. Along the Danube, far beyond the territorial limits of the Empire, the influence of the dignity of the imperial office made itself felt through the person of the monarch who wore the holy crown. In the north there lived the legend of the emperor sleeping in his cave in the *Kyffhauser,* symbol of ultimate law in a Christian world. What the emperor as symbol and legend was to Central Europe, the written constitution became in the United States.

The emperor abdicated in 1806, but did the Empire die? To answer that question I turn to the analysis of the Metternich sys-tem. The Metternich system, which stabilized Central Europe after the Napoleonic wars, was operated in Germany by men whose student training had versed them in the law and tradition of the Empire. At the Congress of Vienna it was an open question whether or not the Empire itself would be restored. The system established at Vienna must be seen both in its Central European and general European aspect. In both it continued some features of the Empire.

In Central Europe was established the complex of the German Confederation and the Hapsburg monarchy; over Europe as a whole, the Concert of the Five Great Powers. The German Confederation was simply a modified adaptation to nineteenth-century conditions of the constitution of the Holy Roman Empire. The essential feature of hierarchy was there; the princes were the only members of the Confederation; their subjects entered it indirectly through the princes. The federal diet consisted of the delegates of the princes, not the representatives of the people. The princes retained their dual capacity as members both of the German Confederation and of the family of European sovereigns. They exercised their right to foreign intercourse under the limitation that they must make no treaties directed against the Confederation or any of its members. The continuous fabric of law was also retained. The Act of the Confederation was a part of the public law of Europe through its incorporation in the final act of Vienna. The constitutions of a number of German states were in turn guaranteed by the Confederation, and the content of all the state constitutions was controlled by the Confederation in that they dared not allow the powers of state diets to impinge on final sovereignty of the princes. This limitation was justified by the final doctrine that the princes must be free to fulfill their obligations to the Confederation. Whereas Woodrow Wilson held that faithfulness to external obligation could be expected only of popular governments, Metternich assumed that it could be expected only of absolute governments.

The Carlsbad decrees exhibited the continuous fabric of legality of the Metternich system. They were drafted by a diplomatic conference, adopted by a federal assembly, and promulgated in each state as state law. They reached the German subject as Bavarian, Prussian, Hessian law, not as federal law. Compare this procedure with that of international labor legislation. An international conference drafts a text of a labor law; the member states are then obligated to submit this draft to their parliaments for a vote. But the American government, unlike the International

Labor Organization, lacks not only the power to compel a state to pass a labor law, but even the power to compel a state legislature to vote yes or no on a specific text. The American legal system is one of concurrent separate systems of law, whereas the tradition of the Empire interwove them. This specific method of enacting uniform laws in a confederation I shall refer to henceforth as the Carlsbad system.

It must be added that the German Confederation assumed the same responsibility that the Empire had once held, to enforce against the princes the right of each of their subjects to due process of law. There was no specific provision for such a guarantee of due process of law in the text of the Federal Act of 1815, but the federal assembly strained the letter of the act to fix this principle as part of the constitution of the Confederation. Article XII of the act permitted small states to combine to establish a common court of third instance. The federal diet deduced from that article the conclusion that every German subject had a right to three instances of appeal. The members of the diet argued that the Confederation must "compel a state to do its duty," for "otherwise there would be a general state of lawlessness which would be contrary to the aim of the Confederation, and defeat the establishment of a general legal order which it is the object of the Confederation to bring about."

What if one of the German princes should prove recalcitrant? The means of executing the will of the Confederation on a prince or his state were those of the Empire—the Confederation would give a mandate to one German state to enforce federal decrees upon another state.

Where were the electors? In many of the drafts for a proposed German constitution that were introduced in the Congress of Vienna there was provision for a directory of the greater German princes, who would function in the Confederation as the electors had functioned in the Empire. The resistance of the small states prevented the adoption of the directory plan; but from that time to the final destruction of the Confederation it was characteristic of all the reform plans that sought to strengthen the Confederation without separating the Austrian Germans from the rest of Germany that they involved the setting up of a directory of the most powerful states.

Even in the Metternich era, the principle which the Empire had legalized in the position of the electors survived as a principle of European politics. The great powers of Europe became, in a sense, a collegium, with claims to special political rights and responsibilities. They were the heirs of the electors. Moreover, the practices of international government in the days of the Pentarchy were not far from those of the Confederation; the Confederation had its Carlsbad Conference, Europe had its Troppau, Laibach, and Verona. The Confederation adopted the principle of intervention by mandate in an unruly state; Europe put the principle into execution against Italy and Spain. Good precedent existed in the rôle of the leading princes of the Circle in the Holy Roman Empire.

The revolutionists of 1848 intended to substitute popular for monarchic sovereignty; they wanted to destroy the Metternich system root and branch. Their attitude toward the later Holy Roman Empire was one of grief and shame; toward the United States, one of open admiration. They learned their political science from Rotteck and Welker's *Staatslexicon,* whose fifteen volumes stood beside the complete edition of Schiller in thousands of German homes. Rotteck's estimate of the relative importance of the United States and the idea of the Empire in Europe may be measured by the fact that he gave almost as many pages in the *Lexicon* to Benjamin Franklin as to Joseph II and Napoleon put together.

The men of the Frankfurt Assembly were constantly alluding to the American example. They borrowed from the American Constitution both in broad matters of principle and in matters of drafting and detail. They defended an article by saying that it resembled the American model, and attacked it by saying it resembled the Confederation or the Empire. America seemed to prove that a great federal state could be based on the sovereignty, and hence the citizenship, of the whole people.

Two key articles of the Frankfurt Constitution that were drawn almost textually from the American model were those which provided for the monopoly of foreign relations in the hands of the new German union, and for the direct elections to the reichstag. On the other hand, there remained in the Frankfurt Constitution equally significant elements that were in the pattern of the old Empire. One of these was a comprehensive list of fundamental rights that the new German union would guarantee to its citizens against acts of the governments of the member states. The members of the Frankfurt Assembly thought that they were imitating the American Constitution in this feature of their draft, for they did not note that the American Bill of Rights, as it existed at that time, limited only the powers of the federal government and not of the states. So a feature of the pattern of the old Empire came into the Frankfurt Assembly of 1848 disguised with the stars and stripes.

In the organization of the army and in leaving the execution of federal law to administration by the states, the Frankfurt Constitution also followed the old pattern.

It is significant that those elements of the Constitution of 1848 which were within the pattern of the Holy Roman Empire were consistent with the maintenance of Austria in the new Germany; but the elements drawn directly from the American Constitution forced the exclusion of Austria from the new Germany. The American elements of the Frankfurt Constitution led to the conclusion that no state could be partly in and partly out of the new Germany, for in such a state the "German people" would not be sovereign and the ruler would not be subject in his foreign relations to the policy of the new Germany. Georg Waitz, in the constitutional committee, concluded that the Austro-Germans could not enter the new Germany unless they formed a state separate from the other Hapsburg lands. Any other solution, said Waitz, "would resemble the unhappy features of the Holy Roman Empire." But this decision meant that the Frankfurt Assembly could neither organize Central Europe nor unite Germany, for neither the Austro-Germans nor the Austrian government were willing to split the monarchy into German and non-German segments.

The principle of sovereignty and citizenship that worked in America could not apply to Central Europe as a whole because the people did not want to be citizens of a Central Europe, but rather of a Hungary, an Austria, or a Germany. The states that the people wanted could only be made by breaking up Central Europe, and the people were not agreed as to how they wanted Central Europe broken up. The Magyars and the Slavs were at war; the Bohemians were disputing with the Germans; the northern Germans could not agree with the Austro-Germans; and therefore the men of 1848 could neither divide Central Europe nor hold it together, and all their labor of constitution-making fell apart in their hands.

After the Frankfurt Constitution of 1848 had been fumbled by Prussia, Schwarzenberg came on the scene with a strong Austrian program of reorganization for Central Europe. No longer, as in 1815, was the Holy Roman Empire a matter of living memory; its jurisprudence was forgotten and its name despised. But the plan that Schwarzenberg backed in 1850, and the plan that Francis Joseph submitted to the Congress of Princes of 1863, were in the pattern of the old Empire, not of the United States. The members of the reformed German Confederation were to be the princes and their states; the larger states were to constitute a directory; though there were to be representatives of the people in a central parliament, they were to be chosen by the diets of the German and Austrian states, not by direct vote; there would be a supreme court which would protect subjects against their own states; the federal government was not to have a monopoly of foreign relations; the princes were to retain their dual capacity as members both of a German union and of the European state system. A constitution along these lines could hold Central Europe together, whereas the Constitution of 1848–49 divided it.

Meanwhile there was a return to the Carlsbad method of uniform legislation, though not in the Carlsbad spirit of conservatism. A uniform commercial code for all Germany was drafted by a commission set up by the Federal Assembly, communicated by the Assembly to the separate states, and adopted by all of them save Luxemburg in 1861.

The Congress of Princes in 1863 failed. Bismarck opposed it on the very ground that the proposed parliament of the reformed Confederation was to consist of delegates of diets, rather than representatives directly elected by the people.

Then came the Bismarck system for Germany, which was essentially the territorial program of 1848, and it brought with it the penalty that it divided the German nation instead of uniting it.

But while Bismarck did not organize Central Europe at the level of constitutional law, he proceeded in the seventies and eighties to build for it a marvelous organization at the level of international law. He not only reunited as allies the Germans whom he had separated from each other, but he held all the surrounding nationalities in his alliance system—Serbia from 1881, Italy from 1882, Rumania from 1883. Russia, which governed part of the Polish nationality, was held in the orbit of Bismarckian diplomacy. The Bismarck system stabilized the relations of the nationalities of Central Europe, though it operated only at the level of international law.

In the World War, while there was a prospect of a German victory, Friedrich Naumann popularized a plan for the reorganization of *Mitteleuropa*. In a sense his plan was a return to the working principles of 1850 and 1863, of Schwarzenberg and Francis Joseph. He would establish a constitutional law fabric under the international law framework of the Dual Alliance. His technique was to be the development of agreements on specific problems, the setting up of coöperative administrative agencies for railways, customs, banking, and so forth and the preparation and adoption of identical laws by the states. His method was the method of Carlsbad, and his proposed institutions for common action on banking, transportation, and so forth had as their remote and forgotten ancestor the Central Investigating Commission at Mainz, established under the Carlsbad decrees to investigate revolutionary plots. Despite the German defeat, this method was used after the war to prepare for the adoption of a common criminal code by Austria and Germany.

The principles actually realized in Central Europe were not those of Naumann, but of Woodrow Wilson. They were a return, pure and simple, to the ideals of 1848. They succeeded this time in breaking up Central Europe, but not in organizing it. The model of the American Constitution was influential in the constitution-making of some of the individual states—notably Germany and Czechoslovakia; but it was not useful in maintaining organization in Central Europe as a whole.

The principal recognition given to the problem of Central Europe as a whole was in the minorities treaties. What were those treaties? They remind one of those articles of the Peace of Westphalia which guaranteed the religious *status quo* of the subjects of the princes of the Holy Roman Empire. The treaties operated against states by giving to injured individuals the protection of super-state authority. They were not in the pattern of the pre-Civil War American Constitution, but rather in the pattern of the constitution of the old Empire. There was no place in Central Europe for the American principle of dual citizenship, for the people of Central Europe did not want to be citizens of Central Europe; the conditions for the application of the American pattern were lacking.

The area of Central Europe, the Holy Roman Empire and its overlapping monarchies, is the principal seat of the modern European nationality problem. To the nineteenth century, Central European nationalism was a domestic problem of three great monarchies; today it is a problem for Europe as a whole.

Reviewing the experience of the monarchies and Europe, we can say that Metternich held Central Europe together with a political system on the pattern of the Holy Roman Empire; that the men of 1848, using the pattern of the United States in their constitution-making, could neither divide it nor organize it; that the reform plan of 1863 attempted reorganization at the constitutional level and failed; that Bismarck divided Central Europe at the constitutional level, but united it at the level of international law; and that the Wilsonian principles left it with neither kind of organization.

The contrast between the two types of federal structure has world meaning. The Wilsonian system of 1918 required for its success a sense of world citizenship in the moral and political sphere, fortified by individualist interests in world commerce. His system was to give to all peoples control of their own states, and he expected them to exercise this control in a double capacity—as citizens of their own state and as citizens of the world—and to hold in their hearts a dual loyalty—to their own country on the one hand, and to world order on the other. It is only on this hypothesis that it can be deduced that democratic governments are specially qualified to maintain the regime of peace.

But the new state and world society is developing in another direction. The individual is increasingly removed from world relations by the interposition of his state. Morally and politically his ideas come from information filtered through the machinery of a propaganda office; his trade relations with business men in other states go through a national control. It took centuries for the German princes to establish themselves as the sole operative link between the Empire and their subjects; this new process of mediatization, this new *Landeshoheit,* is establishing itself with incredibly greater rapidity.

Meanwhile the American system has drawn nearer to the rival pattern, not only in the development of the application of the Fourteenth Amendment as a federal control over the states, but also in the method of bringing state laws to conform to a model established by Congress. Witness the little N.R.A.'s, the little Wagner Acts, and especially the social security laws. Likewise, the British Empire, in developing the right of the dominions to independent foreign policy and giving to each a dual capacity both as a member of the Commonwealth and of the international family of nations, approaches the pattern of the Holy Roman Empire.

What of the League of Nations? It was also somewhat in the Empire pattern. It operated directly upon states; its enforcement scheme was a feeble imitation of the ban of the Empire or of federal execution in the German Confederation, and had nothing in common with the American pattern. But on a crucial point the drafters of the Covenant yielded to small-state pressure and departed from the Empire pattern: this was in the make-up of the Council. Cecil proposed that the Council should consist of the great powers, purely and simply. It would then have been heir to the whole tradition of international political organization since Metternich, and through Metternich it would have been the true heir to the Empire. But small-state pressure in 1919, like the pressure of the small German states in 1815, forced a compromise. The Golden Bull of Woodrow Wilson put into the College of Electors powers whose potential rôle in the high politics of Europe did not justify their presence in that body. Instead of building on the tradition of the old diplomacy, there was an effort to create a new diplomacy and to establish a sacred symbol—sacred like the United States Constitution—in the written Covenant. Today we have the benefit neither of the old order nor of the new.

It is not inconceivable that, if an era of law establishes itself again in the world, it may exhibit more elements of the Holy Roman Empire pattern than of the American pattern: for instance, no attempt at world citizenship; a hierarchic arrangement of states under a directory of a few great world powers; a fabric of law, in which the distinction between international, constitutional and private law has faded, in a society that makes no clear distinction between property rights and political functions. The juridical doctrine to implement such a system is already evolving in the works of Hans Kelsen and Alfred Verdross. We may discover that we will not have world order save by recognizing hierarchies of privilege that are offensive to our present sense of justice. Still, if we weary of our present symbols, find our going political mythology inadequate, and seek another dispensation, let us not forget the old man sleeping in the cave of the *Kyffhauser*.

The Influence of the American Constitution on the Weimar Constitution ⁓ HAJO HOLBORN

SINCE the days when the democratic revolution of 1848–49 attempted to create a federal government in Germany, American and German constitutional history has been linked by certain analogous problems. The chief constitutional problem in Germany during the nineteenth century was the task of bringing into a union a number of states until then connected only by the bonds of a loose confederation. It was but natural that the German statesmen of 1848–49 should have looked to the great model of a union of states on this continent.

Again after 1867 and 1871 the constitutional jurists gave their attention to the United States. Was the new German Reich a confederacy of sovereign princes or a national union? Was the jurisdiction of the new national government confined to the states or did it apply to the individual citizen? These and kindred questions, known from German textbooks as the controversy *Bundesstaat* versus *Staatenbund,* were discussed in terms analogous to those created by American statesmen and lawyers, and the American precedent contributed materially in causing the national interpretation of the Bismarckian constitution to be almost universally accepted. One may say that the American Constitution helped to overcome the traditions of the Holy Roman Empire.

But apart from the federal element there existed little direct connection between the American Constitution and the constitution of the German Empire. The Frankfurt Constitution of 1849 had had much more in common with the general American ideals, and a good many of its champions, like Carl Schurz, proved later that they were able to add to a fuller realization of the precious values of democratic union. The liberal philosophy of the Constitution of 1849 would have brought a close resemblance between the political life of the United States and Germany, though the German Constitution of 1849 still differed from the American in its monarchical character. In the period of Bismarck and William II the monarchical element was made supreme while the liberal part was attenuated. No wonder that the few existing constitutional parallels faded from the public mind.

Mutual dislike of each other's political institutions grew between the two peoples, while their conflicts increased in the sphere of international politics. This was not the only reason, however, for the increasingly critical attitude, at least not in Germany. For there the guardians of the existing constitutional order tried to discover a new justification for the delay of liberal reforms, and they found it in the dark state of public affairs under democratic rule. America with her "machine politics," "spoils system," inefficient bureaucracy, and the corruption of municipal government was placarded to show the superiority of the monarchical government of Germany with its economical and just administration. In America, on the other hand, the arbitrary power of the German monarch and the strong military element in the empire were increasingly stressed.

Thus, when war broke out conceptions had become fixed on either side and the conflict was pronounced a struggle of the ideals of government.

Woodrow Wilson brought the constitutional issue to a head by his notes of October 14 and 23, 1918, in which he restated officially his demand for "the destruction of every arbitrary power anywhere that can separately, secretly, and of its single choice disturb the peace of the world," and intervened directly in German affairs by openly hinting at the deposition of William II. The significance of Wilson's interference with the German developments should not be overemphasized. In fact, the political rôle of William II was finished in any case and it was the emperor's hesitancy in recognizing the situation that contributed more than any other single event to the final outbreak of the revolution, since he appeared to the masses as the chief hindrance to a swift termination of war. Otherwise the parliamentary government of Prince Max of Baden represented the majority of the people and exercised supreme control after the promulgation of the October amendments to the imperial constitution. If William II had abdicated in time, the government might have carried on and might have been able to preserve some of the monarchical traditions by the proclamation of a regency.

There was, however, hardly more than a bare chance for such a policy. The revolution was inevitable, since its motives lay in the disintegration of social conditions rather than in general political considerations. Monarchical government was doomed in Germany, and the history of the post-war period has confirmed this judgment. The interference of Wilson was, therefore, all the more gratuitous. Apparently his advisers still overestimated the strength of monarchical government in Germany. Thus republican government in Germany was not left to develop by its own strength and its antagonists could more easily stigmatize the new order as superimposed by the victorious powers on a defeated nation.

With the downfall of the dynasties in Germany little remained of the old tradition of constitutional life. Not even the Frankfurt Constitution of 1849 could have been revived. One could draw a great deal from its liberal philosophy, embodied in the imposing bill of rights. But the most urgent thing was the creation of a strong national executive, and in such a task the Frankfurt Constitution could no longer serve as a model. A new framework had to be constructed. The constitutions of Switzerland, France, and the United States, as the most notable examples of democratic government, were eagerly perused and among them the American Constitution seemed to contain especially helpful suggestions.

Before proceeding, it is important to survey the wider scene in order to gain a true historical perspective. The Weimar Constitution of 1919 is today generally considered a barren episode in German history. But though the constitutional order of the German republic broke down in 1933, at least two major results of the Weimar republic survive. The first was the success of the democratic statesmen of 1918–19 in stemming the tide of bolshevism. This was chiefly the achievement of social-democratic leaders, like Ebert, but owing to the division existing among the German socialists, they had to rely very largely on the assistance of the old military and civilian bureaucracy. While thus the social-democratic leaders themselves helped to nurture the seeds of the counter-revolution, which dispossessed them in the end, they made Germany for the future immune to Russian enticement.

The second, closely related, historic result of the revolutionary history of those years was the reunification of the German states.

The revolutionary movement of November, 1918, did not start at the center, but flared up in the various provinces engendering a great number of sectional political strongholds. In other words, the revolution of 1918 unleashed all the centrifugal forces still abounding in Germany. After the bolshevist elements had been uprooted, the Berlin government was able to concentrate on the rebuilding of federal government in Germany. Many compromises had to be made at first, but with the convention of the national assembly in Weimar the national forces were able to recover the ground, and more than that, to add substantially to the constitutional unity. To be precise, the Weimar Constitution still retained a federal system, and the old territories preserved certain state rights. But the government of the Reich gained more than the usual attributes of federal government, it had much more of a national character than either the Bismarckian or even the American system. The centralism of the Third Reich rests on foundations laid by the republic.

In drafting the sections of the constitution dealing with the relations of federal and state government, the Weimar assembly was little influenced by foreign prototypes. Probably nobody at that moment was quite aware that the juridical theories about federal government that had been developed in pre-war days and were now further expanded had been originally molded with a view to the American example. But it was different with the framing of those provisions of the constitution that referred to the executive which was to take the place of the monarchical institutions. Here we find a marked influence of the American Constitution.

Before examining the problem as such, the chronological order of events may be recalled. Between November 9, the day of the outbreak of the revolution in Berlin, and of the flight of the emperor to Holland, and February 8, 1919, when the National Assembly in Weimar promulgated a law for the establishment of a provisional Reich government, the Berlin government was in the hands of the so-called "council of people's commissars," who derived their power from the *de facto* law of the revolution. Most of the members of that group were, however, pledged to the restoration of democratic processes of government, and Ebert and his social-democratic friends endeavored to bring about national elections within the shortest possible time.

Though in the end he emerged as master, Ebert could not give much attention to the actual drafting of the constitution. He was fully alive to the desirability of having work started at once, even before the national assembly convened, in order that the democratic leaders might have at their disposal a draft with which they could hasten the discussions of the assembly. But all he could do at the moment was to urge the appointment of a recognized authority on constitutional reform to become head of the Department of Interior. The choice was between two men, Hugo Preuss and Max Weber. On November 14 Preuss was appointed, but the draft constitution prepared by him in the course of the next two months was the outcome of deliberations in which the opinions of other men sometimes counted more.

On January 20, 1919, the day after the elections for the National Assembly had taken place and a few days after the Ebert government had scored its decisive gains in the forceful suppression of the bolshevist revolution, the draft constitution prepared in the Department of Interior was made public. Although most of its sections and articles were changed or remade during the session of the national assembly in Weimar, the section dealing with the office of the president of the Reich was merely reaffirmed in the subsequent discussions.

While the fight between democracy and bolshevism was still raging, the problem of the executive in a democratic government had already been solved by a group of private citizens and experts, and solved in a fashion that was acclaimed by almost all groups of the people. Naturally the public after the revolution gave foremost attention to the men who had striven for a democratic reform before and during the war. It was not a large group of people, but some of the best known patriots and men of learning were among them. Friedrich Naumann, Friedrich Meinecke, Walter Schuecking, Gerhard Anschütz, Hugo Preuss, Max Weber, should be mentioned in the first place. The most powerful figure, however, was the last mentioned, the Heidelberg sociologist. Max Weber had stirred his students by his self-denying search for objective truth, and his political friends by his passionate fervor in the pursuit of his political ideals. He was not closely affiliated with any particular party though he had lent his council to Friedrich Naumann in the planning of the latter's "national-social" pro-

gram. But essentially he was an independent who formed his political aims on the basis of his vast knowledge of political and social sciences. His political writings will be treasured among the
most precious pieces in the history of German political science as
well as of political pamphleteering.

Weber early in life came to feel that the Bismarckian constitution had dried up the sense of political responsibility among the
German bourgeoisie and antagonized the broad masses of the
working population. Moreover, it had produced the autocratic
rule of William II, who was in Weber's opinion a mountebank
who besmirched the achievements and true virtues of a great nation. Weber's extensive studies of political institutions abroad,
especially the observations made during his stay in the United
States, strengthened his belief in the urgent necessity of constitutional reforms. He grew impatient at the sight of the emperor's
fumbling with international affairs and foresaw that Germany under her old constitution was ill prepared to withstand a world-
wide coalition.

The outbreak of the war and the conduct of Germany's wartime policy outdid Weber's worst expectations. His high-strung
patriotism drove him to take up the fight for constitutional reform
in public. In 1917 he published his pamphlet *Parliament and Executive in a Reformed Germany,* which sketched in broad lines a
sweeping program of democratic reform. The pamphlet is his greatest political manifesto for its searching criticism of German politics
and for its profound vision and reasoning. It is also the most significant document for the study of American influence on the constitutional developments in Germany.

Weber's chief aim was the restoration of political leadership by
statesmen to end the rule of unfit monarchs and of a politically
irresponsible caste of military and civil bureaucrats. For this reason
he had turned to democracy and now he tried to refute the predominant arguments voiced in Germany against democratic government. First there was the argument that democracy would
destroy the integrity and efficiency of the civil service. Weber made
it clear that trained civil servants formed an essential element in
the working of modern government and that their rôle would
grow even more important after the war. But their function was

administrative rather than political and accordingly was not in conflict with democratic leadership.

He admitted the weakness of the American civil service but traced it to the fact that such a great number of posts were elective and were thereby laid open to party patronage. But the tide had turned, the introduction of the Civil Service Act showed that the United States would develop in due course a staff of administrative experts. Apart from that, there was a remedy for these consequences of party rule in the operation of direct democracy. The appointments made by the president were in general more satisfactory than those by senators or congressmen. This was owing to the fact that a superior leader was compelled to take general public opinion as well as party interests into account. On a smaller scale this was also true in municipal politics, where the grossest abuses of party rule were rectified by the occasional election of candidates forced upon the parties by a surge of popular indignation.

Popular control, in Weber's opinion, would reassert itself against the invisible rule of party machines to the extent that the parties were made responsible for national affairs. Organized parties will be a source of corruption as long as they are allowed to operate in a sphere of minor public concern which might be due either to lack of interest on the part of the elector or to an existing constitutional weakness. The latter was the case in Germany, where parliament and parties had become a fifth wheel of the chariot. Parties without a policy-determining power in national affairs will never attract the talented men but only second-rate figures. The correcting influence of direct democratic rule is then lacking too. The professional political worker and party man are as important in modern times as expert officials in state administration, but the part played by both these groups has to be counterbalanced by genuine political leadership.

Yet if direct democratic rule is working such miracles, why should one put so much emphasis on the parliament? Would it not be preferable to have only general election of the political leader and in addition occasional plebiscites on legislative questions? Weber took the view that such a form of government would lead in modern conditions to the absolute rule of a bureaucracy, since no single leader is really able to control the working of administration. If such a system of Bonapartistic rule as he thought possible in our age should be coupled with governmental management of economic life, it would become something similar to the New Empire of ancient Egypt, which turned its subjects into mere cogs in all activities of life. The adoption of corporative ideas could not mitigate the universal suppression of individual liberty because they are of no avail against the overwhelming forces of modern industrialism.

The return of the Oriental-Egyptian state in our age was a prophetic vision of Weber and here the most personal motive in his construction of democratic rule became apparent. He felt that the growing significance of the masses, the increasing organization of capitalistic, or for that matter socialistic, society imperils the last footholds of individual liberty. The existence of political parties is the guarantee against the tyrannical exploitation of direct democracy, and where, as in Germany, a two-party system is unlikely of realization, a parliament with broad constitutional authority is indispensable. Weber denied that under a system of parliamentary government the leading statesman would be chosen without a consideration of the masses. Lloyd George's position was largely based on his acclamation by the masses outside the parliament. Not even a more autocratic monarchy is without such examples, as the wartime position of Hindenburg shows.

But parties and parliaments serve a number of useful purposes: they help to steady the rule of the political leader; they control his power and preserve the civil liberties against him; they constitute the arena in which the statesman has to prove his actual knowledge and skill apart from his demagogic qualities; finally, parliamentary procedure makes it possible to depose in a peaceful manner a leader who has lost his sway over the masses. It was for these reasons that Weber in 1917 bent all his energies to bringing about parliamentary control while still recommending the preservation of the monarch as the nominal head of state.

The articles written by him a year afterward in November, 1918, for the *Frankfurter Zeitung* were based on the same ideas and principles. But the monarchy had broken down by then and the war had been lost. This accounted for the revision of Weber's program. Now he proposed to place beside the parliament a popularly elected president with strong constitutional prerogatives. By that he meant more than the usual rights of any head of state, a policy-determining power to be exercised through the appointment of chancellor and ministers, by the right to dissolve the parliament, by vetoing parliamentary legislation, and by initiating referenda and plebiscites. This change of Weber's original plan was motivated not only by the collapse of the monarchy, but by the desperate task of a future German policy. He saw clearly that the huge burden of domestic and foreign war debts was bound to revolutionize the very structure of German society, and that a new political order could be achieved only on a strictly egalitarian basis. The execution of such a great reform would lie very largely in the hands of experts and civil servants and would depend for its success on their efficiency. Only a president elected by the people was likely to live up to this twofold task of protecting the integrity of bureaucracy and of its political course of action. Such a president was to achieve what in Weber's opinion was the precondition of political democracy, namely a larger measure of social equality.

But the new emphasis on the creation of a president did not alter his belief in the necessity of having a politically responsible parliament. Consequently he demanded that the chancellor and ministers should be made responsible for all political acts of the president and that they in turn should need the confidence of the parliament. Thus presidential and parliamentary systems—or as they were somewhat loosely called in Germany: American and French systems—were dovetailed.

Weber's plan was embodied in the appropriate section of the Weimar Constitution. His articles in the *Frankfurter Zeitung* made a deep impression on the public. But he proved himself even more persuasive at the meeting of experts held under the direction of Secretary of Interior Preuss in the second week of December. Quite apart from his imposing personality, he was the only one on the council who had thoroughly studied American government. It was not Preuss, who held similar views, but Weber who convinced the conference of the practicability of such a policy, and thereby ruled out two other possible solutions. The first solution was the construction of a directory or council as highest political body; like the Philadelphia Convention of 1787 and on the same grounds, the Berlin conference of December, 1918, excluded the proposition. The second one was the introduction of an unrestricted presidential system in the executive field. Weber, in contrast, was anxious to have strong checks and balances.

These checks and balances were different from those provided for in the American Constitution. Weber's reading of the American Constitution was not juristic, but the interpretation of a political scientist interested more in the actual than in the written constitution. The juridical theory of the division of powers has been superseded in his scheme by the mutual restriction of indirect and direct democracy and this scheme came near to the true dynamics of American politics.

The plan, however, failed in the history of the German republic. It was this fundamental section of the Weimar Constitution that lead to the collapse of the republic. But this does not mean that the constitution thwarted the realization of democracy. Framing a constitution does not create democracy if this constitution is not implemented by a democratic policy. Weber knew that very well and often intimated that the drafting of the new constitution was a small matter compared with the introduction of radical financial and social legislation. But the democratic parties in Germany did not solve these paramount political problems. Perhaps they could not have done so even under a different leadership after the peace treaty.

In addition, the political leader of democracy during and after the revolution, Friedrich Ebert, was persuaded not to use the opportunities offered to him by the constitution. He agreed to the passing of an *ad hoc* amendment of the constitution that enabled the parliament to elect the first president of the Reich. And we find one more deviation from Weber's plan in the practice of the German republic. By the introduction of proportional representation, the evolution of an adequate party system was blocked and the parliament made ineffective.

Hence the president's office became what the reactionary parties had longed for when they eagerly welcomed its inception. It developed into a safeguard of a military and civil bureaucracy that despised parliamentary control and into a center of all the forces interested in the preservation of old class divisions. In the end, however, it had to recognize the popular egalitarian tendency of which I spoke before and to call in the assistance of a pseudo-egalitarian mass movement.

A modicum of direct democracy can be found even in the Third Reich and yet it is used simply to make arbitrary rule all-embracing. Weber's prediction of what such a system in our days might amount to has become a bitter truth. The difference lies in the human motives. Weber was animated by the ideals of individual liberty. He knew that they were endangered by the progress of industrialism, nationalism, and militarism. In the United States he saw the country that had defended its liberal and democratic ideals most successfully against the onslaught of these modern forces. His critical admiration of the American Constitution rested on the same basis that has made the United States a great nation, namely respect for the dignity of free men.

BIBLIOGRAPHICAL NOTE. The best treatment of the constitutional developments in Germany during the years 1918–19 is to be found in the articles which F. Meinecke and W. Jellinek contributed to the *Handbuch des deutschen Staatsrechts,* edited by G. Anschütz and R. Thoma (Tübingen, 1930–32). The article by F. Meinecke deals with the general political history of the period (I, 95–119), whereas W. Jellinek gives a description of the technical preparation of the Weimar Constitution (I, 119–38). Both authors present bibliographies which make it unnecessary to mention here any of the published sources except Max Weber, *Politische Schriften* (Munich, 1921).

I have used the unpublished documents which W. Jellinek refers to in his article and many others which have not been made public. In the years between 1929–32 I was permitted free access to the German government archives and to many private sources in preparation for a history of the Weimar Constitution. Two articles of mine discuss problems connected with the subject of this paper: "La Formation de la Constitution de Weimar, problème de politique extérieure," Dotation Carnegie, Bulletin No. 6 (Paris, 1931), and "Verfassung und Verwaltung der deutschen Republik: ein Verfassungsentwurf Friedrich Meineckes aus dem Jahre 1918," *Historische Zeitschrift,* CXLVII (1932), 115 ff.

American Influence on British Federal Systems ∾ W. MENZIES WHITELAW

THIS is a broad subject and will have to be treated in a broad way. It will be brought within manageable proportions by considering American influence on only two British federal systems —the Canadian and the Australian—and on only the federal aspects of these two systems. These two have been selected not primarily because they are the constitutions of the two senior dominions, but because in these alone among British federations have American influences been conspicuous and sustained. From time to time other federal systems have been either projected or actually established in other parts of the empire, but in each case these have been primarily the creation of Downing Street, and Downing Street has never shown much aptitude in the reading of the lessons of American history; and even if it had been so disposed, the conditions in these other federated sections of the dependent empire have been too dissimilar to conditions obtaining in the United States to make extensive borrowing possible. What, for instance, could the United States have to teach in regard to the federation of India, or of the Malay States, or even of the Leeward Islands? Each of these was *sui generis*.

I

One of the chief reasons for the extent of American influence on the Canadian and Australian systems was just this similarity of conditions, with the consequent similarity of problems for which these federal systems were expected to provide a solution. Indeed one of the chief difficulties in any attempt to estimate the nature and extent of American influence on these two systems has been due to this very similarity. For, although the similarity has made possible the greatest amount of borrowing, it has equally made it the less necessary to assume that there has been borrowing merely from the fact that there has been a close parallel development.

Of the various elements of similarity, perhaps first place should be accorded to the fact that all three groups of states—American, Canadian, Australian—had previously been British colonial dependencies, and had outgrown that status at the time of their federation. This emergence had in each case produced an emotional mentality in which self-consciousness, idealism, exhilaration, and fear were all readily discernible. In a word, an adolescent mentality. Granted that there were differences between the American states' reaction to their independence and the Canadian and Australian reaction to their autonomy, nevertheless these were differences in degree rather than in kind, and it is equally dangerous to ignore the similarities and to minimize the differences, and a good deal easier.

Less likely to be questioned is the assertion that the Founding Fathers in all three groups brought to their constitutional problems a wealth of practical political experience, and that many of their more fundamental political concepts were identical, because they went back to common English roots. It is interesting to speculate whether Alexander Hamilton would have felt at home had he been able to drop in on the conference at Quebec in 1864, or whether George Brown of the Toronto *Globe* would have been able to adjust himself to the discussions in the Sydney Convention of 1897. If either had felt some unfamiliarity with the language used, both would have been all too familiar with the problems discussed. They would quickly have recognized the strength of the old state particularisms that in each group had grown into such lusty plants, lustiest in those localities where they had had the longest time to grow. Hamilton would doubtless have rejoiced that he had had Rhode Island to placate and not Prince Edward Island, the particularism of Virginia and Massachusetts to manipulate, and not that of Nova Scotia or Quebec. Brown would have regarded the problems of the Australian fathers as child's play compared with that which he had had to face at Quebec. No problems there of race to embitter the issues, no religious conflicts, no differences of language, no maelstrom to the south. Yet he would have recognized the same fundamental problem of building a national structure strong enough to withstand the shocks of internal commotion and external aggression, while guaranteeing to the local states the preservation of their cherished autonomy. Both Hamilton and Brown would have recognized the faint but significant beginnings of a national sentiment, as yet both weak and unreliable, but likely to grow with the passing of the years. Both would have been aware of the conflict between the old state particularism and the new nationalism, but both would have been shrewd enough to see that what paraded itself as nationalism was in some cases merely the desire on the part of the big states to become bigger. They would have recognized in the conflict between the large states and the small the tendency of the large to favor, and of the small to be suspicious of, national integration. For in all three groups there was this fundamental cleavage: between Delaware and Virginia, between Nova Scotia and Upper Canada, between Tasmania and New South Wales.

Had this opposition of large and small states been unrelieved by other cleavages that cut across state boundaries, linking sections and interests within the small states with corresponding sections and interests in the large, it is doubtful whether any of these federations would then have been possible. One of these other lines of cleavage was that between the metropolitan centers of credit and commerce and the hinterland in which agricultural pursuits were likely to be carried on with borrowed capital: the Canadian frontier somewhat more like the hinterland of New England, Australia's more like that of the South. Although these economic groupings inevitably cut across state lines, they tended, on the whole, to leave the creditor mentality in the ascendant in the large states (large that is in population), and the debtor mentality dominant in the small, thus frequently accentuating the conflict between large and small states. In each of the groups there were the beginnings of party political systems, although in the United States the Revolution had temporarily reduced the parties to one. But there was even here the faint beginnings of another two-party system emerging, in which creditor, large-state, national party was being ranged against the debtor, small-state, states-rights party. In none of the groups had there yet been occasion for interstate party coördination.

In all three groups the tariff was a major problem. It was easy to say that one of the chief objects of the federation was the elimination of interstate tariffs. It was more difficult to say who should have the power to regulate the national tariff. This gave an added urgency in all three to the problem of the power to be given to the federal upper house, the states house, as against the federal lower house in matters of financial legislation.

At the time of their federation the population of these three groups was almost the same, between three and four million in each. In area there was at that time considerable difference, but the areas that were potentially theirs, and that were eventually to become theirs, were again almost the same, if we except Alaska from the United States and the Arctic islands from Canada. The Australian states were, of course, much larger than either the Canadian or the American. Victoria, the "postage stamp state," was almost twice the size of the Commonwealth of Pennsylvania, and Western Australia was more than eighty thousand square miles larger than the whole of the present United States east of the Mississippi. The enormously large unoccupied hinterlands of each, reaching away seemingly endlessly to west and north, with relatively a slight population concentrated along the fringe to east and south, were strikingly alike in all three, and it gave to the problems of frontier expansion and control a major place in the setting up of each of these federal systems. All three were, or were to become, of continental proportions, with two oceanic frontages.

But one conspicuous difference must here be noticed: in Australia the whole island was already, at the time of its federation, appropriated among the several states.[1] Each state had its own hinterland, each its own urgent problems of frontier development. The rôle of the West in unifying the East—a process equally evident in Canada and the United States—was not present in Australia, where the unifying effect of the frontier acted directly on the life of each state separately, and to that extent kept the nation as a whole from growing together. In Australia railways had already come to play a dominant rôle in the process of unification, and these were almost exclusively the possession of each individual state. They naturally were used as instruments in the unification of each state, where the state railway systems were like fans with their handles in each case located at the state capital. The problem of the gauges was only one aspect of this situation. This divisive economic factor was accentuated by the historical

[1] The Northern Territory did not become federal until 1911. It had formed part of South Australia since 1863.

fact that in Australia, unlike both Canada and the United States, all the states were established long before the federation.

Then in each group of states there was fear: nebulous, seldom mentioned in specific terms, but seldom out of mind. It was essentially this force that drove the individual states to give up so much of their hard-won statehood. They could hardly otherwise have been lured into any national utopian venture, however attractive.

Finally, in all three groups there had been a previous experience of an unsatisfactory union. In the United States there had been the Confederation, in Canada the undeniably federal aspects of the practice of the Constitution of 1841, and in Australia there had been the Federal Council of 1885. All three, therefore, were saved from having to make a federal system out of whole cloth. In each there were not only the existing state governments on which many aspects of the central government could be modeled, but also these earlier unsatisfactory union schemes to be fixed. The problem was to take their experience of constitutional government and build it into an adequate instrument of federal nationalism. Having so many bricks of their own, it was the less necessary to borrow from the outside.

Over against these outstanding similarities among these three federal systems in the making there stood certain differences hardly less distinct. And if the similarities made it the easier to borrow, differences made it the harder. In the first place there was in both Canada and Australia an assumption of the principle of ministerial responsibility. The Canadians had assumed, apparently without question, that the principles of federalism and ministerial responsibility would be the twin supports of their constitutional edifice. The Australians saw the difficulty in attempting to reconcile these two principles, the British and the American, in one system, but they were determined to make the attempt. Oddly enough they regarded themselves as the first to make such a union of principles, denying that the Canadians had done so. The Australians seemed clearly of the opinion that in Canada the federal principle had been sacrificed to that of ministerial responsibility. Canada, they held, had evolved virtually a unitary type of government. The difficulty in attempting to reconcile ministerial responsibility with a real federalism lay in the fact that under ministerial responsibility the federal executive is responsible to, and therefore dependent upon, a majority in the federal lower house, and this tends inevitably to lower the position of the upper house. Now the federal principle as seen in the American system would seem to involve constitutional parity as between these two branches of the federal legislature, the one representing people as people, and the other states as states. It was the fundamental legislative compromise of the American system, and it was possible because there was no ministerial responsibility. The United States having had, therefore, no such problem could offer no help to the Australians in its solution. In both Canada and Australia the British principle of cabinet responsibility was retained and the federal character of the upper house, the states house, was thereby jeopardized. Matters in this regard were made worse rather than better by the assumption by both dominions of the British principle of the primary responsibility of the lower house in matters of finance.

But if the acceptance of these British principles gave added difficulty to the Canadians and Australians in making a truly federal system, their relative security within the British Commonwealth relieved them from one of America's major problems, the establishment within the federation of a binding contract for its own protection and guarantee. Closely connected with the creation of this contract was the necessity of providing for alterations in the contents of that contract. Canada blithely made its constitution without a single mention of provisions for amendment, assuming that the British Parliament would attend to that, and that the British Parliament would always listen to the parliament of the senior dominion in its requests for amendment. Much water has passed under the bridge since those simple days. Australia, with something of the Canadian difficulty in mind, did make provision for constitutional amendment, but in their method therefor they chose to copy the Swiss rather than the American method, which they fondly believed would provide a more flexible method for constitutional change.

II

These similarities and differences among these three outstanding federations have been enumerated in some detail because they form, as it were, the upper and the lower thresholds, respectively, within which constitutional borrowing was possible. But the influence of one nation on the constitutional life of another may be of a more direct sort. This will occur when two nations are in sufficiently close contact for one to feel the impact of the policies and activities of the other. This need not take the form of a direct attempt of one state to alter the constitution of the other. Certainly there was small concern in the United States over the form the new Canadian constitution was to take, and what evidence there is seems to point in two opposite directions. There is no indication that the United States was at all concerned with the nature of Australian federalism. Indeed one looks in vain even for some indication of pride in the fact that the American Constitution was being used as a model. The United States seemed, at least in these two cases, unaware of its rôle as the mother of federations. Certainly it exhibited nothing of the pride of Great Britain in its rôle as the mother of parliaments. This can be partly explained by the distraction in the United States both in the middle sixties and in the late nineties, when these two other federations were being born.

Perhaps the chief form which American influence took in shaping the Canadian federal system was in the implications of United States economic, political, and military policies. This was by no means limited to the official policies of the government in power. Canadians felt rather the vague fear of the American situation getting out of hand. When they thought, in the middle sixties, of the United States, their minds turned to the Fenians, to the radical Republicans, to the army home from the war. Only to a secondary extent did they fear the results of pressure put on the American government to threaten trade reprisals, abolition of bonding privileges, abolition of reciprocity, and of other forms of pressure to force annexation, especially now that the South could no longer block the extension of the free area. It is not necessary to prove that these menaces were real. The point is that they were heartily believed to be so. They seemed to demand a speedy and a close union; and a speedy and a close union there was. In so far as there was conscious borrowing this was chiefly in the field of warnings to be taken from American experiences, particularly in the exaggeration of states rights into an assumption of states sovereignty. This also seemed to point toward a unified federal system.

However impressive a list of the differences between the American and the Canadian systems may be—and certainly these differences stand out boldly at almost every point—it would be quite wrong to assume that the Canadians studied the course the American Constitution had taken merely to set themselves another course. The danger of such an assumption is all the greater in view of the fact that the copying of American models was so unpopular in Canada in the mid sixties, that as little as possible was said of such borrowing as there was. The bold fact remains, however, that what the Canadians drew from the American system was the federal idea itself, and they drew this not as something conceptual and abstract, nor yet something that had been once, but a living thing which, even in spite of the awful tragedy then drawing to its close, had proved for the first time that a federation of continental proportions was possible. It is significant that when the Canadians thought of a federation they did not have to go to the ancient Greeks, nor to the Iroquois, nor to the Holy Roman Empire, nor even to the Swiss. When they thought of a federation they thought of the United States. Constantly the Canadians reiterated that the Americans had made a mistake in 1787. But that mistake was not held to be the adoption of the federal principle, but in the provisions for its application. The American Civil War had not seemed to them to prove the impossibility of a federation, but only the inadequacy of proper safeguards for national sovereignty.

A list of the differences between the Canadian and American federal systems is impressive; and in each case the Canadian differs from the American in providing a closer form of union. This is all the more striking when placed beside the fact that the provinces were more disparate than the states had been, geographically, racially, historically. One need only mention such factors as the Maine salient, the French character of Quebec, and the Laurentian Shield, to none of which had there been anything comparable in the thirteen states.

In the Canadian constitution the federal government, even without parliamentary authority, was given the blanket power of disallowing any provincial statute whatsoever. Until the end of the Macdonald era this was taken to mean not only a veto on provincial measures *ultra vires* of the province, or local statutes that infringed certain fundamental private rights not otherwise protected in the Act, but any measure that was thought to be prejudicial to national interests. The writer has recently seen a confidential letter by Macdonald justifying the vetoing of a Manitoba statute for building a railway, simply because the proposed line would interfere with traffic on the C.P.R. Secondly, the Canadian federal upper house was to be based on "sectional" rather than "provincial" equality. The distinction was far from being merely technical; it was fundamental, and it made it fundamentally impossible for the Canadian senate to become a "states house." The device of sectional equality in fact gave to each province almost the same legislative representation as if representation in both houses had been based on population. This has made it necessary in Canada to devise a system for making the cabinet federally representative. It has become the invariable practice of the Canadian constitution to have provincial, as well as certain racial and religious, interests represented in the cabinet. To a large extent this has merely pushed the process one step farther back, so that the political party in power is the real federalizing element, and the secret caucus the place in which federal conflicts are resolved. This last has been possible only since the rise of real national parties.

The Canadian fathers laid great stress on the fact that in the Canadian system the American "mistake" of placing the residuum of power in the local legislatures had been avoided. Canada was to be a real nation from the beginning. The control of the federal government was further strengthened by providing that both federal senators and provincial lieutenant governors were to be the appointees of the federal government. Criminal law was also made a federal subject. There were to be no crimes against a province any more than against a municipality. In these outstanding ways, and in others of less importance, the Canadian system differs from the American, and in each case by the strengthening of the central government at the expense of the local.

The Canadian system stands out in equal contrast to the Australian, which uniformly turned away from these Canadian innovations and returned to the American model. This is the more significant because the Australians had both systems constantly in mind as they were evolving their own. And perhaps the borrowing in little things is equally significant with their borrowing in the great. There was, for instance, their extensive use of American names and general terminology. Bryce's *American Commonwealth* had made its appearance just before the first Australian constitutional conference. It was widely read by the fathers, who preferred to use the designation "Commonwealth" for their own federation, rejecting the Canadian term "Dominion." But it is not only in terms and in constitutional mechanics that the Australian and American constitutions follow closely parallel lines. They breathe the same spirit. The Canadian constitution is a conservative constitution, expressing the fundamentally conservative character in the Canadian people. In every sense the Canadian constitution was a Conservative achievement. Both the American and the Australian systems were born in the democratic radicalism of their times. The detailed points of resemblance between Australian and American constitutions have been enumerated too frequently to need repetition here. The similarity was so exact in many respects that the Australian High Court was frequently able to use American Supreme Court decisions and arguments as persuasive authority in constitutional issues.

All this should not, however, be too easily assumed to imply any general liking in Australia for American methods *qua* American. It was rather that in the example of the United States the small states were able to see arguments for steady growth within the framework of states rights and could, therefore, hold tenaciously to these rights without denying the validity of the larger Australian nationalism; whereas the large states were handicapped in having to fall back on the much less spectacular development of the more highly unified Canada. And, of course, the American experiment seemed to be much more strikingly successful in the late nineties when the Australians were creating their federation, than it had in the middle sixties when the Canadians were forming theirs. Then, too, it should be noted that to the Australians the American system was not so much a thing of flesh and blood, of men and political machines, as of documents and textbooks. Only one or two of the Australian fathers had visited the United States, and these had merely passed through as tourists. It is doubtful whether any of the Canadian fathers had not at some time been in the United States, and some of them had been domiciled there. Two had operated newspapers in New York and might have been expected to know rather intimately the working of the American system. To the Australians the American system was Bryce, or Madison's notes, or the expositions of the Federalist. It was utopian.

In one important field American experience failed to provide either of these British federations with useful lessons for their guidance. The American Civil War had been the answer of the United States to secessionist activity. Movements toward secession have appeared in both Canada and Australia. Indeed they may almost be regarded as a distinctive feature of the constitutional development of both. This has doubtless been in part due to the fact that in a federation within an empire such secessionism can be at once useful and safe. It has become in both Canada and Australia a stimulating and innocuous recreation. The experience of the United States not being here available, these dominion agitations have had to borrow from each other. Without any chance of success as against the federation as a whole, and having been consistently cold-shouldered by the British government, the success of these movements has been almost as much beyond the bounds of practical politics as it would now be in the United States. Such movements have become, however, a potent form of pressure politics.

To sum up the American influence on the formation, as distinct from the subsequent growth, of these two British federations we may say that on the Canadian federation this influence was chiefly that of impact, or to put it more accurately, of Canadian determination so to fashion its constitution as to provide a fit instrument for guarding against any possible nefarious activities arising south of their long and exposed southern border; whereas American influence on the Australian constitution was chiefly in the providing of a proved model for it.

III

American influence on Canadian federal development since the formation of the Dominion has in the main followed the pattern of 1864, being determined by impacts more than by imitations. But there has been this fundamental difference, that whereas in the sixties the United States was paradoxically at once weak and menacing, since that time it has with fair consistency grown increasingly strong and benevolent. American high tariffs may have been regretted in Canada, or at times resented, but it is significant that the last outcropping of the annexation menace a quarter of a century ago was in connection with the proposal for reciprocal free trade. On the all-important side of defense it has become almost axiomatic in Canada that the United States is a bulwark along the long southern border, and in no sense itself a menace. Indeed most Canadians are quite unaware that their southern frontier is exposed. It was not always so. Never perhaps more than at present have Canadians been so ready to assume this benevolence on the part of the United States, and it is none the less important in helping to direct Canadian constitutional policy, if we may use such a phrase, on account of its partly selfish character. For, although Canadians receive a sense of security from the presence of a good neighbor on their exposed southern frontier, the United States is also assured of the full support of British arms in the defense of its equally exposed and equally long northern frontier. One may therefore say in a broad way that the threatening attitude of the United States in the sixties seemed to call for a highly centralized Canadian system, but that the subsequent good will of this powerful neighbor has removed much of the reason for its continuance. The benevolence of Great Britain on the one side and of the United States on the other may be regarded as the two greatest obstacles to the growth of Canadian national unity or the retention of the highly centralized system created in the sixties. Without passing moral judgment or attempting to predict, it is possible to read in the decisions of the judicial committee of the privy council in the disputes between central and provincial authorities, in which with fair uniformity the former has been sacrificed to the latter, not so much learned judgments on the law, or perverse policies regarding Canadian development, but merely signs of the times at which these decisions were handed down.

There has been some borrowing by Canada in what may be called federal administrative techniques. But the fundamental difference in the law of the constitution has tended to thwart any disposition there may have been to learn much from American federal experience. The fact that parties in both countries have played a predominant rôle in directing constitutional tendencies has been against such borrowing, for there is little if any feeling of kinship between parties across the border. In the influence which American economic and social policies and practices have exercised on Canadian practices, and indirectly therefore the constitutional forms within which these practices take place, there has been, and there must continue to be, the greatest influence of the United States on the constitutional life of Canada. And this must lead in the long run to the assimilation of such policies, with their constitutional implications. Already there are distinct signs that this process is going on.

For whatever combination of reasons, the Canadian and American federal systems continue to grow more alike. Beginning as almost the antithesis of each other, the American has with fair consistency grown more unified, while the Canadian, at least since the demise of Macdonald, becomes increasingly decentralized. This is not the place to discuss whether this is merely due to the natural tendency of systems at first overbalanced to one side or the other to swing back to a more normal position, and how far to the fact that the conditions in each have actually tended to become more alike. Geography has undoubtedly had something to do with this growing similarity. Canada and the United States are in North America like two slices of an apple. And there is nothing so likely to resemble a half an apple as the other half. In the long run geography is great and will prevail, even over courts. In fact the Supreme Court of the United States and the Judicial Committee of the Privy Council may be regarded as the chosen vessels of Providence, whose historic rôle has been to insist on the inevitable, and to do it in the impressive language of the law.

Conscious borrowing by Canada from the United States has been somewhat retarded undoubtedly by the fact that this has had to be through the medium of some political party. Now the party traditionally least averse to American borrowing has been the Liberal. But this party has also traditionally been the party most favorable to provincial rights, and since the tendency in the United States has been consistently away from states rights, the process of borrowing has been largely thwarted. For many reasons there has not been any perceptible tendency for provinces to learn from states their methods for preserving what rights they may. Quebec may learn from Nova Scotia; it could hardly learn from Rhode Island.

IV

For twenty years after the formation of the Australian federation American influence remained strong in the field of conscious imitation. The most conspicuous form of this was in the adoption of the relevant decisions of the American Supreme Court as persuasive authority in the Australian High Court. There were two special reasons for the extent of this process. In the first place the two constitutions were so nearly alike, often in matters of phrasing as well as in general content, that it was altogether likely that the United States would already have faced problems that Australia eventually came to face in working out its *modus vivendi* as between the federal power and the states. In the second place the Australian High Court at first adopted the principle of constitutional interpretation long accepted in the American Supreme Court. This stood in sharp contrast to the principle of strict literal interpretation applied so consistently by the Judicial Committee. The American principle was based in part on the assumption that the federation must be preserved, and that certain adaptations became from time to time necessary, if the intention of the fathers was to be fulfilled amidst changing circumstances. With the more rigid principles of literal interpretation the Australians had at first little sympathy.

Then came a change. It was due no doubt in part to the changing personnel of the High Court, partly to the influence of Judicial Committee decisions in those cases in which the constitution had made provision for appeal beyond the High Court, partly to the general attitude of Australians to the United States following the World War. It was in the famous Engineers' Case of 1920 that the change in principle of judicial interpretation was clearly laid down by the High Court. Thereafter the constitution of Australia was to be regarded as an Act of the British Parliament, rather than a federal constitution as such. It must therefore be subjected only to the strictest principle of literal interpretation, in which neither the intentions of the fathers nor considerations of expediency, no matter how urgent, could have any place. Since then the Australian High Court has cut itself off from any possible influence from the American Supreme Court. The same tendency is noticed in other fields of possible constitutional change. A Royal Commission reported on constitutional change in 1929. Their elaborate recommendations make almost no mention of American experience. As in Canada, there have been some borrowings in the field of administrative technique, but even these have not been extensive so far as they relate to federal-state relations.

This lack of borrowing does not mean that there have not been some striking parallel developments between Australia and the United States. In the very case in which the High Court so consciously turned away from following the American method of judicial interpretation, the court added substantially to the central power, and correspondingly weakened the power of the states. High Court decisions have in the main tended to further federal and stultify state power, as have those of the Supreme Court of the United States. Strangely enough, the critical change in the principle of judicial interpretation has seemed to make no difference in this tendency. This is the more remarkable when it is recalled that the strict literal interpretations of the judicial committee have tended in Canadian decisions in just the opposite direction. In fact all three of these courts have consistently tended to nullify the essential provision in each of their constitutions which they have been appointed to interpret, in which the residuum of power was supposed to give some ultimate control to the body possessing it. It would seem that the principle of interpretation has had little to do with this tendency. If a court remains long enough in contemplation of any power in the constitution, that tends to become the real residuum of power. The judicial committee of the privy council, for instance, would have made a quite different constitution for Canada had it been as ardent to squeeze the last drop of meaning out of the term "trade and commerce" as it had been to extract the last drop from "property and civil rights." It would seem to be not so much a question of whether interpretations be literal or loose, but what they are literal or loose about. All three courts have in fact been policy-makers, and they have tended to bring all three constitutions into ever closer line with one another.

Another significant parallel development between Australia and the United States has been the growth of uniformity without unity. This process in Australia has been both rapid and extensive. This has undoubtedly been made easier by the small number of states. It has been feasible to have annual, or at least frequent, meetings of different states and federal officials. The annual meeting of parliamentary draftsmen, for instance, has had a great influence on the building up within the Commonwealth of a body of uniform state laws. The premiers' conference has been a notable achievement in the same direction. This has made possible many other forms of interstate activity. A mere list of the departments whose heads or deputy heads meet regularly to coördinate policies would be impressive. The tendency lags in the fields of municipal administration, which in Australia is a veritable jungle, and in land settlement. In other fields it has been consistent and profound. This growth of uniformity has been made the easier by the uniformity in the population itself; also by the fact that all go back to the same constitutional roots in the Colonial Office of the early nineteenth century. An added urge is given to it by the common isolation in the Antipodes, with the consequent sense of the danger of external aggression. The growth of uniformity throughout Australia, within the framework of states rights, constitutes perhaps the most significant factor in its constitutional development. It has been stimulated by at least two interstate bodies, the Australian Loan Council and the Commonwealth Grants Commission. Both of these have become definitely policy-making bodies without intending to become so.

Australia, like Canada and the United States, has been coming increasingly to feel the need for an extension of social services by governmental agencies. The party to feel this most has, of course, been the Labor Party. Now this is the party most in favor of actual unification, and least addicted to states rights. Should they gain control of the federal parliament, there can be slight question that the process of unification would be accelerated. But the other parties have been driven in the same direction. It would seem, therefore, that either in the form of a growing uniformity based on consultation, or of actual unification with perhaps state administrative responsibility, Australia is likely to continue to follow, if it does not come to lead, the American and Canadian tendencies to extend their programs of national social services.

With this is closely linked the tendency toward national supervision and control in business and industrial activities. These movements coupled with increasing responsibilities in the field of national defense are forces common to all three federations and may well be expected to carry them far along the same constitutional road. Even in Canada there are signs that the tide of provincial rights has perhaps run its course and may shortly begin to ebb. And, after all, these cases of parallel development may have greater significance than if the similarity were conditioned on conscious borrowing. When history begins to repeat itself, it leaves to administrators, parliaments, and courts alike a narrowing field for conscious endeavor. Nevertheless, the United States cannot be denied its major rôle in the making of these two British federations, and the success or failure of the American system to remain really federal will continue to have significance for these younger federations; upon the ability of all three countries to retain the essentially federal features of their constitutions may well depend the survival under the stress of modern world conditions of the federal idea itself.

The Judicial Interpretation of the Canadian Constitution ∿ C. P. WRIGHT

THE Constitution of the Dominion of Canada is the product of two conferences. In October, 1864, a conference of representatives of all the provinces and colonies of eastern British North America was held at Quebec; and this conference adopted a series of resolutions which defined all the essential characteristics of the Confederation to be. A second conference, which was attended only by authorized delegates of the three mainland provinces of Canada, New Brunswick, and Nova Scotia, was held in London in December, 1866. The London conference made some subsidiary alterations of the Quebec resolutions and submitted the modified body of resolutions to the colonial secretary; the colonial secretary and the British government accepted the revised resolutions as a compact between the three provinces which did not require the further ratification of the provincial legislatures; the resolutions were translated into the form of a bill, and in March, 1867, this bill was passed into law by the parliament of the United Kingdom, under the title of the British North America Act, 1867.

It was the clearly declared intention of the Quebec and London resolutions to create ". . . a Federal Union under the Crown of Great Britain . . . ," comprising both ". . . a General Government charged with matters of common interest to the whole country, and Local Governments . . . charged with the control of local matters in their respective sections. . . ." The federal aspect of the Canadian Constitution is to be seen principally in a detailed division and specification of legislative jurisdiction, both in the resolutions and in the Act itself, between the parliament of the Dominion on the one hand and the legislatures of the provinces on the other. But in addition to this federal element in the Canadian Constitution, there was also incorporated an "imperial" element, in that the powers with respect to the appointment and removal of provincial lieutenant governors and to the disallowance of provincial legislation, which had hitherto been vested in the crown-in-council itself (that is to say, the British government), were transferred to the governor-general in council (the Dominion government). The combination of these federal and imperial elements of the Constitution would have had the effect of reducing the provinces to little more than municipal status; and such an end was, indeed, intended by some of the principal authors of the Constitution, for the avowed purpose of preventing the creation of "state sovereignties" of the kind that had so recently provoked a civil war in the United States. Yet, strangely enough, the processes of judicial interpretation of the British North America Act, principally by the judicial committee of the privy council, which sits in Downing Street, sublimely removed from the contaminating influences of Canadian politics and also from all other knowledge of Canadian public affairs, has tended in a precisely contrary direction and has created provincial rights and a provincial autonomy very much stronger and wider than the rights and autonomy that the states of the Union now possess.

Both the federal and imperial aspects of the British North America Act have furnished occasions for litigation and judicial interpretation. In the federal field, by far the most important issue has been the conflict of Dominion and provincial jurisdictions in the broad fields of social and economic legislation; and in the imperial field, controversy has centered principally upon the status and powers of the provincial lieutenant governor. Within the limits of this paper, it is possible to consider only the first of these two major issues. But it happens to be the conflict of Dominion and provincial jurisdiction with respect to social and economic legislation that has aroused the greatest concern in Canada at the present time; and there are also several reasons for supposing that a discussion of this question will be of especial interest to a gathering of historians in the United States.

The legislative jurisdiction of the Dominion parliament is established and defined by the British North America Act, section 91, in the following terms:

It shall be lawful for the Queen, by and with the Advice and Consent of the Senate and House of Commons, to make Laws for the Peace, Order and good Government of Canada, in relation to all Matters not coming within the Classes of Subjects by this Act assigned exclusively to the Legislatures of the Provinces; and for greater Certainty, but not so as to restrict the Generality of the foregoing Terms of this Section, it is hereby declared that (notwithstanding anything in this Act) the exclusive Legislative Authority of the Parliament of Canada extends to all Matters coming within the Classes of Subjects next hereinafter enumerated; that is to say,—

and there then follows a schedule of twenty-nine fields of legislation exemplifying and exclusively assigned to Dominion jurisdiction; most of these fields relate to specific aspects of finance, commerce, and navigation (so that they may be generally described as economic), and the broadest of them is:

(2)   The Regulation of Trade and Commerce.

Section 92, which defines the legislative jurisdiction of the provincial legislatures, opens as follows:

92.   In each Province the Legislature may exclusively make Laws in relation to Matters coming within the Classes of Subjects next hereinafter enumerated; that is to say . . .

and there follows a schedule of sixteen fields of provincial jurisdiction, of which the two most important have proved to be:

(13)   Property and Civil Rights in the Province.
.   .   .   .
(16)   Generally all Matters of a merely local or private Nature in the Province.

It will be remarked that the opening declarations of both sections 91 and 92 assign these sixteen enumerated fields of legislation exclusively to the provincial legislatures. Yet, on the other hand, the opening declaration of section 91 also lays it down that seemingly exclusive provincial powers are also to be deemed to be wholly subordinate to any and all of the enumerated specific powers given to the Dominion parliament; and this supremacy of the enumerated powers of parliament is reaffirmed with emphasis at the conclusion of section 91, in the following terms:

And any Matter coming within any of the Classes of Subjects enumerated within this Section shall not be deemed to come within the Class of Matters of a local or private Nature comprised in the Enumeration of the Classes of Subjects by this Act assigned exclusively to the Legislatures of the Provinces.

The complexity of this most labored legal phraseology has rendered it in practice too difficult for members of the judicial committee to comprehend and apply. Yet the purport of it all is not ambiguous. To the Dominion parliament was given the general legislative power in relation to "peace, order, and good government"—practically the words in which the powers of colonial legislatures had been defined for nearly two hundred years before. From this general power were cut away the powers given to the provincial legislatures in relation to matters of a merely local or private nature. And then from these merely local and private powers of the provincial legislatures there were cut away, and restored to the Dominion, all matters coming within any of the Dominion's twenty-nine enumerated, and mainly commercial and economic, powers.

The single leading case that has determined all the subsequent course of judicial interpretation of the British North America Act with respect to social and economic matters came before the judicial committee in 1881. This was the case of *Citizens' Insurance Company* v. *Parsons;* [1] and the constitutional issue involved was the validity of an act of the provincial legislature of Ontario which required the insertion of certain statutory conditions in forms of contract for insurance against losses by fire. Insurance is a difficult field upon the borderlands of commerce which has provided Canada with several of its principal constitutional cases, and unfortunately the board (the conventional term for the membership of the judicial committee in a particular case) was actually—I repeat the words in which a well-known English barrister characterized it to me—"a very weak Board."

In its decision the board first held that the words "Property and Civil Rights" (overlooking the qualifying phrase, "in the Province") were "sufficiently large to embrace, in their fair and ordinary meaning, rights arising out of contract." Upon this showing, the disputed provision in the provincial act lay within the exclusive jurisdiction of the provincial legislature in relation to "Property and Civil Rights." But could the matter be taken away from provincial jurisdiction and given to the exclusive and overriding jurisdiction of the Dominion, under the head, "The Regu-

[1] 7 A.C., 96–126.

lation of Trade and Commerce"? To this question the board returned the answer that "Regulation of Trade and Commerce" would validly include political arrangements in regard to trade, regulation of interprovincial trade, and regulation of trade affecting the whole Dominion; but it would not comprehend the power to regulate by legislation the contracts of a particular business or trade, such as the business of fire insurance in a single province; and accordingly the Dominion jurisdiction in relation to trade and commerce could not in such respects override the provincial jurisdiction in relation to property and civil rights.

The reasoning that led to this double conclusion was ostensibly historical in character. The board quite rightly related the provision in the British North America Act on the subject of property and civil rights to the corresponding words in the Quebec Act of 1774, which had restored the Laws of Canada (the laws of the former French regime) "relative to property and civil rights." But it made no attempt to determine the scope and content in the field of contract either of that older body of law or of its more recent reformulation in 1865 (almost immediately before Confederation) in the elaborated *Civil Code of Lower Canada*. Yet had it done this, it would, or should, have perceived that this portion of the French-Canadian law covers only the forms and essentially legal aspects of contract and does not extend at all to any control over the substance and public implications of specific contracts.

The board was merely negligent in its endeavor to determine the scope of "Property and Civil Rights." But in its attempt to construe the expression "The Regulation of Trade and Commerce" it was utterly fantastic. The only authority which it cited upon this point was the Act of Union with Scotland, of 1707, which contains the words "regulations of trade." The precise wording is not the same, the term in the Act of Union with Scotland is employed in a very special sense, and there is not the slightest evidence of any kinship between the Act of Union with Scotland and the British North America Act. Moreover, an obvious source of the term in the British North America Act—a source which the board entirely disregarded—was the heading, "Trade and Commerce," of a chapter in the *Consolidated Statutes*

of Canada, 1859,[2] which treats, among other things, of such matters of internal regulation as the inspection of staple commodities
—in other words, matters definitely affecting "the contracts of a
particular business or trade."

It is also to be remarked that, apart from any question of their
correctness, these two definitions of "Property and Civil Rights in
the Province" and "Regulation of Trade and Commerce" are of
such extreme breadth that they might well be regarded as *obiter
dicta* with respect to the specific issue. (In point of fact, the Supreme Court of Canada, in its prior hearing of the case, had rendered a majority decision to the same effect as the decision of
the judicial committee, upon the basis of narrower and more
appropriate legal reasoning.) Nevertheless the two definitions
promulgated by the judicial committee in this particular case
have been followed without modification or even criticism in all
subsequent judicial interpretation. The commerce power of the
Dominion parliament, though it was not restricted in the Act
itself by any such qualifying phrase as attaches to the commerce
power of the United States Congress, has thus been reduced by
the interpretation of the judicial committee to a very much narrower compass; and the judicial committee has never adopted
the principle that "the provision regarding the liberty of the
subject is, to some extent, limited by the commerce clause of the
Constitution," which was enunciated in 1899 by the Supreme
Court of the United States.[3]

In the following year, 1882, the case of *Russell* v. *the Queen* [4]
came before the judicial committee, and was decided by very
nearly the same Board as had given the decision in the case of
Citizens' Insurance Company v. *Parsons*. This was the first of a
series of important constitutional cases upon the regulation of
the liquor traffic—another troublesome borderline field. The decision in *Russell* v. *the Queen* upheld the validity of a local option
statute passed by the Dominion parliament, on the ground that:

[2] That is, the former province of Canada.

[3] Addystone Pipe & Steel Company v. U.S., 175 U.S. 211. The Judicial Committee
could not, of course, adopt this principle without some modification, since there is no
Bill of Rights in the British North America Act. Yet in fact the Judicial Committee,
in its decisions of January, 1937 (see below), has spoken of "property and civil rights
in the province" almost as if it did establish a body of individual rights and immunities.

[4] 7 A.C., 329–42.

Few, if any, laws could be made by Parliament for the peace, order, and good government of Canada which did not in some incidental way affect property and civil rights; and it could not have been intended, when assuring to the provinces exclusive legislative authority on the subjects of property and civil rights, to exclude the Parliament from the exercise of the general power whenever any such incidental interference would result from it.

. . . .

Parliament deals with the subject as one of general concern to the Dominion, upon which uniformity of legislation is desirable, and the Parliament alone can so deal with it.

In thus attributing to the provincial legislatures plenary jurisdiction in the field of property and civil rights, this decision went far beyond the conclusion on that point in the case of *Citizens' Insurance Company* v. *Parsons*. Yet despite this very serious error, the decision was favorable in every other respect to Dominion jurisdiction, since it attributed to the Dominion parliament a wide *discretion* in determining whether matters not specifically falling under any of the enumerated heads of section 91 might be regarded as matters of national concern, and a consequent *power* to legislate upon such matters, regardless of any incidental interference with the provincial powers enumerated in section 92. And upon this reading of it, the decision in *Russell* v. *the Queen* may be said to be the judicial ratification of the broad principles enunciated in the resolutions of the Quebec and London conferences.

But the efficacy of this ruling, which was perhaps too broadly and too vaguely stated, was seriously impaired by a train of further decisions, notably in the cases of *Hodge* v. *the Queen* [5] (1883), *In re Dominion Liquor License Acts, 1883–84* [6] (1885), and *Attorney-General for Ontario* v. *Attorney-General for Canada (Ontario Liquor License Act)* [7] (1895–96). All these decisions upheld—or were deemed to uphold—provincial jurisdiction over the liquor traffic; and the principal grounds for the decisions were the jurisdiction given to the provinces in relation to "Municipal Institutions," "Property and Civil Rights in the Province," and "Generally all Matters of a merely local or private Nature in the Province." In the course of the opinion that he delivered on be-

[5] 9 A.C., 147–35.
[6] 4 Cartwright, 342 n.
[7] [1896] A.C., 348–71.

half of the board in the case of 1896, Lord Watson attacked the principle stated in *Russell* v. *the Queen* in the following words, which seem to imply a strong prejudice against the Dominion government and all its powers:

> If it were once conceded that the Parliament of Canada has authority to make laws applicable to the whole Dominion, in relation to matters which in each province are substantially of local or private interest, upon the assumption that these matters also concern the peace, order, and good government of the Dominion, there is hardly a subject upon which it might not legislate, to the exclusion of the provincial legislatures.

The thought expressed in this sentence (notably through the use of the words "substantially" and "assumption") and in this decision of Lord Watson's as a whole, has colored all subsequent interpretation of the British North America Act.

Between 1892 and 1899 Lord Watson played a leading part in the hearing of Canadian appeals and delivered several opinions of the highest consequence, for the most part strongly on the provincial side. Almost all of these decisions, however, related to questions of Dominion and provincial property rights and revenues, so that it is not possible to consider them here. They had the general effect of seriously weakening (by what were perhaps in some instances *obiter dicta*) the "imperial" element of the Dominion government's powers. And they also prepared another interpreter of the British North America Act for the critical part that he was later to play.

In many of the cases for which Lord Watson was a member of the board, one of the leading counsel, and usually on the provincial side, was Mr. R. B. Haldane. Mr. Haldane, as he tells in his reminiscences, succeeded in coming to a very good understanding with Lord Watson. (He was, like Lord Watson, of Scottish origin.) In 1911 Mr. Haldane, then Secretary of State for War, was raised to the peerage, and in 1912 he was made Lord Chancellor. From the time of his elevation to the lords, he took an active part in the work of the judicial committee; and up to the time of his death in 1928 he seems to have possessed the same predominating influence as had Lord Watson in the determination of Canadian appeals, proceeding much further in the same direction.

As a matter of fact, two of Lord Haldane's earliest decisions were adverse to provincial jurisdiction. In 1913, in the case of *Royal Bank of Canada* v. *the King*,[8] he held that certain civil rights might lie outside the jurisdiction of a province; and in 1914, in the case of *John Deere Plow Company* v. *Wharton*,[9] he declared invalid a provincial statute for the regulation of extraprovincial companies.

But from 1916 on, the trend of Lord Haldane's decisions was always in favor of provincial, and against Dominion, jurisdiction. In 1916, in the case of *Attorney-General for Canada* v. *Attorney-General for Alberta*,[10] he declared a Dominion statute for the regulation of the business of insurance to be invalid, on the grounds (1) that it interfered with civil rights in the provinces and (2) that the jurisdiction of the Dominion in relation to the regulation of trade and commerce did not extend to the regulation by licensing of a particular trade in which Canadians would otherwise be free to engage in the provinces. This decision is evidently founded upon the definitions in the case of *Citizens' Insurance Company* v. *Parsons*. Yet, strangely enough, Lord Haldane made no reference to the decision in this case, and considered the decisions of the judicial committee in the liquor traffic cases alone, as if with a set purpose of disparaging the significance of the principle of *Russell* v. *the Queen*.

It was, however, the accident of the war that gave to Lord Haldane the opportunity to make his most unwarrantable contribution to Canadian constitutional law. In 1919 the Dominion parliament had passed two closely related measures, a first law for the creation of a board of commerce, modeled in general upon the Federal Trade Commission of the United States and charged in particular with the administration of a second law against combines and profiteering. The validity of this pair of laws was challenged in the courts, and Lord Haldane delivered the opinion of the Judicial Committee, the case being termed, *In re Board of Commerce Act and Combines and Fair Prices Act*.[11] As in 1916, he held that the subject matter of these two statutes lay within the scope of "property and civil rights" and outside the scope of

---

[8] [1913] A.C., 283–98.
[9] [1915] A.C., 330–44.
[10] [1916] A.C., 588–98.
[11] [1922] 1 A.C., 191–201.

"regulation of trade and commerce." But he now reinforced this conclusion by adding the further and very important doctrine that the general legislative power of the Dominion parliament in relation to "peace, order, and good government"—the definition of colonial legislative power that was formulated in the reign of Charles II, at the very least—could override the enumerated powers given to the provincial legislatures only in special circumstances, such as those of a great war.

Two years later, in 1923, in the case of *Fort Frances Pulp and Power Company, Ltd.,* v. *Manitoba Free Press, Ltd.,*[12] Lord Haldane stated still more positively, though not at all precisely, that only "exceptional necessity" or "national emergency" could give validity to Dominion legislation that overrode provincial powers. At the same time, confronted by the facts of the particular case, he conceded to the Dominion government discretion to determine the duration of the state of emergency of the war.

In 1925, in the case of *Toronto Electricity Commission* v. *Snider and Others,*[13] Lord Haldane delivered his last important opinion, declaring against the validity of a Dominion statute, the Industrial Disputes Investigation Act, which had been passed into law in 1907 and had been continuously administered since that time. This was the first occasion on which a Dominion statute in relation to labor and employment (there have been very few Dominion enactments in this field) had been challenged and declared invalid. Again following the definitions of *Citizens' Insurance Company* v. *Parsons,* Lord Haldane held that the subject matter of the statute lay within "property and civil rights" and outside "regulation of trade and commerce"; and he added that the circumstances of the particular case (not of the passing of the act in question) did not indicate the existence of any national emergency that could evoke the Dominion's jurisdiction in relation to "peace, order, and good government." Perhaps the most remarkable feature of the opinion (in effect Lord Haldane's valedictory to the British North America Act) was the treatment of the principle enunciated in the case of *Russell* v. *the Queen,* which was now virtually repudiated in the following words:

[12] [1923] A.C., 695–708.
[13] [1925] A.C., 395–416.

Their Lordships think that the decision *Russell* v. *The Queen* can only be supported to-day, not on the footing of having laid down an interpretation, such as has sometimes been invoked, of the general words at the beginning of s.91, but on the assumption of the Board, apparently made at the time of deciding the case of *Russell* v. *The Queen,* that the evil of intemperance at that time amounted to one so great and so general that at least for the period it was a menace to the national life of Canada so serious and pressing that the National Parliament was called on to intervene to protect the nation from disaster. An epidemic of pestilence might conceivably have been regarded as analogous . . . Their Lordships find it difficult to explain the decision in *Russell* v. *The Queen* as more than a decision of this order upon facts considered to have been established at its date, rather than upon general law.

These words have often since been quoted, but never with respect. Lord Haldane here evidently failed to discern that the conclusion that the evil of intemperance and the promotion of temperance were matters of national concern had been reached by the Dominion parliament upon the exercise of its own discretion and that the board which heard the appeal of *Russell* v. *the Queen* had done nothing more than to assure itself that the act of parliament in dispute could properly be regarded as a measure of general and uniform character and then to uphold it as a piece of valid legislation.

Hopes of a trend of judicial interpretation more favorable to Dominion jurisdiction were raised in 1931 and 1932. Section 132 of the British North America Act gives to the Dominion all necessary or proper powers for the performance of obligations arising under Empire treaties. (This provision, which originated in the Quebec and London resolutions, is probably attributable to the difficulties that were experienced in procuring legislative enforcement by the several provincial legislatures of the provisions of the Reciprocity Treaty of 1854.) And on the basis of this power, the judicial committee in 1931 gave to the Dominion full powers for the regulation of aerial navigation,[14] and in 1932 (by much more questionable reasoning) full control of radio communication.[15]

It is not necessary to recount the circumstances under which a body of "New Deal" legislation was enacted by the Dominion parliament in 1934 and 1935 and was shortly afterward referred

[14] [1932] A.C. 54.
[15] *Ibid.,* 304.

en bloc to the courts. All that need be said here is that a group of six cases, involving ten statutes or portions of statutes in all, in a complicated structure of appeals and cross-appeals, came before the judicial committee in November, 1936. Three of these cases dealt with matters of the highest social and economic importance, two of them relating to labor and one to the marketing of natural products; and the other three dealt with matters of more limited, yet still substantial, economic concern. The judicial committee pronounced its formal conclusions in January, 1937; and in all three of the principal cases its decisions and reasoning were strongly adverse to the statutes in question and to the Dominion's powers.[16]

The two cases relating to labor embraced a group of three acts providing for a weekly day of rest in industrial undertakings, for the determination of minimum wages, and for the regulation of hours of labor, and an act for the establishment of a national system of unemployment and social insurance. The first three of these matters had previously been made the subjects of draft conventions prepared in general conferences of the International Labor Organization, and the preambles to the statutes directed attention to this foundation for their enactment; in like manner the preamble to the statute on unemployment insurance made reference to the articles on the welfare of labor in the Treaty of Versailles. On behalf of the first three measures, counsel for the Dominion directed their arguments toward establishing that they were valid legislation in fulfillment of international obligations and also (though in only a cursory manner) that they related to matters of "peace, order, and good government" transcending the jurisdiction of the provinces and to an international and inter-provincial "regulation of trade and commerce." And on behalf of the fourth statute they contended that it dealt with unemployment as a matter of national interest and importance affecting the body politic of the Dominion. Nevertheless, in oral argument, one of the counsel for the Dominion conceded that the subject matter of the first three statutes, apart from the existence of the draft conventions, lay within the jurisdiction of the provinces as matters of "property and civil rights"; and he made no attempt to withdraw it from that jurisdiction as a matter of "regulation

16 The reports of all six cases are to be found in [1937] A.C. 326 f.

of trade and commerce." In the presence of a board which had apparently acquired all its knowledge of Canadian constitutional law from the decisions of Lord Watson and Lord Haldane, this double surrender was fatal to the Dominion's case.

In rendering its opinion, the board had no difficulty in deciding that the several draft conventions could not be regarded as "Empire" treaties within the meaning of section 132, and that any justification for the first three statutes must therefore be found within the compass of sections 91 and 92. With respect to the question of "property and civil rights," the admission of Dominion counsel rendered judicial reasoning entirely superfluous; and reference to the doctrine of "emergency" excluded the statutes from consideration as matters of "peace, order, and good government." A summary repetition of the same conclusions was also employed to declare invalid the unemployment insurance act.

The third case of cardinal importance concerned the Natural Products Marketing Acts, which authorized the establishment of producers' marketing boards operating under government regulation. These acts also were declared invalid on the ground that they related to transactions completed within the province and falling exclusively within the scope of "property and civil rights"; and this invalidation was rendered all the more serious by reason of previous decisions of the judicial committee and the Supreme Court of Canada adverse to the establishment of marketing agencies upon the basis of provincial jurisdiction. In the field of marketing, therefore, the judicial committee has now thus created a "twilight zone," within which neither the Dominion nor the provinces can legislate effectually except by recourse to the complex and dubious processes of concurrent legislation.

From the decisions in these three major cases (the three minor cases do not call for particular consideration) three principal conclusions can be drawn. Firstly, in the sphere of constitutional law, the authority of the Dominion parliament with regard to matters of the highest economic and social concern has been reduced to the most exiguous and ineffectual limits, thanks to the execrable decision in the case of *Citizens' Insurance Company* v. *Parsons* and to its uncritical acceptance ever since. Secondly, in the sphere of politics, it would appear that the judicial committee is not willing to concede to the parliament of Canada any real discretion in determining what matters can be deemed to be questions of Canadian concern. And thirdly, in the sphere of international relations, the status of the Dominion of Canada as an international personage has been most seriously limited, by the refusal of the judicial committee to concede to the parliament of Canada full powers of legislation for the performance of any international obligations the Dominion assumes in its own right. For this last injury, however, the blame would seem to rest not so much upon the judicial committee as upon the Imperial Conference of 1926, which omitted to give full and conclusive legal effect to its resolutions upon the international aspects of Dominion status. But the guilt for the judicial murder of the Canadian Constitution and the judicial—shall I say infanticide?—of the Canadian nation rests primarily upon the judicial committee itself.

The Frontier and the Constitution
in South Africa ～ C. W. DE KIEWIET

THE distinction between the Old Empire and the New Empire is a real one. In the one the great colonies of settlement gained their independence by a revolutionary process; in the other they gained it by a constitutional process. The one enshrined its independence in a unique and sovereign document; the other wove it out of a tissue of deliberately vague and indecisive assumptions. Before the modern Empire could make a revolution, its revolution had happened. Yet the distinction between the Old Empire and the New is sometimes made uncritically to imply that the one is incompatible with the other, that the Old Empire, for example, came to an end in 1783, while the New Empire took its rise only in 1815. The Napoleonic Wars helped to strengthen the impression of a confused interregnum stretching between the two colonial epochs like a jungle in which the colonial movement of the eighteenth century got lost and spent its strength before the imperial renaissance of the nineteenth century got under way.

Actually the nineteenth-century Empire went to school with its predecessor. The influence, for example, of the Declaration of Independence and of the Constitution of the Thirteen Colonies upon the thought and practice of the major colonies of the British Empire in the nineteenth century was close and constant. From the great stock of ideas, phrases and beliefs that the Revolution and the Constitution produced, colonial and imperial statesmen borrowed with the greatest freedom. There was hardly a speech on important colonial matters that did not show, consciously or unconsciously, its debt to the pregnant years between 1776 and 1787. The Whig interpretation of the Revolution created an atmosphere in which it was not unseemly for men in England and the Empire to look to the seceded colonies for precept and example. Certainly the attitude of those who were afraid that the New Empire would collapse like the Old, and of those who were afraid that it would not, enabled British thought to look upon the

Revolution not so much as a disaster to be forgotten, but as a lesson to be remembered.

It is, however, within the individual colonies that the influence of the American scene is of special interest. The colonists of the greater settlements of the nineteenth century never forgot that the Americans had once been colonists of Great Britain too. It became a habit with them to compare their material and political circumstances with those of the great republic in search of analogies and likenesses, as if to discover the portents in themselves of similar happenings and a similar career. Of American influence in Canada it would be invidious to speak. It is at once so inevitable and vast. But in New Zealand, Australia, and South Africa, American history was feelingly understood and followed. When the early Australian colonists in the beginning of the century contemplated the great girth of their continent, it was a vision of another America of the southern seas that they beheld, until the lessons of climate and geography finally dispelled their dream. In so many things were the American and colonial frontiers alike. There was the same spontaneous achievement of what was elsewhere a radical formula—one man, one vote, one value; the same love of demagogic eloquence, the same social conservatism, the same political radicalism, and the same suspicion of distant and central governments, whether federal or British. There was the same refusal to be confined by fixed frontiers and lines. Australian squatters and South African Boers [1] denied all obedience to the ancient principle *ne exeat regno,* even as there was no power, legal or physical, that could hold back the American pioneer. And everywhere, in greater or lesser degree, the frontier produced that sectionalism which is so essential in understanding the theory and practice of the American Constitution.

The full extent of the influence of American constitutional practice and thought upon the nineteenth-century Empire has still to be clearly determined. That it was great will not be denied. Australia actually adopted a federal form of association. Even New Zealand, so obviously destined for unitary government, flirted with federalism till 1875. Nowhere did the adoption of a federal constitution seem more logical and proper than in South Africa.

[1] C. W. de Kiewiet, *British Colonial Policy and the South African Republics* (London, 1929), pp. 11-12.

It was a land in which every individual seemed set on escaping the tyranny of his neighbor's smoke, and every community sought to wall itself off against its neighbor. Between 1850 and 1890 there were, at one time and another, upwards of twelve distinct colonies and republics. So extreme came to be the individualism of these communities, so set were they upon the defense of their separate privileges, that the only conceivable solution of the problem of closer association seemed to be in a loose federation. It was of a federation of states that Sir George Grey spoke in his famous dispatch in 1858 on South African politics.[2] It was for a federation, loose as a bundle of sticks, provided only that it ended disunion, that Lord Carnarvon pleaded vainly in 1875.[3] The brief notes for a South African constitution which Cecil Rhodes penned shortly before his death read like a rough summary of the American Constitution.

It is not easy to appreciate the truth that this brittle separatism was fortuitous. It had none of the inevitability of American or Australian sectionalism. In South Africa the frontier was not a line, nor a special part of the country, more distant or more primitive than the rest. The frontier began a hundred miles from Cape Town, and from there on was continuous and a thousand miles deep. The Dutch farmers of the Natal uplands, of the Basuto border, the Karroo, and the Transvaal Bushveld, were all the same in language, habits, and pursuits. Colonization developed from a single center, not from thirteen as in America, or half a dozen as in Australia. Between Dutch and English there was no geographical division, as there was between English and French in Upper and Lower Canada. For all its vast size, South Africa was climatically and geographically remarkably uniform.

It was the political workings of men that superimposed upon this basic uniformity of climate and soil a disastrous political disharmony. The exodus of Boers from the Cape Colony in 1836, known as the Great Trek, revealed an Empire that was without the constitutional machinery needed to meet the crisis produced when a body of settlers refused to be bound by the narrow limits of the King's government. Between rebellion and outright independence the pre-Victorian Empire had not yet found the middle road

[2] C.O. 48/390, Grey to Lytton, Nov. 19, 1858.
[3] C. W. de Kiewiet, *The Imperial Factor in South Africa* (Cambridge, 1937), Ch. V.

which the later Empire found in dominion status. Almost simultaneously the French in Canada expressed themselves in rebellion and the Dutch in South Africa marched off into the wilderness. The British government simply did not know how it could yield to the Boers without sacrificing their allegiance, or hold them without using violence. In America the federal government followed in the wake of trans-frontier settlement, erecting territories, and ultimately acknowledging and admitting them as states. In South Africa such a process would have been an invaluable aid in solving the problems of the frontier. An established and admitted doctrine of Manifest Destiny for the subcontinent would have permitted British authority to be extended naturally to all settlement beyond the frontier. But the British government did not look upon the hinterland as guaranteed to its colonists, and even shrank, as it did in Australia, from colonizing the wilderness.

There was, however, one interest that drew it deeply into the life of the colonists. A genuine concern with the lot of the native population caused it to make an unusually comprehensive attempt to govern the relations of the colonists with the natives. Herein was the chief offending of the Home government in the eyes of the South African settlers. The acute separatism of the nineteenth century was in large measure due to the desire of the frontier communities to restrict the power of the British government to interfere in their affairs. And the British government was itself afraid of the responsibilities into which its humanitarian sentiments might lead it. It was always, therefore, fighting on two fronts, against the colonists who wanted too little interference with the natives, and the "Aborigines Protection" people who wanted too much. It ran the double risk of incurring too much expense and robbing the British taxpayer's purse, or of assuming too little responsibility and violating his conscience.

As long as there had been merely the Cape Colony, numbering its natives in thousands, the effort to realize a liberal native policy had not been unsuccessful. But the Great Trek, which in America would have involved a sudden bound of the frontier from Pittsburgh to the middle of Nebraska and Oklahoma, brought millions of natives into contact with European settlement. It created a problem so vast that the British government shrank back from it. Although it was like the federal government in that it was paramount and could therefore exercise jurisdiction, it was unlike the federal government in that it could diminish its authority, and even withdraw it altogether. Thus, against its own philanthropic scruples, it finally encouraged and helped the two most important frontier communities, the Transvaal in 1852 and the Orange Free State in 1854, to establish their separate independence.[4] Separatism was, therefore, a device welcomed by the republics and by Downing Street for the same reason, that it lessened the influence and authority of the Home government upon South Africa's frontier.[5]

In 1872 the British government proceeded still further in the direction of political dismemberment by rushing the Cape Colony prematurely into self-government. Thus the major British colony too was given an instrument with which to pursue its own sectional interests, and was permitted to appeal to the principles of its constitution in defense of a narrow and selfish interpretation of its rights, in a manner that emphasized difference and rivalry to the detriment of similarity and independence.

The development of colonial self-government is unquestionably the leading achievement of imperial statesmanship in the nineteenth century. Yet it is a serious question whether the principle of self-government did not become a doctrinaire conception, so that opinion was uneasy about any policy that did not envisage early responsibility. The grant of self-government is traditionally regarded as one of those achievements in the history of a colonial community that mark its arrival at political adulthood, where refusal of responsibility becomes tyrannous and a denial of the indefeasible political rights of Englishmen. Burke's rounded periods on the sensitiveness of the constitution to national needs, the tone set by Macaulay of pride in the progress of the constitution, and the self-satisfaction of much imperialist sentiment, have encouraged certain general assumptions which, though not false in themselves, confuse the historical view of constitutional development in the Empire. There is room for some correction of the one-sided view which the Durham "classicists" have imposed upon constitutional history. The Durham Report asked that men should

---

[4] It is interesting to note that the framers of the constitutions of Natal, the Orange Free State, and the Transvaal had before them copies or summaries of the United States Constitution.

[5] *Cambridge History of the British Empire*, VIII, 391.

"follow out consistently the principles of the British constitution," granting to the colonies "more of equality, of freedom and local independence." In this spirit much constitutional history has been written, and the illusion has been created that all colonial life was borne to a fuller and freer destiny upon a broadening tide of constitutional liberties. Yet in South Africa it is not possible to regard constitutional development simply as a growth from immaturity to responsibility.

Self-government for a single colony, like independence for the single republics, was an incomplete answer to the problems of South Africa. Actually it proved an obstruction to a wider liberty. The superficial liberalism of the grant of 1872 concealed the frustration that had caused the British government to thrust it upon the Cape Colony. In a practical sense, nineteenth-century liberalism combined a willingness to encourage nations and colonies to assume control of their own affairs with an equal distaste for undertaking duties for others. It was a policy that characteristically and deliberately elevated its own needs and desires into virtues. "Free institutions," wrote John Stuart Mill, "are next to impossible in a country made up of different nationalities." Could self-government be lightheartedly applied to a land in which the white population was intent upon erecting the strictest social and political barriers between itself and the native population? Before 1872 British policy was confronted with the choice between oppressing the whites through despotism and oppressing the natives through democracy. To give a normal political liberty to the whites imposed an abnormal restriction of liberty on the natives. It was the natural perplexity of a policy which condoned interference on the grounds of humanity and denounced it on the grounds of liberty.

The grant of 1872, with its uncritical and specious faith in the solvent action of responsible institutions, greatly weakened the position in South Africa of the British government. By relinquishing control over the parent community of them all, it abandoned an invaluable strategic position. It weakened the paramountcy which *de jure* or *de facto* it had exercised over republics and colonies. It became almost an alien influence,[6] whose activities were branded as unwarranted interference, and whose advice was

[6] E. A. Walker, *Lord de Villiers and His Times*, p. 128.

rejected as doctrinaire ignorance of local conditions. When Lord Carnarvon attempted between 1874 and 1878 to bring about federation in South Africa, he stumbled over the resistance of both the Cape Colony and the republics.[7] It was the weakened constitutional position of the British government that caused it to use violence against the Transvaal by annexing it in 1877. Its subsequent defeat and withdrawal left a legacy of ill-will that dangerously deferred the achievement of closer political understanding between the different states. The ideal of a constructive native policy for the entire country was doomed. The grating and grinding of the separate communities grew worse as the century neared its end. Attempts to alleviate the country's ills merely inflamed them. Yet when they were ignored they became a pestilence that had to be stamped out in war.

In the Boer War Great Britain won a victory that ended her influence in South Africa. This paradoxical war was fought not to hold South Africa but to relinquish it. It actually showed Great Britain in the last stages of retreat from the humanitarian position which it had tried to hold. In all the wars that the century had seen, none were fought to benefit the natives. The greatest of them all was fought as if the natives did not exist. Herein lay the victory that the defeated Dutch won. The terms of peace [8] promised that no attempt would be made to alter the political status of the natives until responsible government had been granted to the ex-republics. That promise ended all hope that the British government could remain in the country in an advisory capacity, acting as a court of review in matters vitally affecting the native population. Upon the new order that was to follow the Boer War the doctrines of the frontier were destined to exercise a dominant influence. The future of South Africa was in the hands of republics that had lived in exile for two generations, and had ended that exile in defeat.

In native matters the frontier at all times thought in terms of repression. European settlement had advanced upon the native tribes determined to break their cohesion and their economic stability. It borrowed from the philanthropists their aversion to savage ways, but shared little of their desire to enlighten or to eman-

---

[7] C. W. de Kiewiet, *The Imperial Factor in South Africa, passim.*
[8] Cd. 109 of 1902; Cd. 1163 of 1902.

cipate. White civilization was deliberate in its effort to turn the natives into a black proletariat. Its legislation sought to restrict and to bind, not to relieve or to liberate. Its endeavor was to replace stability by instability, to batter strength down into weakness, so that it could subject the natives to its needs. Economically it drew the natives deeply into white society. Socially and politically it cast them forth. The Transvaal Constitution declared uncompromisingly that there should be "no equality between white and black either in Church or State." The frontier was not fond of devices and expedients. It expressed itself positively in war and dispossession, and was entirely frank in declaring its determination to possess the best land of the natives, to control their labor, and to deny them any share in the governance of the state.

From Sir George Grey onward the chief argument for closer union had been that it would permit enlightened handling of the native problem. In other words, only the united efforts of all communities, pooling the wisdom of their best statesmanship, could cope with so perverse a problem. Such phrases, sentimentally attractive, were practically misleading. When at long last South Africa sought and found unity, it sought it rather for the strength than the wisdom that it gave. By the end of the century a long process of military defeat, confiscation, eviction, and taxation had subjected the natives to a regime of legal disabilities, squalid living conditions, chronic underpayment and acute overpopulation. And yet their loins remained strong. Unlike the North American Indians, they refused to be swept away by the white man's frontier. They continued to multiply, and therefore they still had a future. What was that future to be? Had white society, in its own despite, set their feet after all on the rung of progress? Would they go on to seek entry into skilled employment? Would they seek to penetrate more deeply into white society, and take on progressively the white man's clothes, his speech, and finally his political rights? These were the great issues that the Boer War had touched not at all, and that the British government, while the country lay helpless at its feet, might have attempted to solve. Lord Milner's suggestion that all South Africa should be reduced to the status of a Crown colony at least offered the possibility of an interregnum during which the British government might try to liberalize native policy.[9] But the cataclysm of the war was the beginning of a new era. The self-governing institutions with which the former republics were endowed within five years of the peace placed no restrictions upon their control over native policy. And white society was convinced that it needed a still stronger guarantee of its racial supremacy. Because the natives were now not a military but a social menace, a new weapon other than the rifle had to be forged. What was called for was a more emphatic concentration of political power in the hands of the white community, not to rule more wisely but to rule more firmly.

This need furnished one of the strongest reasons for the adoption in 1910 of a unitary constitution. The purpose of this paper, it will now be sufficiently clear, has been to explain how a country, apparently so clearly destined to adopt a form of government comparable to that of America, was influenced negatively rather than positively by American example. What was it that led South Africa to adopt union when neither the Australian nor the American colonies had ever been so utterly estranged from one another, and when two generations of political thought had looked upon federalism as alone attainable? In such a complex society as South Africa had become, the explanation cannot be simple. By 1908 it was plain, just as it had been plain in America by 1787, that the country could no longer live without a central regulating power. If that power could not be Great Britain—and Great Britain hankered after such a position not at all—then that power had to be found in South Africa itself. The practical demands of railways, commerce, and natives had produced a world of problems with which the individual communities were incompetent to deal.[10] Actually the country suffered from a Nomansland of problems upon which no community could encroach without the certainty of quarreling with its neighbors. It was because the errors of past generations had destroyed the foundations of unity, and left a quicksand of suspicion and resentment in which all previous efforts at compromise and adjustment had foundered, that the work of the National Convention was so remarkable. In the acuteness of the issues with which they dealt, if not in the magnitude, the con-

[9] Cd. 1162 of 1902.
[10] R. H. Brand, *The Union of South Africa* (Oxford, 1909), Ch. II.

stitution makers of South Africa bear some little comparison with the great ones of 1787.

Among the considerations that led the Convention to follow New Zealand rather than the United States, natives undoubtedly held first place. In its deliberations the unpopularity of the American Constitution, and especially of the Supreme Court, was almost startling.[11] Both the regime of separate states and the power of the courts to review the actions of the legislature were regarded as weaknesses of the American Constitution that South Africa should avoid. A country confronted, as it was convinced, by the menace of a large native population could not afford to leave such breaches in its political armament. The Convention was frankly afraid of a politically minded court which, through its power of judicial review, would be able to exercise, as the American Supreme Court has exercised, a legislative function, or, more significantly still, to compel a reconciliation between legislative enactment and constitutional principle. These fears were felt rather than expressed. What might not a South African supreme court do with a "due process" clause in applying it to the place of the natives in society? It is true that the National Convention did not seem to comprehend the flexibility of the American Supreme Court in adjusting itself to the dominant currents of national sentiment, even to the point in times of great crisis of making itself the willing instrument of national policy. What they did, however, comprehend was that in a unitary constitution the power of the courts to interpret the constitution is emphatically qualified or even denied. Union, as opposed to federation, permitted the strongest guarantees in favor of the politically powerful whites.[12] Though the constitution was written, it was placed under the control of parliament itself.

The Union Constitution expelled the metropolitan point of view, and upheld the doctrines of the frontier. Had the British government insisted on being a responsible party to the negotiations, or on winning a place for Downing Street in the new Constitution, as Lord Carnarvon had tried to do in the South Africa

---

[11] Sir E. H. Walton, *The Inner History of the National Convention of South Africa* (London, 1912).

[12] It is significant that the Constitution or Grondwet of the Transvaal placed by far the greatest emphasis on the legislature. In practice, if not in strict theory, the legislature was above the constitution.

Act of 1877, it is positive that each colony would have been concerned with withholding rather than yielding, so that a loose and unconvinced federation might have been the utmost that the Convention could achieve. Any attempt to keep the political future open to the native population would have wrecked the cause of union. But the British government had abandoned its place in South Africa. There was consequently no longer any reason for the frontier to seek protection behind particularism for its social and political beliefs. Thus the frontier came out of its exile, and agreed to make whole the torn fabric of South African life. Union was the triumph of the *Voortrekker* and republican spirit. It was built upon the characteristic view of the frontier that the foundation of society is race and the privileges of race, and not civilization and the rights of civilized men. The terms upon which the former republics insisted closed the door to all hopes that the natives might one day achieve a larger share in the affairs of their land. That the Cape Colony was allowed to keep its native franchise was not a true liberal gesture. It was a concession to precedent, and the maximum concession that could be made. Even it was not fully safeguarded against future attack.

Since Union, the extrusion of the "Imperial factor" from South Africa, and of the native from the Constitution have been important issues. He who would truly understand the workings of the Union's institutions must know that among the leading problems are still those that estranged frontier and mother country just a hundred years ago. Such is the tenacity of the frontier spirit, that in a dominion so wealthy, powerful, and influential, the ideals of the trekkers, like the political thought of the American West, persist strongly. Though they are now debated more decorously on a constitutional level, the issues of the nineteenth century are live and present issues still. In 1837 the trekkers were fleeing from British jurisdiction and British allegiance. In 1937 General Hertzog, the leader of the government and the Nationalist Party, came to London in quest of a South African nationality that would in practice extinguish British allegiance and so far weaken Great Britain's constitutional position as to make South Africa all but a sovereign and independent state. Though there are still those whose ambition is set upon a complete break with the Empire, the leading political party is seeking the road to independence without the breach of secession. Of all the dominions, South Africa has been the most unwilling to accept the intentional indefiniteness of the Empire's constitution. It is of all dominions the most eager to hasten as quickly as possible the normal gradualness of imperial development, whereby constitutional courtesies grow to be privileges, and mature into sovereign rights. The American constitutional historian knows axiomatically that he cannot study the English elements in American institutions without recognizing that they have been adapted to American conditions. In South Africa the constitutional historian must remember that, in the matters with which this paper has tried to deal, he is beholding the adaptation of institutions that are English rather than Dutch to ends that are Dutch rather than English.

In native matters likewise the legislation of the Union has sought more fully to realize what the manifesto of the trekking Boers in 1836 termed "the proper relations between master and servant." The swift modernization that the great mining industry caused, afforded means of physical coercion that the previous century had never dreamed of. Yet white society did not cease to consider itself menaced. Steadily the demand grew for the exercise of timely precaution to avert any challenge to the supremacy of the whites. Inequality in economic and political life, inequality in the Constitution, has thus been the key to most legislation on native matters since Union.

"The white people of South Africa," said Lord Selborne in 1907, how prophetically we cannot yet tell, "are committed to such a path as few nations had trod before them, and scarcely one trod with success."

Federalism in Latin America ⚜

C. H. HARING

THERE are four so-called federal republics in Latin America: Argentina, Brazil, Mexico, and Venezuela. Of the two considered elsewhere in this volume, one, Brazil, is represented as coming by a federal organization legitimately; the other, Mexico, as an artificial creation. Between the other two republics, Argentina and Venezuela, the same distinction may be drawn. Argentina has been genuinely, perhaps inevitably, federalistic; in Venezuela, since the middle of the nineteenth century, federalism has been imposed by doctrinaire thinkers, political theorists, who considered federalism the ideally perfect form of democracy; their country therefore must have it, at least on paper.

Federalism was also tried for short periods of time in several other republics: in Colombia for about thirty years before 1886; in Chile for a few years in the first decade of its independent history; in Central America immediately after independence, when the provinces of the former captaincy general of Guatemala tried to hang together under a federalist regime, provinces which have dreamed ever since of recovering their former unity. In Peru, under President Leguia's constitution of 1919, a step toward federalism was taken in the establishment of three regional legislatures with limited powers. But as these three regions were not considered to be sovereign entities, perhaps we should not call this federalism. In one country, Bolivia, because of the strength of local, particularist sentiment and jealousies, and the wide separation of centers of population, one might have expected to find an outcropping of federalism. But such, as a matter of fact, possibly for a variety of reasons, has not been the case.

One might surmise that in the four present-day federal republics, this form of government would be most effective in the nations in which the development was a natural one—and this seems to be borne out by the observations of history. Federalism has been more effective in Argentina and Brazil than in Venezuela and Mexico.

In both of these latter countries presidential autocracy, more or less disguised, has been the rule. Constitutional forms have generally been used, or misused, merely to maintain in office, whether in the national or state governments, a small political clique dominated by some great *caudillo*.

None of the Latin-American nations were prepared for a federal organization when the day of independence arrived. They had always lived under a highly centralized regime, under viceroys or captains general appointed by and responsible alone to a despotic sovereign in Europe. And at the end of the colonial epoch, with the administrative reforms introduced by the Spanish Bourbons, especially the system of *intendentes,* this centralization was greater than ever before. The contrast between the situation in the Latin-American communities and that in Anglo-Saxon America was patent enough, and has often been stressed by historians. Yet the example of the new federal republic in North America—and, interestingly enough, of Mexico in the 1820s—was very powerful, in spite of the counter attractions of the highly centralized, bureaucratic organization which Napoleon had devised for France, and with which some of the early Latin-American political thinkers were familiar. And as every patriot wanted the very best for his own country, regardless of any consideration of its appropriateness to the social, material, and geographic conditions prevailing in that country, it was probably inevitable that in some places the federal experiment should be made—as happened even in Chile in the years 1826–28. Federalism and liberalism were considered by many as virtually synonymous; centralism and conservatism were the cause of all evils.

The social, political, and geographical circumstances which made federalism inappropriate will be touched upon in the paper on Mexico by Professor Mecham. Some of them prevail still in some areas of Latin America. They still constitute obstacles to the federal union of the Central American republics. And in Colombia two generations ago they led to disaster—almost to the political dissolution of the republic.

One disqualification could be pleaded more easily a hundred years ago than it can today: that is, the utter and complete lack of political experience among those who devised the first constitutions —inexperience in formulating the terms of the constitutional document, and inexperience in administering the institutions which that document provided for. There was an abysmal ignorance of political science, and a fatal attraction of words and phrases in place of genuine political principles. Words and phrases still play an unmerited rôle in all societies, whether Latin or Anglo-Saxon. But the educated classes of Latin America have now a century of experience behind them—often a bitter one—and that experience is reflected, not only in the increasing stability of Latin-American governments (taking a long view of their history) but also in the greater realism reflected in recent constitutional changes—as in Uruguay, Chile, and Colombia during the past two decades. A century ago, however, men of political experience and administrative ability were rare. There were too few to provide the personnel for a centralized administration, let alone for the more scattered and complex machinery involved in the government of a group of federalized states.

Brazil today seems to be at the crossroads. She has just passed through—or entered upon—a crisis in her political history. Highly decentralized in spirit and organization during the three centuries of colonial rule, on achieving independence from Portugal she happily retained a monarchical form of government under a prince of the Portuguese royal house. But it was a centralized monarchy, and one of its weaknesses was the stress and strain caused by the persistence of provincial sentiments and ambitions. When the monarchy was overthrown in 1889, the republic which took its place, as was to be expected, was a federal republic, with a constitution fashioned after that of the United States. Yet provincial jealousies persisted, an equilibrium between the states was not attained; and this is the basic explanation of the Revolution of 1930 which put Getulio Vargas in the presidency.

After four years as chief of a provisional government under which federalism was practically nullified, and over three as president under a revised federal constitution, Vargas chose in November, 1937, to declare himself dictator, for reasons best known to himself. Although a hastily written temporary constitution imposed by presidential decree declares Brazil to be "a Federal State constituted by the indissoluble union of the [existing] States, Federal District and Territories," the opportunities for presidential interference and control are unlimited, and in Brazil today federal-

ism is virtually nonexistent. What the future will bring forth
no one can tell. At least I have no aspirations to the rôle of
prophet. And the censor in Brazil takes good care to keep from us
any information concerning the actual state of public opinion in
that country at this moment. The Brazilians are a liberty-loving
people, and the republic till now has been a loose federation of
autonomous states jealous of their rights. Whether President Vargas can maintain a centralized, dictatorial government sufficiently
strong to overcome the historic particularism of Brazil is a major
question—and I have my doubts.

The Latin-American republic in which federalism is presumed
to have functioned most successfully is Argentina. The River Plata
region in colonial days, it is true, was no more decentralized in government than was any other part of the Spanish American empire.
But certain circumstances made for the existence in 1810 of a strong
local, particularist, sentiment: the scant population of the country,
and the separation of the various centers of population by great
open spaces dominated by hostile nomad Indians; the very recent
promotion of Buenos Aires to be the political capital, residence of
a viceroy; its ambition to dominate the interior provinces, which
till then had been more closely allied with Chile on the one hand
and with Upper Peru on the other; its ambition also to dominate
the up-river provinces, which till then had enjoyed equal contacts
with the outside world, so as to force them into economic dependence upon the one great seaport; the consequent absorption by
Buenos Aires of the financial and commercial activities of the country, causing the interior provinces to experience a notable decay;
also the monarchism of the Porteño leaders, the success of whose
plans would have sealed the hegemony of the capital on the Rio
de la Plata. Buenos Aires as the symbol of a traditional loyalty
the other provinces had at least endured; they saw no reason why
the inhabitants of Buenos Aires should constitute themselves the
sole heirs of the monarchy.

It was preëminently these circumstances which made possible
the rule of the provincial *caudillos,* and the anarchy that prevailed
during the years immediately preceding Rosas and during most of
the time that he dominated the country. The educated urban class
was inclined toward unitary principles of government, but the
country at large remained steadfastly federalist. When the con-

stituent assembly, dominated by Buenos Aires, in 1819 produced a
centralized constitution, most of the provinces repudiated it. In
1826 followed another constitution which provided for a limited
amount of decentralization through the deliberations of provincial
assemblies. The governors, however, were to be appointed by the
national executive, and there was no pretense of sovereign states
rights. Again it was repudiated, and upon the ruins of a civil war
Juan Manuel de Rosas imposed a dictatorship extending over the
entire country. Yet he always considered himself to be a federalist
—most of the members of the unitary party he killed or drove into
exile. He believed that his stern rule, by destroying the disruptive,
centrifugal forces represented by the provincial *caudillos,* was a
necessary preliminary to a national federalist organization. Mean-
time the Pacto Federal, a treaty drawn up and subscribed to by the
provinces of Buenos Aires, Santa Fé, and Entre Rios in 1831, remained the sole legal evidence of national union.

Thus the federalistic provinces, outmaneuvered in the constituent congresses of 1819 and 1826, awaited only the elimination of
the greatest of the *caudillos,* Rosas, to organize the country definitely on a federal basis in 1853. All parties, *porteño* or *arribeño,*
in this respect at least were of one mind. Or perhaps it would be
more accurate to say that the educated classes, relieved of the in-
cubus of Rosas, took refuge in federalism as the only formula by
which the country could be united other than by a dictatorship.
And the constitution they devised, under the inspiration and leadership of Juan Bautista Alberdi, reflected more closely that of the
United States than has the constitution of any other South American nation. It happens also to be the oldest surviving constitution
south of the Rio Grande.

One observes today in Argentina the same course of development
as in the other two effectively federalist states of America, the United
States and Brazil: that is, the tendency of the federal government
to increase its authority and influence at the expense of "states
rights." In Argentina it has been more marked than in this country. It is due in part to the poverty and social backwardness of
many of the autonomous provinces, and to the concentration of the
wealth and intelligence of the nation in the great city of Buenos
Aires. There has been a marked inclination of all the provinces,
rich and poor, to lean more and more heavily upon the national

treasury. The federal government has for years made grants to the less favored provinces for internal improvements, such as irrigation works in the country and sanitary systems in the towns. During the past thirty years it has participated more and more in the support and control of primary and normal schools, a responsibility which under the constitution should belong to the provincial governments; so that educational progress in the country at large is due almost entirely to the initiative and activity of the government in Buenos Aires. Very recently, in 1934, when the system of taxation was remodeled and simplified, the federal government assumed entire responsibility for collecting most of the internal taxes formerly belonging to the provinces. The proceeds are now distributed to the provinces on a quota basis, adjustable every ten years. This radical innovation has resulted in more efficient administration and in largely increased revenues. The provinces have profited greatly. Yet it only emphasizes the propensity to federal encroachment upon provincial autonomy. And it has the effect of giving to the national administration an undue, if not overwhelming, influence in the politics of many of the provincial governments.

I said that in most of the Latin-American states after independence political experience and administrative ability were too uncommon to provide for the effective management of a decentralized, federalist type of government. The remark applies also to Argentina. The economic and social stagnation, the lack of population and resources, of many of the provinces carry their inevitable corollary of political disorders. Domination by selfish and corrupt political bosses or cliques, with consequent graft, bribery, intimidation, or open violence, are only too common. They are the signs of a raw and incipient democracy.

And this has given excuse for frequent interventions by the federal government—in Argentina as in Mexico and Brazil—intervention permitted by the Argentine constitution (as by our own) to maintain a republican form of government in the several states. In recent times in Argentina it has been used chiefly for ulterior purposes: to displace provincial governors and the members of provincial legislatures unfriendly to the national administration, and to put the province under the rule of a federal *interventor*, who in the succeeding elections will see to it that individuals acceptable to the national government are chosen. Owing to the vagaries of provincial politics, pretexts are generally not difficult to find. The device was used in a wholesale manner by President Irigoyen after the Radical Party for the first time came into power in 1916 —twenty interventions during the six years of his first administration. But it has been used in equally scandalous fashion by the Conservative minority which ruled the republic before 1916 and which has been in control again since the Revolution of 1930. The most recent and one of the most notorious instances has been the federal intervention in the important province of Santa Fé, from October of 1935 to the middle of 1937. It prepared for, and helped to make easier, the Conservative victory in the national elections of last September. Federal intervention is one of the abuses of Argentine political practice which makes impossible that equilibrium between the federal and provincial governments which was anticipated by the members of the Constituent Congress eighty-five years ago.

Whether the federal form of national organization was the most desirable for Argentina in 1853, and since, may easily be questioned. That it was the necessary basis of any common agreement among the politically conscious elements in the nation at that time, it would be difficult to dispute. But the whole course of Argentine political evolution—at least since 1880, when Julio Roca became president—has been in the direction of centralization, of a unitary type of government; or perhaps, one might better say, of that mixed type which, stopping short of provincial sovereignty, combines centralized control with decentralized administration, and which was the ideal striven for by Bernardino Rivadavia and his unitary allies in 1826.

As Dr. Rodolfo Rivarola wrote, as early as 1908, in the preface of his volume *Del régimen federativo al unitario,* "La palabra *federación* ha perdido ya su acepción etimológica; solamente la *unidad* expresa a la vez el orden, la fuerza, y la justicia."

PART FOUR

The Constitution in the Nuclear and Space Age

Some Reflections on Current Constitutional Controversy* ∾ LOUIS HENKIN

THE Constitution of the United States has, from its beginning, known the recurrent tides of controversy. Today controversy is again at the flood, and it includes different controversies between different controversialists. There has, of course, been controversy between Justices of the Supreme Court. There have been strong words in constitutional clothing by state legislators and governors and some Southern congressmen against the Supreme Court, and, unusually, even some words back by the Court, in *Cooper v. Aaron*.[1] And there have been differences rising perhaps to the level of not-always-polite controversy among the professors.

Note an omission. At one time, one might have reflected also on sharp constitutional disagreements between members of Congress. Such controversy hardly exists today. One reason is that legislators have apparently discontinued reflecting on the constitutionality of their own actions. It is a rare occasion when even an isolated member of Congress manifests that his oath to support the Constitution of the United States requires that he consider whether or not the Constitution permits particular legislation, or incidental legislative activity. It is a rare committee of Congress that deems it part of its function in considering a bill or conducting a hearing to reach a judgment as to how its actions square with the limitations and obligations of the Constitution. Even state legislators, some of whom have no hesitation in challenging constitutional interpretations of the Supreme Court, do not appear to indulge the more fruitful practice of attending

* Reprinted by permission of the *University of Pennsylvania Law Review*.
[1] 358 U.S. 1 (1958).

dispassionately, in advance of legislative action, to how this action would conform to the Constitution as it has become, even—if you will—as the Supreme Court is likely to make it. One may well reflect a little sadly on such legislative omissions, and upon their relevance to so-called presumptions of constitutionality and to the institution of judicial review.

But this is digression, even if perhaps relevant digression. Turning to issues which are current, we will concern ourselves with controversy within the Supreme Court of the United States and with controversies among professors about the controversies of the Justices. In sum, one might assert, first, that there has been a change in the subject matter of constitutional controversy; second, that there has been a corresponding, if not a consequent, change in the issues that divide the Justices of the Supreme Court; and third, that there has been a change also in the criticism of the Court, leading to controversies among the critics.

THE CHANGING ISSUE OF THE CONSTITUTION

Let us begin by examining the constitutional stuff of which today's controversies are made; and we approach that examination by noting yesterday's battlefields which are today quiet. It has long been apparent that the constitutional provisions in controversy today are not those of a generation ago, specifically the judicial generation which passed in 1936. Principally, the extent of the power of Congress is hardly in question. The once-big issue, the scope of permissible action by Congress in matters affecting interstate commerce, is no longer an issue. "To regulate commerce with foreign nations and among the several states" has gone as far as words will go, and relation or relevance to commerce has been stretched—or recognized—where it never had been before. If the commerce power were not enough, other powers have magnified to render it highly unlikely that any foreseeable congressional act would be declared to fall outside the Constitution's authorizations to Congress. Congress long ago learned that it can tax anything, and can prohibit or regulate by taxing—apparently even if regulation is the principal motive.[2]

[2] See, *e.g.*, United States v. Kahriger, 345 U.S. 22 (1953); Sonzinsky v. United States, 300 U.S. 506 (1937).

Permissible congressional action under the fourteenth amendment has grown, as the concept of "state action" and state responsibility has grown, maybe even to include forms of state inaction. The so-called war powers and their ramifications during war, and in the aftermath of war, and in anticipation of war, or in the fear of war, or in defense against possible war, have led some to wonder whether there is anything beyond the scope of *that* power of Congress. And the newly labeled "foreign affairs power" of Congress has led at least me to wonder whether Congress might not be able to legislate on anything which affects the relations of the United States with other nations, in a world in which everything seems to affect in some way the relations of the United States with other nations.[3]

There has, then, been no controversy worthy of that characterization about the scope of the powers of Congress—not even at the height of the Bricker episode, when "states-righters" found themselves building up the powers of Congress in order to show that cutting down the treaty power to the size of the powers of Congress could not have any serious consequence, while lawyers of a generally "nationalist" hue found themselves denigrating the powers of Congress in order to show the danger of the proposed constitutional amendment. The Bricker controversy, it is true, reflected as well as enhanced states-rights sentiment, which has had important effect on whether, and how, Congress will exercise its powers. But these are political limitations, not constitutional ones; they are self-imposed, not clamped upon an unwilling Congress by a superior Supreme Court.

As to the states, too, the area of controversy has changed. Some of the old battlefields are almost quiet. It is true that in regard to some old issues majorities, over strong dissent, have recently upheld the power of states to tax net income from interstate commerce,[4] as well as the states' power to tax some instrumentalities having relation to the federal government.[5] But in both areas, it seems clear, this power can be nullified by Congress. And in both areas the majority of the Court may have acted on the basis that "it's only money" and may have assumed that Congress concurs

[3] Henkin, *The Treaty Makers and the Law Makers: The Law of the Land and Foreign Relations*, 107 U. PA. L. REV. 903, 922-30 (1959).

[4] Northwestern States Portland Cement Co. v. Minnesota, 358 U.S. 450 (1959).

[5] United States v. City of Detroit, 355 U.S. 466 (1958).

in allowing the states the increased revenue, even where the United States Government ultimately pays the bill. There may well remain small questions as to the power of the states to act when Congress is silent, or speaks unclearly. But in matters relevant to the nation—and increasingly few matters are not—the states, in an ultimate sense, act only by the grace of Congress.

The constitutional issues involving the powers of the state, then, revolve not about the tenth amendment, but about the fourteenth; they relate not to the issues of federation, but to the relation of the state to the citizen, of the state's power of government to the individual's liberties. Here too there has been change. The big issue of the last generation was "substantive due process," implementing inherent limitations on government, on the police power. The revolution brought by *Nebbia* and *Parrish* in effect rendered the police power plenary.[6] Laissez faire is not a constitutional requirement and the welfare state is equally consistent with constitutional principles. There are no inherent limitations on the role of government. There are only prohibitions, prohibitions like those in the Bill of Rights for the protection of individuals and minorities. In regard to the states, only those in the original Constitution are particularized; others can only be spun out of "equal protection" and the oracular ambiguity of "due process of law." In economic matters, there remains a minimum of limitation in substantive due process, a prohibition of confiscation, and—perhaps—of regulation wholly arbitrary and capricious. But no recent case has invalidated economic or social legislation for violation of due process. If the equal protection clause was used—some think misused—in one case to strike down an economic regulation,[7] it is not likely that there will be many such occasions for the Court to find objectionable "discrimination" or class legislation.

The constitutional issues today, then, are no longer primarily about the scope of governmental power, federal or state, but about the meaning and scope of prohibitions on that power. For the federal government the issues are about the meaning and application of prohibitions on ex post facto laws and bills of

6 Nebbia v. New York, 291 U.S. 502 (1934); West Coast Hotel Co. v. Parrish, 300 U.S. 379 (1937).
7 Morey v. Doud, 354 U.S. 457 (1957).

attainder; of "Congress shall make no law abridging the freedom of speech"; of "unreasonable searches and seizures"; of being "twice put in jeopardy," and being "compelled to be a witness against himself"; of "due process of law," and whether private property was "taken for public use"; of "cruel and unusual punishments." There are differences about whether to infer further prohibitions—for example, whether Congress is forbidden to take away a man's citizenship against his will. Even when Justices seem to be disagreeing about the scope of the power of Congress to make rules for the government and regulation of the land and naval forces, it is only in a context where the disagreement is really as to whether civilians associated with the armed services abroad can be tried without the protections which the Bill of Rights grants to those accused of crime by the United States.[8]

Similar controversy is engendered by challenges to actions of the states. There are the same disputes as to the meaning of specific prohibitions on the states—bills of attainder, ex post facto laws. And still alive is an old controversy—in its contemporary manifestation exemplified by *Adamson v. California*[9]—whether the Bill of Rights was made applicable to the states by the fourteenth amendment. *Adamson* in 1947 represented the high water mark for the dissident view, when four Justices expressed themselves for total "incorporation," although they differed among themselves as to whether the due process clause should have some additional independent content. Today only Mr. Justice Black and Mr. Justice Douglas frankly adhere to this view.[10] For the

---

[8] Kinsella v. Singleton, 361 U.S. 234 (1960); Reid v. Covert, 354 U.S. 1 (1957).

[9] 332 U.S. 46 (1947).

[10] Because it is recent, and perhaps insufficiently noted, a new footnote to this controversy is worthy of mention. Mr. Justice Brennan, at the end of the last term of Court, apparently decided to seize a case in which Mr. Justice Stewart was not sitting, Ohio *ex rel.* Eaton v. Price, 364 U.S. 263 (1960), to set forth what Justice Stewart meant in a majority opinion handed down the same day, Elkins v. United States, 364 U.S. 206 (1960). The view he announced was that where due process is deemed to afford a protection which is also contained in the Bill of Rights, the protection against the state has the same scope as the protection against Congress. For this position one may cite language in earlier cases which seemed to put the question as whether a particular provision in the Bill of Rights was incorporated in the due process clause. If so, says Justice Brennan, those provisions which are found to be incorporated must mean the same thing in their incorporated form against the states as they do in the Bill of Rights against the federal government. Justice Brennan admits that there are

majority, following a series of cases culminating in *Palko v. Connecticut*,[11] the due process clause forbids to the states action which "shocks the conscience of Mankind," which violates "the concept of ordered liberty."[12]

So the controversy has raged about this "ordered liberty." Is ordered liberty violated by involuntary blood tests for alcohol; by putting Willie Francis into the electric chair a second time after an abortive first attempt to electrocute him; by failure to provide counsel to indigents in noncapital cases; by admitting evidence obtained by unreasonable search and seizure; by trying Hoag

cases which would not be consistent with his interpretation, but he considers them erroneous. Mr. Justice Frankfurter, chief spokesman today for the traditional view of due process, would not agree. In addition to a number of holdings, he would say, the logic of the doctrine and its derivation in the language of the fourteenth amendment do not support Justice Brennan's view. If the due process clause accords some of the protections also accorded by the Bill of Rights, surely it is not because the framers of that amendment had made a selection among the Bill of Rights for application to the states, but because the amendment contains a concept, applicable to the states, some of the content of which coincides with some of the protection in the Bill of Rights. It is difficult to see why in regard to any particular "right" the concept of ordered liberty must be found to afford exactly the same protection as has been found in the explicit language of the earlier amendments. It is yet to be seen whether Justice Stewart will adopt what four of his brethren say he means; if he does, there will be new constitutional jurisprudence, another heap of rejected cases, including the renowned Betts v. Brady, 316 U.S. 455 (1942), and a sharp reduction of the differences between the prohibitions on the federal government in the Bill of Rights, and those on the states in the fourteenth amendment.

[11] 302 U.S. 319 (1937).

[12] One might note that "substantive" rights guaranteed by the Bill of Rights are, in the view of all the Justices, also protected by the fourteenth amendment, while the "procedural" safeguards are, for the majority, guaranteed only if they are implied in the concept of "ordered liberty." If one accepts these categories, there may still be doubt whether this nice division is coincidence, or an understandable consquence of the spirit and the language of the fourteenth amendment. It has never been quite clear how the Court was reading and applying the language of the due process clause. When the Court says that this clause requires of the states that they respect "ordered liberty," is that requirement found in the word "liberty," in the phrase "due process of law," or, somehow, in the clause as a whole? When the Court holds that the clause protects, against state infringement, the freedoms of the first amendment, is it saying that freedom of speech is an aspect of "ordered liberty," just as is the right not to be convicted of a crime on the basis of a coerced confession? One might have suggested that the "substantive" provisions of the Bill of Rights, *e.g.*, the freedoms of the first amendment, or the right to be secure from unreasonable search and seizure, are included in the "liberty" which, together with life and property, are the subjects of protection. As to the procedural safeguards in the later amendments of the Bill of Rights, or other procedures not mentioned in the Bill of Rights, the question for the Court is whether a particular procedure is implied in "due process," in accepted notions of fairness, in "ordered liberty." It has sometimes seemed that such careful "parsing" of the clause in the fourteenth amendment might lead to greater consistency, or at least greater clarity. The opinions of the Court, however, do not fit comfortably into this linguistic analysis.

for the robbery of one victim after he had been acquitted of robbery upon other alleged victims in the same incident?[13]

We do not consider any of the disputes in detail. But patterns are discernible and some generalizations have some warrant. Several Justices, in most instances a minority, seek to broaden the various prohibitions against the federal government; and the same Justices, for the most part, seek to extend the requirements of ordered liberty to approximate the expanding specifics of the Bill of Rights. They would find bills of attainder and ex post facto laws in situations where historically, others insist, the prohibitions would not apply.[14] They would extend the concept of "punishments" to consequences other than those meted out by judicial sentence after criminal trial and find some of these to be cruel or unusual.[15] They would extend the right of the people to be secure against unreasonable search and seizure to a right to be secure against inspections by officials who are not police officials searching for contraband or evidence of crime.[16] They would extend the right to counsel to investigations which are not strictly criminal in nature.[17] They would extend to new situations the prohibition against double jeopardy.[18] Most significant perhaps they would push the protections of the first amendment— freedom of communication, association, religion, which are also protected by the fourteenth—to a preferred position, sometimes tantamount to erecting a presumption of unconstitutionality for legislation on these subjects.[19] Mr. Justice Black, and perhaps Mr. Justice Douglas, would seem ready to go yet further— to the position that communication and association are absolutely immune to regulation, leaving at least libel and the well-worn "shouting fire in a theatre" somehow to fend for themselves.[20]

[13] Breithaupt v. Abram, 352 U.S. 432 (1957); Louisiana *ex rel.* Francis v. Resweber, 329 U.S. 459 (1947); Betts v. Brady, 316 U.S. 455 (1942); Wolf v. Colorado, 338 U.S. 25 (1949); Hoag v. New Jersey, 356 U.S. 464 (1958).

[14] See Flemming v. Nestor, 363 U. S. 603 (1960); Garner v. Board of Pub. Works, 341 U.S. 716 (1951); *cf.* United States v. Lovett, 328 U.S. 303 (1946).

[15] See Trop v. Dulles, 356 U. S. 86 (1958).

[16] See Frank v. Maryland, 359 U.S. 360 (1959).

[17] See *In re* Groban, 352 U.S. 330 (1957).

[18] See Gore v. United States, 357 U.S. 386 (1958); Green v. United States, 355 U.S. 184 (1957); *cf.* Hoag v. New Jersey, 356 U.S. 464 (1958).

[19] The cases are many, *e.g.*, Beauharnais v. Illinois, 343 U.S. 250 (1952); Kovacs v. Cooper, 336 U.S. 77 (1949).

[20] See, *e.g.*, their opinion in the obscenity cases, Roth v. United States, 354 U.S. 476, 508 (1957), and in Beauharnais v. Illinois, 343 U.S. 250, 267 (1952). Compare their respective opinions in Dennis v. United States, 341 U.S. 494, 579, 581 (1951).

Those who seek to increase the limitations on both federal and state governments also seek, to that end, to discard some distinctions based on the separate sovereignty of the states. They seem prepared, for instance, to find double jeopardy when one is tried by both a state and the federal government, where the same act violates both state and federal law.[21] They are not satisfied that the federal privilege against self-incrimination does not exempt one from testifying in federal proceedings to matters which may incriminate under state law, nor from testifying in state proceedings to matters which may incriminate under federal law.[22] They have barred the admission in federal courts of evidence unlawfully obtained by state officials.[23]

INSTITUTIONAL CONCOMITANTS OF CONSTITUTIONAL CHANGE

The accent on controversy may perhaps divert attention from the fact that these differences, while sharp and sometimes deep, are in an agreed and limited area of conflict; outside this area is a large domain of constitutional development which is settled beyond present dispute.

Although the Bill of Rights is 170 years old, it was little invoked and infrequently given effect in constitutional litigation before the last three or four decades. It is interesting to speculate whether this was because a Congress fighting for its still-limited powers was careful not to trench on the rights of individuals whom the still-powerful states would have championed; because in the context of the times the limited powers of Congress did not in fact produce legislation in the forbidden areas of the early amendments, or proliferate criminal prosecutions with which so much of the Bill of Rights is concerned; or because, quite differently, the Bill of Rights as then interpreted represented a standard commonly recognized, and one which the Congress was not disposed to violate. In regard to the first amendment, in

---

[21] See Abbate v. United States, 359 U.S. 187 (1959); Bartkus v. Illinois, 359 U.S. 121 (1959).

[22] See Knapp v. Schweitzer, 357 U.S. 371 (1958); Feldman v. United States, 322 U.S. 487 (1944); United States v. Murdock, 284 U.S. 141 (1931).

[23] See Elkins v. United States, 364 U.S. 206 (1960); *cf.* Rea v. United States, 350 U.S. 214 (1956).

particular, it took foreign war and fear of foreign sympathies to move Congress to impinge on political rights, and after the alien and sedition laws in John Adams' administration there were none of that kind until the First World War.

The Bill of Rights, it will be recalled, was an attempt to preserve for the citizen protections only recently won in England, and some not then yet won there but achieved in the Colonies. In addition, the due process clause, innocent in its simplicity, was to assure that there would be rule of law, the law of the land, the common law and procedure of England. The Bill of Rights offered these assurances against the central government; similar guarantees against the states were put into state constitutions.

The fourteenth amendment is eighty years younger than the Bill of Rights. It has its independent history and its different origins in a victory for the nation over the states. There is significance in the fact that, like the Bill of Rights, the fourteenth amendment was not important for the protection of civil rights or liberties until a few decades ago—substantive due process to protect liberty born as substantive due process to protect property was dying. New doctrines and changing world forces led to the increased exercise of repressive governmental power by the nation and by the states, raising issues of individual liberty against both governments. And inevitably—if not necessarily in accord with constitutional language, or history, or logic—how the Bill of Rights governed the federal government has affected how the fourteenth amendment governed the states. In regard to both the federal government and the states, the protections for the individual have grown steadily. The Bill of Rights being long established and in comparatively explicit terms, there was of course a considerable headstart against the federal government, and there was no states-rights' sentiment to hinder the Court in developing and extending protections. Prohibitions on the states, virtually nonexistent before the Civil War, had to await the slow pouring of content into ambiguous phrases, in the face of resistance by local interests to a federal Supreme Court applying a not-popular constitutional amendment. But the long evolution of our common-law constitution continues and the controversies noted are part of the process. The protections of the Bill of Rights grow; those of the fourteenth amendment grow too; they remain less, although the differences are narrowing. The developing concept of ordered liberty reduces the consequences of the failure of the Constitution to make all of the provisions of the Bill of Rights applicable to the states. Due process, the phrase once designed to assure mere lawfulness by government, has become the headstone of the corner of individual protection.

The changing issues of constitutional controversy, then, are yet another reflection of the fact that the Constitution under which we live today has changed from that of our fathers. They reflect also, I would suggest, significant change in the role of the institutions of our federal government. I offer for your consideration some generalizations, valid, I think, as indicating trends, tendencies, emphases.

Constitutionally, our federal government continues to become a national government.

In regard to the central government, one may say, with only a modicum of exaggeration and simplification, that the United States has become a national society with a national economy, its interests thoroughly intertwined with those of other nations, particularly in time of international crisis; that legislatively, at least, the federal government has become a national government; that the power of Congress has moved from a limited power derived from enumerated clauses measured out by the Supreme Court, towards a plenary power based on national need as seen in the light of political judgment. It is the Congress, no longer the Supreme Court, that ultimately can make the important decisions of federalism. Once the Court, although itself a branch of the federal government, stood between the Congress and the states as an impartial arbiter, meting out to each its proper share of governmental power. Congress no longer needs the Court to protect the nation against encroachment by the states; the states can no longer invoke the Court to protect them against encroachment by Congress. State and local interests must look for their protection to the Congress itself, as, indeed, the Constitution originally contemplated—particularly to that body of "ambassadors" of the states, the United States Senate.

The Supreme Court is no longer defining and adjusting the frontiers between the powers of governments; it is defining and redefining prohibitions on government on behalf of the individual.

The issues for the Court are no longer which government, state or federal, can act, or whether a particular act is within the power of government. The issue is whether a particular act is prohibited to government by the Bill of Rights or the fourteenth amendment, or those other provisions of the Constitution which afford protection to the individual against the action of his governments. With the exception of the infrequent case reflecting the constitutional separateness of one state from another, the Court hardly acts any longer to adjust and maintain the mechanism of federation under the Constitution; it acts, in constitutional matters, to mediate between the requirements of government asserted by the Legislature, the Executive, and sometimes the Judiciary, and the protection for the individual and the minority promised by a written constitution. The Court does not mediate between two powerful competing interests. It stands in the path of powerful representative government in the name of an ideal—the liberties of the individual.

The constitutional issues before the Court, then, begin to resemble those of a unitary state with a written constitution. Indeed, one may suggest that the Court's constitutional role grows less dissimilar to that of the courts of Great Britain. For when we frequently say, lightly, that Great Britain has no written constitution, we forget some very precise constitutional documents like Magna Charta, the Bill of Rights, the Act of Settlement, the Habeas Corpus Act, the Act of Toleration, and the Parliament and Representation Acts. Parliament lives by these. The courts enforce them upon the Executive. If in principle the courts cannot apply them as limitations on Parliament, we have seen that in the United States, too, the Court now only rarely applies our Constitution to limit or prohibit acts of Congress.

In any event, one may fairly suggest that the Supreme Court, which originally and only yesterday was needed primarily to resolve the conflicts of federation, is now available—although, and perhaps in part because, the issues of federalism are evaporating—to assume an increasing role in the conflict between the alleged requirements of government and the claimed liberties of the individual.

The Court is not concerned with governmental experiment; it worries about unfairness to individuals.

When the Supreme Court strikes at governmental action it is frequently striking at an act of administrators, not at an act of the legislature—as in many of the criminal cases under the Bill of Rights or the fourteenth amendment. If behind such an act of the executive there is an act of the legislature, it is frequently an old act. If it is a new act, it is not an act of social experimentation based on hope, but very likely one of repression rooted in fear—like contemporary internal security legislation. The Court is not now a conservative body standing athwart new legislative experimentation, economic or social. It is more frequently a body challenging established institutions. The Court is engaged in raising state practices, often long established, to new levels of ordered liberty, or, in federal cases, raising to new levels the protection against the federal government found in old words in the Bill of Rights.

When the Court protects the criminally accused, even when it is struggling with security legislation in the name of political freedom, it is protecting individuals or small minorities against majority action deemed unfair; it is not frustrating social and economic programs of direct moment to large numbers of people. This makes the role of the Court seem less intrusive. On the other hand, there is less general sympathy for the Court's work, since insufficient numbers of the public identify with the rights vindicated. In regard to the states, it is, of course, not without significance that the enforcement of prohibitions for the protection of individuals and minorities is administered by a federal supreme court under a federal constitution. Even there few constitutional actions of the Supreme Court are calculated to arouse legislatures thwarted in programs of importance to meet new problems.

The constitutional issues before the Court relate largely to the states.

The federal government has learned, generally, to meet the

explicit standards of the Bill of Rights. It has been more amenable to reform than some of the now fifty states. And the Court has been able to raise federal standards in other ways—through its influence on the promulgation of rules of procedure, as well as under its supervisory powers in decisions like *McNabb v. United States*[24] *and Rea v. United States;*[25] and Congress has generally acquiesced. There has therefore been far less need for invoking the Constitution against the federal government. For years after May 18, 1936, [26] not a single act or provision of Congress was invalidated. In 1943 there was *Tot v. United States,*[27] a minor and isolated instance. Since then, I count five other occasions on which the Supreme Court invalidated provisions of general acts of Congress, four of them in the last six years dealing with or related to the armed forces.[28] The civilian-soldier as a permanent aspect of our society is new; inevitably his constitutional status, and that of associated civilians, has required clarification, adjustment, and development.

Because the Court's active constitutional role today is largely directed to curbing the states, and because the Court no longer protects the states from congressional inroads, the Court is more obviously and exclusively a branch of the federal government. Because it is less frequently at odds with Congress—even in the security cases, the Court has so far avoided declaring any action of Congress invalid, and one sometimes suspects many in Congress are pleased to have the Court save them from follies which they deem politically necessary—the Court may feel more confident to act firmly vis-à-vis the states on behalf of the federal government, as in bringing up to today's date the meaning of the Constitution in regard to the Negro. The Court shares with

[24] 318 U.S. 332 (1943).
[25] 350 U.S. 214 (1956).
[26] See Carter v. Carter Coal Co., 298 U.S. 238 (1936).
[27] 319 U.S. 463 (1943).
[28] See United States *ex rel.* Singleton, 361 U.S. 234 (1960); Trop v. Dulles, 356 U.S. 86 (1958); Reid v. Covert, 354 U.S. 1 (1957); Toth v. Quarles, 350 U.S. 11 (1955). I am counting also United States v. Cardiff, 344 U.S. 174 (1952), although it is not clear whether the Court invalidated the provision, or merely construed it as not applicable to the defendant. In United States v. Lovett, 328 U.S. 303 (1946), the Court threw out special legislation providing that no part of an appropriation should be used to pay the salaries of three named individuals. Bolling v. Sharpe, 347 U.S. 497 (1954), invalidated an act of Congress interpreted as requiring school segregation in the District of Columbia.

Congress the role of keeping the states in line, even if there has not been between Court and Congress any clear division and assumption of responsibility. In those few constitutional decisions which have broad impact on the states, the states do not have in the Court a means for political resistance or self-defense such as they have within Congress against congressional legislation; nor can the states frequently move Congress to undo what the Court has done, even where Congress could constitutionally do so.

The Court increasingly reviews findings of fact.

Increasingly, differences of fact determine whether a constitutional right was violated. While all constitutional issues may involve matters of degree, the Court's business under "due process," "equal protection," "cruel and unusual" punishments, "unreasonable" searches and seizures, and other constitutional phrases of more or less ambiguity, requires it to determine anew in every case whether the inevitably different facts of this case exceed the forbidden degree. Occasionally, some Justices, at least, appear to be on the verge of testing, under due process of law, the adequacy of evidence to support a verdict or other conclusion.[29] If the Court should yield to this temptation, it could, of course, render every case a constitutional case for the Court's review.

Is the Court's jurisprudence changing?

One may also ask whether the changing issues of constitutional adjudication and the changing role of the Court may not be effecting modifications in the Court's jurisprudence: in its application of the requirements of case or controversy, and of standing, even of "substantial federal question" properly preserved and presented, and of the absence of adequate nonfederal ground; in the doctrine of "political questions"; in the Court's exercise of judicial review, as exemplified in the so-called "presumption of constitutionality" and the policy of "judicial self-restraint"; as well as in related practices like the interpretation of statutes to avoid constitutional doubt. One cannot make many bricks from

[29] *Cf.* Thompson v. Louisville, 362 U.S. 199 (1960); Konigsberg v. State Bar, 353 U.S. 252 (1957).

the few straws available, but one may hazard a guess that students of a later generation will be taught a jurisprudence different in these respects from the one we learned.

There are other consequences also for the institution that is the Supreme Court. It is again the subject of controversy, but for the most part this is directed at its role in other than constitutional cases (even when the attacks are motivated by passion aroused by *Brown v. Board of Educ.*).[30] The periodic efforts to curb its jurisdiction have been vindictive, and directed at its so-called misinterpretations of statutes or abuse of its supervisory powers, rather than at any alleged perversion of the Constitution. Problems of racial segregation apart, the Court's calendar and docket contain few major constitutional cases having wide community repercussions. There have been legislation and legislative attempt to undo judicial interpretations of statute; there has been no occasion to seek constitutional amendment to undo the Court's constitutional interpretations.

The consequences which I have suggested—acceptable, I hope, as tentative generalizations—may be multiplied, and these consequences have further consequences. Perhaps we are only stressing the obvious results of changes in the life of the nation: the Court's constitutional activity must reflect the change in political relationships between the federal and state governments, and the consequent changes in their respective spheres of activity. Where the Court is obviously adopting revised meanings for the Constitution, as in *Brown v. Board of Educ.* or *Shelley v. Kraemer*,[31] it is also reflecting deep change in today's United States and in

[30] 347 U.S. 483 (1954), 349 U.S. 294 (1955). It may seem incredible that one can speak for half an hour on current constitutional matters and say almost nothing about *Brown v. Board of Educ.* My justification is that too much has already been said; and that our theme is constitutional controversy. The segregation cases have achieved remarkable unanimity on the Court, and even the critics—those who deal with the issues rationally—have not engendered much controversy. It is nevertheless appropriate to note for our purposes that those cases also involve prohibitions on the states in the name of individual and minority rights; that the cases have important impact on the states, not on the federal government, and on only some states, not all; that the Court rather than Congress is acting for the federal government; that the Court is striking at established patterns in an attempt to raise standards of equal protection and ordered liberty. And the Negro cases, as much as any other group, suggest the possibility of changing Supreme Court jurisprudence, particularly in regard to standing, presumptions of constitutionality, respect for state findings of fact, and "adequate" nonfederal grounds.

[31] 334 U.S. 1 (1948).

the world of which it is a part. It is obvious that the Supreme Court is not out of this world.

THE CONTROVERSY OF THE PROFESSORS

We will return to the constitutional divisions on the Court today. I should like to get back to them through some reflections about the criticism of the Court by its best critics.

Professorial criticism of the Court is hardly new. Professor Frankfurter, for example, and even more the late Professor T. Reed Powell, frequently held a mirror to the Justices, although it is not always apparent that all the Justices looked into it. It has been remarked, again recently by Dean Griswold, that no one has appeared to pick up Powell's mirror.

Perhaps that was inevitable. Perhaps the professor-critic's role had to change with the change in the constitutional issues before the Court, and in the times of the Justices. Professor Powell was the ideal critic for the comparatively unsophisticated jurisprudence of a comparatively unsophisticated Court majority. He was not demanding that the Court replace their values with his. He could show the Justices what assumptions they were finding in the Constitution, often without being aware that they were making any assumptions. He could identify the texts of economic interest which lay behind their pretexts of doctrine. With dispassionate surgical deftness, he could trace the circles in their reasoning, spear their tautologies, make blatant their inconsistencies, scorn their distinctions where there were no differences and their failures to distinguish where there were. He could mock their juggling of concepts and categories when they should have been looking hard at hard facts.

If Justices of a former day deserved their chastisement, they were perhaps also deserving of classic forgiveness, for it is not beyond doubt that they knew what they did. The Court is more sophisticated today. Justices are subject less to charges of naïveté than of cynicism. And so the critics they deserve are different—and the criticism. In any event, after a lull while the Court and its jurisprudence were changing, the professors are again giving attention to the Court. The professors have been virtually unanimous in defense of the Court against the passionate outbursts of those gored by *Brown v. Board of Educ.* They were only less than unanimous when others, perhaps also motivated by anger over school integration, made other irresponsible attacks, especially when these took the form of attempts to limit the jurisdiction of the Court by congressional legislation. Then the professors criticized in turn. Perhaps because the professors felt obliged to show that their defense of the Court was not uncritical; perhaps because they felt that their defense of the Court gave them the right to criticism of a more responsible character; perhaps because the Court again cried for criticism—the law schools have begun to play again the role of loyal critic.

There has been criticism—and defense—of the handling of particular cases—for example, the FELA and Jones Act cases. There has been criticism of sloppy judicial procedures, of inadequate consideration and unacceptable analysis, of opinions that are enigmatic, unmeaningful, misleading. From some quarters there has been criticism that the Court, or some members of it, have shamelessly become too much a political body, too little a judicial one; that they have abused the opportunity of their position to remold this country nearer to their hearts' desires; that they have legislated more than interstitially, have distorted interpretation into legislation, have given statutes and legislative materials readings that were not fair readings—in order to achieve a result in the case before them that conformed to their political desires, not to those of the legislature. From other sources has come criticism of another kind—that the Court, or Justices on it, were dragging long chains of the dogmas of the quiet past; were indifferent or hostile to the demands of individual liberty and minority rights; were abdicating their constitutional role of checking oppressive majorities; were retarding the realization of the American ideal.

These and other criticisms have had their rebuttals. Particularly when the criticism was against one "wing" of the Court, there were counterattacks against the other, especially by those who see every Supreme Court Justice alive as either a liberal or a little conservative. For today's purpose, however, we would eschew most of these controversies and deal only with some that revolve around the Court's role in constitutional decision.

Perhaps Judge Hand began the current round in his rare incursion into the academic universe. Speaking of judicial review he agreed, one might say, that the Court may properly determine the frontiers of power of Congress or of the states.[32] It should not, however, intrude when the Legislature is acting within the general orbit of its powers, merely to substitute the Court's choice between values for the choice of the Legislature. If the generalizations we suggested earlier about the changing constitutional issues are correct, on Judge Hand's position, the issues coming before the Court today require judicial restraint—at least where acts of the Legislature rather than those of the Executive are concerned.

Then Professor Wechsler demanded of the Court "neutral principles" of adjudication, and looked for them—and had difficulty finding them—in several leading cases where he sympathized with the result: *Brown v. Board of Educ., Shelley v. Kraemer,* the Negro voting cases.[33] Professor Pollak sought to help Professor Wechsler find neutral principles for reaching the results in those cases.[34] Recently, two articles, one by Professors Mueller and Murray Schwartz, one by Professors Miller and Howell, questioned the very demand for neutral principles.[35] Most recent were Dean Griswold's strictures against "result-oriented" decisions.[36]

THE CALL FOR PRINCIPLE

Perhaps a word in the controversy must be said as foundation for the reflections to follow. It seems to me inevitable that we start where Professor Wechsler starts. His term "neutral principles" has been variously interpreted, and at least part of the

[32] Hand, *The Bill of Rights* (1958).

[33] Wechsler, "Toward Neutral Principles of Constitutional Law," 73 *Harv. L. Rev.* 1 (1959).

[34] Pollak, "Racial Discrimination and Judicial Integrity: A Reply to Professor Wechsler," 108, *U. Pa. L. Rev.* 1 (1959).

[35] Mueller & Schwartz, "The Principle of Neutral Principles," 7 *U.C.L.A.L. Rev.* 571 (1960); Miller & Howell, "The Myth of Neutrality in Constitutional Adjudication," 27 *U. Chi. L. Rev.* 661 (1960).

[36] Griswold, *Foreword:* "Of Time and Attitudes—Professor Hart and Judge Arnold, The Supreme Court, 1959 Term," 74 *Harv. L. Rev.,* 81 (1960). The controversy between Professor Hart and once-Professor Thurman Arnold, while not irrelevant, does not turn on different views as to the Court's role in constitutional adjudication. Hart, "Foreword: The Time Chart of the Justices, The Supreme Court, 1958 Term," 73 *Harv. L. Rev.,* 84 (1959); Arnold, "Professor Hart's Theology," 73 *Harv. L. Rev.* 1298 (1960).

disagreement with him is due, perhaps, to misunderstanding. But if I interpret him correctly, it would seem that Professor Wechsler demands what my colleague Paul Mishkin and I have called, in the title to an article we have never written, "The Return to Doctrine": Professor Wechsler calls for principle, generally applied, except where the Constitution is admittedly, or can be interpreted as being, partisan. Surely, to begin with the absurd, the Court ought not to decide for appellant against respondent, in constitutional cases as in others, because appellant has bribed the Court, or is a political leader, or is a nice fellow— unless judgment for the payer of bribes, or the political leader, or the nice fellow, were to be accepted as a general principle of adjudication. Surely decision should not go in a specific case, nor should special constitutional preference be given, to the rich man, or the white man, or the protestant man, or the poor man, or the insurance company, or the labor union, or the black man; or the Quaker, or the Witness—unless one can fairly say that the Constitution granted such a preference. Neutral principle, then, means, I take it, "principle," "doctrine," a rule of general application. Neutral principle also means that the principles which the Court announces must be logically and consistently applied. It means, for example, that if the due process clause no longer precludes economic regulation and does not prevent a state from barring "yellow-dog contracts," it does not prevent a state from adopting a "right to work" law, unless relevant differences can afford a distinguishing principle.[37] It means that if a state can require the Ku Klux Klan to disclose its membership, a state can be barred from requiring membership lists from the NAACP only if the Court can set forth relevant distinctions between the two cases.[38] It means, on the other hand, Professor Wechsler might rightly say, that one cannot continue to nod respect to language and history and admit that the fourteenth amendment applies only to state action, but go on to treat private action as state action when it is a Negro complaining. Or, again, one cannot find judicial enforcement of racial discrimination to be for-

[37] See Lincoln Fed. Labor Union v. Northwestern Iron & Metal Co., 335 U.S. 525 (1949).
[38] See Bryant v. Zimmerman, 278 U.S. 63 (1928); NAACP v. Alabama *ex rel.* Patterson, 357 U.S. 449 (1958).

bidden state action in one circumstance, and not in another, unless one can build a rational distinction between the two kinds and contexts of judicial action that is relevant to the concept of state action.

It happens that I, like Professor Pollak, believe that the particular cases which bother Professor Wechsler can be justified on "neutral principles," although the Court perhaps did not do so effectively. But Professor Wechsler's basic thesis seems to me unchallengeable. It is a thesis which should perhaps go without saying, but one cannot assert confidently that it does not need to be said. One cannot be sure that the object of his attack is a man of straw, as long as courts continue to give basis for his fears, and writers even seek to rationalize a principle of "anti-principle." Professor Wechsler's seems to me to be the inevitable reaction, long overdue. Long ago critics of the Court began "to remove the fig leaf," to stress that judges were fallible mortals with prejudices, who talked "principle" that was really a rationalization for achieving prejudged results; or, at least, that judges tended to find in the general language of the Constitution the notions they brought to it about the proper role of government and the rights of the individual. It was perhaps inevitable that some should carelessly press this necessary cautionary reminder to the judgment that there is, can be, and ought to be no doctrine, that all adjudication is empirical, *ad hoc,* and that the appellate judge, at least in constitutional cases, has no rule other than his own predilections. But is it not time to insist that this is not so, and that not even the most extremist proponent of the empirical view really intended any such absurdity? Is it not clear that even strictly political actions of political bodies cannot be entirely *ad hoc,* and that the judge's role under a written constitution differs from the politician's at least in substantial degree? Can it be denied, for instance, that every Justice has at some time decided a constitutional case contrary to his political sympathies, although judges may differ radically in how hard they will struggle to achieve a disinterested result?

Sometimes, it appears that those who deny doctrine believe that they are supporting an "activist" view in constitutional adjudication. But the cases which bother Professor Wechsler in particular were unanimous decisions, or at least decisions which did not reflect any basic "activist" division in the Court, and which quickly became accepted by all. The current divisions of the Court, to which we have referred, are not differences as to whether principles exist, or whether they should be neutral or general. All members of the Court assume that there is doctrine and act on that assumption. All participate in the writing of opinions, the citation of cases, even the distinguishing of other cases; do these not presuppose a rational application of principle by a continuing judicial institution? If there is any among today's Justices who rejects doctrine, he pays to the rest the homage of hypocrisy by joining in the rational process of adjudication on the assumption that principles exist. In large areas of the Constitution today judges do not even differ as to what the principles are—as in those once-issues in which the Court has long denied review and litigants no longer seek it. Where the judges now divide they are differing not as to whether principles exist, but as to what are the applicable and controlling principles.

The denial of principle is, I sometimes think, the snicker of the cynic. To him the entire process of decision is a sham. The judicial opinion is ritual, not reason, and principles are incantations to be invoked. To those who believe, on the other hand, that the game has rules and the rules have purpose, that the process has reason, principle is the essential reason. The judicial opinion is a vital aspect of the process. One might do worse for the beginning of a definition than to suggest that judicial doctrine and principle are those reasons for reaching a result which can be stated in a judicial opinion.

THE INGREDIENTS OF CONSTITUTIONAL DECISION

We assume that there is and must be doctrine, that in the current divisions of the Court there are, in largest part, doctrinal differences. Criticism of the work of the Court, then, must deal with these differences, must consider whether competing doctrines are equally acceptable, and how the proper or preferable doctrine is to be selected.

Sometimes, when discussing one of the Court's constitutional divisions, I amuse myself by asking a student, "Who is right?" Sometimes a wise student rejoins by asking what the question means. Some would suggest that "Who is right?" is a silly question. They might say that different judges are applying different values—and there is no basis, except one's own values, for choosing between the differing values of different judges.

I might grant them their proposition, within narrow limits. But even if I were not trying to decide who is right, even if I were only trying to equip myself to choose between their values, I, as a litigant, citizen, critic, or legislator seeking constitutional amendment or legislative curbs on the Supreme Court, might wish to know what these values are. In fact, however, it should be clear that values, and choices between values, are not fungible, and that not all values are equally available to the judge. Judges are not entirely at large in choosing among values. If in some constitutional cases, indeed, either answer may have something to be said for it, surely we cannot accept that all constitutional cases can with equal propriety be decided either way.

Like others who have spoken on this subject,[39] I believe that the Court owes an obligation to the integrity of the judicial process in constitutional cases to articulate the bases for its decisions—what ingredients have gone into the judgment, in what weights, absolute and comparative. The writing of an opinion will help assure that the decision is based on principle, and will help make clear what the principle is. Whether or not the Court meets this obligation, the critic of the Court, too, must seek to identify the ingredients of decision, to expose those which are choices between competing values, to examine the extent to which this choice is open to the judge, to evaluate the choice made.

I do not suggest that this is an easy task, that it can be done with any hope of precision, that the process of criticism itself can escape criticism for the critic's assumptions, articulated or unarticulated, and the critic's choices. But the attempt is essential if the critics are to be able to speak to the Court, or to each other. Here I should like to reflect briefly on what seem to be principal ingredients in constitutional adjudication, and on how the Court handles them.

[39] Early criticism of inadequate per curiam and other opinions was Professor Brown's in "Foreword: Process of Law, The Supreme Court, 1957 Term," 72, *Harv. L. Rev.*, 77 (1958).

Let us begin by stressing the extent to which the judge, in constitutional adjudication, does not have free choice between values or results. There are some elements in decision, that may also be called principles or values, which, all must agree, limit the judge's choice. Take, for instance, the very fact of a written Constitution, and the kinds of substantive provisions in our Constitution. A judge is inevitably bound by the system of government which is the context in which he sits. We may demand of him commitment to the philosophy of government that he, in his part, also represents. The fact that the Constitution which he invokes is written means that he must pay a substantial respect to the words in it, no matter how much he may feel that the society would be better if they had not been written, or if different words were in the Constitution. If language can be used at all, there must be large areas of agreement on the meaning of words. Words are ambiguous but the area of ambiguity is not without narrow limits; in many provisions, at least, the words of the Constitution have a minimum core of unambiguity which cannot be avoided. Surely, then, the Court does not have unlimited latitude to say what the Constitution is; the Court does not possess an equivalent alternative to the amending process provided in the Constitution. Words limit the choices open to the Court. We can demand that Justices give words their due.

There are other institutional factors, or principles, or values, which also limit the Court's freedom in choosing among values. The fact that it is established as, and called, a "judicial body," not an "appellate legislature," suggests that its choice between values is not as free as was that of the legislature whose action it reviews. We do not pretend to define the difference in role between judiciary and legislature, or to define even the special differences between these roles in constitutional cases—in distinction from their roles in the development of private law. But surely there must be more to justify a court in invalidating a statute than that the judge, had he been in the legislature, would have voted for value *B* as more desirable than value *A*.

These factors—the written Constitution, the unambiguous minimum core of meaning in its words, the quality of a court in contradistinction to a legislature—will be generally accepted, I believe, as limitations on the Court's free choice between values, although there may be disagreement as to how stringent the limitations are, in general or in a particular case. There are other ingredients, with greater uncertainty as to their import, and greater disagreement as to how heavily they weigh. There are words between the lines of the Constitution, and the history of these lines and of these words, the story of what was said about them by those who said and heard them. There is "the statute as a whole," the pattern of the Constitution, the division of power between nation and state, the distribution of functions among the branches of the national government, and the limitations on these powers. In addition to the pattern as established, there is the pattern that became, the federalism that grew and the special shape it took as the result of the Civil War, and the Civil War amendments, and the interpretations of these amendments. There are the great admonitions—of Marshall, that it is a constitution we are exponding; of Holmes, that in interpreting the Constitution we must consider what this country has become. That it is a constitution suggests that it is alive and grows; it suggests also that there are principles of growth; it does not, of course, mean that any Justice is free to make it "grow" however and wherever he will.

We have been recently reminded that our ancestors did not expel George III in order to offer an American throne to Clio, the Muse of History.[40] We may all agree that they did not. But do we, perhaps, owe more and better to history than did our ancestors? Or perhaps, not being revolutionaries, can we as easily escape history? That it is a constitution we are expounding also means that our ancestors wrote the document for us as well as for themselves. We are not new men, without umbilical cords. To be aware of how we got here does not mean to be tied by the dogmas of the past. The rearview mirror is not primarily to warn us that we are being chased. It suggests, it has been said, that you cannot successfully navigate the future unless you keep always framed beside it a small, clear image of the past. Clio deserves no throne; but may she not claim a corner seat at the conference table?

The ingredients we have mentioned are admittedly proper, even if the weights to be given them are hardly agreed by either

40 Cahn, Book Review, N.Y. Herald Tribune, Oct. 16, 1960, p. 8, col. 3.

Justices or critics. Even these disagreements, I would urge, are within limits which emphasize that the Justices are not at large in their choices. There are, however, ingredients of another kind, more difficult to appraise and to criticize. Sometimes it is clear that what determines how the agreed ingredients we have noted are used—what determines, ultimately, the decision—are other ingredients whose claim to inclusion is not always articulated and justified. I do not mean anything sinister like bias to a particular litigant, or even a class of litigants. I refer to implicit or assumed philosophies of government which Justices find or put in the Constitution.

What one might call meta-constitutional assumptions are not new to constitutional adjudication, although the need to justify them has not always been equally felt or satisfied. Way back, for example, in *Calder v. Bull*,[41] Mr. Justice Chase suggested that there are inherent limitations on government, apart from the Constitution, deriving from natural justice. Mr. Justice Marshall, too, in *Fletcher v. Peck*,[42] suggested that even without a constitutional prohibition there are things a legislature cannot do; for example, it could not take private property without compensation. Later Justices were less frank, or perhaps less aware. When Justice Holmes said in dissent in *Lochner v. New York*[43] that the fourteenth amendment did not enact Herbert Spencer's Social Statics, it is not beyond possibility that Mr. Justice Peckham and his majority in that case did not know what Holmes was talking about.[44] They could not, perhaps, conceive that one could read the Constitution without finding there, or assuming, that particular view of the role of government which accorded with their ideas of the natural and inevitable. Important deviations from laissez faire were violations of the natural limitations upon government which, if they did not rise to constitutional stature be-

---

[41] 3 U.S. (3 Dall.) 386 (1798).

[42] 10 U.S. (6 Cranch) 87 (1810).

[43] 198 U.S. 45, 74 (1905).

[44] A friend once asked Mr. Justice Holmes: "What about your colleague, Justice Peckham?" "Oh," answered Holmes, "he is a handsome, charming fellow and a delightful raconteur." "I don't mean that," continued his questioner, "I mean what is he like intellectually speaking?" "Intellectually?" replied Holmes. "I never thought of him in that connection.

"Now that you ask me, however, I would say that his major premise is 'God damn it.' "

fore, were put or confirmed there by the fourteenth amendment.

Lochner v. New York and its assumed limitations on government are long dead. But there are now prohibitions on governmental action which Justices have found in the Constitution, also subject to the charge that the Justices are putting them there. We are all agreed that the fourteenth amendment did not enact Herbert Spencer or Adam Smith, the "liberalism" of another day, as limitations on majority government; many of us seem prepared to assume that the Constitution did enact John Stuart Mill's *On Liberty*. The Court has found, or put, ideas of proper relation between individual liberty and governmental order in the first amendment and in the fourteenth. If the language of the first amendment offers more of a "peg" for Mill than, to our trained eye, the words "liberty or property" provide for Herbert Spencer or Adam Smith, one must admit that the language cannot bear the whole weight, even as to the federal government, even less as to the states. And, though we give every weight to the ancestral influence of John Locke and to the later Jefferson, history too does not provide the necessary support.[45] The views of Mill afford a philosophy of government which you and I may share, but it is likely that this philosophy was not shared by those who wrote either of those amendments, and is not shared by the majority of the citizenry today, surely not by majorities of the legislatures which pass acts which the Court invalidates in the name of these amendments. When the Court gives these protections a preferred position and, assuming a different role for the Supreme Court in relation to legislation, applies a different presumption as to the constitutionality of legislative action, the Court may also be doing something with which you and I sympathize. But it is important that the Justices, and the professors, admit it and justify it. There have of course been attempts at justifications—in Stone's famous footnote;[46] in Cardozo's "matrix" metaphor;[47] even Judge Hand's strictures on judicial review admit that here it is less likely that the legislature has balanced

---

[45] See Levy, *Legacy of Suppression*, 100-04, 266-67, 299-306 (1960), Cahn, supra note 36.

[46] United States v. Carolene Prods. Co., 304 U.S. 144, 152 n.4 (1938).

[47] Palko v. Connecticut, 302 U.S. 319, 326-27 (1937).

values impartially and in good judgment.[48] But granting some justification for "preferred position," the nature and degree of the preference remain to be agreed. Somewhere, some Justices at least seem to see an ideal image of the nation, of the "democracy" which we are not but are ever becoming; and they see theirs as the principal role in realizing that image. Perhaps the Court cannot even attempt to educate us as to what is the ideal image of ourselves as a nation, what is this "democracy" toward which our Constitution is being headed. The critic may still demand such education; he may also demand that the Court keep in mind that democracy implies respect for majorities as well; he may ask whether the Court is the one to lead the reluctant rest to that promised democracy. The critic is entitled to ask, although he be himself hard put to give a confident answer, how much this ideal of freedom is to weigh in a balance with language, or history, or the respect due to legislatures, or the respect due to federalism when action of a state is involved.

THE PROCESS OF CONSTITUTIONAL ADJUDICATION

The choice of values in today's divisions then can be criticized —on the ground of insufficient respect to institutional limitations; too little or too much weight to other factors admittedly relevant; the injection of factors not admitted, the degree of their influence not justified; a preference by some Justices for results which fit an image of the nation not projected by the Constitution and which the Justices cannot prove to be justified by history, need, the philosophy of the people, or anything other than the Justices' faith or inclination. The criticism is not to be directed at any one judge, or even exclusively at one faction. Inevitably, of course, the burden of justification is greater—if indeed justification is inherently possible—when a Justice allows his ideal to outweigh the traditional ingredients of adjudication.

These criticisms, of course, assume adjudication on principle, the kind of general principle which I believe Professor Wechsler demands. There is another respect, however, in which the current divisions may be examined, and some of the Justices found wanting, in respects which do not meet Professor Wechsler's demands.

[48] Hand, *The Bill of Rights*, 69 (1958).

For the demands of doctrine we have suggested also require respect for the qualities of principled adjudication, for the integrity of judicial process. The law, if we may adapt Cardozo, is "not only as the past has shaped it in judgments already rendered, but as the future ought to shape it in cases yet to come."[49] The judge, as Cardozo said of the lawyer, "must be historian and prophet all in one."[50] We have suggested that the claims of history—where we started, how we came, what we have become—are not always given their due in the development of constitutional doctrine. If the Court has not always been fair to its role as historian, it is sometimes even less fair to its role as prophet. For that should suggest that a decision is to live for some indefinite while, that a doctrine is to have some durable life and have application to other cases of common character. Neutral principles need not be eternal, but they ought to offer hope for survival. If lines are to be drawn, we may have to accept that there may be two cases, barely on either side of a fine line, with opposite results. We may have to accept also that in the light of experience and hindsight, the Court may later see fit to redraw the line. But still its decisions must draw a line, must establish a principle of decision to which the Court is then prepared to give general application. It is obvious, of course, that the Court only decides the case before it, but in deciding that case it must give reason that promises applicability to the next case. Too often, it is fair to say, the Court, intent on disposing of the case before it, has inadequately considered that the reasons it gives, and the doctrine it announces, will and ought to apply to tomorrow's case in indistinguishable circumstances. No doubt some of the Court's critics read more into judicial opinions than is there, and are later surprised when the Court tells us that its earlier decision was limited. Still, greater awareness by the Justices, greater care in giving reasons for decision, would have spared it criticism when the Court moved from *Dennis* to *Yates*, from *Watkins* back to *Barenblatt*, from *Nelson* and *Sweezy* to *Uphaus*.[51]

---

[49] Cardozo, *Law and Literature*, 137 (1931).

[50] *Id*. at 166.

[51] Dennis v. United States, 341 U.S. 494 (1951); Yates v. United States, 354 U.S. 298 (1957); Watkins v. United States, 354 U.S. 178 (1957); Barenblatt v. United States, 360 U.S. 109 (1959); Pennsylvania v. Nelson, 350 U.S. 497 (1956); Sweezy v. New Hampshire, 354 U.S. 239 (1957); Uphaus v. Wyman, 360 U.S. 72 (1959).

But the criticism reaches deeper. Can the Court announce, in *Lambert v. California*,[52] that ignorance of the law is a constitutional excuse, without writing an opinion which would adequately distinguish ignorance which has been held not to be an excuse, and give due account to the generally applied view that scienter is not a constitutional requirement? Or take *Shelley v. Kraemer*, a case that concerned Professor Wechsler and has troubled others. The Court announced, as the basis for decision to reverse enforcement by a state court of a restrictive covenant, that judicial action is state action. That some judicial action is state action was long clear, for example, from state criminal convictions invalidated for lack of procedural due process. But some believe that the Court was invalidating as "state action" discrimination which was not the state's but that of private individuals. They believe also that there is some judicial action that enforces private discrimination which the Court would not be prepared to invalidate. Is the Court prepared, for example, to find forbidden "state action" when a state court imposes a sentence, or grants a recovery, for trespass, to give effect to private racial discrimination? Or when a state court probates and administers a discriminatory will? If, as many assume, the Court is not prepared to invalidate the judgments of state courts in these situations, surely then the reason for the decision in *Shelley v. Kraemer* cannot be merely that judicial action is state action. I, too, suspect that the Court is not prepared to follow where its opinion might seem to lead. I believe that one can perhaps write an opinion in *Shelley v. Kraemer* which can draw distinctions that would tolerate the action of a state giving effect to discriminatory bequests but not to restrictive covenants; or distinctions that in special contexts might tolerate the enforcement of religious discrimination, but recognize no comparable and permissible racial discrimination; or distinctions that would recognize the state's right to give effect to social discrimination in one's home, but not in one's business—and show the relevance of these distinctions to the proper role of government and thereby to the concept of "state action." Perhaps I am wrong, perhaps such an opinion cannot be written—at least not without establishing some new "inherent" concepts about the respective areas of permissible

[52] 355 U.S. 225 (1957).

government regulation and of inviolable individual liberty. The Court clearly has not written a satisfying opinion. It leaves the impression that the Court is expanding and contracting words; it does not reflect adequate recognition that the requirement of "state action" contains important principles of relation in the federal system, and important principles of relation between government and individual. Inadequate efforts to write adequate opinions cry for criticism, not least because they lend support to the cynics to purvey the impression that reason is unnecessary, that opinions have to be indulged but do not really matter.

CONCLUSION

The issues in constitutional controversy today do not generally reflect an ordeal of battle between powerful political forces. They represent primarily the degree to which the Court will opt for liberty over "democracy," will champion an ideal—the rights and liberties of individuals and small groups—against the forces of representative government. The changing issues have reflected and effected changes in institutions and relations between them, changes between state and nation, between Court and legislature, between Court and critic.

The answers to constitutional questions do not lend themselves readily to the judgment of right and wrong. We can only hope and ask for scrupulous adherence to the process due constitutional adjudication—the principled application of principle, man-made principle, the exposition of the ingredients of decision, of the respective weights given them, of the choices they represent. Whether or not he likes the result, the critic must review this process. He too must adhere to neutral principles, to neutral principles of criticism—he cannot merely choose sides and vote for his sympathies, or for his judicial favorites. The critic must demand equally of all judges in all cases respect for the rules of judging. Perhaps then we can demand for our criticism and for our own controversies the attention of the Justices.

The Founding Fathers: A Reform Caucus in Action* ∼ JOHN P. ROCHE

OVER the last century and a half, the work of the Constitutional Convention and the motives of the Founding Fathers have been analyzed under a number of different ideological auspices. To one generation of historians, the hand of God was moving in the assembly; under a later dispensation, the dialectic (at various levels of philosophical sophistication) replaced the Deity: "relationships of production" moved into the niche previously reserved for Love of Country. Thus in counterpoint to the Zeitgeist, the Framers have undergone miraculous metamorphoses: at one time acclaimed as liberals and bold social engineers, today they appear in the guise of sound Burkean conservatives, men who in our time would subscribe to *Fortune,* look to Walter Lippmann for political theory, and chuckle patronizingly at the antics of Barry Goldwater. The implicit assumption is that if James Madison were among us, he would be President of the Ford Foundation, while Alexander Hamilton would chair the Committee for Economic Development.

The "Fathers" have thus been admitted to our best circles; the revolutionary ferocity which confiscated all Tory property in reach and populated New Brunswick with outlaws has been converted by the "Miltown School" of American historians into a benign dedication to "consensus" and "prescriptive rights." The Daughters of the American Revolution have, through the ministrations of Professors Boorstin, Hartz, and Rossiter, at last found ancestors worthy of their descendants. It is not my purpose here to argue that the "Fathers" were, in fact, radical revolutionaries; that proposition has been brilliantly demonstrated by Robert R. Palmer in his *Age of the Democratic Revolution.* My concern is with the further position that not only were they revolutionaries,

* Reprinted by permission of *The American Political Science Review.*

but also they were democrats. Indeed, in my view, there is one fundamental truth about the Founding Fathers that *every* generation of Zeitgeisters has done its best to obscure: they were first and foremost superb democratic politicians. I suspect that in a contemporary setting, James Madison would be Speaker of the House of Representatives and Hamilton would be the *eminence grise* dominating (*pace* Theodore Sorenson or Sherman Adams) the Executive Office of the President. They were, with their colleagues, *political men*—not metaphysicians, disembodied conservatives or Agents of History—and as recent research into the nature of American politics in the 1780s confirms,[1] they were committed (perhaps willy-nilly) to working within the democratic framework, within a universe of public approval. Charles Beard *and* the filiopietists to the contrary notwithstanding, the Philadelphia Convention was not a College of Cardinals or a council of Platonic guardians working within a manipulative, pre-democratic framework; it was a *nationalist* reform caucus which had to operate with great delicacy and skill in a political cosmos full of enemies to achieve the one definitive goal—popular approbation.

Perhaps the time has come, to borrow Walton Hamilton's fine phrase, to raise the Framers from immortality to mortality, to give them credit for their magnificent demonstration of the art of democratic politics. The point must be reemphasized; they *made* history and did it within the limits of consensus. There was nothing inevitable about the future in 1787; the *Zeitgeist,* that fine Hegelian technique of begging causal questions, could only be discerned in retrospect. What they did was to hammer out a pragmatic compromise which would both bolster the "National interest" and be acceptable to the people. What inspiration they got came from their collective experience as professional politicians in a democratic society. As John Dickinson put it to his fellow delegates on August 13, "Experience must be our guide. Reason may mislead us."

---

[1] The view that the right to vote in the states was severely circumscribed by property qualifications has been thoroughly discredited in recent years. See Chilton Williamson, *American Suffrage from Property to Democracy, 1760–1860* (Princeton, 1960). The contemporary position is that John Dickinson actually knew what he was talking about when he argued that there would be little opposition to vesting the right of suffrage in freeholders since "The great mass of our Citizens is composed at this time of freeholders, and will be pleased with it." Max Farrand, *Records of the Federal Convention,* Vol. 2, p. 202 (New Haven, 1911). (Henceforth cited as *Farrand.*)

In this context, let us examine the problems they confronted and the solutions they evolved. The Convention has been described picturesquely as a counter-revolutionary junta and the Constitution as a *coup d'etat,*[2] but this has been accomplished by withdrawing the whole history of the movement for constitutional reform from its true context. No doubt the goals of the constitutional elite were "subversive" to the existing political order, but it is overlooked that their subversion could only have succeeded if the people of the United States endorsed it by regularized procedures. Indubitably they were "plotting" to establish a much stronger central government than existed under the Articles, but only in the sense in which one could argue equally well that John F. Kennedy was, from 1956 to 1960, "plotting" to become President. In short, on the fundamental *procedural* level, the Constitutionalists had to work according to the prevailing rules of the game. Whether they liked it or not is a topic for spiritualists—and is irrelevant: one may be quite certain that had Washington agreed to play the De Gaulle (as the Cincinnati once urged), Hamilton would willingly have held his horse, but such fertile speculation in no way alters the actual context in which events took place.

I

When the Constitutionalists went forth to subvert the Confederation, they utilized the mechanisms of political legitimacy. And the roadblocks which confronted them were formidable. At the same time, they were endowed with certain potent political assets. The history of the United States from 1786 to 1790 was largely one of a masterful employment of political expertise by the Constitutionalists as against bumbling, erratic behavior by the opponents of reform. Effectively, the Constitutionalists had to induce the states, by democratic techniques of coercion, to emas-

[2] The classic statement of the *coup d'etat* theory is, of course, Charles A. Beard, *An Economic Interpretation of the Constitution of the United States* (New York, 1913), and this theme was echoed by Vernon L. Parrington, Merrill Jensen and others in "populist" historiographical tradition. For a sharp critique of this thesis see Robert E. Brown, *Charles Beard and the Constitution* (Princeton, 1956). See also Forrest McDonald, *We the People* (Chicago, 1958); the trailblazing work in this genre was Douglas Adair, "The Tenth Federalist Revisited," *William and Mary Quarterly,* Third Series, Vol. VIII (1951), pp. 48–67.

culate themselves. To be specific, if New York had refused to join the new Union, the project was doomed; yet before New York was safely in, the reluctant state legislature had *sua sponte* to take the following steps: (1) agree to send delegates to the Philadelphia Convention; (2) provide maintenance for these delegates (these were distinct stages: New Hampshire was early in naming delegates, but did not provide for their maintenance until July); (3) set up the special *ad hoc* convention to decide on ratification; and (4) concede to the decision of the *ad hoc* convention that New York should participate. New York admittedly was a tricky state, with a strong interest in a *status quo* which permitted her to exploit New Jersey and Connecticut, but the same legal hurdles existed in every state. And at the risk of becoming boring, it must be reiterated that the *only* weapon in the Constitutionalist arsenal was an effective mobilization of public opinion.

The group which undertook this struggle was an interesting amalgam of a few dedicated nationalists with the self-interested spokesmen of various parochial bailiwicks. The Georgians, for example, wanted a strong central authority to provide military protection for their huge, underpopulated state against the Creek Confederacy; Jerseymen and Connecticuters wanted to escape from economic bondage to New York; the Virginians hoped to establish a system which would give that great state its rightful place in the councils of the republic. The dominant figures in the politics of these states therefore cooperated in the call for the Convention.[3] In other states, the thrust towards national reform was taken up by opposition groups who added the "national interest" to their weapons system; in Pennsylvania, for instance, the group fighting to revise the Constitution of 1776 came out four-square behind the Constitutionalists, and in New York, Hamilton and the Schuyler *ambiance* took the same tack against George Clinton.[4] There was, of course, a large element of person-

---

[3] A basic volume, which, like other works by Warren, provides evidence with which one can evaluate the author's own opinions, is Charles Warren, *The Making of the Constitution* (Boston, 1928). The best brief summary of the forces behind the movement for centralization is Chapter 1 of *Warren* (as it will be cited hereafter).

[4] On Pennsylvania see Robert L. Brunhouse, *Counter-Revolution in Pennsylvania* (Harrisburg, 1942) and Charles P. Smith, *James Wilson* (Chapel Hill, 1956), ch. 15; for New York, which needs the some sort of microanalysis Pennsylvania has received, the best study is E. Wilder Spaulding, *New York in the Critical Period, 1783–1789* (New York, 1932).

ality in the affair: there is reason to suspect that Patrick Henry's opposition to the Convention and the Constitution was founded on his conviction that Jefferson was behind both, and a close study of local politics elsewhere would surely reveal that others supported the Constitution for the simple (and politically quite sufficient) reason that the "wrong" people were against it.

To say this is not to suggest that the Constitution rested on a foundation of impure or base motives. It is rather to argue that in politics there are no immaculate conceptions, and that in the drive for a stronger general government, motives of all sorts played a part. Few men in the history of mankind have espoused a view of the "common good" or "public interest" that militated against their private status; even Plato with all his reverence for disembodied reason managed to put philosophers on top of the pile. Thus it is not surprising that a number of diversified private interests joined to push the nationalist public interest; what would have been surprising was the absence of such a pragmatic united front. And the fact remains that, however motivated, these men did demonstrate a willingness to compromise their parochial interests in behalf of an ideal which took shape before their eyes and under their ministrations.

As Stanley Elkins and Eric McKitrick have suggested in a perceptive essay,[5] what distinguished the leaders of the Constitutionalist caucus from their enemies was a "Continental" approach to political, economic and military issues. To the extent that they shared an institutional base of operations, it was the Continental Congress (thirty-nine of the delegates to the Federal Convention had served in Congress[6]), and this was hardly a locale which inspired respect for the state governments. Robert de Jouvenal observed French politics half a century ago and noted that a revolutionary Deputy had more in common with a non-revolutionary Deputy than he had with a revolutionary non-Deputy,[7] similarly one can surmise that membership in the Congress under the Articles of Confederation worked to establish a continental frame of reference, that a Congressman from Pennsylvania and one from South Carolina would share a universe of discourse

[5] Stanley Elkins and Eric McKitrick, "The Founding Fathers: Young Men of the Revolution," *Political Science Quarterly*, Vol. 76, p. 181 (1961).

[6] *Warren*, p. 55.

[7] In *La Republique des Camarades* (Paris, 1914).

which provided them with a conceptual common denominator *vis à vis* their respective state legislatures. This was particularly true with respect to external affairs: the average state legislator was probably about as concerned with foreign policy then as he is today, but Congressmen were constantly forced to take the broad view of American prestige, were compelled to listen to the reports of Secretary John Jay and to the dispatches and pleas from their frustrated envoys in Britain, France and Spain.[8] From considerations such as these, a "Continental" ideology developed which seems to have demanded a revision of our domestic institutions primarily on the ground that only by invigorating our general government could we assume our rightful place in the international arena. Indeed, an argument with great force—particularly since Washington was its incarnation—urged that our very survival in the Hobbesian jungle of world politics depended upon a reordering and strengthening of our national sovereignty.[9]

Note that I am not endorsing the "Critical Period" thesis; on the contrary, Merrill Jensen seems to me quite sound in his view that for most Americans, engaged as they were in self-sustaining agriculture, the "Critical Period" was not particularly critical.[10] In fact, the great achievement of the Constitutionalists was their ultimate success in convincing the elected representatives of a majority of the white male population that change was imperative. A small group of political leaders with a Continental vision and essentially a consciousness of the United States' *international* impotence, provided the matrix of the movement. To their standard other leaders rallied with their own parallel ambitions. Their great assets were (1) the presence in their caucus of the one authentic American "father figure," George Washington, whose prestige was enormous;[11] (2) the energy and talent of their leadership (in which one must include the towering intellectuals

---

[8] See Frank Monaghan, *John Jay* (New York, 1935), ch. 13.

[9] "[T]he situation of the general government, if it can be called a government, is shaken to its foundation, and liable to be overturned by every blast. In a word, it is at an end; and, unless a remedy is soon applied, anarchy and confusion will inevitably ensue." Washington to Jefferson, May 30, 1787, *Farrand*, III, 31. See also Irving Brant, *James Madison, The Nationalist* (New York, 1948), ch. 25.

[10] Merrill Jensen, *The New Nation* (New York, 1950). Interestingly enough, Prof. Jensen virtually ignores international relations in his laudatory treatment of the government under the Articles of Confederation.

[11] The story of James Madison's cultivation of Washington is told by Brant, *op. cit.*, pp. 394–97.

of the time, John Adams and Thomas Jefferson, despite their absence abroad), and their communications "network," which was far superior to anything on the opposition side;[12] (3) the preemptive skill which made "their" issue The Issue and kept the locally oriented opposition permanently on the defensive; and (4) the subjective consideration that these men were spokesmen of a new and compelling credo: *American* nationalism, that ill-defined but nonetheless potent sense of collective purpose that emerged from the American Revolution.

Despite great institutional handicaps, the Constitutionalists managed in the mid-1780s to mount an offensive which gained momentum as years went by. Their greatest problem was lethargy, and paradoxically, the number of barriers in their path may have proved an advantage in the long run. Beginning with the initial battle to get the Constitutional Convention called and delegates appointed, they could never relax, never let up the pressure. In practical terms, this meant that the local "organizations" created by the Constitutionalists were perpetually in movement building up their cadres for the next fight. (The word organization has to be used with great caution: a political organization in the United States—as in contemporary England[13]—generally consisted of a magnate and his following, or a coalition of magnates. This did not necessarily mean that it was "undemocratic" or "aristocratic," in the Aristotelian sense of the word: while a few magnates such as the Livingstons could draft their followings, most exercised their leadership without coercion on the basis of popular endorsement. The absence of organized opposition did not imply the impossibility of competition any more than low public participation in elections necessarily indicated an undemocratic suffrage.)

The Constitutionalists got the jump on the "opposition" (a collective noun: oppositions would be more correct) at the outset with the demand for a Convention. Their opponents were caught in an old political trap: they were not being asked to approve

---

[12] The "message center" being the Congress; nineteen members of Congress were simultaneously delegates to the Convention. One gets a sense of this coordination of effort from Broadus Mitchell, *Alexander Hamilton, Youth to Maturity* (New York, 1957), ch. 22.

[13] See Sir Lewis Namier, *The Structure of Politics at the Accession of George III*, 2d ed. (New York, 1957); *England in the Age of the American Revolution* (London, 1930).

any specific program of reform, but only to endorse a meeting to discuss and recommend needed reforms. If they took a hard line at the first stage, they were put in the position of glorifying the *status quo* and of denying the need for *any* changes. Moreover, the Constitutionalists could go to the people with a persuasive argument for "fair play"—"How can you condemn reform before you know precisely what is involved?" Since the state legislatures obviously would have the final say on any proposals that might emerge from the Convention, the Constitutionalists were merely reasonable men asking for a chance. Besides, since they did not make any concrete proposals at that stage, they were in a position to capitalize on every sort of generalized discontent with the Confederation.

Perhaps because of their poor intelligence system, perhaps because of over-confidence generated by the failure of all previous efforts to alter the Articles,[14] the opposition awoke too late to the dangers that confronted them in 1787. Not only did the Constitutionalists manage to get every state but Rhode Island (where politics was enlivened by a party system reminiscent of the "Blues" and the "Greens" in the Byzantine Empire)[15] to appoint delegates to Philadelphia, but when the results were in, it appeared that they dominated the delegations. Given the apathy of the opposition, this was a natural phenomenon: in an ideologically non-polarized political atmosphere those who get appointed to a special committee are likely to be the men who supported the movement for its creation. Even George Clinton, who seems to have been the first opposition leader to awake to the possibility of trouble, could not prevent the New York legislature from appointing Alexander Hamilton—though he did have the foresight to send two of his henchmen to dominate the delegation. Incidentally, much has been made of the fact that the delegates to Philadelphia were not elected by the people;

[14] The Annapolis Convention, called for the previous year, turned into a shambles: only five states sent commissioners, only three states were legally represented, and the instructions to delegates named varied quite widely from state to state. Clinton and others of his persuasion may have thought this disaster would put an end to the drive for reform. See Mitchell, *op. cit.*, pp.362–67; Brant, *op. cit.*, pp. 375–87.

[15] See Hillman M. Bishop, *Why Rhode Island Opposed the Federal Constitution* (Providence, 1950) for a careful analysis of the labyrinthine political course of Rhode Island. For background see David S. Lovejoy, *Rhode Island Politics and the American Revolution* (Providence, 1958).

some have adduced this fact as evidence of the "undemocratic" character of the gathering. But put in the context of the time, this argument is wholly specious: the central government under the Articles was considered a creature of the component states and in all the states but Rhode Island, Connecticut and New Hampshire, members of the national Congress were chosen by the state legislatures. This was not a consequence of elitism or fear of the mob; it was a logical extension of states'-rights doctrine to guarantee that the national institution did not end-run the state legislatures and make direct contact with the people.[16]

II

With delegations safely named, the focus shifted to Philadelphia. While waiting for a quorum to assemble, James Madison got busy and drafted the so-called Randolph or Virginia Plan with the aid of the Virginia delegation. This was a political master-stroke. Its consequence was that once business got underway, the framework of discussion was established on Madison's terms. There was no interminable argument over agenda; instead the delegates took the Virginia Resolutions—"just for purposes of discussion"—as their point of departure. And along with Madison's proposals, many of which were buried in the course of the summer, went his major premise: a new start on a Constitution rather than piecemeal amendment. This was not necessarily revolutionary—a little exegesis could demonstrate that a new Constitution might be formulated as "amendments" to the Articles of Confederation—but Madison's proposal that this "lump sum" amendment go into effect after approval by nine states (the Ar-

16 The terms "radical" and "conservative" have been bandied about a good deal in connection with the Constitution. This usage is nonsense if it is employed to distinguish between two economic "classes"—*e.g.*, radical debtors versus conservative creditors, radical farmers versus conservative capitalists, etc.—because there was no polarization along this line of division; the same types of people turned up on both sides. And many were hard to place in these terms: does one treat Robert Morris as a debtor or a creditor? or James Wilson? See Brown, *op. cit., passim.* The one line of division that holds up is between those deeply attached to states'-rights and those who felt that the Confederation was bankrupt. Thus, curiously, some of the most narrow-minded, parochial spokesmen of the time have earned the designation "radical" while those most willing to experiment and alter the *status quo* have been dubbed "conservative"! See Cecelia Kenyon, "Men of Little Faith," *William and Mary Quarterly*, Vol. 12, p. 3 (1955).

ticles required unanimous state approval for any amendment) was thoroughly subversive.[17]

Standard treatments of the Convention divide the delegates into "nationalists" and "states'-righters" with various improvised shadings ("moderate nationalists," etc.) , but these are *a posteriori* categories which obfuscate more than they clarify. What is striking to one who analyzes the Convention as a case-study in democratic politics is the lack of clear-cut ideological divisions in the Convention. Indeed, I submit that the evidence—Madison's *Notes,* the correspondence of the delegates, and debates on ratification—indicate that this was a remarkably homogeneous body on the ideological level. Yates and Lansing, Clinton's two chaperones for Hamilton, left in disgust on July 10. (Is there anything more tedious than sitting through endless disputes on matters one deems fundamentally misconceived? It takes an iron will to spend a hot summer as an ideological *agent provocateur.*) Luther Martin, Maryland's bibulous narcissist, left on September 4 in a huff when he discovered that others did not share his self-esteem; others went home for personal reasons. But the hard core of delegates accepted a grinding regimen throughout the attrition of a Philadelphia summer precisely because they shared the Constitutionalist goal.

Basic differences of opinion emerged, of course, but these were not ideological; they were *structural.* If the so-called "states'-rights" group had not accepted the fundamental purposes of the Convention, they could simply have pulled out and by doing so have aborted the whole enterprise. Instead of bolting, they returned day after day to argue and to compromise. An interesting symbol of this basic homogeneity was the initial agreement on secrecy: these professional politicians did not want to become prisoners of publicity; they wanted to retain that freedom of maneuver which is only possible when men are not forced to take public stands in the preliminary stages of negotiation.[18]

---

[17] Yet, there was little objection to this crucial modification from any quarter—there almost seems to have been a gentlemen's agreement that Rhode Island's *liberum veto* had to be destroyed.

[18] See Mason's letter to his son, May 27, 1787, in which he endorsed secrecy as "a proper precaution to prevent mistakes and misrepresentation until the business shall have been completed, when the whole may have a very different complexion from that in which the several crude and indigested parts might in their first shape appear if submitted to the public eye." *Farrand,* III, 28.

There was no legal means of binding the tongues of the delegates: at any stage in the game a delegate with basic principled objections to the emerging project could have taken the stump (as Luther Martin did after his exit) and denounced the convention to the skies. Yet Madison did not even inform Thomas Jefferson in Paris of the course of the deliberations[19] and available correspondence indicates that the delegates generally observed the injunction. Secrecy is certainly uncharacteristic of any assembly marked by strong ideological polarization. This was noted at the time: the *New York Daily Advertiser*, August 14, 1787, commented that the " . . . profound secrecy hitherto observed by the Convention [we consider] a happy omen, as it demonstrates that the spirit of party on any great and essential point cannot have arisen to any height."[20]

Commentators on the Constitution who have read *The Federalist* in lieu of reading the actual debates have credited the Fathers with the invention of a sublime concept called "Federalism."[21] Unfortunately *The Federalist* is probative evidence for only one proposition: that Hamilton and Madison were inspired propagandists with a genius for retrospective symmetry. Federalism, as the theory is generally defined, was an improvisation which was later promoted into a political theory. Experts on "federalism" should take to heart the advice of David Hume, who warned in his *Of the Rise and Progress of the Arts and Sciences* that " . . . there is no subject in which we must proceed with more caution than in [history], lest we assign causes which never existed and reduce what is merely contingent to stable and universal principles." In any event, the final balance in the Constitution between the states and the nation must have come as a great disappointment to Madison, while Hamilton's unitary views are too well known to need elucidation.

It is indeed astonishing how those who have glibly designated James Madison the "father" of Federalism have overlooked the solid body of fact which indicates that he shared Hamilton's

---

[19] See Madison to Jefferson, June 6, 1787, *Farrand*, III, 35.

[20] Cited in *Warren*, p. 138.

[21] See, *e.g.*, Gottfried Dietze, *The Federalist, A Classic on Federalism and Free Government* (Baltimore, 1960); Richard Hofstadter, *The American Political Tradition* (New York, 1948); and John P. Roche, "American Liberty," in M. Konvitz and C. Rossiter, eds., *Aspects of Liberty* (Ithaca, 1958).

quest for a unitary central government. To be specific, they have avoided examining the clear import of the Madison-Virginia Plan,[22] and have disregarded Madison's dogged inch-by-inch retreat from the bastions of centralization. The Virginia Plan envisioned a unitary national government effectively freed from and dominant over the states. The lower house of the national legislature was to be elected directly by the people of the states with membership proportional to population. The upper house was to be selected by the lower and the two chambers would elect the executive and choose the judges. The national government would be thus cut completely loose from the states.[23]

The structure of the general government was freed from state control in a truly radical fashion, but the scope of the authority of the national sovereign as Madison initially formulated it was breathtaking—it was a formulation worthy of the Sage of Malmesbury himself. The national legislature was to be empowered to disallow the acts of state legislatures,[24] and the central government was vested, in addition to the powers of the nation under the Articles of Confederation, with plenary authority wherever " . . . the separate States are incompetent or in which the harmony of the United States may be interrupted by the exercise of individual legislation."[25] Finally, just to lock the door against state intrusion, the national Congress was to be given the power

[22] "I hold it for a fundamental point, that an individual independence of the states is utterly irreconcilable with the idea of an aggregate sovereignty," Madison to Randolph, cited in Brant, *op. cit.*, p. 416.

[23] The Randolph Plan was presented on May 29, see *Farrand*, I, 18–23; the state legislatures retained only the power to *nominate* candidates for the upper chamber. Madison's view of the appropriate position of the states emerged even more strikingly in Yates' record of his speech on June 29: "Some contend that states are sovereign when in fact they are only political societies. There is a gradation of power in all societies, from the lowest corporation tó the highest sovereign. The states never possessed the essential rights of sovereignty . . . . The states, at present, are only great corporations, having the power of making by-laws, and these are effectual only if they are not contradictory to the general confederation. The states ought to be placed under the control of the general government—at least as much so as they formerly were under the king and British parliament." *Farrand*, I, 471. Forty-six years later, after Yates' "Notes" had been published, Madison tried to explain this statement away as a misinterpretation: he did not flatly deny the authenticity of Yates' record, but attempted a defense that was half justification and half evasion. Madison to W. C. Rives, Oct. 21, 1833. *Farrand*, III, 521–24.

[24] Resolution 6 gave the National Legislature this power subject to review by the Council of Revision proposed in Resolution 8.

[25] Resolution 6.

to use military force on recalcitrant states.[26] This was Madison's "model" of an ideal national government, though it later received little publicity in *The Federalist.*

The interesting thing was the reaction of the Convention to this militant program for a strong autonomous central government. Some delegates were startled, some obviously leery of so comprehensive a project of reform,[27] but nobody set off any fireworks and nobody walked out. Moreover, in the two weeks that followed, the Virginia Plan received substantial endorsement *en principe;* the initial temper of the gathering can be deduced from the approval "without debate or dissent," on May 31, of the Sixth Resolution which granted Congress the authority to disallow state legislation " . . . contravening *in its opinion* the Articles of Union." Indeed, an amendment was included to bar states from contravening national treaties.[28]

The Virginia Plan may therefore be considered, in ideological terms, as the delegates' Utopia, but as the discussions continued and became more specific, many of those present began to have second thoughts. After all, they were not residents of Utopia or guardians in Plato's Republic who could simply impose a philosophical ideal on subordinate strata of the population. They were practical politicians in a democratic society, and no matter what their private dreams might be, they had to take home an acceptable package and defend it—and their own political futures—against predictable attack. On June 14 the breaking point between dream and reality took place. Apparently realizing that under the Virginia Plan, Massachusetts, Virginia and Pennsylvania could virtually dominate the national government—and probably appreciating that to sell this program to "the folks back home" would be impossible—the delegates from the small states dug in their heels and demanded time for a consideration of alternatives. One gets a graphic sense of the inner politics from John Dickinson's reproach to Madison: "You see the conse-

[26] *Ibid.*

[27] See the discussions on May 30 and 31. "Mr. Charles Pinkney wished to know of Mr. Randolph whether he meant to abolish the State Governts. altogther . . . Mr. Butler said he had not made up his mind on the subject and was open to the light which discussion might throw on it . . . Genl. Pinkney expressed a doubt . . . Mr. Gerry seemed to entertain the same doubt." *Farrand*, I, 33–34. There were no denunciations—though it should perhaps be added that Luther Martin had not yet arrived.

[28] *Farrand*, I, 54. (Italics added.)

quences of pushing things too far. Some of the members from the small States wish for two branches in the General Legislature and are friends to a good National Government; but we would sooner submit to a foreign power than . . . be deprived of an equality of suffrage in both branches of the Legislature, and thereby be thrown under the domination of the large States."[29]

The bare outline of the *Journal* entry for Tuesday, June 14, is suggestive to anyone with extensive experience in deliberative bodies. "It was moved by Mr. Patterson [*sic*, Paterson's name was one of those consistently misspelled by Madison and everybody else] seconded by Mr. Randolph that the further consideration ·of the report from the Committee of the whole House [endorsing the Virginia Plan] be postponed til tomorrow, and before the question for postponement was taken. It was moved by Mr. Randolph seconded by Mr. Patterson that the House adjourn."[30] The House adjourned by obvious prearrangement of the two principals: since the preceding Saturday when Bearley and Paterson of New Jersey had announced their fundamental discontent with the representational features of the Virginia Plan, the informal pressure had certainly been building up to slow down the streamroller. Doubtless there were extended arguments at the Indian Queen between Madison and Paterson, the latter insisting that events were moving rapidly towards a probably disastrous conclusion, towards a political suicide pact. Now the process of accommodation was put into action smoothly—and wisely, given the character and strength of the doubters. Madison had the votes, but this was one of those situations where the enforcement of mechanical majoritarianism could easily have destroyed the objectives of the majority: the Constitutionalists were in quest of a qualitative as well as a quantitative consensus. This was hardly from deference to local Quaker custom; it was a political imperative if they were to attain ratification.

III

According to the standard script, at this point the "states'-rights" group intervened in force behind the New Jersey Plan,

---

[29] *Ibid.*, p. 242. Delaware's delegates had been instructed by their general assembly to maintain in any new system the voting equality of the states. *Farrand*, III, 574.
[30] *Ibid.*, p. 240.

which has been characteristically portrayed as a reversion to the *status quo* under the Articles of Confederation but with minor modifications. A careful examination of the evidence indicates that only in a marginal sense is this an accurate description. It is true that the New Jersey Plan put the states back into the institutional picture, but one could argue that to do so was a recognition of political reality rather than an affirmation of states'-rights. A serious case can be made that the advocates of the New Jersey Plan, far from being ideological addicts of states'-rights, intended to substitute for the Virginia Plan a system which would both retain strong national power and have a chance of adoption in the states. The leading spokesman for the project asserted quite clearly that his views were based more on counsels of expediency than on principle; said Paterson on June 16: "I came here not to speak my own sentiments, but the sentiments of those who sent me. Our object is not such a Governmt. as may be best in itself, but such a one as our Constituents have authorized us to prepare, and as they will approve."[31] This is Madison's version; in Yates' transcription, there is a crucial sentence following the remarks above: "I believe that a little practical virtue is to be preferred to the finest theoretical principles, which cannot be carried into effect."[32] In his preliminary speech on June 9, Paterson had stated " . . . to the public mind we must accommodate ourselves,"[33] and in his notes for this and his later effort as well, the emphasis is the same. The *structure* of government under the Articles should be retained:

> 2. Because it accords with the Sentiments of the People
>   [Proof:] 1. Coms. [Commissions from state legislatures defining the jurisdiction of the delegates]
>   2. News-papers—Political Barometer. Jersey never would have sent Delegates under the first [Virginia] Plan—
>
> Not here to sport Opinions of my own. Wt. [What] can be done. A little practicable Virtue preferrable to Theory.[34]

This was a defense of political acumen, not of states'-rights. In fact, Paterson's notes of his speech can easily be construed as an argument for attaining the substantive objectives of the

[31] *Ibid.*, p. 250.
[32] *Ibid.*, p. 258.
[33] *Ibid.*, p. 178.
[34] *Ibid.*, p. 274.

Virginia Plan by a sound political route, *i.e.*, pouring the new wine in the old bottles. With a shrewd eye, Paterson queried:

Will the Operation and Force of the [central] Govt. depend upon the mode of Representn.—No—it will depend upon the Quantum of Power lodged in the leg. ex. and judy. Departments—Give [the existing] Congress the same Powers that you intend to give the two Branches, [under the Virginia Plan] and I apprehend they will act with as much Propriety and more Energy . . .[35]

In other words, the advocates of the New Jersey Plan concentrated their fire on what they held to be the *political liabilities* of the Virginia Plan—which were matters of institutional structure—rather than on the proposed scope of national authority. Indeed, the Supremacy Clause of the Constitution first saw the light of day in Paterson's Sixth Resolution; the New Jersey Plan contemplated the use of military force to secure compliance with national law; and finally Paterson made clear his view that under either the Virginia or the New Jersey systems, the general government would " . . . act on individuals and not on states."[36] From the states'-rights viewpoint, this was heresy: the fundament of that doctrine was the proposition that any central government had as its constituents the states, not the people, and could only reach the people through the agency of the state government.

Paterson then reopened the agenda of the Convention, but he did so within a distinctly nationalist framework. Paterson's position was one of favoring a strong central government in principle, but opposing one which in fact *put the big states in the saddle.* (The Virginia Plan, for all its abstract merits, did very well by Virginia.) As evidence for this speculation, there is a curious and intriguing proposal among Paterson's preliminary drafts of the New Jersey Plan:

Whereas it is necessary in Order to form the People of the U. S. of America in to a Nation, that the States should be consolidated, by which means all the Citizens thereof will become equally intitled to and will equally participate in the same Privileges and Rights . . . it is therefore resolved, that all the Lands contained within the Limits of each state individually, and of the U. S. generally be considered as

---

[35] *Ibid.*, pp. 275–76.

[36] "But it is said that this national government is to act on individuals and not on states; and cannot a federal government be so framed as to operate in the same way? It surely may." *Ibid.*, pp. 182–83; also *ibid.* at p. 276.

constituting one Body or Mass, and be divided into thirteen or more integral parts.

Resolved, That such Divisions or integral Parts shall be styled Districts.[37]

This makes it sound as though Paterson was prepared to accept a strong unified central government along the lines of the Virginia Plan if the existing states were eliminated. He may have gotten the idea from his New Jersey colleague Judge David Brearley, who on June 9 had commented that the only remedy to the dilemma over representation was " . . . that a map of the U. S. be spread out, that all the existing boundaries be erased, and that a new partition of the whole be made into 13 equal parts."[38] According to Yates, Brearley added at this point, " . . . then a government on the present [Virginia Plan] system will be just."[39]

This proposition was never pushed—it was patently unrealistic —but one can appreciate its purpose: it would have separated the men from the boys in the large-state delegations. How attached would the Virginians have been to their reform principles if Virginia were to disappear as a component geographical unit (the largest) for representational purposes? Up to this point, the Virginians had been in the happy position of supporting high ideals with that inner confidence born of knowledge that the "public interest" they endorsed would nourish their private interest. Worse, they had shown little willingness to compromise. Now the delegates from the small states announced that they were unprepared to be offered up as sacrificial victims to a "national interest" which reflected Virginia's parochial ambition. Caustic Charles Pinckney was not far off when he remarked sardonically that " . . . the whole [conflict] comes to this": "Give N. Jersey an equal vote, and she will dismiss her scruples, and concur in the Natil. system."[40] What he rather unfairly did not add was that the Jersey delegates were not free agents who could adhere to their private convictions; they had to take back, sponsor and risk their reputations on the reforms approved by the Convention —and in New Jersey, not in Virginia.

[37] *Farrand*, III, 613.
[38] *Farrand*, I, 177.
[39] *Ibid.*, p. 182.
[40] *Ibid.*, p. 255.

Paterson spoke on Saturday, and one can surmise that over the weekend there was a good deal of consultation, argument, and caucusing among the delegates. One member at least prepared a full length address: on Monday Alexander Hamilton, previously mute, rose and delivered a six-hour oration.[41] It was a remarkably apolitical speech; the gist of his position was that *both* the Virginia and New Jersey Plans were inadequately centralist, and he detailed a reform program which was reminiscent of the Protectorate under the Cromwellian *Instrument of Government* of 1653. It has been suggested that Hamilton did this in the best political tradition to emphasize the moderate character of the Virginia Plan,[42] to give the cautious delegates something *really* to worry about; but this interpretation seems somehow too clever. Particularly since the sentiments Hamilton expressed happened to be completely consistent with those he privately—and sometimes publicly—expressed throughout his life. He wanted, to take a striking phrase from a letter to George Washington, a "strong well mounted government";[43] in essence, the Hamilton Plan contemplated an elected life monarch, virtually free of public control, on the Hobbesian ground that only in this fashion could strength and stability be achieved. The other alternatives, he argued, would put policy-making at the mercy of the passions of the mob; only if the sovereign was beyond the reach of selfish influence would it be possible to have government in the interests of the whole community.[44]

From all accounts, this was a masterful and compelling speech, but (aside from furnishing John Lansing and Luther Martin with ammunition for later use against the Constitution) it made little impact. Hamilton was simply transmitting on a different wavelength from the rest of the delegates; the latter adjourned after his great effort, admired his rhetoric, and then returned to business.[45] It was rather as if they had taken a day off to attend the opera. Hamilton, never a particularly patient man or much of a

[41] J. C. Hamilton, cited *ibid.*, p. 293.

[42] See, *e.g.*, Mitchell, *op. cit.*, p. 381.

[43] Hamilton to Washington, July 3, 1787, *Farrand*, III, 53.

[44] A reconstruction of the Hamilton Plan is found in *Farrand*, III, 617–30.

[45] Said William Samuel Johnson on June 21: "A gentleman from New-York, with boldness and decision, proposed a system totally different from both [Virginia and New Jersey]; and though he has been praised by every body, he has been supported by none." *Farrand*, I, 363.

negotiator, stayed for another ten days and then left, in considerable disgust, for New York.[46] Although he came back to Philadelphia sporadically and attended the last two weeks of the Convention, Hamilton played no part in the laborious task of hammering out the Constitution. His day came later when he led the New York Constitutionalists into the savage imbroglio over ratification—an arena in which his unmatched talent for dirty political infighting may well have won the day. For instance, in the New York Ratifying Convention, Lansing threw back into Hamilton's teeth the sentiments the latter had expressed in his June 18 oration in the Convention. However, having since retreated to the fine defensive positions immortalized in *The Federalist,* the Colonel flatly denied that he had ever been an enemy of the states, or had believed that conflict between states and nation was inexorable! As Madison's authoritative *Notes* did not appear until 1840, and there had been no press coverage, there was no way to verify his assertions, so in the words of the reporter, " . . . a warm personal altercation between [Lansing and Hamilton] engrossed the remainder of the day [June 28, 1788]."[47]

IV

On Tuesday morning, June 19, the vacation was over. James Madison led off with a long, carefully reasoned speech analyzing the New Jersey Plan which, while intellectually vigorous in its criticisms, was quite conciliatory in mood. "The great difficulty," he observed, "lies in the affair of Representation; and if this could be adjusted, all others would be surmountable."[48] (As events were to demonstrate, this diagnosis was correct.) When he finished, a vote was taken on whether to continue with the Virginia Plan as the nucleus for a new constitution: seven states voted "Yes"; New York, New Jersey, and Delaware voted "No"; and Maryland, whose position often depended on which delegates happened to be on the floor, divided.[49] Paterson, it seems, lost de-

---

[46] See his letter to Washington cited *supra* note 43.
[47] *Farrand,* III, 338.
[48] *Farrand,* I, 321.
[49] Maryland's politics in this period were only a bit less intricate than Rhode

cisively; yet in a fundamental sense he and his allies had achieved their purpose: from that day onward, it could never be forgotten that the state governments loomed ominously in the background and that no verbal incantations could exorcise their power. Moreover, nobody bolted the convention: Paterson and his colleagues took their defeat in stride and set to work to modify the Virginia Plan, particularly with respect to its provisions on representation in the national legislature. Indeed, they won an immediate rhetorical bonus; when Oliver Ellsworth of Connecticut rose to move that the word "national" be expunged from the Third Virginia Resolution ("Resolved that a *national* Government ought to be established consisting of a *supreme* Legislative, Executive and Judiciary"[50]), Randolph agreed and the motion passed unanimously.[51] The process of compromise had begun.

For the next two weeks, the delegates circled around the problem of legislative representation. The Connecticut delegation appears to have evolved a possible compromise quite early in the debates, but the Virginians and particularly Madison (unaware that he would later be acclaimed as the prophet of "federalism") fought obdurately against providing for equal representation of states in the second chamber. There was a good deal of acrimony and at one point Benjamin Franklin—of all people—proposed the institution of a daily prayer; practical politicians in the gathering, however, were meditating more on the merits of a good committee than on the utility of Divine intervention. On July 2, the

---

Island's: the rural gentry, in much the same fashion that Namier described in England, divided up among families—Chases, Carrolls, Pacas, Lloyds, Tilghmans, etc.—and engaged in what seemed, to the outsider, elaborate political Morris dances. See Philip A. Crowl, *Maryland During and After the Revolution* (Baltimore, 1943). The Maryland General Assembly named five delegates to the Convention and provided that "the said Deputies or such of them as shall attend . . . shall have full Power to represent this State," *Farrand*, III, 586. The interesting circumstance was that three of the delegates were Constitutionalists (Carroll, McHenry and Jenifer), while two were opposed (Martin and Mercer); and this led to an *ad hoc* determination of where Maryland would stand when votes were taken. The vote on equality of representation, to be described *infra*, was an important instance of this eccentricity.

[50] This formulation was voted into the Randolph Plan on May 30, 1787, by a vote of six states to none, with one divided. *Farrand*, I, 30.

[51] *Farrand*, I, 335–36. In agreeing, Randolph stipulated his disagreement with Ellsworth's rationale, but said he did not object to merely changing an "expression." Those who subject the Constitution to minute semantic analysis might do well to keep this instance in mind; if Randolph could so concede the deletion of "national," one may wonder if any word changes can be given much weight.

ice began to break when through a number of fortuitous events[52] —and one that seems deliberate[53]—the majority against equality of representation was converted into a dead tie. The Convention had reached the stage where it was "ripe" for a solution (presumably all the therapeutic speeches had been made), and the South Carolinians proposed a committee. Madison and James Wilson wanted none of it, but with only Pennsylvania dissenting, the body voted to establish a working party on the problem of representation.

The members of this committee, one from each state, were elected by the delegates—and a very interesting committee it was. Despite the fact that the Virginia Plan had held majority support up to that date, neither Madison nor Randolph was selected (Mason was the Virginian) and Baldwin of Georgia, whose shift in position had resulted in the tie, was chosen. From the composition, it was clear that this was not to be a "fighting" committee: the emphasis in membership was on what might be described as "second-level political entrepreneurs." On the basis of the discussions up to that time, only Luther Martin of Maryland could be described as a "bitter-ender." Admittedly, some divination enters into this sort of analysis, but one does get a sense of the mood of the delegates from these choices—including the interesting selection of Benjamin Franklin, despite his age and intellectual wobbliness, over the brilliant and incisive Wilson or the sharp, polemical Gouverneur Morris, to represent Pennsylvania. His passion for conciliation was more valuable at this juncture than Wilson's logical genius, or Morris' acerbic wit.

There is a common rumor that the Framers divided their time

---

[52] According to Luther Martin, he was alone on the floor and cast Maryland's vote for equality of representation. Shortly thereafter, Jenifer came on the floor and "Mr. King, from Massachusetts, valuing himself on Mr. Jenifer to divide the State of Maryland on this question . . . requested of the President that the question might be put again; however, the motion was too extraordinary in its nature to meet with success." Cited from "The Genuine Information, . . . " *Farrand*, III, 188.

[53] Namely Baldwin's vote *for* equality of representation which divided Georgia—with Few absent and Pierce in New York fighting a duel, Houston voted against equality and Baldwin shifted to tie the state. Baldwin was originally from Connecticut and attended and tutored at Yale, facts which have led to much speculation about the pressures the Connecticut delegation may have brought on him to save the day (Georgia was the last state to vote) and open the way to compromise. To employ a good Russian phrase, it was certainly not an accident that Baldwin voted the way he did. See *Warren*, p. 262.

between philosophical discussions of government and reading the classics in political theory. Perhaps this is as good a time as any to note that their concerns were highly practical, that they spent little time canvassing abstractions. A number of them had some acquaintance with the history of political theory (probably gained from reading John Adams' monumental compilation *A Defense of the Constitutions of Government,*[54] the first volume of which appeared in 1786), and it was a poor rhetorician indeed who could not cite Locke, Montesquieu, or Harrington *in support* of a desired goal. Yet up to this point in the deliberations, no one had expounded a defense of states'-rights or the "separation of powers" on anything resembling a theoretical basis. It should be reiterated that the Madison model had no room either for the states or for the "separation of powers": effectively *all* governmental power was vested in the national legislature. The merits of Montesquieu did not turn up until *The Federalist;* and although a perverse argument could be made that Madison's ideal was truly in the tradition of John Locke's *Second Treatise of Government,*[55] the Locke whom the American rebels treated as an honorary president was a pluralistic defender of vested rights,[56] not of parliamentary supremacy.

It would be tedious to continue a blow-by-blow analysis of the work of the delegates; the critical fight was over representation of the states and once the Connecticut Compromise was adopted

[54] For various contemporary comments, see *Warren,* pp. 814–818. On Adams' technique, see Zoltan Haraszti, "The Composition of Adams' *Defense,*" in *John Adams and the Prophets of Progress* (Cambridge, 1952), ch. 9. In this connection it is interesting to check the Convention discussions for references to the authority of Locke, Montesquieu and Harrington, the theorists who have been assigned various degrees of paternal responsibility. There are no explicit references to James Harrington; one to John Locke (Luther Martin cited him on the state of nature, *Farrand,* I, 437); and seven to Montesquieu, only one of which related to the "separation of powers" (Madison in an odd speech, which he explained in a footnote was given to help a friend rather than advance his own views, cited Montesquieu on the separation of the executive and legislative branches, *Farrand,* II, 34). This, of course, does not prove that Locke and Co. were without influence; it shifts the burden of proof, however, to those who assert ideological causality. See Benjamin F. Wright, "The Origins of the Separation of Powers in America," *Economica,* Vol. 13 (1933), p. 184.

[55] I share Willmoore Kendall's interpretation of Locke as a supporter of parliamentary supremacy and majoritarianism; see Kendall, *John Locke and the Doctrine of Majority Rule* (Urbana, 1941). Kendall's general position has recently received strong support in the definitive edition and commentary of Peter Laslett, *Locke's Two Treatises of Government* (Cambridge, 1960).

[56] The American Locke is best delineated in Carl Becker, *The Declaration of Independence* (New York, 1948).

on July 17, the Convention was over the hump. Madison, James Wilson, and Gouverneur Morris of New York (who was there representing Pennsylvania!) fought the compromise all the way in a last-ditch effort to get a unitary state with parliamentary supremacy. But their allies deserted them and they demonstrated after their defeat the essentially opportunist character of their objections—using "opportunist" here in a non-pejorative sense, to indicate a willingness to swallow their objections and get on with the business. Moreover, once the compromise had carried (by five states to four, with one state divided), its advocates threw themselves vigorously into the job of strengthening the general government's substantive powers—as might have been predicted, indeed, from Paterson's early statements. It nourishes an increased respect for Madison's devotion to the art of politics, to realize that this dogged fighter could sit down six months later and prepare essays for *The Federalist* in contradiction to his basic convictions about the true course the Convention should have taken.

V

Two tricky issues will serve to illustrate the later process of accommodation. The first was the institutional position of the Executive. Madison argued for an executive chosen by the National Legislature and on May 29 this had been adopted with a provision that after his seven-year term was concluded, the chief magistrate should not be eligible for reelection. In late July this was reopened and for a week the matter was argued from several different points of view. A good deal of desultory speechmaking ensued, but the gist of the problem was the opposition from two sources to election by the legislature. One group felt that the states should have a hand in the process; another small but influential circle urged direct election by the people. There were a number of proposals: election by the people, election by state governors, by electors chosen by state legislatures, by the National Legislature (James Wilson, perhaps ironically, proposed at one point that an Electoral College be chosen by lot from the National Legislature!), and there was some resemblance to three-dimensional chess in the dispute because of the presence of two other variables, length of tenure and re-eligibility. Finally, after opening, reopening, and re-reopening the debate, the thorny problem was consigned to a committee for resolution.

The Brearley Committee on Postponed Matters was a superb aggregation of talent and its compromise on the Executive was a masterpiece of political improvisation. (The Electoral College, its creation, however, had little in its favor as an *institution*—as the delegates well appreciated.) The point of departure for all discussion about the presidency in the Convention was that in immediate terms, the problem was non-existent; in other words, everybody present knew that under any system devised, George Washington would be President. Thus they were dealing in the future tense and to a body of working politicians the merits of the Brearley proposal were obvious: everybody got a piece of cake. (Or to put it more academically, each viewpoint could leave the Convention and argue to its constituents that it had *really* won the day.) First, the state legislatures had the right to determine the mode of selection of the electors; second, the small states received a bonus in the Electoral College in the form of a guaranteed minimum of three votes while the big states got acceptance of the principle of proportional power; third, if the state legislatures agreed (as six did in the first presidential election), the people could be involved directly in the choice of electors; and finally, if no candidate received a majority in the College, the right of decision passed to the National Legislature with each state exercising equal strength. (In the Brearley recommendation, the election went to the Senate, but a motion from the floor substituted the House; this was accepted on the ground that the Senate already had enough authority over the executive in its treaty and appointment powers.)

This compromise was almost too good to be true, and the Framers snapped it up with little debate or controversy. No one seemed to think well of the College as an *institution;* indeed, what evidence there is suggests that there was an assumption that once Washington had finished his tenure as President, the electors would cease to produce majorities and the chief executive would usually be chosen in the House. George Mason observed casually that the selection would be made in the House nineteen times in twenty and no one seriously disputed this point. The vital aspect of the Electoral College was that it got the Convention over the hurdle and protected everybody's interests. The future was left to cope with the problem of what to do with this Rube Goldberg mechanism.

In short, the Framers did not in their wisdom endow the United States with a College of Cardinals—the Electoral College was neither an exercise in applied Platonism nor an experiment in indirect government based on elitist distrust of the masses. It was merely a jerry-rigged improvisation which has subsequently been endowed with a high theoretical content. When an elector from Oklahoma in 1960 refused to cast his vote for Nixon (naming Byrd and Goldwater instead) on the ground that the Founding Fathers intended him to exercise his great independent wisdom, he was indulging in historical fantasy. If one were to indulge in counter-fantasy, he would be tempted to suggest that the Fathers would be startled to find the College still in operation—and perhaps even dismayed at their descendants' lack of judgment or inventiveness.[57]

The second issue on which some substantial practical bargaining took place was slavery. The morality of slavery was, by design, not at issue;[58] but in its other concrete aspects, slavery colored the arguments over taxation, commerce, and representation. The "Three-Fifths Compromise," that three-fifths of the slaves would be counted both for representation and for purposes of direct taxation (which was drawn from the past—it was a formula of Madison's utilized by Congress in 1783 to establish the basis of state contributions to the Confederation treasury) had allayed some Northern fears about Southern over-representation (no one then foresaw the trivial role that direct taxation would play in later federal financial policy), but doubts still remained. The Southerners, on the other hand, were afraid that Congressional control over commerce would lead to the exclusion of slaves or to their excessive taxation as imports. Moreover, the Southerners were disturbed over "navigation acts," *i.e.*, tariffs, or special legislation providing, for example, that exports be carried only in

---

[57] See John P. Roche, "The Electoral College: A Note on American Political Mythology," *Dissent* (Spring, 1961), pp. 197–99. The relevant debates took place July 19–26, 1787, *Farrand*, II, 50–128, and September 5–6, 1787, *ibid.*, pp. 505–31.

[58] See the discussion on August 22, 1787, *Farrand*, II, 366–375; King seems to have expressed the sense of the Convention when he said, "the subject should be considered in a political light only." *Ibid.* at 373.

American ships; as a section depending upon exports, they wanted protection from the potential voracity of their commercial brethren of the Eastern states. To achieve this end, Mason and others urged that the Constitution include a proviso that navigation and commercial laws should require a two-thirds vote in Congress.

These problems came to a head in late August and, as usual, were handed to a committee in the hope that, in Gouverneur Morris' words, " . . . these things may form a bargain among the Northern and Southern states."[59] The Committee reported its measures of reconciliation on August 25, and on August 29 the package was wrapped up and delivered. What occurred can best be described in George Mason's dour version (he anticipated Calhoun in his conviction that permitting navigation acts to pass by majority vote would put the South in economic bondage to the North—it was mainly on this ground that he refused to sign the Constitution):

The Constitution as agreed to till a fortnight before the Convention rose was such a one as he would have set his hand and heart to. . . . [Until that time] The 3 New England States were constantly with us in all questions . . . so that it was these three States with the 5 Southern ones against Pennsylvania, Jersey and Delaware. With respect to the importation of slaves, [decision-making] was left to Congress. This disturbed the two Southernmost States who knew that Congress would immediately suppress the importation of slaves. Those two States therefore struck up a bargain with the three New England States. If they would join to admit slaves for some years, the two Southernmost States would join in changing the clause which required the ⅔ of the Legislature in any vote [on navigation acts]. It was done.[60]

On the floor of the Convention there was a virtual love-feast on this happy occasion. Charles Pinckney of South Carolina attempted to overturn the committee's decision, when the compromise was reported to the Convention, by insisting that the South needed protection from the imperialism of the Northern states. But his Southern colleagues were not prepared to rock the boat and General C. C. Pinckney arose to spread oil on the suddenly ruffled waters; he admitted that:

It was in the true interest of the S[outhern] States to have no regulation of commerce; but considering the loss brought on the commerce of the Eastern States by the Revolution, their liberal conduct towards the views of South Carolina [on the regulation of the slave trade] and the interests the weak Southn. States had in being united with the strong Eastern states, he thought it proper that no fetters should be imposed on the power of making commercial regulations; *and that his constituents, though prejudiced against the Eastern States, would be reconciled to this liberality.* He had himself prejudices agst the Eastern States before he came here, but would acknowledge that he had found them as liberal and candid as any men whatever. (Italics added)[61]

Pierce Butler took the same tack, essentially arguing that he was not too happy about the possible consequences, but that a deal was a deal.[62] Many Southern leaders were later—in the wake of the "Tariff of Abominations"—to rue this day of reconciliation; Calhoun's *Disquisition on Government* was little more than an extension of the argument in the Convention against permitting a congressional majority to enact navigation acts.[63]

VI

Drawing on their vast collective political experience, utilizing every weapon in the politician's arsenal, looking constantly over their shoulders at their constituents, the delegates put together a Constitution. It was a makeshift affair; some sticky issues (for example, the qualification of voters) they ducked entirely; others

---

[61] August 29, 1787, *Farrand*, II, 449–50.

[62] *Ibid.*, p. 451. The plainest statement of the matter was put by the three North Carolina delegates (Blount, Spaight and Williamson) in their report to Governor Caswell, September 18, 1787. After noting that "no exertions have been wanting on our part to guard and promote the particular interest of North Carolina," they went on to explain the basis of the negotiations in cold-blooded fashion: "While we were taking so much care to guard ourselves against being over reached and to form rules of Taxation that might operate in our favour, it is not to be supposed that our Northern Brethren were Inattentive to their particular Interest. A navigation Act or the power to regulate Commerce in the Hands of the National Government . . . is what the Southern States have given in Exchange for the advantages we Mentioned." They concluded by explaining that while the Constitution did deal with other matters besides taxes—"there are other Considerations of great Magnitude involved in the system"—they would not take up valuable time with boring details! *Farrand*, III, 83–84.

[63] See John C. Calhoun, *A Disquisition on Government* (New York, 1943), pp. 21–25, 38. Calhoun differed from Mason, and others in the Convention who urged the two-thirds requirement, by advocating a functional or interest veto rather than some sort of special majority, *i.e.*, he abandoned the search for quantitative checks in favor of a qualitative solution.

they mastered with that ancient instrument of political sagacity, studied ambiguity (for example, citizenship), and some they just overlooked. In this last category, I suspect, fell the matter of the power of the federal courts to determine the constitutionality of acts of Congress. When the judicial article was formulated (Article III of the Constitution), deliberations were still in the stage where the legislature was endowed with broad power under the Randolph formulation, authority which by its own terms was scarcely amenable to judicial review. In essence, courts could hardly determine when " . . . the separate States are incompetent or . . . the harmony of the United States may be interrupted"; the National Legislature, as critics pointed out, was free to define its own judisdiction. Later the definition of legislative authority was changed into the form we know, a series of stipulated powers, *but the delegates never seriously reexamined the jurisdiction of the judiciary under this new limited formulation.*[64] All arguments on the intention of the Framers in this matter are thus deductive and *a posteriori,* though some obviously make more sense than others.[65]

The Framers were busy and distinguished men, anxious to get back to their families, their positions, and their constituents, not members of the French Academy devoting a lifetime to a dictionary. They were trying to do an important job, and do it in such a fashion that their handiwork would be acceptable to very diverse constituencies. No one was rhapsodic about the final document, but it was a beginning, a move in the right direction,

[64] The Committe on Detail altered the general grant of legislative power envisioned by the Virginia Plan into a series of specific grants; these were examined closely between August 16 and August 23. One day only was devoted to the Judicial Article, August 27, and since no one raised the question of judicial review of *Federal* statutes, no light was cast on the matter. A number of random comments on the power of the judiciary were scattered throughout the discussions, but there was another variable which deprives them of much probative value: the proposed Council of Revision which would have joined the Executive with the judges in *legislative* review. Madison and Wilson, for example, favored this technique—which had nothing in common with what we think of as judicial review except that judges were involved in the task.

[65] For what it may be worth, I think that judicial review of congressional acts was logically on all fours with review of state enactments and that it was certainly consistent with the view that the Constitution could not be amended by the Congress and President, or by a two-thirds vote of Congress (overriding a veto), without the agreement of three-quarters of the states. *External* evidence from that time supports this view, see Charles Warren, *Congress, the Constitution, and the Supreme Court* (Boston, 1925), pp. 41–128, but the debates *in* the Convention prove nothing.

and one they had reason to believe the people would endorse. In addition, since they had modified the impossible amendment provisions of the Articles (the requirement of unanimity which could always be frustrated by "Rogues Island") to one demanding approval by only three-quarters of the states, they seemed confident that gaps in the fabric which experience would reveal could be rewoven without undue difficulty.

So with a neat phrase introduced by Benjamin Franklin (but devised by Gouverneur Morris)[66] which made their decision sound unanimous, and an inspired benediction by the Old Doctor urging doubters to doubt their own infallibility, the Constitution was accepted and signed. Curiously, Edmund Randolph, who had played so vital a role throughout, refused to sign, as did his fellow Virginian George Mason and Elbridge Gerry of Massachusetts. Randolph's behavior was eccentric, to say the least—his excuses for refusing his signature have a factitious ring even at this late date; the best explanation seems to be that he was afraid that the Constitution would prove to be a liability in Virginia politics, where Patrick Henry was burning up the countryside with impassioned denunciations. Presumably, Randolph wanted to check the temper of the populace before he risked his reputation, and perhaps his job, in a fight with both Henry and Richard Henry Lee.[67] Events lend some justification to this speculation: after much temporizing and use of the conditional subjunctive tense, Randolph endorsed ratification in Virginia and ended up getting the best of both worlds.

Madison, despite his reservations about the Constitution, was the campaign manager in ratification. His first task was to get the Congress in New York to light its own funeral pyre by approving the "amendments" to the Articles and sending them on to the state legislatures. Above all, momentum had to be main-

---

[66] Or so Madison stated, *Farrand*, II, 643. Wilson too may have contributed; he was close to Franklin and delivered the frail old gentleman's speeches for him.

[67] See a very interesting letter, from an unknown source in Philadelphia, to Jefferson, October 11, 1787: "Randolph wishes it well, & it is thought would have signed it, but he wanted to be on a footing with a popular rival." *Farrand*, III, 104. Madison, writing Jefferson a full account on October 24, 1787, put the matter more delicately— he was working hard on Randolph to win him for ratification: "[Randolph] was not inveterate in his opposition, and grounded his refusal to subscribe pretty much on his unwillingness to commit himself, so as not to be at liberty to be governed by further lights on the subject." *Ibid.*, p. 135.

tained. The anti-Constitutionalists, now thoroughly alarmed and no novices in politics, realized that their best tactic was attrition rather than direct opposition. Thus they settled on a position expressing qualified approval but calling for a second Convention to remedy various defects (the one with the most demagogic appeal was the lack of a Bill of Rights). Madison knew that to accede to this demand would be equivalent to losing the battle, nor would he agree to conditional approval (despite wavering even by Hamilton). This was an all-or-nothing proposition: national salvation or national impotence with no intermediate positions possible. Unable to get congressional approval, he settled for second best: a unanimous resolution of Congress transmitting the Constitution to the states for whatever action they saw fit to take. The opponents then moved from New York and the Congress, where they had attempted to attach amendments and conditions, to the states for the final battle.[68]

At first the campaign for ratification went beautifully: within eight months after the delegates set their names to the document, eight states had ratified. Only in Massachusetts had the result been close (187–168). Theoretically, a ratification by one more state convention would set the new government in motion, but in fact until Virginia and New York acceded to the new Union, the latter was a fiction. New Hampshire was the next to ratify; Rhode Island was involved in its characteristic political convulsions (the Legislature there sent the Constitution out to the towns for decision by popular vote and it got lost among a series of local issues);[69] North Carolina's convention did not meet until July and then postponed a final decision. This is hardly the place for an extensive analysis of the conventions of New York and Virginia. Suffice it to say that the Constitutionalists clearly outmaneuvered their opponents, forced them into impossible political positions, and won both states narrowly. The Virginia Convention could serve as a classic study in effective floor management: Patrick Henry had to be contained, and a reading of the debates discloses a standard two-stage technique. Henry would

---

[68] See Edward P. Smith, "The Movement Towards a Second Constitutional Convention in 1788," in J. F. Jameson, ed., *Essays in the Constitutional History of the United States* (Boston, 1889) , pp. 46–115.

[69] See Bishop, *op. cit., passim.*

give a four- or five-hour speech denouncing some section of the Constitution on every conceivable ground (the federal district, he averred at one point, would become a haven for convicts escaping from state authority!);[70] When Henry subsided, "Mr. Lee of Westmoreland" would rise and literally poleaxe him with sardonic invective (when Henry complained about the militia power, "Lighthouse Harry" really punched below the belt: observing that while the former Governor had been sitting in Richmond during the Revolution, *he* had been out in the trenches with the troops and thus felt better qualified to discuss military affairs).[71] Then the gentlemanly Constitutionalists (Madison, Pendleton and Marshall) would pick up the matters at issue and examine them in the light of reason.

Indeed, modern Americans who tend to think of James Madison as a rather dessicated character should spend some time with this transcript. Probably Madison put on his most spectacular demonstration of nimble rhetoric in what might be called "the Battle of the Absent Authorities." Patrick Henry in the course of one of his harangues alleged that Jefferson was known to be opposed to Virginia's approving the Constitution. This was clever: Henry hated Jefferson, but was prepared to use any weapon that came to hand. Madison's riposte was superb: First, he said that with all due respect to the great reputation of Jefferson, he was not in the country and therefore could not formulate an adequate judgment; second, no one should utilize the reputation of an outsider—the Virginia Convention was there to think for itself; third, if there were to be recourse to outsiders, the opinions of George Washington should certainly be taken into consideration; and finally, he knew from privileged personal communications from Jefferson that in fact the latter *strongly favored* the Constitution.[72] To devise an assault route into this rhetorical fortress was literally impossible.

---

[70] See *Elliot's Debates on the Federal Constitution* (Washington, 1836), Vol. 3, pp. 436–438.

[71] This should be quoted to give the full flavor: "Without vanity, I may say I have had different experience of [militia] service from that of [Henry]. It was my fortune to be a soldier of my country. . . . I saw what the honorable gentleman did not see—our men fighting. . . . " *Ibid.*, p. 178.

[72] *Ibid.*, p. 329.

VII

The fight was over; all that remained now was to establish the new frame of government in the spirit of its framers. And who were better qualified for this task than the Framers themselves? Thus victory for the Constitution meant simultaneous victory for the Constitutionalists; the anti-Constitutionalists either capitulated or vanished into limbo—soon Patrick Henry would be offered a seat on the Supreme Court[73] and Luther Martin would be known as the Federalist "bull-dog."[74] And irony of ironies, Alexander Hamilton and James Madison would shortly accumulate a reputation as the formulators of what is often alleged to be our political theory, the concept of "federalism." Also, on the other side of the ledger, the arguments would soon appear over what the Framers "really meant"; while these disputes have assumed the proportions of a big scholarly business in the last century, they began almost before the ink on the Constitution was dry. One of the best early ones featured Hamilton versus Madison on the scope of presidential power, and other Framers characteristically assumed positions in this and other disputes on the basis of their political convictions.

Probably our greatest difficulty is that we know so much more about what the Framers *should have meant* than they themselves did. We are intimately acquainted with the problems that their Constitution should have been designed to master; in short, we have read the mystery story backwards. If we are to get the right "feel" for their time and their circumstances, we must in Maitland's phrase, " . . . think ourselves back into a twilight." Obviously, no one can pretend completely to escape from the solipsistic web of his own environment, but if the effort is made, it is possible to appreciate the past roughly on its own terms. The first step in this process is to abandon the academic premise that because we can ask a question, there must be an answer.

[73] Washington offered him the Chief Justiceship in 1796, but he declined; Charles Warren, *The Supreme Court in United States History* (Boston, 1947), Vol. 1, p. 139.

[74] He was a zealous prosecutor of seditions in the period 1798–1800; with Justice Samuel Chase, like himself an alleged "radical" at the time of the Constitutional Convention, Martin hunted down Jeffersonian heretics. See James M. Smith, *Freedom's Fetters* (Ithaca, 1956), pp. 342–43.

Thus we can ask what the Framers meant when they gave Congress the power to regulate interstate and foreign commerce, and we emerge, reluctantly perhaps, with the reply that (Professor Crosskey to the contrary notwithstanding)[75] they may not have known what they meant, that there may not have been any semantic consensus. The Convention was not a seminar in analytic philosophy or linguistic analysis. Commerce was *commerce*—and if different interpretations of the word arose, later generations could worry about the problem of definition. The delegates were in a hurry to get a new government established; when definitional arguments arose, they characteristically took refuge in ambiguity. If different men voted for the same proposition for varying reasons, that was politics (and still is); if later generations were unsettled by this lack of precision, that would be their problem.

There was a good deal of definitional pluralism with respect to the problems the delegates did discuss, but when we move to the question of extrapolated intensions, we enter the realm of spiritualism. When men in our time, for instance, launch into elaborate talmudic exegesis to demonstrate that federal aid to parochial schools is (or is not) in accord with the intentions of the men who established the Republic and endorsed the Bill of Rights, they are engaging in historical Extra-Sensory Perception. (If one were to join this E. S. P. contingent for a minute, he

[75] Crosskey in his sprawling *Politics and the Constitution* (Chicago, 1953) , 2 vols., has developed with almost unbelievable zeal and intricacy the thesis that the Constitution *was* designed to establish a centralized unitary state, but that the political leadership of the Republic in its formative years betrayed this ideal and sold the pass to states'-rights. While he has unearthed some interesting newspaper articles and other material, it is impossible for me to accept his central proposition. Madison and the other delegates, with the exceptions discussed in the text *supra*, did *want* to diminish the power of the states and create a vigorous national government. But they were not fools, and were, I submit, under no illusions when they departed from Philadelphia that this end had been accomplished. The crux of my argument is that *political realities* forced them to water down their objectives and they settled, like the good politicians they were, for half a loaf. The basic difficulty with Crosskey's thesis is that he knows *too* much—he assumes that the Framers had a perfectly clear idea of the road they were taking; with a semantic machete he cuts blandly through all the confusion on the floor of the meeting to the *real* meanings. Thus, despite all his ornate research apparatus, there is a fundamentally nonempirical quality about Crosskey's work: at crucial points in the argument he falls back on a type of divination which can only be described as Kabbalistic. He may be right, for example, in stating (without any proof) that Richard Henry Lee did *not* write the "Letters from a Federal Farmer," but in this country spectral evidence has not been admissible since the Seventeenth Century.

might suggest that the hard-boiled politicians who wrote the Constitution and Bill of Rights would chuckle scornfully at such an invocation of authority: obviously a politician would chart his course on the intentions of the living, not of the dead, and count the number of Catholics in his constituency.)

The Constitution, then, was not an apotheosis of "constitutionalism," a triumph of architectonic genius; it was a patch-work sewn together under the pressure of both time and events by a group of extremely talented democratic politicians. They refused to attempt the establishment of a strong, centralized sovereignty on the principle of legislative supremacy for the excellent reason that the people would not accept it. They risked their political fortunes by opposing the established doctrines of state sovereignty because they were convinced that the existing system was leading to national impotence and probably foreign domination. For two years, they worked to get a convention established. For over three months, in what must have seemed to the faithful participants an endless process of give-and-take, they reasoned, cajoled, threatened, and bargained amongst themselves. The result was a Constitution which the people, in fact, by democratic processes, did accept, and a new and far better national government was established.

Beginning with the inspired propaganda of Hamilton, Madison and Jay, the ideological build-up got under way. *The Federalist* had little impact on the ratification of the Constitution, except perhaps in New York, but this volume had enormous influence on the image of the Constitution in the minds of future generations, particularly on historians and political scientists who have an innate fondness for theoretical symmetry. Yet, while the shades of Locke and Montesquieu *may* have been hovering in the background, and the delegates *may* have been unconscious instruments of a transcendent *telos*, the careful observer of the day-to-day work of the Convention finds no over-arching principles. The "separation of powers" to him seems to be a by-product of suspicion, and "federalism" he views as a *pis aller*, as the farthest point the delegates felt they could go in the destruction of state power without themselves inviting repudiation.

To conclude, the Constitution was neither a victory for abstract theory nor a great practical success. Well over half a million men had to die on the battlefields of the Civil War before certain constitutional principles could be defined—a baleful consideration which is somehow overlooked in our customary tributes to the farsighted genius of the Framers and to the supposed American talent for "constitutionalism." The Constitution was, however, a vivid demonstration of effective democratic political action, and of the forging of a national elite which literally persuaded its countrymen to hoist themselves by their own boot straps. American pro-consuls would be wise not to translate the Constitution into Japanese, or Swahili, or treat it as a work of semi-Divine origin; but when students of comparative politics examine the process of nation-building in countries newly freed from colonial rule, they may find the American experience instructive as a classic example of the potentialities of a democratic elite.

Epilogue

Afterthoughts on Constitutions ᨏ

CARL BECKER

ON THIS memorable occasion, devoted so largely to the celebration of the one hundred and fiftieth anniversary of the adoption of the Constitution of the United States, it may not be amiss for one who knows little about the minutiae of particular constitutions, to hazard some remarks about constitutions in general—a subject which, according to Mr. Stuart Chase, has no discoverable "referent," for which no identifying "operation" is at present available. This is a difficulty, no doubt, but it has its advantages: it permits me to be discursive, and to begin with the first thing that occurs to me.

As a historian, the first thing that occurs to me, naturally, is to begin at the beginning. The beginning is, of course, the first constitution, which might be the Code of Hammurabi (about 1900 B. C.) except for two valid objections. One is that by verbal definition the Code of Hammurabi is a code and not a constitution. The other is even more important. To begin with the Code of Hammurabi would violate the academic tradition which requires us to believe that everything significant for enlightenment and progress has its origin with the ancient Greeks. Fortunately, all the constitutions collected by Aristotle, except the constitution of Athens, are lost. Thus the prestige of the Greeks is preserved, and I can do them customary homage by reverently pronouncing the names of Solon and Cleisthenes—the original Fathers, the framers of the earliest constitutional bulwarks of democratic liberty.

The next thing that occurs to me is that constitutions are of various sorts. Besides constitutions made for real communities, I recall several made for unreal, or nonexistent communities. Of these, the most famous, no doubt, is Plato's *Republic,* which suffices to recall More's *Utopia,* Bacon's *Atlantis,* Cyrano's *States in the Moon,* and many others, not forgetting the Great Society of the future described by H. G. Wells in the ninth book of his

Outline of History. But then, since for classification there is some special magic in the number three, there ought to be a third kind of constitution. I think at once of those constitutions which, although appertaining to real communities, are themselves, if not unreal, at least somewhat intangible and illusive. Of these, the English constitution is by far the most intriguing.

The English, if hard pressed, will admit that they have a constitution, but they profess not to know precisely what it is. If you insist upon knowing at any rate where it may be found, they may be heard, with clipped and reticent embarrassment, to mutter something about the Magna Carta and all that rot. A shy people, the English, but a practical people. A practical people, and therefore extremely subtle theorists—after the event: Jesuits lost to the theological, but gained for the political, realm. Ask an English jurist whether the English constitution anywhere forbids the king to make a statute on his sole authority, and he will very likely say that the question is an improper one, since it does not really arise until a statute, alleged to have been made by the king on his sole authority, comes before the court for adjudication. Actually confronted with this inconvenient predicament, the court would, no doubt, require adequate evidence to convince it that the statute before it had in fact been enacted by the king on his sole authority; and, no doubt, the only evidence which the court would regard as adequate for that purpose, would be a bill proclaiming that His Majesty, the king, with the advice and consent of his faithful lords and commons, doth ordain—whatever it is that he ordains. In short, nothing would convince an English court that the king had enacted a statute on his own, except a document proving beyond any doubt whatever that he had done no such thing. Such is the practical English mind. Such is the English constitution. It presumably exists, but the English refuse to define it beforehand: its true meaning is never revealed except on those rare occasions that call for a fresh interpretation of its provisions. In this respect, I may say in parenthetical confidence, it does not, after all, differ much from the written constitution with which we are all most familiar.

Since one thing leads to another, I am reminded by this that the Constitution of the United States, whatever else it may be, is a written constitution. As such, it is not, when seen in its historical setting, an isolated phenomenon. On the contrary, the century which elapsed between 1775 and 1875 was preëminent for the great number of written constitutions which were drafted and adopted, and, alas, not infrequently abandoned. A few years before 1787, nearly all of the thirteen states adopted such constitutions, besides uniting in a common government under the Articles of Confederation. A few years later, in 1791, the French began their spectacular feat in constitution-making. Between 1791 and 1875 Taine counts thirteen French constitutions adopted in relatively rapid succession. I can find only twelve, but maybe Taine is right. It doesn't really matter. The point is that for facility, speed, and endurance in constitution-making, France holds the record. Yet other nations also ran. During the nineteenth century, nearly every country of Europe, to say nothing of Canada, Australia, the Latin-American countries, and the several states of the American Union, adopted one or more constitutions. How many constitutions were carefully drafted, solemnly adopted, and often abandoned between 1775 and 1875 I do not profess to know. But at all events very many—more, I should guess, than during all the preceding centuries of human history.

It may be that at last I have hit upon a significant fact—this sudden epidemic of constitution making, lasting for a brief century, and then dying away almost as suddenly as it began. It could hardly have been a mere academic exercise in literary discourse, although often enough it has that appearance. Some deep-seated disturbance there must have been, some failure of metabolism in the body politic. "It is obvious to all," said Tocqueville, writing about 1835, "that a great democratic revolution is going on among us." True enough. The century of constitution making was also a century of revolution—in its most obvious aspects, a political revolution. Marxists will tell us that it was essentially an economic revolution. I agree. I even insist upon it; but only to point out that those who made the revolution were scarcely aware of the fact, or rather were convinced that economic and social ills would readily yield to political remedies. What is the proper basis of political authority? What are the proper limits of governmental power? What are the fundamental and imprescriptible rights of citizens? These were the all-absorbing questions of that time. The purpose of a written constitution was to provide authoritative answers to these questions, to delimit with precision the realms of social compulsion and individual liberty. It was taken for granted that when every man was free, all men would be equal; when all men were equal, everyone would have enough; when everyone had enough, no one would any longer be unjust or inhumane.

What astonishes us today is the widespread and persistent belief that these desired ends could be attained by these means. The failure of many constitutions did not abate the profound conviction that, with a little more enlightenment and insight, the right one, the true Palladium of Liberty, could be constructed. This conviction, since we can no longer share it, seems to us naïve; and we wonder what could have inspired so much optimistic faith in the power of the written word, such a childlike trust in the capacity of the human mind to create and guarantee rights and obligations by official definition.

Answers occur to us, of course. We think at once of the eighteenth century, the Age of Enlightenment, the age that pinned its faith to Natural Law, to the universal and imprescriptible Rights of Man, and to human reason as a sure instrument for discovering and interpreting those rights *sub specie aeternitatis*. But that is an old story, too familiar to need retelling here, and indeed not to be itself well understood except in terms of some more general frame of reference. Let us then, for the moment dispensing with the testimony of independent witnesses not self-deceived, take a little flight into the blue, and look down upon the Age of Reason as it lies in the long perspective of five or six millennia of history. In short, let us run the risk of going mildly philosophical and visionary.

In the long history of man on the earth, there comes a time when he remembers something that has been, anticipates something that will be, knows the country he has traversed, wonders what lies beyond—the moment when he is aware of himself as a differentiated, lonely item in the world. Sooner or later there emerges for him the most devastating of all facts; namely, that in an indifferent universe which endures, he alone aspires, struggles to attain, and attains only to be defeated in the end. But to be wholly defeated is intolerable. Of necessity, therefore, he creates ideal worlds of semblance, Utopias of other time or place in which all has been, will be, or may be well. The nature and location of Utopia will depend upon many things, but especially upon what is known or imagined about other times and places. He cannot place Utopia in the moon if he thinks the moon an evil spirit, or in Cathay if he has never heard of Cathay, or in past or future times unless past or future times can be imagined radically different from the present. The nature and location of Utopia, like all thinking, will be largely conditioned by the perspective, long or short, in which men can see themselves acting in time and space. Let us call this the time-and-space frame of reference.

The gradual expansion of the time-and-space frame of reference is of great, but not sufficiently noted, importance in the history of thought. The ancient Sumerians, for example, were in many ways a highly civilized people, but their social thinking was hampered by the fact that they lived in a very narrow time-and-space world. For them the "four quarters of the world" were comprised within the countries of western Asia; for them the. decisive event in history was the Great Flood, previous to which nothing was known (so far as we are aware) except that eight supermen reigned during a period of 240,000 years. Other ancient peoples were less limited than the Sumerians in this respect. But generally speaking, all ancient peoples lived and thought in what must seem to us a restricted and stifling time-and-space frame of reference: little was known of a long-time past; little was known about the extent or the behavior of the outer world of nature.

In ancient societies, accordingly, Utopia, as a necessary compensation for a precarious existence in a world not amenable to man's control, was most easily projected into the unknown past, pushed back to the beginning of things, to the creation of the world—to the time of P'an Ku and the eighteen celestial emperors, to the Garden of Eden, or the Golden Age of King Chronos when men lived like gods, free from toil and grief. From this happy state of first created things, there had obviously been a decline and fall, occasioned by disobedience and human frailty, decreed as punishment by implacable Fate or the angry gods. The mind of man was, therefore, afflicted with pessimism, oppressed by nostalgia for the lost golden age, a sense of guilt for having betrayed the divine purpose, a feeling of inadequacy for bringing the sinful and perverse world back to its original innocence and purity. To men who felt insecure in a changing world, and helpless in a world always changing for the worse, the future had little to offer. It could be contemplated only with resignation, mitigated by hope of some miraculous intervention of the gods, or the return of the godlike kings, to set things right again, yet with no assurance that from this setting right there would not be another falling away.

This pervasive pessimism was gradually dispelled in the Western world, completely so during the course of the intellectual revolution occurring roughly between the fifteenth and the eighteenth centuries—a revolution which, by emancipating the minds of men from resignation to Fate and the angry gods, enabled them to transfer the golden age from the past to the future. This significant transformation was made possible by a notable extension of historical and scientific knowledge. A group of learned men, differentiated from the ancient priests and scribes, and resolutely dispensing with the assistance of the gods, set themselves to discover how as a matter of fact the outer world of nature behaved, and what as a matter of fact had occurred in times past.

The result of this twofold enterprise was an unprecedented expansion of the time-and-space frame of reference within which men could form a pattern of human activities in relation to the world in which they occurred. Accumulated knowledge of history, filling in time past with a continuous chain of credible events from remote beginnings, gradually banished all lost golden ages, and enabled men to live without distress in a changing world of human relations, since they could regard it as not necessarily changing for the worse. At the same time, more competent observation of the heavenly bodies disclosed a universe infinitely extended, while more exact measurement of the action of material things disclosed an outer world of nature indifferent to man indeed, yet behaving, not as the unpredictable sport of the gods, but in ways understandable to human reason, and, therefore, ultimately amenable to man's control.

Within this enlarged and transformed time-and-space world, there was room for men to stand more aloof from themselves, to view themselves more objectively, in longer perspective: to see themselves as infinitesimal in a universe of infinite spaces, as temporary and negligible in an endless series of passing generations.

This enlarged view was at first bewildering, no doubt. Men were a little "frightened by the eternal silence of the infinite spaces"; they still courted the favor of communal gods, still looked back with envious admiration to the golden age of classical antiquity. But not for long. If the moderns were still inferior to the ancients, it seemed not unlikely that accumulating experience, added to what the Greeks knew, would presently redress the balance in favor of the moderns. If the silence of the infinite spaces reduced man to insignificant proportions in the cosmic scheme, it was reassuring, was it not, to reflect that the reason of man was sufficiently ingenious to have discovered that insignificance. Still more reassuring to know that the outer world of nature, however indifferent to man's fate, was equally indifferent to its own, and for that reason would lend itself, without anger or retaliation, to rational manipulation in the service of human needs.

Thus the conditions were fulfilled which made it possible for men to conceive of Utopia as a future state of their own devising. Living in a world of nature that could be regarded as amenable to man's control, and in a world of social relations which need not be regarded as an inevitable decline and fall from original perfection, they could formulate the modern idea of progress: the idea that man, by deliberate intention and rational direction, can set the terms and indefinitely improve the quality of his mundane existence.

The eighteenth century was the moment in human history when men experienced the first flush and freshness of this resplendent idea, the moment when its engaging implications were first fully understood, the moment when, not yet brought to the harsh appraisal of experience, it could be accepted with unclouded optimism. Never had the universe seemed less mysterious, more simply constructed, more open and visible, more eager to yield its secret to common-sense questions. Never had the nature of man seemed less perverse, or the mind of man less perverted; never had the will and intelligence of man seemed more pliable to the pressure of rational persuasion. All the insoluble riddles that man had ever propounded seemed on the point of solution, all the frustrations that had ever impeded his search for salvation seemed on the point of being resolved. Evils had only to be accurately noted to lose half their menace, and ideal ends were already half accomplished as soon as they were correctly defined.

The great secret was at last out: God was not angry. God the Father was seen to be no more than a benevolent investment trust in perpetuity, a well-disposed First Cause, who had created the world on a simple rational plan, and had endowed man with a spark of the divine reason capable of discovering to his advantage the laws of nature and his own being. To bring his ideas, his actions, and his institutions into harmony with the universal laws of nature, was man's simple allotted task.

Upon this optimistic note, the revolutionary age opened. Its distinguishing characteristic is the idea that revolution itself is in the nature of things. Revolution no longer needs apology, since it has ceased to be a blasphemy and has become a right. Revolutionists are no longer intriguers bargaining under cover for power, but accredited agents of Destiny, whose mission it is to harmonize the social structure with the law of nature and of nature's God. Possessed of these credentials, the character of the Constitution seems predetermined. Since social evils are the result of ignorance or neglect of the natural rights of man, the first task of political science is to define these rights, the second to devise a mechanism of government suited to guarantee them. The natural rights are easily defined, since they are self-evident: all men are created equal, and are endowed by their Creator with certain inalienable rights, among which are life, liberty, and the pursuit of happiness. The all-inclusive right is liberty: freedom of thought, so that the truth may prevail; freedom of occupation, so that careers may be open to talent; freedom of self-government, so that no man may be compelled against his will.

The making of the Constitution, as Barère said, was the work of weeks, since its principles were the result of a century of enlightenment, and little more was required than to transcribe on the tablets of the law the eternal truths engraved on the hearts of all men. Legislators were recorders: the Constitution did not create rights, it merely recognized them; it did not restrain natural human impulses, it merely gave them the right of way.

For more than half a century, this naïve faith retained its prestige, suffering some defeats and disillusionments, but playing its appointed rôle in great revolutionary days in many countries, presiding at the installation of many constitutional bulwarks of human liberty. Yet it could not forever withstand the attrition of slow-footed time and drab experience without losing much of its original glamour. After the great days of 1848 we note a perceptible drop of the idealistic temperature. The failure of so many revolutions and constitutions as a panacea for social and economic ills disclosed the fact that the nature of man was far more perverse, the mind of man far less responsive to rational persuasion and humane impulses, than the Age of Enlightenment had supposed.

There was, it seemed, a "higher law" than the constitution, a law, whatever it might be, which could not be appeased by the rational definition and official proclamation of the imprescriptible rights of man. The ends most passionately desired by men turned out to be tribal rather than universal in character. National aspirations could be better, or at least more quickly, achieved by blood and iron than by speeches and resolutions of majorities: blood drawn by the lash better compensated by blood shed by the sword than by the sweet reasonableness of congressional debate.

After 1848, constitutions could still be constructed, but they ceased to carry a sacred or mystical sanction. They were not Palladiums of Liberty, but political bargains—a device of Orleanist monarchists to outwit the Bonapartists, a compromise to enable Magyars and Austrians to manage their respective barbarians, a species of political blackmail to win German liberals to the cause of Prussian domination.

One hundred and fifty years have passed since the Age of Enlightenment declared its faith in the perfectibility of man. One hundred and fifty years during which men have endeavored to create Utopia by the application of intelligence to the mastery of nature and the organization of social relations. What remains today of the optimistic faith which inspired this effort? Whatever remains, it is not an excess of optimism. We find ourselves presented, not with Utopia, but with a disturbing paradox: whereas the effort to subject the outer world of nature to human control has proceeded with unanticipated success and mounting confidence, every effort to shape the world of social relations to humane ends by rational means has ended in confusion and defeat. We know so much more, and are so much less sure, than the Age of Enlightenment. We have learned that man is far more complex than things, and far less tolerant of rational manipulation and control.

What confuses our purposes and defeats our hopes is that the simple concepts upon which the Age of Enlightenment relied with assurance have lost for us their universal and infallible quality. Natural Law turns out to be no more than a convenient and temporary hypothesis. Imprescriptible rights have such validity only as prescriptive law confers upon them. Liberty, once identified with emancipation of the individual from governmental restraint, is now seen to be inseparable from the complex pattern of social regulation. Even the sharp, definitive lines of reason and truth are blurred. Reason, we suspect, is a function of the animal organism, and truth no more than the perception of discordant experience pragmatically adjusted for a particular purpose and for the time being.

Looked at in this gray light, constitutions are seen to be documents historically conditioned, the imperfect and temporary products of time and place. Whatever the intention of their framers may have been, their meaning is determined by the ingenuity of judges, God helping them, to luff and fill before the shifting winds of social opinion. Constitutions, if we have them, we retain from force of habit; but we do not make new ones if we can help it. Having lost the universal formula for their construction, the task is too formidable.

We have lost the formula, yet something remains of the old faith. What remains is the conviction that man's fate rests with man himself, since nature is indifferent and the gods unavailing. His fate will be what he makes or fails to make it. He may will to make it fair, but we are not sure his intelligence is adequate to the task. Adequate or not, he must rely upon it, since it is the only guide he has.

We still hold, therefore, to the belief that man can, by deliberate intention and rational direction, shape the world of social relations to humane ends. We hold to it, if not from assured conviction, then from necessity, seeing no alternative except cynicism or despair. Some there are who, perplexed and angry, abandon the method of rational persuasion for irresponsible force and the assistance of communal or dialectical gods, beating at once, with equal gusto and emotional abandon, the tom-tom and the heads of their opponents. But this recourse is not for those who still cherish the value of truth and the increase of knowledge, since it is, after all, no more than veiled despair or cynicism disguised.

Like it or not, we are confronted once more with the necessity of making constitutions. Since we have learned that constitutions are inseparable from the complex pattern of social regulation, we may call them codes rather than constitutions. Call them what we please, they will inevitably differ in character from the constitutions that derive from the Age of Enlightenment. They will be shaped by an experimental and pragmatic rather than by an absolute conception of rights. They will be based less upon universal principles than upon statistical tables, will be concerned less with invariable natural law and more with temporary but insistent concrete needs. They will be less suited, no doubt, to the nature of man but better adapted, let us hope, to the frailties and vagaries of men.

Index

Index

AAA case (1936), 197

Absolutism assailed by Melville, 257

Académie de Peinture et de Sculpture, founded by Le Brun, 92

Académie des Sciences, 91, 92

Académie Française, 92

Acherley, Roger, 43, 44, 45

Acta Constitutiva (Mexico), 358, 359, 360, 361

Acta de Guadalajara (Mexico), 356

Acto Addicional (Brazil) of 1834, 372, 373

Act of Mediation, Swiss, 267

Act of Settlement, English, clause providing for divorce of executive and legislative, 41

Act of the (German) Confederation, 276

Act of Union with Scotland, 319

Adams, Henry, 211

Adams, John, 46, 126n, 155, 387; defense of balance, 39; criticism of Locke, 52; appeal from acts of parliament to monarchy, 55; influence, 57; excluded non-propertied man from franchise, 108; opinion of the poor and of the rich, 110; quoted, 129, 227

Adams, Samuel, 53; interpretation of Locke, 54

Addison, Joseph, 39; on poverty and riches, 111

Addystone Pipe & Steel Company v. *U.S.*, 320n

Adkins case, 164

Aerial Navigation (Canada), regulation of, 325

Africa, South, *see* South Africa

Agreement of the People (England), 126n, 127n, 149

Agricultural interests, influence upon political systems in the United States, in Canada, 161, 162, 299

Agricultural society of eighteenth century, attitude toward the poor, 111

Aguila mexicana, El, 353

Alamán, Lucas, quoted, 359, 360

Alberdi, Juan Bautista, 345

Alexander I, Czar, 267

Alfieri, Vittorio, definition of the people, 109

Allen, C. K., 23

Allgeyer v. *Louisiana*, 184n, 185, 186

Amendment, constitutional: provision for, in the United States, 217; in Canada, 302

Amendments to the United States Constitution, *see under numbers*, e.g., Fourteenth Amendment; *also under* Bill of Rights

America, mineral wealth, 79; democratic form of government suited to, 107; religious life in colonial, 132-41; influence of the Thirteen Colonies, 329; contrast between Latin-American and Anglo-Saxon situations, 342

America, Latin, *see* Latin America

American Commonwealth (Bryce), 306

American industry: and the Constitution, 79-103; progress of, bound to strengthen state and increase wealth of people, 79 f.; expectation of rapid development after removal of British restrictions, 80

American Revolution, leaders influenced by English speculative thought, 50; movement that culminated in, 55; influence of, 329

Ames, Fisher, quoted, 203

Anglicanism in American colonies, 136

Annonay, France, paper mills, 85

Anschütz, Gerhard, 289

Antonio, Dom, bishop of Pará, 378

Anzin, France, coal mining, 94

Apatzingán, Constitution of, 350

Apprentices (English), Statute of, 67, 71, 72n, 86, 87

Apprenticeship (English), seven-year, 86, 87

Argenson, M. A. d', on poverty, 109; on liberty, 114

Argentina, federal system, 341, 344 ff.; unitary and federalist conflict, 344 f.; constitution, 345; influence of federal government at expense of "states rights," 345; political parties, 345, 347; federal intervention, 346; government activities, schools, 346; evolution toward unitary type of government, 347

Aristocracy, tone of, in cult of reason, 130; of property, 199
Aristotelians, 144
Aristotle, balanced government, 45; constitutions collected by, 387
Arnold, Thurman, 193, 211
Articles of Confederation, 301, 389; impositions on interstate commerce, 90
Artificers, Statute of, *see* Apprentices
Assembly (English) of 1254, 30
Assize of Clarendon, 9
Athens, constitution of, 387
Atlantis (Bacon), 387
Attorney-General for Canada v. Attorney-General for Alberta, 323
Attorney-General for Ontario v. Attorney-General for Canada, 321
Augustine, Saint, followers of, 123; theory of obligation, 144; City of God, 144
Austin, John, quoted, 227
Austin, Stephen F., 361
Australia, American influence on formation of federal system, 297-303, 305-7, 330; conditions and problems similar to American, 298, 330; railways, 300; population, and area, 300; Federal Council of 1885, 301; differences making borrowing from American system difficult, 301; provision for constitutional amendment, 302; turned from Canadian innovations to American federal model, 305; High Court, 306, 310; movements toward secession, 307; American influence on development of federal system, 310-13; Constitution regarded as act of British parliament, 310; power of federal system v. power of states, 311; growth of uniformity without unity, 311; social services, supervision of business, 312
Australian Loan Council, 312
Austria, maintenance of, in the new Germany, 279; program of reorganization for Central Europe, 280
Austro-Germans, relation to Germany, 279
Authority, constituted, defined and limited, 3
Autocracy, distinguished from despotism, 7; presidential, in South America, 342, 343
Ayres, Venancio, 376

Babbitt, Irving, 253
Bacon, Francis, 23, 24; on king's prerogative, 12; *Atlantis*, 387

Bacon, Leonard, quoted, 255
Baden, Constitution of, 267
Baer, George F., 205n
Bagehot, Walter, 46; popularized convention of cabinet government, 49
Bainton, Roland, "The Appeal to Reason and the American Constitution," 121-30
Balance, political, 37-49; between abstract moral qualities, 37; origins of the theory, 39; state of perfect, a state of war, 47; arguments of critics of, 48; provided in Constitution, 58; Adam Smith's doctrine, 59; *see also* Checks and balances
Bar, *see* Lawyers
Bar Association of New York, 228
Barbacena, Marquez de, 371; quoted, 372
Barbosa, Ruy, 376, 377, 378
Barère de Vieuzac, Bertrand, 394
Barons, royal administration transferred to committee of, 11
Battle Abbey, ancient custom of, 8
Bavaria, Constitution of, 267
Baxter, Richard, 69, 148
Beard, Charles A., viii, 28, 79, 209, 220; "Historiography and the Constitution," 159-66; *Economic Interpretation of the Constitution*, 201
Becerra, Juan L., 358
Becker, Carl, 217, "Afterthoughts on Constitutions," 387-97
Bennet, A. A., quoted, 256
Bentham, Jeremy, 49, 129
Berlin conference (1918), 293
Berruecos (Mexican political leader), quoted, 359
Bible popularized by Puritans, 138
Biel, Gabriel, 122n
Biglow Papers, quoted, 125
Bill of Rights (England), 48, 151, 265
Bill of rights (Frankfort Constitution), 287
Bill of Rights (United States), 4, 217, 279, 358-62; reason as basic for, 121, 125; opinions of framers of the Constitution, 127; philosophical differences between Constitution and, 143-56; intellectual background, 155; Jefferson fought for, 156; converted into charter of property protection, 203; *see also amendments under numbers, e.g.*, First Amendment
Bill of Rights (Virginia), 53, 55
Bills of rights, Hamilton's argument on, 156; state, 169, 217

Billy Budd (Melville), 258

Binkley, Robert C., "The Holy Roman Empire v. the United States: Patterns for Constitution-Making in Central Europe," 271-84

Bishops, English, the third estate, 41

Bismarck, Otto von, political system, 271, 280, 282, 290; opposition to Congress of Princes, 280

Black, Hugo La Fayette, 243

Blackstone, Sir William, 37, 218; his constitution a mathematical symbol, 49; vogue of his *Commentaries* in America, 56; found balance in British constitution, 59

Blatchford, Samuel, 181, 182

Bocanegra, José María, 353, 358; quoted, 362

Bodin, Jean, theory of balance, 39

Boers, independence of, 330; exodus from Cape Colony, 331, 332; policy toward natives, 332, 339, 340; peace terms, Boer War, 335

Boer War, 335, 336

Bolingbroke, Henry St. John, 1st viscount, philosophy of government, 45

Bolivia, federalism, 341

Bolshevism halted in Germany, 287, 289

Bonaparte, *see* Napoleon

Bonham, Thomas, reëxamination of the case of, 15-24; imprisonment of, unjustified, 20, 21; fine illegal, 21

Bracton, Henry, 218; on king's prerogative, 10; constitutional doctrine, 11

Bradford, William, 134

Bradley, Joseph P., 176, 177, 178, 183, 184

Brandeis, Louis D., 242, 243

Bravo, Nicolás, 357

Brazil, federalism in, 341, 343, 345, 346, 367-84; political history, 343; colonial period, 367; independence, 368; unity its greatest accomplishment, 368; empire, 368-78; Constitution, of 1823, 369; of 1824, 369, 371, 372, 383; political parties, 370, 374, 375, 377; debates on federalism, 371; autonomy of provinces, 371, 372, 373, 374; project for federal union with U.S., 372; Acto Adicional of 1834, 372, 373; emancipation of slaves, 376; advent of the republic, 378; how federalism worked out in practice, 378-84; Constitution of 1891, 378, 379, 380, 383; status of states, 379, 381-83; Constitution of 1934, 379, 380, 381; of 1937, 379, 380-84; executive, 379, 380, 381, 383; fascism, 380; electoral college, 381

Brearley Committee, 404

Brearley, Judge David, 397

Brewer, David Josiah, 185; quoted, 227

Brissot de Warville, Jacques Pierre, on property, 115

British Empire, American influence on federal systems, 297-313; emergence of colonial dependencies, 298; security of states within, 302; influence of American institutions upon colonies of, 329; *see also names of units, e.g.,* Australia; Canada; England; etc.

British North America Act: history of, 315; federal and imperial aspects, 316; resulting litigation and judicial interpretation, 316, 318-28; legislative jurisdiction of parliament established and defined by, 316; property and civil rights provision, 319; decision which has colored interpretation of, 322; gives Dominion treaty-obligation powers, 325

Brown, George, 298

Bruun, Geoffrey, "The Constitutional Cult in the Early Nineteenth Century," 261-69

Bryce, James, *American Commonwealth*, 306

Buckley, Lord Justice, 192n

Buenos Aires, domination by, 344, 345, 346; treaty, 345

Bundesstaat v. Staatenbund, 285

Bunyan, John, 69

Burgesses, English: writs for election of, text, 31; election of, with binding authority, 31, 34, 36; had no place in original parliament, 33

Burke, Edmund, 206, 209, 212; quoted, 25, 26; contribution to art and practice of government, 49; Conciliation Speech, 56; contempt for swinish multitude, 110

Burlamaqui, Jean Jacques, 122

Burr, Aaron, quoted, 191

Business law, *see* Corporation law

Business supervision and control in Australia, 312

Bustamante, Carlos María, 352, 353, 357, 358, 359; quoted, 362

Butler, Joseph, Bishop, 48

Cabinet (Canada), representation in, 305

Cabinet government, English, 11, 13; recognized by Burke, popularized by Bagehot, 49

Cabinet responsibility in Canada, principle of, 302

Cádiz, Constitution of, 350

Calhoun, John C., 162, 220, 251, 252

California, laundry ordinance case, 178

Calvinism, 125, 127n, 136, 137, 138, 145, 147

Cambridge University, field of practice for medical students, 15, 18

Camp, George Sidney, 248

Campbell, John Archibald, 170, 179, 183; arguments in *Slaughter House Cases*, 171-76, 184, 189

Campos, Francisco, 380

Canada, American influence on formation of federal system, 297-305; population and area, 300; Constitution of 1841, 301; makes Constitution without provision for amendment, 302; annexation menace, 303, 308; federal power over provincial statutes, 304; representation in legislature and in cabinet, 305; federal system differs from Australian, 305; Constitution a conservative achievement, 306; movements toward secession, 307; litigation over Dominion and provincial jurisdiction, 308, 318 ff.; southern frontier, 308; becomes increasingly decentralized, 309; historic rôle of Judicial Committee, 309 (*see also* Judicial Committee); judicial interpretation of Constitution, 310, 311, 316, 318-28; regulation of trade and commerce, 311, 317, 318 ff.; problems of property and civil rights, 311, 317, 318 ff.; social services, supervision of business, 312; history of Constitution; Quebec and London conferences, 315; British North America Act, 315, 316, 318-28; federal and imperial elements in Constitution, 315; Dominion and provincial jurisdictions, 316; supremacy of enumerated powers of parliament, 317; French-Canadian laws, 319; Supreme Court decisions, 320, 327; New Deal legislation, 325; international relations impaired, 328; the French in rebellion, 332

Canterbury, Archbishop of, his ship seized for Church of Battle, 8

Cape Colony, exodus from, 331, 332; native policy, 332, 339; self-government, 333; grant of 1872, 334; resists federation, 335

Capitalists, acquire ownership of industries in England, 87; epithets hurled at in United States, 201

Capitalist system, 118; maintenance of, under the forms of a democracy, 192; supported by American sense of property and vested rights, 196; defended by liberalism, 200; control by vested interests, 203; ready to keep minority rule or scrap democratic framework? 206; *see also* Minority rule

Captaincies, hereditary, in Brazil, 367, 368

Cardozo, Benjamin N., 243, 376, 378; quoted, 242

Carlsbad Decrees, 276, 281

Carlsbad system, 277, 280

Carnarvon, Henry Howard Molyneux Herbert, Lord, 331, 335, 338

Carneiro, Levi, quoted, 367

Cartwright, John, 107

Casa Mata, Plan de, 351, 352, 353, 355, 357

Case of Proclamations, 10

Catholicism, liberal, 206

Caudillos (Argentina), 344, 345

Caus, S. de, 92

Cavendish's Case, 12

Cecil of Chelwood, Edgar Algeron Cecil, Viscount, 283

Central America, federalism, 341, 342

Central Europe, *see* Europe, Central

Central Investigating Commission at Mainz, 281

Centralist party, Mexico, 352; leaders of, 358

Centralization, United States driven toward, 197; Latin-American colonies, 342; predominant in Mexico, 349, 350, 364, 365; passes off scene in Mexico, 364, 365

Channing, William Ellery, quoted, 250

Charles I, of England, 40; constitution, 41

Charles II, of England, Restoration, 70; interest in Royal Society, 91

Charters granted by monarchs, 267, 268

Chase, Salmon P., 220, 229

Chase, Stuart, 387

Checks and balances, 9, 11, 12, 37, 38; demand for restoration of, 4; swept away by Parliament Act of 1911, 13 f.; English upholders of, members of an opposition, 42; Franklin's opinion of, 58n; plan for, in Germany, 294; *see also* Balance, political

Child Labor Cases, 221

Chile, federalism, 341, 342, 343

Chisholm suit, 274

Index

Choate, Joseph H., 242

Christian Dictionary (Baxter), 69

Christianity, *see* Religion

Churches versus the church, in America, 133, 134

Church of England: and Puritanism, 132; settlement of North America an incident to disruption of, 133

Citizenship, Central Europe, 279

Citizenship, United States: protected by Fourteenth Amendment, 169, 173; dual capacity, 272, 282, 283; equality, 272

Citizens' Insurance Company v. *Parsons*, 318, 320 ff.

Civic virtue, doctrine of, 155

Civil Code of Lower Canada, 319

Civil law violating rights of man is void, 6, 9

Civil liberty, 112; judicial guardianship of, 198; defended by liberalism against society, 200

Civil rights and property, Canadian jurisdiction over, 311, 317, 318 ff.

Civil service, influence of democracy upon, 290; weakness of American, 291

Civil Service Act, 291

Civil War (United States), 307; in light of historical facts, 165; effect upon Constitution and courts, 168; dooms aristocratic theory, 200

Clayton Act, 221

Cleisthenes, 387

Coal trade, of vital importance to London, 86

Cohen, Morris R., 227

Coke, Sir Edward, 147n, 218; on king's prerogative, 10; dictum in Dr. Bonham's case, 15 ff.; retreat from earlier position, 17; *Institutes*, 17, 22, 23; quoted, 18; arguments on interpretation of statute, 19 ff.; precedents on statutes repugnant and impossible, 22

Colbert, J. B., 69

Colepepper, Sir John, quoted, 40; three estates, 40; significance of his remarks, 41

Collectivism, distinguished from mercantilism, 63

Colleges founded by Puritans, 140

Colombia, federalism, 341, 342, 343; constitution supplies juridical basis for Confederation of the Equator, 370

Colonial dependencies, emergence into federal systems, 298

Colonial self-government, an achievement of imperial statesmanship, 333; failure in South Africa, 334

Combines and Fair Prices Act, 323

Commager, Henry Steele, "Constitutional History and the Higher Law," 225-45

Commentaries (Blackstone), 56

Commerce, Board of, Act (Canada), 323

"Commerce," defined, 97

Commercial code, uniform, for all Germany, 280

Committee government (England), 11

Common law, superseded and defeated by negative statutes, 17; power to void act of parliament, 19, 21; liberty under, 48; *see also* Natural law

Commonwealth, theory of, 147; Australia's designation, 306

Commonwealth Grants Commission, 312

Commonwealths, "very and true," 69

Concert of the Five Great Powers, 276

Condensation symbols, 211

Congress of Princes (Germany), 280

Confederation, *see* Articles of Confederation

Confederation of the Equator, 369

Conkling, Roscoe, 180, 242

Conservatism, Canadian, 306

Conservatives (Argentina), 347

Consolidated Statutes of Canada, 319

Constitution, *see* United States Constitution

Constitutional Convention, delegates, *see* Founding Fathers

Constitutional cult in the early nineteenth century, 261-69; close of era, 266; de Tocqueville's diagnosis an epitaph on, 268

Constitutional democracy, *see* Democracy

Constitutional interpretation, principle of, 310, 311; *see also* Judiciary; Supreme Court

Constitutionalism, negative feature, 3, 4; modern tendencies, 5; growth traced from feudal law, 6; threatened, 14

Constitutional law, importance of "due process" in, 167-90; Fourteenth Amendment comes into, 178; "equal protection of the laws" comes into, 179; power of judicial supremacy, 191; how judicial supremacy was built up and maintained, 192 ff.; natural law transformed into, 228; doctrine of the higher law, 228, 244; inadequacy of the teaching of, 243

Constitutions: medieval, 6, 40; papal, 266; European revolutionary, 267; patterns for constitution-making in Central Europe, 271-84; three most notable examples of democratic, 287; oldest in Latin America, 345; earliest, 387; made for nonexistent communities, 387; France holds record in making, 389; reasons for century of, 389 ff.; purpose of written, 389; cease to carry mystical sanction and become political bargains, 395; seen to be documents historically conditioned, 396; meaning determined by judges, 396; continuous necessity for, shaped by experimental and pragmatic conception of rights, 397; *see also under countries, e.g.,* England; Germany; South Africa; United States; etc.

Constitutions, state (United States): place limits upon majority principle, 217; provision for amendment, 217; adopted before 1787, 389

Continental Congress of 1774, 55

Contract, freedom of, 71, 197; in corporation law, 174, 185, 186, 190; sanctity of, 196, 197

Cooley, Thomas M., 194, 225, 243

Córdova, Treaty of, 350

Corporation as person, 154, 180, 181, 204

Corporation law, the path of due process of law, 167-90; freedom of contract, 174, 185, 186, 190; most famous dissent, 186; power of judiciary when private right balanced against general good, 187; formula for safeguarding business against regulatory power of state, 187

Corporative state, 224

Corwin, Edward S., 201, 211, 218, 220; quoted, 232 f.

Council of League of Nations, 283

Council or directory as highest political body in Germany, 293

Counties, knights of the English, summoned to attend parliament, 30

Courts, *see also* High Court; Judicial Committee; Supreme Court

Courts and the Constitution: a reëxamination of the case of Dr. Bonham, 15-24

Courts of law, English, 147n; Parliament as a court, 148

Covarrubias (Mexican political leader), 359

Craftsmen, French, brought under authority of gilds, 84

Crawford, William H., quoted, 219n

Crawley, Sir Francis, 13

Creditor-national party in English dominions, 299

Crescent City Company, 177, 178, 180, 184

Criminal law a federal subject in Canada, 305

Cromwell, Oliver, 147, 149, 150n, 151

Cunha, Carneiro da, 371

Cyrano de Bergerac, Savinien, *States in the Moon*, 387

Danby Case, 41

Daniel, Justice, 18

Day, William Rufus, 186

Debtor-states-rights party in British dominions, 299

Decembrists, 268n

Declaration of Independence, 55, 168; Locke's philosophy, shaped by Jefferson, 216; influence upon British colonies, 329

Declaration of Rights (Virginia), 155

Declaration of the Rights of Man, 262, 263, 265

Deism, 247, 250

De Lolme, Jean Louis, 46; belief in political rights based on property rights, 108; on liberty, 112

Democracy, deflation of more idealistic conception of, 56; concepts of, in the eighteenth century, 105-11; suited to small territories only, 106; Spinoza's theory of, 153; distinguished from liberalism, 199; struggle with antidemocratic forces, 199; basis and premise of, 200; epithets hurled at, and by, mass movements, 200 f.; antithesis between democratic impulse and judicial power, 202; corporate groups ready to scrap framework of? 206; why is judicial review encouraged by? 236; constitutional, of nineteenth century, 247-58; realistic, and romantic, 248; foundations of democratic faith, 249 ff.; doctrines of the ruling creed assailed, 256; studies of Martineau and de Tocqueville, 268; arguments voiced in Germany against, 286, 290; three most notable examples, 287; Max Weber's ideas, 290 ff.; *see also* Federalism

Democracy (Camp), 248

"Denial of justice," 274

Despotism, checks on, 4, 13, 14; distinguished from autocracy, 7; a present danger, 14

Determinism, doctrine of, 137; elements of, in history, 164

Dialogue of the Exchequer, 7, 9

Díaz, Porfirio, 365

Dickens, Charles, 249

Dickinson, John, 57; quoted, 127, 128, 232n, 382, 393

Dictators, Latin America, 343, 345, 373, 379, 380

Diderot, Denis, *Encyclopédie*, 109

Dillon, John F., quoted, 225n

Diós Cañedo, Juan de, 358

Directory or council as highest political body in Germany, 293

Discourses on Government (Sidney), 54

Divine right of judges, 193

Doctrine of law, fashioning of, 167

Dodd, William E., 165

Dodington, Bubb, 47

Dominium politicum, 12

Dooley, Mr., 238

Dred Scott Case, 168, 171n, 219

Dual Alliance, international law framework, 281

Due process of law: historical path, 167-90; lineage of phrase, 168; makes its judicial entry, 170; set down in law reports as an alternative reading to the police power, 178; Court admissions that legislation must meet standards of, 180; as buttress about corporate interest, 180; ideas out of which shaped, 189; twisted from a procedural to a substantive meaning, 204; not transformed without a challenge, 222; clause not new in Constitution but new as a limitation upon states, 230; literature on, 231n; right of, in the United States, 274; in Holy Roman Empire, 274; German Confederation, 277

Durham Report, quoted, 333 f.

Dutch in South Africa, *see* Boers

Ebert, Friedrich, 287, 288, 289, 294

Echevarri, General J. A., 351

Economic enterprise, government interference with, 91

Economic groupings accentuate conflict between states, 299

Economic interests, influence upon constitution makers, 161 ff.; upon judges, 163; protection of, the object of government, 165

Economic Interpretation of the Constitution (Beard), 201

Economic legislation, Canada, conflict in field of, 316; assigned to Dominion jurisdiction, 317

Economic liberty, danger of, 117

Economic opportunity, equitable distribution of, in medieval community, 67

Economy, controlled, mercantilism the old English pattern of, 63-77

Economy, national, preceded by municipal, 66

Education, initiated by Puritans, 140; control of, in Latin America, 346, 381

Edward I, of England, 31; negotiating for a subsidy, 34; fiscal motive behind innovations affecting parliament, 35

Edward III, of England, task of commons under, to vote supply, 35

Edwards, J. G., 31, 32

Elections, efforts to decrease ministerial influence over in England, 45

Electors, Holy Roman Empire, 272; German Confederation, 277

Eleventh Amendment, 274

Elizabeth, queen of England, Statute of Apprentices, 67; challenged Earl of Northumberland in case of mines, 86; attitude toward religious anarchy, 132, 139

Ellesmere, Sir Thomas Egerton, Lord, 22, 23, 24

Elliott, W. Y., 193; "The Constitution as the American Social Myth," 209-24

Emerson, Ralph Waldo, philosophy of, with quotations, 248-54; greatest preacher of democratic faith, influence, 254

Enclosure movement, 71; attitude of Tudors and early Stewarts toward, 68

Engineers' Case of 1920, 310

England: representative institutions in medieval, 25-36; thirteenth-century economic and social development, 30; monarchy restored on Colepepper's words, 41; influence of seventeenth-century philosophy of, upon America, 50, 53; mercantilism, the old English pattern of, a controlled economy, 63-77; political action designed to meet immediate situation, 65; burden of administration shifted to justices of the peace, 70; Restoration marks abandonment by crown of any social and eco-

England (*Continued*)

nomic program, 70; mercantilism controlled by county and city magnates, 71; contrasted with earlier version, 71; command of the seas, 76; national defense and foreign trade, 76; quarrels with colonies, 76; support of study of experimental science, 91; Puritanism in, 132, 134, 136, 147; corporative state, 224; attitude toward revolutionary philosophy, 265; wealth, *see* Economic conditions

Agriculture, indifference to interests of, 66; favored by Statute of Apprentices, 67; controlled economy in matters of, abandoned, 72

Commerce, foreign trade, 72 ff., 75, 76; domestic trade, 73; freedom of interior commerce, 90

Constitution, notion of parliamentary mandate foreign to, 25; checks and balances, 46; continually changed, 49; principles of, the common rights of man, 53; primary and auxiliary (political) rights, 113; foundations of constitutional philosophy, 147 ff.; Whigs take over defense of, 151; symbolism, 216; elusive, and people unable to define, 388

Economic conditions, wage earners, 72, 73; bullionists, 75; private wealth, 88, 89

Economic policy, mercantilism, 63-77; toward food stuffs, 66; concept of national economy an extension of municipal concept, 66, 68; Statute of Apprentices an attempt to define, in a single law, 67 (*see also* Statute of Apprentices); controlled economy increasingly hard to impose, 69; effect of Restoration upon, 70; dictated by parliament, 71; freedom of contract favored as against statutory restrictions, 71; nothing done to define a consistent, 72; official attitude toward wage earners, 72; persistence of mercantilism in area of foreign trade, 74, 76; during fifty years before American Revolution, 76; changes a result of industrial expansion, 93

Finance, gold standard, 88; rôle played by public credit in promoting industry, 102

Government, by committee, 11; rests upon consent of propertied classes, 48; move away from absolute monarchy to parliamentary government, 83; new rôle in economic life, 93; representative monarchy best suited to in eighteenth century, 106; conflict and confusion of political theories, 147 ff.

Industries, municipal control of, 67; controlled economy in matters of, abandoned, 72; industrial history in relation to the American Constitution, 79-103; leadership in mining and heavy manufactures, 81, 91, 97; why they developed more rapidly than in France, 81 ff.; government control diminished, 86; private ownership of minerals, 86 f.; government policy of encouraging private ventures, 89; granting patents for new inventions, 91; Statute of Monopolies, 91; industrial leadership over France, 92; supremacy little affected by government policies, 93; funding of public debts promotes, 102

Laws, interpretation of, in judicial decisions, 65; Statute of Apprentices, 67, 71, 72n, 86, 87; judges favor freedom of contract, 71; Navigation Laws, 76; penal statutes, 87; neglect in execution of, 87; Statute of Monopolies, 91

Parliament, *see* Great Britain, parliament

Taxation, funds raised by, 88; duties on coastwise traffic in coal, 90

English, a practical people and subtle theorists, 388

Enlightenment, the, 129, 226, 229, 390, 395, 396

Epic symbols, 211

Epithets hurled at democratic movements, and propertied groups, 201

Equality, doctrine of, 55, 57, 272

"Equal protection of the laws" comes into constitutional law, 179

Equilibrating commonwealth, 153

Erasmus, Desiderius, 124, 128

Espinosa (Mexican political leader), 360

Estates, balance between three equal, 37 ff.

Europe, constitutional cult in early nineteenth century, 261-69; influence of United States Constitution, 261, 263, 268; revolutionary constitutions, 267

Europe, Central, patterns for constitution-making in, 271-84; number of

Europe, Central (*Continued*)
  political systems and languages in, 271;
  Holy Roman Empire, 271 ff.; Metternich system, 271, 275 f., 282; revolutionists of 1848, 271, 278, 280, 282, 285;
  Bismarck system, 271, 280, 282, 290;
  Naumann's *Mitteleuropa* projects, 271,
  281; Wilson's political system, 271, 276,
  281 f., 286; Schwarzenburg's program
  of reorganization, 280, 281; minorities
  treaties, 281; *see also* Austria; Germany; Holy Roman Empire
Exaltados in Brazil, 371
Executive, judicial veto on delegation of
  power to, 222; office of president, German Reich, 289, 292, 294; federal, responsibility of in British dominions,
  302; presidential autocracy in South
  America, 342, 343; plural, in Mexico,
  352, 354; powers of, in Brazil, 379, 381,
  383; selection, 381

Farías, Valentín Gómez, 358
Farrapos, revolution of, in Brazil, 373
Fascism, European, strengthens minority
  rights argument, 198, 205, 207; in
  Brazil, 380
Federal Act of 1815, German, 277
Federal Council of 1885, Australia, 301
Federalism, doctrine of, 195, 196; Ameri-
  can influence on British systems, 297-
  313; federations created by Downing
  Street unlike American system, 297; in
  Latin America, 341-47; Mexico, 349-
  65; Brazil, 367-84
Federalist, The, 59, 60, 102, 307
Federalist papers, 219
Federalist Party, in the United States,
  199; in Mexico, 352, 358
Federalist-Whig-Republican school of
  thought, 161
Feijó of Brazil, 371n
Felice, F. B. de, on liberty and property,
  114
Feudalism, constitutionalism traced
  from, 6; negative check on government
  inhering in rights of vassals, 7
Feudal law, disputed point touching
  rights and obligations of tenants, 10
Field, Stephen Johnson, 176, 177, 178,
  179, 183
Fifteenth Amendment, 169
Fifth Amendment, 168, 231n
Filmer, Sir Robert, 216
First Amendment, Puritan background,

131-41; clause confirming religious lib-
  erty, 131
"First church" in colonial communities,
  133, 134
Fitzhugh, George, quoted, 252
Fitzsimons, Thomas, 82
Folklore of Capitalism, The (Arnold),
  211
Foreign intercourse, right to, in German
  states, 273, 276
"Formation de la Constitution de Weimar, La . . ." (Holborn), 295
Fortescue, Sir John, 12
*Fort Frances Pulp and Power Company,
  Ltd.*, v. *Manitoba Free Press, Ltd.*, 324
Founding Fathers, adopt clauses in Constitution which favor private interests,
  79, 80, 100, 102
Fourteenth Amendment, 163, 164, 274,
  283; meaning confused by general and
  abstract language, 169; unity with
  Thirteenth, 169, 173; provisions covering rights of citizens, 169, 173; meaning becomes concern of the Court, 170;
  invoked in *Slaughter House Cases*,
  172 ff.; comes into constitutional law,
  178; result of conspiracy between politicians and industrialists? 180; protection of, first accorded to a corporation,
  189; converted into charter of property
  protection, 203
France: king's ordinances seldom touched
  private law, 7; unfavorable to experimental science and technical improvement, 92; distrust of French for value
  of new forces, 92; representative monarchy best suited to, in eighteenth century, 106; contempt felt in, for proletariat, 108, 109; revolutionary ideology,
  261 ff.; and United States, attitude
  toward one another, 261; constitutional acts of the Revolution, 262;
  Rights of Man, 262, 263; imperial adventure, 264; romance of the revolution over, 264; charter granted by
  Louis XVIII, 267
  Constitutions, 263, 264, 267, 287; revo-
    lutionary, 263; Napoleonic, 264;
    Constitution of 1793, 267; holds
    record in constitution making, 389
  Economic policy, Colbert's controlled
    economy, 69; concerned in trying to
    overcome economic superiority of
    England, 82; liberty of private cap-
    ital restricted, 84; private merchants
    become creditors of crown, 88

France (*Continued*)
Finance, 88, 96
Industries, industrial history in relation to the American Constitution, 79-103; industrial progress compared with England's, 81 ff., 92; interference of government in, 83, 84, 85, 96, 97; large-scale, neglected by clergy and nobility, 87; financed by mercantile classes, 88; period of rapid development, 94
Laws, care in execution of, 87
Taxation, financial burdens imposed on private enterprise, 87; industries handicapped by tolls and duties, 89; relief from, 96
Franchise, in Colonial America based on property qualifications, 107 ff.
Francis Joseph, of Austria, 280, 281
Frankfurt Assembly, 278 f.
Frankfurt Constitution, 278, 279, 280, 285, 287
Frankfurter, Felix, quoted, 240
Frankfurter Zeitung, Max Weber's articles in, 292, 293
Franklin, Benjamin, 52, 69, 123, 124n, 128, 130, 278; clung to principle of hereditary monarchy, 55; attitude toward native industries, 80n; motion regarding canals defeated, 99; quoted, 101
Free city (Greek), defined, 143
Freedom (Hoover), 118
Freedom of contract, 71, 197; in corporation law, 174, 185, 186, 190
Freedom of speech and press, 131; theories of, 143 ff.; defined by Spinoza, 153n
French-Canadian laws, 319
French Revolution, 212, 215, 247; constitutional acts, 262
Freyre, Felisbello, 382n
Frontier, influence upon colonial religious freedom, 134; South African and its influence, 331 ff., 339
Fugitive Slave Law, 251
Fundamental law behind the Constitution, 3-14, 53

Gabriel, Ralph Henry, "Constitutional Democracy: a Nineteenth-Century Faith," 247-58
Garrison, William Lloyd, 251
General Will, doctrine of, 155
German Confederation, 276 ff., 280; constitutions guaranteed by, 276; Federal Act of 1815, 277
Germany: Romantic movement and *Volkgeist*, 129n; attitude toward revolutionary creed, 264; constitutions of Baden, Bavaria, and Württemberg, 267; unwritten constitution of Holy Roman Empire, 273; Frankfurt Constitution, 278, 279, 280, 285, 287; maintenance of Austria in, 279; whether states could be partly in and partly out of, 279; uniform commercial code, 280; monarchical system, 285 ff.; constitutional development, 285-95; post-war revolution, 286, 288; critical attitude toward U.S., 286; Weimar republic, 287 ff., 294; Weimar Constitution of 1919, 287-95; Third Reich, 288, 295; *see also* Europe, Central: Holy Roman Empire
Gerry, Elbridge, refused to sign Constitution, 99n
Glassmakers, French, 95
Gold standard, principle of a fixed, in England and in France, 88
Good neighbor policy approved in Brazil, 380
Good Society, The (Lippmann), 204
Goths, balanced government, 45
Gough, J. W., 153n
Grant of 1872 (South Africa), 334
Great Britain, *see* Australia; British Empire; Canada; England; South Africa
Great Britain, parliament: knights of the shires summoned to attend, 30; distinction between original functions of parliament and of the commons in parliament, 32; main business under the three Edwards, 32; fiscal motive behind innovations affecting, 34; independence demanded, 42, 45; genesis of parliamentary reform, 43; economic and social policy proceeded from, 71; as a court of law, 148; confusion of ideas concerning, 150; acts of, *see* Statutes
Commons, House of, beginnings of representative government in England, 25-36; commons denounced, 26; petitioners, not judges in parliament, 33; judicial functions as determining factor in rise of, 33; established control over vital functions of government, 35; power to legislate and impeach, 42; class which dominated, 70, 71; crown impotent without support of, 83; challenged right of crown to im-

Great Britain *(Continued)*
pose taxes, 88; tendency toward supremacy of, 216
Lords, House of, most independent assembly, 26; as legislative body and court of last resort, 42
Great Powers, European, 272, 276, 278; in League of Nations, 283
Great Trek (South Africa), 331, 332, 339
Greek constitutional theory, 143-45, 153
Greek constitutions, 387
Greek republic, slave base, 200
Green, Justice, 225
Green, John Richard, 28
Green, T. H., 155
Grey, Sir George, 331, 336
Grimke, Frederick, quoted, 253
Grotius, Hugo, 122, 145-46, 154
Guadalajara, Mexico, 356, 357, 360, 361; *see also* Jalisco
Guatemala, 341

Habeas Corpus, effect upon liberty, 48
Haldane, R. B., 322; decisions, 323 ff.
Haller, William, "The Puritan Background of the First Amendment," 131-41; *Rise of Puritanism in Pulpit and Press*, 136n
Hamilton, Alexander, 91, 124n, 162, 191, 236, 298, 388, 398, 399, 412, 414; appeal from acts of parliament to monarchy, 55; work for balanced state, 60; promotes ratification by states, 80; use of word industry, 98; appeals to English history in dealing with public finance, 101; quoted, 156, 227; dream of an aristocracy of property, 199
Hamilton, Walton H., "The Path of Due Process of Law, 167-90"; mentioned, 201
Hammurabi, Code of, 387
Handbuch des deutschen Staatsrechts (Anschütz and Thoma, ed.), 295
Hapsburg monarchy, 276
Haring, C. H., "Federalism in Latin America," 341-47
Harlan, John Marshall, 186, 187; quoted, 233
Harrington, James, on proportioning of political power, 39, 48; influence of his *Oceana*, 54; respect for property, 54, 59; theory of commonwealth, 152; John Adams a reincarnation of, 155
Harvard College, 140
Harvard Law School Library, inscription, 218

Hay, William, 44
Heckscher, Eli, 67
Henry II, of England, assizes not definitions of rights, 9
Henry III, of England, reigned but did not rule, 11; writs for election of burgesses, 31; fiscal motive behind innovations affecting parliament, 34
Henry VIII, of England, act regulating practice of medicine, 18; England an industrial backwater under, 81
Henry, Patrick, 54, 385, 409-412
Herder, Johann Gottfried von, quoted, 265
Hertzog, General J. B. M., 339
Hidalgo y Costilla, Miguel, 349
Hierarchy, principle of, in Germany, 272, 276, 284
High Court, Australia, influence of American Supreme Court, 306, 310; constitutional interpretation, 310
Higher law, theory of, 23; and constitutional history, 225-45; characterization, 226; elaborated and transformed into constitutional law, 228, 244; invoked on behalf of property, 229, 231; what constitutes legislation, 232; judicial decisions based on considerations of, 235; *see also* Moral order; Natural law
Hindenburg, Paul von, 292
Historiography and the United States Constitution, 159-66, 235
History, conception of, 160; elements of determinism in, 164; importance of economic interests, 165
Hobbes, Thomas, 152, 153n, 154, 213, 215, 216
Hodge v. *the Queen In re Dominion Liquor License Acts*, 321
Holborn, Hajo, "The Influence of the American Constitution on the Weimar Constitution," 285-95; articles on German republic, 295
Holker, John, 82
Hollanda (Brazilian deputy), 371
Holmes, Oliver Wendell, 223, 228, 240n, 243; remark on constitution, 42; quoted, 163, 233, 237, 244, 262; most famous dissent in legal history, quoted, 186
Holy Commonwealth, A (Baxter), 148
Holy Roman Empire, pattern of, contrasted with that of U.S., 271-84; number of political systems and languages, 271; hierarchy, 272; system of law, 273; unwritten constitution, 273; success in

Holy Roman Empire (*Continued*) maintaining collective security, 275; U.S. Constitution helped to overcome traditions of, 285; *see also* Austria; Europe, Central; Germany

Hoover, Herbert, 221; conservatism, 118

Hughes, Charles Evans, 191

Human nature, assumptions about, by social-contract theorists, 215

Human perfectibility, 264, 266

Hume, David, 124, 129; skepticism, 59

Hunton, Philip, 37, 47

Ideas and interests, association of, in history of Constitution, 160-66

Idea structures and the judicial power, 193, 195

Ideology and Utopia (Mannheim), 161

Iguala, Plan de, 350

Immunities, personal, 113

Impeachment, judicial abuse never rebuked by, 236

Imperial Conference (British), of 1926, 328

Independents, political theory of, 149, 150

Individualism, basic for the inalienable rights of man, 125; revolt of Romantic movement against, 129; enhanced by Puritanism, 140; ethics of, 214

Individual liberty, and doctrine of minority rights, 197, 198; as doctrine of the democratic faith, 252 ff.

Industrial Disputes Investigation Act, (Canada), 324

Industrial history of England and France in relation to the Constitution, 79-103

Industry, the State as a partner in, 223

Initiative, referendum and recall, 221

In re Board of Commerce Act and Combines and Fair Prices Act, 323

Insurance, unemployment (Canada), 326

Insurance litigation, in the United States, 183; in Canada, 318, 323

"Integralista" Party (Brazil), 380n

Interests and ideas, association of, in history of Constitution, 160-66

Interest structures and the judicial power, 193

International Labor Organization, 276, 326

International relations, right of states to (Germany), 273, 276; status of (Canada), 328

Interstate Commerce Act, 180

Interstate commerce in Constitution, 100

Investment, reasonable *v.* confiscatory return on, 232

Ireton, Henry, 148n, 149; quoted, 150n

Irigoyen, Hipólito, 347

Isolation, American tradition of, 273

Italy, in Bismarck system, 281

Iturbide, Agustín de, Emperor of Mexico, 349-57 *passim*

Jackson, Andrew, 220, 247

Jalisco, Mexico, 356, 359; *see also* Guadalajara

Jansenists, 92

Jars, Gabrielle, 82

Jarvis, William C., quoted, 253

Jefferson, Thomas, 130n, 162, 168, 174, 195, 196, 202, 218, 219, 227, 253, 268, 387; praise of Locke, 52; proclaimed rights of people born free and equal, 55; concept of democracy, 106; on right of British electors to give law to U.S., 112; quoted, 128, 129; fought for Bill of Rights, 156; application of Locke's philosophy to Declaration of Independence, 216

Jeffersonian — Jacksonian — Democratic school of thought, 162

Jeffersonians, 201, 202

Jellinek, Georg, 126-27n

Jellinek, W., 295

Jesuits, 92

Jews, assembly of, 34

João, Dom, of Brazil, 368, 369

John Deere Plow Company v. Wharton, 323

Johnson, Samuel, 52

Joint-stock companies, beginning of, 74

Joseph II, of Austria, 278

Judges, *see* Judiciary

Judicial Committee of Privy Council (Great Britain), decisions in disputes between central and provincial authorities in Canada, 308, 318 ff.; historic rôle, 309; constitutional interpretation in Canada, 310, 311, 316, 318-28; judicial murder of Canadian Constitution by, 328

Judicial power, as an act of usurpation, 191; how built up and maintained, 192 ff.; formal ideology, 193; protected and supported by property, 196; antithesis between democratic impulse and, in Constitution, 202; erected into commanding position, 219; why encouraged by democracy, 236

Judicial review, doctrine of, 218, 219; power of, unpopular in South Africa, 338

Judiciary, wide powers of statutory interpretation, 24; belief in an independent, 38; king's powers should be limited by, 108; interpretations influenced by ideas and interests of, 163; power of, when private right balanced against general good, 187; masters of the art of political manipulation, 191; divine right of, 193, 237; F. D. Roosevelt's "reform" of, 198n, 221, 222, 231n; personification symbols of the Founding Fathers, 219; need of judicial self-restraint, 223; choice of precedents, 233; elective *v.* appointive, 236; decisions often political, reflect public opinion, 238; judicial *v.* political atmosphere, 239; factors which determine choices made by, 241; professional training and equipment, 242; *see also* Supreme Court

Juries, local English, used for governmental business, 29

Jury system distinguished from system of representative government, 29

Justice, *see also* Right and justice

Kelsen, Hans, 284

Kent, James, 194, 229; quoted, 243n

Kiewiet, C. W. de, "The Frontier and the Constitution in South Africa," 329-40

King, Rufus, 60

King of England, legal limits to prerogative, 7, 9, 10, 12, 13; right to autocratic rule, 11; regal and legal prerogative; discretionary powers, 13; in Colepepper's three estates, 40; power to legislate and choose administrative officers, 42; need for understanding between people and, 47; office of, 108, 148

Knights of the English shires, writs for election of, 31; had no place in original parliament, 33

Labor, revolution in status of, 173; man's right in his own, 174

Labor and employment litigation, 185, 235, 324, 326

Laboring classes, in England under Mercantilism, 72, 73

Labor legislation, 185, 221, 235

Labor Party (Australia), 312

Laissez faire, 189, 190, 196, 198; distinguished from mercantilism, 63; the

English official attitude by 1700, 72; of eighteenth century, 118; in respect to religion, 138; judicial reaction to ideas of, 237, 238, 239

Languages, political, in Central Europe, 271

Languedoc, France, textile enterprises, 95

Laski, Harold J., 116

Latin America, federalism, 341-47; lack of political experience, 342; colonial government; contrast with situation of Anglo-Saxon America, 342; *see also names of units, e.g.,* Brazil; Mexico

Laundry ordinance, 178

Law, not an accurate index to economic policy of a government, 64; administration of, not always conclusive, 65; how precedent is established and doctrine fashioned, 167; Aaron Burr's definition, 191; linked with religion, 212; phonographic theory, 227, 243; symbols of reason and consistency, 239; systems of Holy Roman Empire and United States contrasted, 273

Law, civil: violating rights of man is void, 6, 9

Law, common: superseded by negative statutes, 17; power to void act of parliament, 19, 21; liberty under, 48

Law, fundamental: behind the Constitution of the United States, 3-14; protest in developments converging on Constitution in name of, 53

Law, private: in France, seldom touched by king's ordinances, 7

Law of nature, *see* Nature, law of

Laws (Plato), 143

Lawyers, rule by, 219; influence on bench, 241 f.

Leacock, Stephen B., 384

League of Nations, pattern of, 283

Leão, Carneiro, 371

Le Brun, Charles, 92

Le Creusot, France, metallurgy, 94

Legislative representation in Canada, 305

Legislative supremacy, limits on, 216

Legislature, Locke's theory of, rejected by Americans, 53; judicial review of work of, 167, 182; problem of power to be given upper and lower house (Canada), 300; responsibility in matters of finance (Canada), 302; constitutional parity as between branches (Canada), 302

Legislatures, local (Canada), residuum of power in, 305

Leguia, Augusto B., 341

Lerner, Max, 211; "Minority Rule and the Constitutional Tradition," 191-207; "Lippmann Agonistes," 204n

Levellers, political theory of, 149, 150

Leviathan, The (Hobbes), 152, 213, 215

Lex Rex (Rutherford), 148

Liberalism, development of, 118; nineteenth-century, 118, 334; distinguished from democracy, 199; as defense of the capitalist power, 200; confusing rationalizations flowing from premises of, 203 ff.; in Mexico, 364, 365

Liberal Party, Canada, 309; Brazil, 370, 371, 374, 375, 377

Liberties, auxiliary or political, 113

Liberties, essential or personal, 113

Liberty: concepts of, in the eighteenth century, 111-16; economic, danger of, 117; natural, 152 (*see also* Rights of man); to acquire property, 179; individual, and doctrine of minority rights, 197, 198; what constitutes, in the economic order? 232; American philosophy of, 252 ff.; reasons for apotheosis of, 254

Life and Death of Mr. Badman (Bunyan), 69

Life, liberty, and property, 114

Lilburne, John, quoted, 150

Limited governmental powers, doctrine of, 195, 198, 217; *see also* Government, constitutional

Lincoln, Abraham, 220

Lippmann, Walter, attack on majority principle, 204, 207

"Lippmann Agonistes" (Lerner), 204n

Liquor traffic, jurisdiction over (Canada), 320, 325

List, Friedrich, 91

Livre tournois, gold value, 88, 96

Llave, D. Pablo de la, 358

Lloyd George, David, 292

Lochner v. *New York*, 163, 185-87

Locke, John, 126n, 127n, 129, 130, 161, 195; influence in America, 52, 216, 247; theory of legislative authority rejected by Americans, 53; political philosophy, 54, 105, 124, 213-18 *passim*, 223; theory of property, 54, 57, 154, 215, 216, 223; influence in establishing price for gold, 89

London, regulation of practice of medicine in, 15 ff.

London conference, 315, 321, 325

Lothrop, Samuel Kirkland, quoted, 255

Louis IX, decision on committee government, 11

Louis XIV, enactments increasingly effective, 83

Louis XVIII, charter granted by, 267

Louisiana, statutes and resulting litigation, 171 ff., 183

Lower class, contempt felt for, in eighteenth century, 108 ff.

Luther, Martin, 390, 400, 401, 412

Mably, Gabriel Bonnot de, on democracy, 110; on property rights, 115

Macdonald, Sir John Alexander, 304, 305, 309

Machiavelli, Niccolò, 39

McIlwain, Charles H., 27, 28, 34, 218; "The Fundamental Law behind the Constitution of the United States," 3-14

MacIver, R. M., "European Doctrines and the Constitution," 50-61

Mackworth, Sir Humphrey, description of constitution, 41

Madison, James, 37, 39, 124n, 126n, 141, 165, 308, 389-395, 399, 400, 403, 411, 412, 414; work for balanced state, 60; responsibility for form of Constitution, 80; belief in government support of manufactures, 101; concept of democracy, 106

Magistrate, office of, 147, 148

Magna Carta, legal limitation, 10; effect upon liberty, 48

Maine, Sir Henry Summer, 196, 205n

Maistre, Joseph de, 206

Majorities, Supreme Court as barricade against, 202

Majority movements of eighteenth century, 198; defeated by judicial review, 198

Majority principle, struggle between minority rule and, 201; dangers in new interpretation of, 204-7; in Locke's doctrine, 216, 217; rights put beyond reach of, by United States Constitution, 218

Majority rule, expansion of federal powers through, 221

Malebranche, Nicolas de, 92

"Man and citizen," 116

Mandate, intervention by (Germany), 275, 277, 278

Manitoba, statute for building railway, 305

Mannheim, Karl, 161

Manoel, João, 377

"Manufactures," use of term, 98

Marbury case, 228

Mardi (Melville), 257

Marketing acts, litigation, 327

Marshall, John, 191, 196, 219, 220, 228, 229; quoted, 250

Martineau, Harriet, 268

Martin, Percy Alvin, "Federalism in Brazil," 367-84

Maryland, colonial church, 133

Mason, George, 126n; refused to sign Constitution, 99n

Massachusetts, colonial religion, 133, 140

Max, Prince, of Baden, 286

Maverick, Maury, 212

Mecham, J. Lloyd, "The Origins of Federalism in Mexico," 349-65

Medicine, regulation of practice of, in London, 15 ff.; outside of London, act regulating practice, 18; Coke's interpretation of regulations, 19; imprisonment confined to those guilty of incompetent or improper practice, 20

Meinecke, Friedrich, 289, 295

Melville, Herman, 256-58

Mercantilism, the old English pattern of a controlled economy, 63-77; prevalence of, when Constitution was written, 195

Merchants, English, professional status, 74; self-seeking interests, 75

Metropolitan centers of credit and commerce *v.* agricultural hinterland, 299

Metternich political system, 271, 275 f., 282

Mexico: federal system, 341, 349-65; federal intervention, 346; centralism, 349, 350, 364, 365; Spanish Constitution of 1812, 350, 351, 352, 354, 362, 363; Constitution, of Apatzingán, 350; of Cádiz, 350; struggle of provinces for independence, 351, 353, 355-57, 363; elections, 351, 357; deposition of Iturbide, 352, 353; Constitution of 1814, 353; Centralist and Federalist parties, 352 f., 358; federal government proclaimed, 354; victorious at polls, 357; Acta Constitutiva, 358, 359, 360, 361; federalism granted, 359; adopted by Congress, 360; normal processes of federation reversed, 363; status of states, 363, 365; Constitution, of 1824, 363, 364; of 1836, 364; Organic Bases of 1843, 364; Constitution, of 1857, 365; of 1917, 365

Michels, Robert, 209

Middle Ages, growth of constitutionalism, 6, 40; distinction between autocracy and despotism, 77; prosperity not identified with material wealth, 67; group interest, 67

Middle classes, 116

Mier, Servando Teresa de, 352, 354, 358; speech opposing federalism, 360; quoted, 361

Mill, John Stuart, quoted, 334

Miller, Samuel Freeman, 176, 177, 178, 182, 183

Milner, Alfred Milner, Viscount, 336

Milton, John, 54; quoted, 141; political theory of, 147n

Minas Geraes, Brazil, 368, 381

Minimum wage case, 163, 164

Ministerial responsibility (Canada), principle of, 301

Ministers of Crown (England), efforts to decrease influence of, 42, 45; practices of, excoriated, 42

Minnesota milk rate case, 181-83, 184

Minorities treaties, 281

Minority rights, doctrine of, Court's zeal for, 195, 197, 198; defended by liberalism, 200

Minority rule, and the constitutional tradition, 191-207; struggle with majority will and its effect upon American life, 201; two senses in which aided by judiciary, 202; subtlety in new defense of, 204-7; corporate groups ready to scrap democratic framework for sake of? 206; *see also* Capitalist system

Mirsky, D. M., quoted, 268n

Mission, doctrine of, 255, 257

Mitteleuropa projects of Naumann, 271, 281

Monarchy, representative and despotic, 106; German system, 285 ff.; Mexican, 349, 352

Monopolies, "due process" invoked in cases against, 171; breakdown of doctrine to protect natural rights of men against, 187

Monopolies, Statute of (England), 91

Montesquieu, Charles de Secondat de, 155, 218; elaborator of theory of checks and balances, 46; doctrine of division of powers, 60; views on French government, 108; on liberty, 111

Montpellier, France, sugar industry, 95

Morales, Juan Bautista, 358

Moral obligation, theories of, 144 ff., 154

Moral order, doctrine of, 248, 249, 251, 253, 255, 256

More, Sir Thomas, 68; *Utopia*, 387

Morelos, José María, 350

Morris, Gouverneur, 80, 101, 401, 403, 409; quoted, 124n, 406

Morris, Robert, 82

Müller, Adam, 206

Municipal economy preceded national economy, 66

"Municipal Institutions," jurisdiction *in re*, 321

Myers, Gustavus, 241

Mystical conception of body politic, 206

Myth, definition, functions, 210; *see also* Social myth

Nabuco, Joaquim, 376, 377

Napoleon Bonaparte, 264, 267, 271, 278, 342

Napoleonic constitutions, 264

Natal, South Africa, Constitution, 333n

National Assembly in Weimar, 288, 289

National Convention, South Africa, 337

Nationalism, conflict with state particularism, 299, 306

Nationalist Party (South Africa), 339

Nationality problem, European, 282

Natural law, Coke's appeal to, 16; found to be basis for government, 122; literature on, 122n; animals excluded from sphere of, 125; relation to rights of man; 126n (*see also* Rights of man); Germany's disruption of tradition, 129n; refuge in jurisprudence, 230; *see also* Higher law

Natural power, identified with natural law, 153n

Natural Products Marketing Acts, 327

Natural right, *see* Nature, law of

Natural rights, *see* Rights of man

Nature (Emerson), 248

Nature, law of, 392, 393, 395, 396, 397; governments and their acts judged by conformity to, 5; state may not promulgate civil law contrary to, 6, 9; appeal to, identical with appeal to divine law, 150

Nature, state of, in Locke's theory, 213, 214, 215, 216

Naumann, Friedrich, 289; *Mitteleuropa* projects, 271, 281

Navigation Laws, 76

Nef, John U., "English and French Industrial History after 1540 in Relation to the Constitution," 79-103

Negroes, acts denying privileges of citizenship to, challenged, 168; South African policy toward, 332, 335 ff.; *see also* Slavery

New Deal (Canada), legislation, 325

New Deal (United States), 221, 222; decisions, 233n, 239

Newfoundland, control of fiscal system, 383

Newton, Sir Isaac, 123, 247

New York state, hours of labor legislation, 185

New Zealand, American influence upon, 330; influence upon South Africa's National Convention, 338

Non appellando, privilege of, 274

Notestein, Wallace, 65

Novalis (pseudonym of G. F. P. von Hardenberg), quoted, 265

Obligation, theories of, 144 ff., 154

Oceana (Harrington), 54

Ockhamites, 145

Ontario Liquor License Act, 321

Orange Free State, independence, 333

Ordinances and statutes, English, precedent for distinction between, 9

Organic Bases of 1843 (Mexico), 364

Origin and destiny, doctrine of, 255

Otis, James, 225

Ouro Preto, Visconde de, 377

Overton, Richard, "Remonstrance to Parliament," 149; quoted, 149n, 151n

"Own" in Roman law, 144

Pacto Federal (Argentina), 345

Paine, Thomas, 212, 247; *Common Sense* proclaimed America the asylum of mankind, 56; advocacy of equal representation, 108

Papal States, organic statute for, 266

Pareto, Vilfredo, 209

Pargellis, Stanley, "The Theory of Balanced Government," 37-49

Parker, Henry, quoted, 148

Parliament, *see* Great Britain, Parliament

Parliament Act of 1911, 14

Parliament and Executive in a Reformed Germany (Weber), 290

Parliamentary government, German, plan for, 291, 293, 294

Parliamentary mandate, *see* Mandate

Particular rights, relation between constitutional right and, 150, 151

Parties, political, 291, 292; beginnings of system, 299; Canadian, 305; Latin American, 345, 347; Mexican, 352, 358, 364

Pascal, Blaise, 92

Paterson, of New Jersey, 394-400

Paz (Mexican political leader), 360

"Peace, order, and good government," jurisdiction *in re*, 324, 326

Peace of Westphalia, 271, 273

Peckham, Rufus W., 184, 185

Pedro I, Dom, of Brazil, 368, 369, 370

Pedro II, Dom, of Brazil, 370, 371n, 373, 374n

Peel, Sir Robert, 26

Peerage, as legislative body and court of last resort, 42

Peerage Bill, 43

Peers, royal power of creating, infringed independence of lords, 43

Pennsylvania, colonial church, 133

People, the, governments the trustees and servants of, 56, 57; the final arbiters of government, 58; eighteenth-century concept of, 116

Pernambuco, Brazil, 369, 370

Person, concept of an artificial, 152, 154; corporation as, 154, 180, 181, 204

Personal rights, 105

Personification symbols, 211, 216

Peru, federalism, 341

Peters, Hugh, 134

Philosophical differences between the Constitution and the Bill of Rights, 143-56

Phonographic theory of the law, 227, 243

Physiocrats, attitude toward industrial progress, 80n; demanded economic liberty, 113

Pilgrim's Progress (Bunyan), 60

Pinckney, Charles, 397, 406

Piratini, Republic of, 373

Pius VII, quoted, 266

Plato, 212; *Republic*, 143, 214, 387

Platonism, 143, 144, 147, 153

Platonists, Scottish, 155

Plucknett, Theodore F. T., 22

Poland, Constitution, 267

Police power of state, conflict with due process, 175, 177, 178, 180, 185, 186, 187, 190, 230; defined by Shaw, 230; possibilities of, *in re* property, 230; higher-law concept of, prevented, 244

Political history, defined, 160

Politics, concerned with governing power, 38; meaning of social myths for, 210-14

Politische Schriften (Weber), 295

Pollard, A. F., *Factors in American History*, 5

Pollock, Sir Frederick, 16

Porteño leaders, Argentina, 344

Portugal, rule over Brazil, 368

Postlethwayt, M., 93

Pound, Roscoe, 227; quoted, 232, 239

Powell, T. R., 209, 212

Pownall, Thomas, quoted, 47

Pragmatic Sanction of 1723, 273

Precedents, legal, 167; choice of, 233

Predestination, doctrine of, 137

Prerogative of king, *see* King

Presbyterian political theory, 147, 148

President, *see* Executive

"President's Political Philosophy, The" (Thompson), excerpts, 204n

Preuss, Hugo, 289, 293

Price, Richard, advocate of complete representation, 107; on liberty, 112, 113

Priesthood, ancient, political function, 210

Princes, Holy Roman Empire, 272 ff.; German Confederation, 276; Congress of (Germany), 280

Private enterprise, regulation of, in France and in England, 87; financial burdens, 87, 88

Private ownership of industries, 87

Private property, *see* Property

"Privileges and immunities," 178, 179

Privy Council, Judicial Committee, *see* Judicial Committee

Progress, philosophy of, 253

Prolegomena to the Right of War and Peace (Grotius), excerpts, 145

Proletarian class, 110; *see also* Lower class

Property, political leadership vested in, 54; principle of liberty released from bracket of, 55; Locke's liberty conjoined with, 58; franchise based on, 107 ff.; natural rights reduced to right of, 114; limited, 115; doctrines of right- and left-wing radicals, 118; Locke's concept of, 154, 215, 216, 223; safeguarded by Court, 179 ff., 231; sanctity of, 195, 198; sense of, provides status for age of capitalism, 196; protection and support accorded judicial power, 196; an aristocracy of, 199; Constitution shown as representing property interests, 201; Bill of Rights and Fourteenth Amendment converted into charter for protection of, 203; higher law invoked on behalf of, 229, 231; con-

Property (*Continued*)
cept of, broadened by courts, 230; what is clothed with a public interest? 232; private rights, Holy Roman Empire, 273; Canada's jurisdiction over civil rights and, 311, 317, 318 ff.

Provinces, Argentina, status of, 344 ff.

Provinces, Brazil, autonomy, 371, 372, 374; legislative power, 372, 373

Provinces, Canada, litigation over Dominion and provincial jurisdiction, 308, 318 ff.; rights and autonomy, 316

Provinces, Mexico, as units in a centralistic state, 349; struggle for independence, 351, 353, 355-57; pretensions to independence, idle, 363

Provinces, *see also* States

Provisions of Oxford, 11

Public purpose, what action constitutes a? 232

Pufendorf, Samuel, 154

Puritan background of the First Amendment, 131-41

Puritanism, rise of, in England, 132, 134, 136; character of, in New England, 135; literature, 136, 138; attacks upon, 136; doctrine of predestination, 137; a cause of popular education, 140; political theory, 147 ff.

Quebec Act of 1774, 319

Quebec conference, 298, 315, 321, 325

Querétaro Constitutional Convention, 365

Quintana, General Luis, 357

Race, belief in privileges of (South Africa), 339

Radical Party (Argentina), 347

Radicals, English, advocate universal suffrage, 106

Radio Communication, control of (Canada), 325

Railroad litigation, 180, 181

Railways, Australian, 300

Ramos Arizpe, Miguel, 358, 361

Rayón, Ignacio, 349

Read, Conyers, "Mercantilism: The Old English Pattern of a Controlled Economy," 63-77

Reason, Age of, 121, 123, 125, 390

Reason, appeal to, and the United States Constitution, 121-30; three meanings, 121; as a faculty of man, 121, 128; as a quality of the universe, 125; as a temper in the conduct of human affairs, 128; pitfalls, 130

Reciprocity Treaty of 1854 (Canada), 325

Reconstruction period, legislation and resulting litigation, 170 ff.

Reforms, accomplishment of, in France and in England, 114

Religion, shift from religious to secular concept, 122, 124, 126; Puritan background of the First Amendment, 131-41; becomes occasion for disunion in England, 132; condition of religious life in colonial America, 132-41; linked with law, 212; influence upon American democracy, 248; requirements to be met by a secular national, 248

Religious liberty, in American colonies, 126n; made law by First Amendment, 131; prevalence of, before written into law, 135; assumptions underlying doctrine of, 135

Report on Manufactures (Hamilton), 98, 101, 102

Representation, actual, distinguished from virtual, 25, 27; equal, 106, 107; popular, an essential feature of English parliaments, 33; in cabinet (Canada), 305; legislative (Canada), 305

Representative government in England, beginnings of, 25-36; system a matter of political necessity, 36

Republic, German, 287 ff.; collapse of, 294

Republic (Plato), 143, 214, 387

Republica Anglorum, De (Smith), 147n

Republican constitution of 1793 (France), 263

Republicanism, Greek, 143-45, 153

"Repugnancy," 21, 24

"Reserved" rights regarded as natural, 155

Restoration Era (England), constitutional progress, 268

Revolution, post-war, in Germany, 286, 288; Revolutionary ideology, 263 ff.; right of revolution, 216, 220, 394; American contribution to, 261; Germany's attitude toward, 264; England's, 265; constitutions, 267; de Tocqueville's diagnosis, 268; Revolutionists of 1848 (Central Europe), 271, 278, 282, 285

Revolution of Ayutla (Mexico), 364

Revolutions, social, meaning of, 213; *see also* American Revolution; French Revolution

Rhodes, Cecil, 331

Richardson, H. G., 32; quoted, 33

Richelieu, Armand Jean du Plessis, Cardinal, 92

Richmond, Charles Lennox, 3d Duke of, universal suffrage bill, 107; universal suffrage and property, 115

Riezler, Kurt, conception of history, 160

Right, classical theory of, 143-45, 153

Right, private, order of king against, 9

Right and justice, principles of, may not be contravened by acts of parliament, 17, 19

Rights, auxiliary or political, 105, 113

Rights, essential or personal, 105, 113

Rights, established, the basis of protest, 55

Rights embodied in ancient custom never spoken of as "made," 9

Rights of assembly and petition, 131

Rights of man: more binding than "civil" law, 6; established within the Constitution, 53, 54, 55; doctrine of natural rights the ground of revolution and foundation of a new order, 55; term, 113; natural rights reduced to right of property, 114; origin of concepts, 126n; classical and other theories, 143 ff.; defined as an institutional moral structure? 151; or in terms of particular acts? 152; solutions of greatest philosophers, 152-55; doctrine written into state constitutions, 169; guaranteed by Fourteenth Amendment, 169, 174; accorded protection of the Constitution, 179; breakdown of protection against corporate monopoly, 187; myth of natural rights and judicial supremacy, 219; natural rights defined, 394

Rights of Man, French declaration, 262, 263, 265

Rio Grande do Sul, Brazil, 373, 374, 376, 381

Rise of Puritanism in Pulpit and Press (Haller), 136n

Rivadavia, Bernardino, 347

Riva Palacio, Vicente, 357, 361, 362

Rivarola, Rodolfo, quoted, 347

Roca, Julio, 347

Roman Stoicism, 122, 125, 144, 147

Romantic movement, 129

Roosevelt, Franklin Delano, 202, 380; court reorganization plan, 198n, 221, 222, 231n; critique of his Roanoke Island speech, 204; quoted, 231n

Roosevelt, Theodore, 220; quoted, 231n

Rosas, Juan Manuel de, 344, 345, 373

Roure, Agenor de, 374

Rousseau, Jean Jacques, 57, 113, 126n, 127n, 155, 195, 214, 215, 216; contempt for proletariat, 109; on best form of government, 109; on liberty, 112; on property rights, 115

Rowles v. *Mason*, 17, 22, 23

Royal Bank of Canada v. *the King*, 323

Royal College of Physicians, jurisdiction over practice of medicine in London, 15 ff.; power to fine and imprison, 20, 23; should not assess fines in which it shares, 20

Royal Society, incorporated, 91

Rumania, in Bismarck system, 281

Russell v. *the Queen*, 320, 322, 323, 324

Russia, despotic monarchy recommended for, in eighteenth century, 106; charter, 268; in orbit of Bismarckian diplomacy, 281

Rutherford, Samuel, 148

Saint-Gobain, France, glass-making in, 94

Saint-Just, Louis de, quoted, 263

Salgado, Plinio, 380n

Salvemini, Gaetano, "The Concepts of Democracy and Liberty in the Eighteenth Century," 105-19

San Luis Potosí, Mexico, 356; revolt in, 357

Santa Anna, Antonio López de, insurrection resulting in overthrow of Iturbide, 351; activities, 357; made dictator, exiled, 364

Santa Fé, Argentina, 345, 347

São Paulo, Brazil, 381

Sapir, Edward, 211

Saraïva (Brazilian parliamentarian), 378

Sayles, George, 32

Schmitt, Carl, 127n

Schneider, Herbert W., "Philosophical differences between the Constitution and the Bill of Rights," 143-56

School control in Latin America, 346, 381

Schuecking, Walter, 289

Schurz, Carl, 285

Schwarzenberg, Felix, Prince von, program of reorganization for Central Europe, 280, 281

Scotists, 145

Secession, movements toward (British Dominions), 307

Second Treatise on Government (Locke), 52

Sectionalism produced by frontier, 330

Selborne, William Waldegrave Palmer, Lord, quoted, 340

Self-determination, 111

Self-government, 116; principle of, 144, 333; failure in South Africa, 334

Semanario politico literario, 350

Separation of powers, urged for parliament, 150; erected by United States Constitution, 218

Septennial Act, argument for balance used against, 43

Serbia, in Bismarck system, 281

Sévigné, Madame de, 92

Seward, William Henry, 250

Sharpe, Gregory, 44

Shaw, Lemuel, 229

Sherman, Roger, quoted, 127

Sherman Act, 180, 221

Ship-Money Case, 13

Shires, *see* Counties

Sidney, Algernon, 54

Siete Leyes of 1836 (Mexico), 364

Slaughter House Cases, 171-78, 188

Slaves, status of, 57

Slavery, Brazil, abolished in, 376

Slavery, United States, abolition of, 168, 169; defense of, 199; controversy over, 251

Smith, Adam, 63, 72, 76, 117, 155; economic doctrine, 59; on interior commerce, 90

Smith, Sir Thomas, 147n

Social Contract (Rousseau), 112

Social contract theory, 55, 155, 213 ff.

Social legislation, Canada, conflict in field of, 316, 326

Social legislation, United States, treatment by Court, 189; outlawed by judiciary, 203

Social myth, Constitution as the American, 209-24

Social revolutions, meaning, 213

Social services, national (Canada), 312

Society for Constitutional Information, 112

Society for Establishing Useful Manufactures, creation of, advocated, 102

Society for Promoting Constitutional Information, 107

Socrates, 212

Sol, El, 352

Solon, 387

Sommer, Frank, 236n

Sophists, constitutional theory, 143

Sorel, Georges, 209

South, the, radicalism of, 55; *see also* States, Southern

South Africa: the frontier and the Constitution, 329-40; American influence, 330; the Great Trek, 331, 332, 339; influence of frontier, 331, 339; individualism of separate colonies and republics, colonization, 331; efforts to bring about federation, 331, 335; Great Britain's attitude toward problems of, 332 ff.; policy toward natives, 332, 335 ff.; constitutions of provinces, 333n, 336, 338n; political dismemberment, 333; grant of 1872, 334; Great Britain's loss of influence in, 334, 339; reasons for adopting union, 337; Union Constitution, 337, 338; influenced negatively by American example, 337; positively by New Zealand, 338; fear of court with power of judicial review, 338; present quest for nationality, 339

South Africa Act of 1877, 338

South Sea Bubble, 74

Spanish Constitution of 1812, 267, 350, 351, 354, 362

Spencer, Herbert, 237; *Social Statics*, 187, 238

Spinoza, Baruch, 153, 154

State, protection of business against regulatory power of, 167, 187; as a partner in industry, 223; corporative, 224

State regulation, what is of a nature to justify? 232

States, conflict between large and small, 299, 306

States, Australia: power stultified by Court, 311

States, Brazil: status under federalism, 379, 381, 383; power of large, 381; problem of lesser, 382

States, Mexico: status of provinces before federation, 349, 351, 353, 355-57, 363; created by national representative body, 363; federal domination over, 363, 365

States, United States: bills of rights, 169, 217; Reconstruction period, legislation, 170; litigation, 170 ff.; legal sphere set apart from federal government, 273, 274, 275; federal control over, 274, 283; rights of citizens against, 274

States, *see also* Provinces

States in the Moon (Cyrano de Bergerac), 387

States rights, and federalism, theory of, 196; Argentina, 345

Statute of Apprentices, 67, 86, 87; results of failure to enforce, 71; wage earners fight against repeal, 72n

Statute of Monopolies, 91

Statutes, precedent for distinction between ordinances and, 9; disallowance of, on ground of conflict with Constitution, 15; negative, superseded and defeated common law, 17; power of common law to void repugnant and impossible, 19, 21; may be interpreted contrary to words, 24; legislative power over provincial (Canada), 304

Statutory interpretation, common-law rules of, 21

Stephen, Leslie, quoted, 117

Stephenson, Carl, "The Beginnings of Representative Government in England," 25-36

Stoicism, 122, 125; compared with Greek republicanism, 144, 147

Stone, Harlan F., 223; quoted, 164, 194

Story, Joseph, 229; quoted, 231n, 250, 256

Stuarts, early: attitude toward enclosure movement, 68; fought against increasing commercialism, 69; at loggerheads with their parliaments, 70; poverty, 70; effort to guard social interest from exploitation, 86; right to license and control manufactures, 86

Suffrage, universal: advocated by radicals, 106, 107; republic based on, least remote from democracy, 109; United States made first experiments in, 110

Summa de Legibus of Normandy, 9

Superiority, illusion of, 249, 256

Supernaturalism permeates American thought, 249

Supreme Court, Canada: decisions, 320, 327

Supreme Court, United States: review of work of the legislature, 167, 182; the path of "due process" through, 167-90; meaning of Fourteenth Amendment becomes concern of, 170; Roosevelt's reorganization plan, 198n, 221, 222, 231n; rationalizations used to confuse and defend, 203; legislature reduced to "creature of the Constitution" by, 218; rôle of, as expounder of the Constitution, 219 f., 222, 360, 361; the "epic symbol" of the social myth, 219; usurpation of power by, condemned, 222; function of, in importing higher law doctrine into Constitution, 231; property protected by judicial legisla-

tion, 231; as authority for Australian High Court, 306, 310; historic role, 309; constitutional interpretation, 311; power of judicial review unpopular in South Africa, 338; flexibility, as willing instrument of national policy, 338; *see also* Judiciary

Sutherland, George, 37; quoted, 242

Swift, Jonathan, 37

Switzerland, Act of Mediation, 267; Constitution, 287; method for constitutional change, 302

Sydney Convention of 1897, 298

Symbolism of Constitution and Supreme Court, 193

Symbolism (Whitehead), 212, 214, 224n

Symbols, interrelated, built up by Constitution and Supreme Court, 193; definition, object, 211

Symbols of Government (Arnold), 211

Taft, William Howard, 164, 225

Taine, H. A., 389

Taney, Roger B., 168, 219

Tariff regulation an object of federation, 299

Tawney, R. H., 69

Taxation (Argentina), 346

Tax avoidance cases, 180, 181

Temperance, promotion of, 325

Tenants, feudal law touching rights and obligations of, 10

Tenth Amendment, revival of, to hamstring federal powers, 222

Territories, conversion of weak states into (Brazil), 382

Thayer, James B., 12

Thirteenth Amendment, unity with Fourteenth, 169, 173

Thomas Aquinas, Saint, 144

Thompson, Dorothy, attack on majority principle, 204, 207

Thoreau, Henry, 253

Thorne, S. E., "The Constitution and the Courts," 15-24

Tiradentes, conspiracy of, 368

Tocqueville, Alexis de, 268; quoted, 261, 389

Tornel y Mendivil, José Maria, quoted, 355

Toronto Electricity Commission v. *Snider and Others*, 324

Tory doctrine of government, 42

Tout, T. F., 10

Trade organizations, changing character of English, 74; fight against, 75

Traders, *see* Merchants

Trade wars of eighteenth century, 74

Transcendentalism, and the higher law, 228-30, 244; of Emerson, 248, 249

Transvaal, South Africa, independence, 333; annexation, 335; constitution, 336, 338n

Tucker, Josiah, 37, 82; opinion on backwardness of France in economic development, 83

Tudors, economic and social policy of, 66, 68, 69, 86

Turgot, A. R. J., 108

Turnbull, George, quoted, 45

Turner, Frederick Jackson, 165

Unions preceding federation, in the United States and British dominions, 301

Unitary government, Argentina's evolution toward, 347; in Brazil, 368 ff.

Unitary party (Argentina), 344, 345

United States: adoption of English economic policies desirable, 97; influence of England and France upon economic thought, 101; not a democracy, 106; made first experiments in universal suffrage, 110; doctrine of origin and destiny of, 255; and revolutionary France; attitude toward one another, 261; first visitors to study democracy in, 268; principle of equality, 272; legal system, 273, 277; concurrent separate systems of law, 277; Germany's critical attitude toward, 286; civil service, 291; population and area at time of federation, 300; unaware of rôle as mother of federations, 303; northern frontier; British good will, 308; federal social services and supervision of business, 312; Brazilian project for federal union with, 372

Commerce, Congress authorized to regulate, 97; control strengthens central government, 100

Congress powers conferred by Constitution, 97, 100

Federal system, pattern of, contrasted with that of Holy Roman Empire, 271-84; influence in Central Europe, 271, 278; legal sphere of states set apart from, 273, 274, 275; control over states, 274, 283; influence on British federal systems, 297-313, 330; similarity of conditions and problems a chief reason for extent of influence, 297, 330; Australian borrowings, 305; grows more unified, 309; growth of uniformity without unity, 311; negative influence upon South Africa, 337; influence in Latin-America, 342, 343, 345; influence upon Mexico, 349, 350, 352, 354, 359, 361, 362, 363, 365; influence upon Brazil, 368, 369, 372, 376, 378; *see also* United States, Constitution

United States Constitution: fundamental law behind, 3-14; and the courts, reexamination of the case of Dr. Bonham, 15-24; influence of European doctrines, 50-61 (*see also* Locke, John; Natural law; Reason; Rights of man); political developments—1st stage, protest in name of fundamental law within existing order, 53; 2d stage, doctrine of natural rights the ground of revolution and foundation of new order, 55; 3d stage, establishment of state, 56; answer to problem of statesmanship, 58; embodiment of Montesquieu's doctrine of division of powers, 60; fabric profoundly new, 60; English and French industrial history in relation to, 79-103; policies conducive to private interests of delegates, 79, 80, 100, 102; development of industry an objective in preparing, 79; influence of industrial history upon, 93; commerce clause, 97; extension of post offices and post roads clause to cover cutting of canals defeated, 99; financial clauses, aids to the wealthy, 99, 100; forbade capitation or other direct tax, 99; works of authors and inventors protected by, 100; economic sections, 100, 102; as product of the appeal to reason, 121-30; why toleration not affirmed in primary form, 131; philosophical differences between Bill of Rights and, 143-56; intellectual background that of seventeenth-century England, 155; historiography, 159-66; treatment of, conditioned by personality, time, and circumstances, 159; interpretation of, involves an interpretation of history in general, 160; influence of economic interests, 161 ff.; conception of, by two schools of thought, 161; rights of man accorded protection of, by Court, 179; dates from 1905 *in re* public control of business, 188; minority rule and the constitutional tradition, 191-207; judi-

United States Constitution (*Continued*)
cial power not expressly granted in, 191; but has written itself into, 192; prevailing political and economic thought at time of birth, 195; flexibility, adaptation to changes intended, 201; shown as representing property interests, 201; as the American social myth, 209-24; places limits upon majority principle, 217, 218; history of, and the higher law, 225-45; center of controversy during slavery dispute, 251; worship of, 252; influence in revolutionary Europe, 261, 263, 268; not fitted into framework of international law, effect upon states, 273; influence on Frankfort Constitution, 278, 279, 285; extent of influence in post-World War Europe, 281; connection with Constitution of German Empire, 285; influence on Weimar Constitution, 288, 290, 293; provision for amendment, 302; unpopular in South Africa, 338; *see also* United States, federal system

Amendments, *see under* numbers, *e.g.*, Fourteenth Amendment; *also under* Bill of Rights

Interpretation of, *see* Judiciary; Supreme Court

Universal law, *see* Nature, law of

Uruguay, constitutional change, 343

Utopia, 387, 390; Puritan, 134, 138, 139, 140; faith in democratic, 268; in ancient societies, 391; as a future state, 393; methods used in attempts to create, 395

Utopia (More), 68

Vargas, Getulio, 343, 344, 379, 380

Vasconcellos, Bernardino de, 371n

Veiga, Evaristo da, 371n

Venezuela, 360; federal system, 341

Vera Cruz, Plan de, 351

Verdross, Alfred, 284

"Verfassung und Verwaltung der deutschen Republik . . ." (Holborn), 295

Versailles, Treaty of, welfare of labor, 326

Vested interests, control by, 203

Vested rights, 197

Victoria, Australia, 300

Vienna, Congress of, 275, 277

Viner, Jacob, 75

Virginia, Bill of Rights, 53, 55; colonial church, 133, 136; Declaration of Rights, and constitution, 155n

Voltaire, F. M. A. de, admiration of English discoveries, 82 f.; on liberty and property, 114; views on acquired wealth, 117

Voluntarism, 145, 154

Wage case influenced by ideas and interests of judge, 163, 164

Wage earners, *see* Laboring classes

Wages, English justices of the peace empowered to fix rate of, 86

Waite, M. R., 180, 181

Waitz, George, 279

Wales, offered area of free trade, 90

Walmesley, Sir Thomas, quoted, 17

Walpole, Sir Robert, belief in independency, 42; opposition to, 43

Walwyn, William, 151n; quoted, 149n, 150

Warren, James, 54

Washington, George, 199, 386, 411

Watson, William Watson, Lord, 322, 327

Wealth, taxes on (in France), 87, 88; eighteenth-century concept, 116; a danger to be suppressed, 117

Wealth of Nations (Smith), 60, 64, 72, 76, 172

Weber, Max, at National Assembly in Weimar, 289, 293; political ideas, 290-95; writings, 290, 292, 293, 295

Webster, Daniel, 162, 194, 242, 251, 252

Weimar Constitution, history of, 287-95

Wells, H. G., Great Society described by, 387; *Outline of History*, 388

West, rôle in unifying East, 300

Westphalia, Peace of, 271, 273, 281

Whig doctrine of government, 42; Locke's justification of, 154

Whigs, take over defense of constitution, 151

White, E. D., 186

White, A. B., 29

Whitehead, Alfred N., quoted, 211, 214, 224

Whitelaw, W. Menzies, "American Influence on British Federal Systems," 297-313

Whitman, Walt, quoted, 256

Wilkes, John, demands equal representation, 106

William II, of Germany, 286, 290

William and Mary College, Blackstone's works taught at, 56

Williams, Roger, 126n

Wilson, James, 82, 124, 127; responsibility for form of Constitution, 80; interpretation of commerce clause, 99

Wilson, Thomas, 69

Wilson, Woodrow, 220, 221; Central European political system, 271, 276, 281 f., 286; League of Nations, 283; interference with German developments, 286, 287

Winthrop, John, 148n

Wordsworth, William, quoted, 263

World citizenship, 273, 282, 283

Wright, C. P., "The Judicial Interpretation of the Canadian Constitution," 315-28

Württemberg, Constitution, 267

Yancey, William Lowndes, 251

Year Books, medieval, 12

Yick Wo v. *Hopkins,* 179, 180

Yucatan, Mexico, 355

Zavala, Lorenzo de, 358

harper ✦ torchbooks

American Studies: General

HENRY STEELE COMMAGER, Ed.: The Struggle for Racial
Equality   TB/1300
CARL N. DEGLER, Ed.: Pivotal Interpretations of American
History   TB/1240, TB/1241
A. S. EISENSTADT, Ed.: The Craft of American History:
Recent Essays in American Historical Writing
            Vol. I TB/1255; Vol. II TB/1256
CHARLOTTE P. GILMAN: Women and Economics ‡ TB/3073
MARCUS LEE HANSEN: The Immigrant in American His-
tory   TB/1120
JOHN HIGHAM, Ed.: The Reconstruction of American
History △   TB/1068
ROBERT H. JACKSON: The Supreme Court in the American
System of Government   TB/1106
LEONARD W. LEVY, Ed.: American Constitutional Law:
Historical Essays   TB/1285
LEONARD W. LEVY, Ed.: Judicial Review and the Supreme
Court   TB/1296
LEONARD W. LEVY: The Law of the Commonwealth and
Chief Justice Shaw   TB/1309
RALPH BARTON PERRY: Puritanism and Democracy
                                                 TB/1138
ARNOLD ROSE: The Negro in America   TB/3048

American Studies: Colonial

BERNARD BAILYN, Ed.: The Apologia of Robert Keayne:
Self-Portrait of a Puritan Merchant   TB/1201
BERNARD BAILYN: The New England Merchants in the
Seventeenth Century   TB/1149
JOSEPH CHARLES: The Origins of the American Party
System   TB/1049
CHARLES GIBSON: Spain in America †   TB/3077
LAWRENCE HENRY GIPSON: The Coming of the Revolu-
tion: 1763-1775. † Illus.   TB/3007
PERRY MILLER & T. H. JOHNSON, Eds.: The Puritans: A
Sourcebook   Vol. I TB/1093; Vol. II TB/1094
EDMUND S. MORGAN, Ed.: The Diary of Michael Wiggles-
worth, 1653-1657   TB/1228
EDMUND S. MORGAN: The Puritan Family   TB/1227
RICHARD B. MORRIS: Government and Labor in Early
America   TB/1244
WALLACE NOTESTEIN: The English People on the Eve of
Colonization: 1603-1630. † Illus.   TB/3006
JOHN P. ROCHE: Origins of American Political Thought:
Selected Readings   TB/1301
JOHN SMITH: Captain John Smith's America: Selections
from His Writings. Ed. with Intro. by John Lankford
                                                 TB/3078

American Studies: From the Revolution to 1860

MAX BELOFF, Ed.: The Debate on the American Revolution, 1761-1783: A Sourcebook △   TB/1225

RAY A. BILLINGTON: The Far Western Frontier: 1830-
1860. † Illus.   TB/3012
EDMUND BURKE: On the American Revolution. ‡ Edited
by Elliott Robert Barkan   TB/3068
WHITNEY R. CROSS: The Burned-Over District   TB/1242
GEORGE DANGERFIELD: The Awakening of American Na-
tionalism: 1815-1828. † Illus.   TB/3061
WILLIAM W. FREEHLING, Ed.: The Nullification Era: A
Documentary Record ‡   TB/3079
FRANCIS GRIERSON: The Valley of Shadows: The Coming
of the Civil War in Lincoln's Midwest   TB/1246
JAMES MADISON: The Forging of American Federalism.
Edited by Saul K. Padover   TB/1226
JOHN C. MILLER: Alexander Hamilton and the Growth of
the New Nation   TB/3057
RICHARD B. MORRIS, Ed.: The Era of the American Revo-
lution   TB/1180
FRANCIS S. PHILBRICK: The Rise of the West, 1754-1830. †
Illus.   TB/3067

American Studies: Since the Civil War

W. R. BROCK: An American Crisis: Congress and Recon-
struction, 1865-67 ° △   TB/1283
W. A. DUNNING: Reconstruction, Political and Economic:
1865-1877   TB/1073
ROBERT GREEN MCCLOSKEY: American Conservatism in
the Age of Enterprise: 1865-1910   TB/1137
VERNON LANE WHARTON: The Negro in Mississippi:
1865-1890   TB/1178
A. RUSSELL BUCHANAN: The United States and World War
II. † Illus.   Vol. II TB/3044; Vol. II TB/3045
FOSTER RHEA DULLES: America's Rise to World Power:
1898-1954. † Illus.   TB/3021
ROBERT L. HEILBRONER: The Limits of American Capital-
ism   TB/1305
SIDNEY HOOK: Reason, Social Myths, and Democracy
                                                 TB/1237
WILLIAM E. LEUCHTENBURG: Franklin D. Roosevelt and
the New Deal: 1932-1940. † Illus.   TB/3025
ARTHUR S. LINK: Woodrow Wilson and the Progressive
Era: 1910-1917. † Illus.   TB/3023
GEORGE E. MOWRY: The Era of Theodore Roosevelt and
the Birth of Modern America: 1900-1912. † TB/3022
RUSSEL B. NYE: Midwestern Progressive Politics: 1870-
1958   TB/1202
WILLIAM PRESTON, JR.: Aliens and Dissenters: Federal
Suppression of Radicals, 1903-1933   TB/1287
JACOB RIIS: The Making of an American. ‡ Edited by
Roy Lubove   TB/3070
PHILIP SELZNICK: TVA and the Grass Roots: A Study in
the Sociology of Formal Organization   TB/1230
IDA M. TARBELL: The History of the Standard Oil Com-
pany: Briefer Version.‡ Edited by David M. Chalmers
                                                 TB/3071
GEORGE B. TINDALL, Ed.: A Populist Reader ‡   TB/3069

† The New American Nation Series, edited by Henry Steele Commager and Richard B. Morris.
‡ American Perspectives series, edited by Bernard Wishy and William E. Leuchtenburg.
* The Rise of Modern Europe series, edited by William L. Langer.
** History of Europe series, edited by J. H. Plumb.
¶ Researches in the Social, Cultural, and Behavioral Sciences, edited by Benjamin Nelson.
§ The Library of Religion and Culture, edited by Benjamin Nelson.
Σ Harper Modern Science Series, edited by James R. Newman.
° Not for sale in Canada.
△ Not for sale in the U. K.

History: Ancient

A. ANDREWES: The Greek Tyrants △ TB/1103
ADOLF ERMAN, Ed.: The Ancient Egyptians TB/1233
MICHAEL GRANT: Ancient History ° △ TB/1190
SAMUEL NOAH KRAMER: Sumerian Mythology TB/1055
NAPHTALI LEWIS & MEYER REINHOLD, Eds.: Roman Civilization.   Vol. I TB/1231; Vol. II TB/1232

History: Medieval

P. BOISSONNADE: Life and Work in Medieval Europe △ TB/1141
HELEN CAM: England Before Elizabeth △ TB/1026
NORMAN COHN: The Pursuit of the Millennium △ TB/1037
GALBERT OF BRUGES: The Murder of Charles the Good. Trans. with Intro. by James Bruce Ross TB/1311
DENO GEANAKOPLOS: Byzantine East and Latin West △ TB/1265
DENYS HAY: Europe: The Emergence of an Idea TB/1275
DENYS HAY: The Medieval Centuries ° △ TB/1192
J. M. HUSSEY: The Byzantine World △ TB/1057
FERDINAND LOT: The End of the Ancient World TB/1044
MARSILIUS OF PADUA: The Defender of the Peace. Trans. with Intro. by Alan Gewirth TB/1310
CHARLES PETIT-DUTAILLIS: The Feudal Monarchy in France and England ° △ TB/1165
HENRI PIRENNE: Early Democracies in the Low Countries TB/1110
STEVEN RUNCIMAN: A History of the Crusades. △ Vol. I Illus. TB/1143; Vol. II Illus. TB/1243; Vol. III Illus. TB/1298
FERDINAND SCHEVILL: Siena TB/1164
SULPICIUS SEVERUS et al.: The Western Fathers △ TB/309
HENRY OSBORN TAYLOR: The Classical Heritage of the Middle Ages TB/1117
J. M. WALLACE-HADRILL: The Barbarian West TB/1061

History: Renaissance & Reformation

JACOB BURCKHARDT: The Civilization of the Renaissance in Italy. △ Illus.   Vol. I TB/40; Vol. II TB/41
JOHN CALVIN & JACOPO SADOLETO: A Reformation Debate. △ Edited by John C. Olin TB/1239
FEDERICO CHABOD: Machiavelli and the Renaissance △ TB/1193
G. CONSTANT: The Reformation in England △ TB/314
G. R. ELTON: Reformation Europe, 1517-1559 ** ° △ TB/1270
JOHN NEVILLE FIGGIS: The Divine Right of Kings. Introduction by G. R. Elton TB/1191
FRANCESCO GUICCIARDINI: Maxims and Reflections of a Renaissance Statesman (Ricordi) TB/1160
J. H. HEXTER: More's Utopia TB/1195
HAJO HOLBORN: Ulrich von Hutten and the German Reformation TB/1238
JOHAN HUIZINGA: Erasmus and the Age of Reformation. △ Illus. TB/19
JOEL HURSTFIELD, Ed.: The Reformation Crisis △ TB/1267
ULRICH VON HUTTEN et al.: On the Eve of the Reformation: "Letters of Obscure Men" TB/1124
PAUL O. KRISTELLER: Renaissance Thought TB/1048
NICCOLÒ MACHIAVELLI: History of Florence and of the Affairs of Italy TB/1027
J. E. NEALE: The Age of Catherine de Medici ° △ TB/1085
ERWIN PANOFSKY: Studies in Iconology △ TB/1077
J. H. PARRY: The Establishment of the European Hegemony: 1415-1715 △ TB/1045
J. H. PLUMB: The Italian Renaissance △ TB/1161
A. F. POLLARD: Henry VIII ° △ TB/1249
A. F. POLLARD: Wolsey ° △ TB/1248
A. L. ROWSE: The Expansion of Elizabethan England. △ Illus. TB/1220
GORDON RUPP: Luther's Progress to the Diet of Worms ° △ TB/120
FERDINAND SCHEVILL: The Medici. Illus. TB/1010
FERDINAND SCHEVILL: Medieval and Renaissance Florence. Illus.   Vol. I TB/1090; Vol. II TB/1091
G. M. TREVELYAN: England in the Age of Wycliffe, 1368-1520 ° △ TB/1112
VESPASIANO: Renaissance Princes, Popes, and Prelates: The Vespasiano Memoirs TB/1111

History: Modern European

MAX BELOFF: The Age of Absolutism, 1660-1815 △ TB/1062
ROBERT C. BINKLEY: Realism and Nationalism, 1852-1871. * Illus. TB/3038
ASA BRIGGS: The Making of Modern England, 1784-1867: The Age of Improvement ° △ TB/1203
CRANE BRINTON: A Decade of Revolution, 1789-1799. * Illus. TB/3018
D. W. BROGAN: The Development of Modern France. ° △ Vol. I TB/1184; Vol. II TB/1185
J. BRONOWSKI & BRUCE MAZLISH: The Western Intellectual Tradition: From Leonardo to Hegel △ TB/3001
ALAN BULLOCK: Hitler, A Study in Tyranny ° △ TB/1123
E. H. CARR: The Twenty Years' Crisis, 1919-1939 ° △ TB/1122
GORDON A. CRAIG: From Bismarck to Adenauer ° △ TB/1171
DENIS DIDEROT: The Encyclopedia: Selections. Ed. and trans. by Stephen Gendzier TB/1299
FRANKLIN L. FORD: Robe and Sword TB/1217
RENÉ FUELOEP-MILLER: The Mind and Face of Bolshevism TB/1188
M. DOROTHY GEORGE: London Life in the Eighteenth Century △ TB/1182
LEO GERSHOY: From Despotism to Revolution, 1763-1789. * Illus. TB/3017
C. C. GILLISPIE: Genesis and Geology: The Decades before Darwin § TB/51
ALBERT GOODWIN: The French Revolution △ TB/1064
ALBERT GUÉRARD: France in the Classical Age TB/1183
J. H. HEXTER: Reappraisals in History △ TB/1100
STANLEY HOFFMANN et al.: In Search of France TB/1219
DAN N. JACOBS, Ed.: The New Communist Manifesto & Related Documents. Third edition, revised TB/1078
LIONEL KOCHAN: The Struggle for Germany: 1914-45 TB/1304
HANS KOHN: The Mind of Germany △ TB/1204
WALTER LAQUEUR & GEORGE L. MOSSE, Eds.: International Fascism: 1920-1945 ° △ TB/1276
WALTER LAQUEUR & GEORGE L. MOSSE, Eds.: The Left-Wing Intellectuals between the Wars, 1919-1939 ° △ TB/1286
WALTER LAQUEUR & GEORGE L. MOSSE, Eds.: 1914: The Coming of the First World War ° △ TB/1306
FRANK E. MANUEL: The Prophets of Paris: Turgot, Condorcet, Saint-Simon, Fourier, and Comte TB/1218
L. B. NAMIER: Facing East △ TB/1280
L. B. NAMIER: Personalities and Powers △ TB/1186
DAVID OGG: Europe of the Ancien Régime, 1715-1783 ** ° △ TB/1271
JOHN PLAMENATZ: German Marxism and Russian Communism ° △ TB/1189
RAYMOND W. POSTGATE, Ed.: Revolution from 1789 to 1906: Selected Documents TB/1063
PENFIELD ROBERTS: The Quest for Security, 1715-1740. * Illus. TB/3016
GEORGE RUDÉ: Revolutionary Europe, 1783-1815 ** ° △ TB/1272
LOUIS, DUC DE SAINT-SIMON: Versailles, The Court, and Louis XIV △ TB/1250
A. J. P. TAYLOR: From Napoleon to Lenin ° △ TB/1268
A. J. P. TAYLOR: Habsburg Monarchy, 1809-1918 ° △ TB/1187
G. M. TREVELYAN: British History in the Nineteenth Century and After: 1782-1919 ° △ TB/1251
H. R. TREVOR-ROPER: Historical Essays ° △ TB/1269
ELIZABETH WISKEMANN: Europe of the Dictators, 1919-1945 ** ° △ TB/1273